The Changing World
of Christianity

PETER LANG
New York • Washington, D.C./Baltimore • Bern
Frankfurt • Berlin • Brussels • Vienna • Oxford

DYRON B. DAUGHRITY

The Changing World of Christianity

The Global History of a Borderless Religion

PETER LANG
New York • Washington, D.C./Baltimore • Bern
Frankfurt • Berlin • Brussels • Vienna • Oxford

Library of Congress Cataloging-in-Publication Data

Daughrity, Dyron B.
The changing world of Christianity: the global history of a borderless religion /
Dyron B. Daughrity.
p. cm.
Includes bibliographical references and index.
1. Christianity. I. Title.
BR121.3.D38   270—dc22   2010010384
ISBN 978-1-4331-0523-4 (hardcover)
ISBN 978-1-4331-0452-7 (paperback)

Bibliographic information published by **Die Deutsche Nationalbibliothek**.
Die Deutsche Nationalbibliothek lists this publication in the "Deutsche
Nationalbibliografie"; detailed bibliographic data is available
on the Internet at http://dnb.d-nb.de/.

FSC

Mixed Sources

Product group from well-managed
forests, controlled sources and
recycled wood or fiber

Cert no. SCS-COC-002464
www.fsc.org
©1996 Forest Stewardship Council

Cover photo: Etchmiadzin Cathedral, Armenia
Author photo on back cover courtesy of Ron Hall

The paper in this book meets the guidelines for permanence and durability
of the Committee on Production Guidelines for Book Longevity
of the Council of Library Resources.

© 2010 Peter Lang Publishing, Inc., New York
29 Broadway, 18th floor, New York, NY 10006
www.peterlang.com

Printed in the United States of America

Contents

List of Illustrations

Acknowledgments

The idea for this book came about when I realized I needed a more suitable textbook to organize a course I teach on World Christianity. There are some fine texts out there, but I needed something to fit my lecture style and arrangement. In this course, I lecture on trends in Christianity all around the world, moving geographically from one cultural block to another. I also deliver a few introductory lectures that lay out the changing nature of the field, as well as a general history of how Christianity got to where it is today—the largest and most global religion on the planet. I hope this book will benefit other scholars of Christianity who have struggled to present this leviathan of a topic amidst all of the pedagogical forces rapidly shaping this still-emerging discipline. While I believe this book contributes to the current scholarship, it has been written especially with students in mind. I have attempted to organize the material without simplifying it. One of my chief goals is to assist students in their endeavors to understand World Christianity, from North Korea to South America, from South Africa to North Carolina.

Christianity is increasingly being taught from a global perspective. This rather new approach was a long time coming. For generations, most university syllabi presented the history of Christianity mainly from Western European and North American perspectives. This has changed radically in the recent past. Many scholars have been involved in charting a new course for the discipline. In my own career, the scholars who have changed, and are still changing, my thinking are numerous, but I owe a special debt to the work of Stephen Neill, Philip Jenkins, Lamin Sanneh, Andrew Walls, and David Barrett. These towering scholars have transformed how people think about Christianity. Today, Christianity is the most numerically prominent religion in Western Europe, Eastern Europe, North America, Latin America, Africa, and Oceania. Of the eight cultural blocks of the world, Christianity ranks first in six of them. Today, there are far more Christians in Africa than in Western Europe or North America. The region of Latin America and the Caribbean is easily the most Christianized part of the world. These facts represent a changing of the guard. This book attempts to engage these realities and perhaps push the conversation a little farther along. I think of this book as a hybrid:

an introductory text to the changing realities in the field, yet a contribution to knowledge in the way the material is presented.

This book has the distinction of being written from the vantage points of three distinct offices: my old office which was demolished, an interim office graciously loaned to me, and my new office which is located one floor above my old one. Perhaps this will give the book an even broader perspective. The most challenging part, however, was transporting the books to and from the various locations. Students snickered at this professor as he trekked across campus with a stack of books, balancing them as if in a circus act. Several trips, carts, and boxes later, the books are finally, alas, out of my possession and back in the libraries from whence they came.

My colleagues at Pepperdine have been a constant source of encouragement and joy during the writing of this book. It is difficult to call what we do "work" in light of such a pleasant and congenial atmosphere. I owe special gratitude to the Religion Division, which has accepted me with open arms since my arrival in 2007. Randy Chesnutt, the division Chairman during the writing of this work, is a fount of encouragement through his patience and cheerful support.

I look forward to sharing this book with my excellent students and perhaps even taking note of their corrections! I hope my enthusiasm for the topic will infect them with curiosity, causing them to further stimulate my own thinking on how this religion continues to move in mysterious ways. I make special mention of one of my graduate students, Corey Williams, who spent considerable time gathering facts, calculating numbers, organizing data, and helping in many and various ways. One of these days I plan to shake his hand with those sublime words, "Welcome to the guild."

Stan Litke deserves my profound thanks for his hard work during the final stages of this book. Pepperdine University has contributed much by offering a course release for new faculty, and by allowing me several venues in which to present some of my research. I have also benefitted a great deal from Pepperdine's highly resourceful Associate Provost for Research, Lee Kats.

The stable, and growing, force during the writing of this book was my family: Sunde, Clare Soleil, Ross, and Mande Mae. The last one happened to be born right around chapter three. My wife Sunde has made my joy complete for many years now. My parents and grandparents introduced me to Christianity and made it a good thing, not a bad thing, in my life. For that I am very grateful.

Now unto him that is able to do exceeding abundantly above all that we ask or think, according to the power that worketh in us. Unto him be glory in the church by Christ Jesus throughout all ages, world without end. Amen. (Eph. 3:20-21)

World Religion

PEOPLE

Total Population:	6,709,393,092
Total Median Age:	28.1 years
Life Expectancy:	66.26 years
Fertility Rate:	2.61 children born/woman

RELIGION

Top Religion Percentages:
Christian (33.33%)
Muslim (20.87%)
Hinduism (13.41%)
Nonreligious (11.71%)
Buddhist (5.78%)
Chinese Universalist (5.83%)
Indigenous Religions (4.21%)
Atheist (2.27%)
Neoreligionist (1.61%)
Sikh (0.35%)
Jewish (0.226%)
Baha'i (0.114%)
Confucianism (0.097%)
Shinto (0.055%)
Taoist (0.05%)

Number of Christians: 2,236,255,415

Major Christian Groupings:
Catholic (49%)
Protestant/Independent (40%)
Orthodox (11%)

World Rankings 2010[1]

Population

1. Asia (3,767,141,703)
2. Africa (973,699,893)
3. Latin America/Caribbean (580,413,248)
4. Western Europe (389,846,133)
5. Eastern Europe (356,470,738)
6. North America (337,044,380)
7. Middle East (270,398,623)
8. Oceania (34,373,095)

Median Age

1. Western Europe (41.1)
2. Eastern Europe (38.1)
3. North America (37)
4. Oceania (33.1)
5. Asia (28.9)
6. Latin America/Caribbean (26.9)
7. Middle East (24.7)
8. Africa (19.4)

Life Expectancy

1. Western Europe (79.6)
2. North America (78.44)
3. Oceania (77.77)
4. Latin America/Caribbean (73.14)
5. Middle East (71.9)
6. Asia (70.67)
7. Eastern Europe (70.15)
8. Africa (50.05)

Fertility Rate

1. Africa (4.72)
2. Middle East (2.88)
3. Latin America/Caribbean (2.42)
4. Asia (2.35)
5. Oceania (2.26)
6. North America (2.05)
7. Western Europe (1.56)
8. Eastern Europe (1.38)

Number of Christians

1. Latin America/Caribbean (537,579,955)
2. Africa (453,085,307)
3. Asia (348,299,020)
4. Western Europe (304,430,845)
5. Eastern Europe (284,328,648)
6. North America (274,505,073)
7. Oceania (27,410,997)
8. Middle East (6,611,769)

Percent of Christians

1. Latin America/Caribbean (92.62%)
2. North America (81.44%)
3. Eastern Europe (79.76%)
4. Oceania (79.74%)
5. Western Europe (78.09%)
6. Africa (46.53%)
7. Asia (9.25%)
8. Middle East (2.45%)

CHRISTIANITY: THE LARGEST FAITH

Yㅣ̲ou are about to embark on a study of the largest religious institution in
the history of humankind. In addition to having more devotees than
any other religion, it is also the most global, most diverse, and perhaps
most influential religion in history. Several of the world's major cultural blocks
are today largely Christian: North America, Latin America and the Caribbean,
Eastern and Western Europe, sub-Saharan Africa, Oceania, and parts of Asia.
The enormity and global influence of the Christian faith emphasizes why
Christianity should be studied carefully, and from as many angles as possible.
In a globalizing world, it is important to understand major movements and
trends that affect human civilizations. The purpose of this book is to understand how Christianity—originally a Middle Eastern faith—became the largest,
most international religion in the world. The intent is to give readers a global
perspective of a religion that has grown and receded, pulsating back and forth,
over the course of two millennia. The roots of Christianity, however, go back
even further. The Christian faith is based on the core texts and beliefs of Judaism—an ancient religion roughly twice as old as Christianity.

When we look at a vast, complex institution like Christianity, we must do
so with respect to people. Religious institutions are comprised of living,
breathing human beings. The institution of the church has been passed down
from generation to generation: mothers to sons, teachers to young children,
clergy to laity, and friends to friends. Christianity consists of people. In this
book we will be dealing with churches, movements, demographics, and cities.
However, a religious institution is not some mechanistic force; it is you and
me and our parents and close friends.

Christianity began as a movement amongst Jews. Jesus was not a Christian; he was Jewish. All of the apostles were Jews. The early years of Christianity were dominated by Jews. In short order, however, Christianity began to be
adopted by Gentiles, or, non-Jews.

The life of Jesus is of monumental significance. The years of his life are
traditionally dated from 0 to 33 AD or so.[1] His life is the dividing line of his-

tory in much of the world. Entire civilizations operate by this understanding—a little over 2000 years ago Jesus was born. Anything in recorded history that happened "before Christ"—that is, before his birth—is usually known as "BC" and anything that happened after his birth is normally construed "AD" or "Anno Domini" which is Latin for "Year of the Lord." There is an increasing tendency in scholarship to use the expressions "BCE" (Before the Common Era) and "CE" (the Common Era) so as to avoid the politically charged reference to "the Lord." However, whichever system one chooses, the common denominator is the life of Jesus Christ.

While Christianity is the largest faith today, this is not necessarily going to be the case forever; nor, obviously, has it always been the case. Christianity's rise to global prominence can be traced through quarterly estimations, using the years 500, 1000, 1500, and 2000 as our guide.[2] It began as a distinct movement shortly after Christ's death in the first century AD. By the year 500 there were approximately 43 million Christians alive, which would have been about 22% of the world's population. In the year 1000, approximately 19% of the world was Christian. In the year 1500, that number had not changed much and was still hovering right around 19%. However, the year 1500 marks a period of major Christian expansion, particularly in the voyages of the Spanish and Portuguese to the Americas. By the late 1800s, approximately one-third of humanity was Christian. In the year 2000, most estimates claimed that 33% of the world's inhabitants were Christians.

Will Christianity grow? Will it die? Either scenario is possible. Both have happened in various regions of the world at different epochs of world history. Our task for this book is to understand the past and present state of Christianity, and perhaps make a few predictions about the future based on current trends.

Christianity: The Largest Religion in the World

There are around seven billion people in the world right now. One-third (33%) are Christian, one-fifth (20%) are Muslim, one-eighth (13%) are Hindu, and one-seventeenth (6%) are Buddhist. These are the only religions in the world that are statistically significant; in other words these are the only religions that contain more than one percent of the world's population. Judaism, Sikhism, Baha'i Faith and all other religions in the world each amount to less than half of one percent.[3]

This might come as something of a surprise because the world is often thought of as an extremely diverse place when it comes to religion. Actually, the world is not as diverse as one might think. When we combine Christianity and Islam, two faiths that trace their roots to Judaism, we will see that over half of humanity (54%) is either Christian or Islamic. Cultural geographers point out that these two religions prevail over 70% of the Earth's inhabited territory.[4] Christianity and Islam are, truly, world religions. Christianity is more diverse and more global—as we will see momentarily—but both of these religions can be found virtually anywhere on the earth.

It is also important to point out that people rarely switch religions. When this does happen, it is newsworthy, and can deeply impact the future demographics of a particular region in the world. However, the vast majority of humans practice the faith of their parents. It has been estimated that over 99% of people in the history of humanity practiced the religion of their parents. While it is fairly common for people to convert to new doctrines or take a fresh perspective on their own faith, outright conversion to an entirely different religion is, however, very rare indeed. Humans tend to associate with their parents' general faith orientation. People may shift from one form of their religion to another—for example from Presbyterian to Pentecostal—but these are not considered to be changes in religion. These would be characterized better as changes in emphasis since the core beliefs remain relatively unchanged. Those who deny the religion of their parents and make an outright conversion to another religion are exceptional throughout history.

Religions tend to be associated with countries or regions of the world. People in India tend to be Hindu. People in Latin American tend to be Christian. People in the Middle East tend to be Islamic. This is not a hard and fast rule, but it is certainly a general tendency. A good example is the United States of America. Nearly 80% of Americans consider themselves to be Christian. Only about 5% of Americans describe themselves as Jewish, Muslim, Buddhist, or some other faith. Statistically speaking, America is a mainly Christian nation. Imagine if by the year 2100, America was 50% Islamic. That would be highly unlikely. It is significant to point out, however, that this sort of thing has happened in human history. While rare, it will probably happen again. Why? In a word, the answer is proselytization—the concept of consciously attempting to convert someone else to one's own faith. Christians often refer to this as "evangelism."

Some readers may not be very acquainted with the world's major religions; taking a brief look at them may prove useful. While this book is not directly about world religions, it will certainly help to say a few words about the others that are prominent in the world today. We begin by looking at that religion that claims 13% of the world's inhabitants: Hinduism—the third largest religion in the world.

Hinduism: A Regional Faith

Hinduism named after the Indus River in India, should not really be considered as a worldwide religion because it does not have large numbers of adherents all over the globe. Hinduism is better understood as the main religion of India. India is the second most populated country in the world after China, and predictions based on fertility rates tell us that by 2035 India will be the most populated country in the world. The vast majority of Hindus however are located in India, and Hinduism is more of an ethnic faith. One is born a Hindu or not born a Hindu. Judaism is similar: generally speaking, either one's mother is a Jew—making him or her Jewish—or one's mother is not Jewish, making that person a Gentile (not Jewish). Hinduism is like that. People do not normally convert to Hinduism. There are a few exceptions; for example George Harrison of the Beatles became a Hindu during his life. This is rare, however. If a Caucasian person, for example, converts to Hinduism, the normal question might be, "Why did that Westerner convert to Hinduism?" Hinduism is not a missionary faith; it is passed on through kinship. Nearly three quarters of Indians are Hindu.

One additional point here: some scholars argue that Hinduism is not really a religion. They say Hinduism is probably best described as a large family of local religions practiced by the majority of Indians. Hinduism has many, many gods, possibly millions of gods, and followers of this faith tend to choose various gods for *puja*, or, Indian worship. Hindus are unified primarily by geography, history, and the belief that there are many gods that can be worshipped in this life. Ultimately, however, by worshipping those various and different gods, Hindus believe they are worshipping the one true reality, a notion Hindus define as *Brahman*.

The Rise and Fall of Buddhism

Christianity, Islam, and Buddhism are what we can more properly call world religions. They are open to anyone and welcome converts from any background. Historically, they have had tens of thousands of missionaries who traveled across mountains, lakes, deserts, and even oceans in search of converts to their message. Buddhism, a religion born in India around 500 BC, at one time in its history grew very rapidly. It spread from North India to Nepal, south to Sri Lanka, southeast to Myanmar, Thailand, Laos, Cambodia and Vietnam—even as far as Malaysia and Indonesia. By 500 AD—about a millennium after its inception—Buddhism had made many converts in China. Shortly after that, it made its way into Korea and eventually into Japan, at the eastern edge of Asia. While Buddhist missionaries headed east, the religion tended to recede in India. It got absorbed into the Indian culture and stopped being a distinct religion for the most part. There are still Buddhists in India, but the percentage is less than 1% of the population. There is a similar story in China. Chinese Buddhism reached its zenith around the year 1000 AD.[5] After that, Buddhism slowly became absorbed into the larger Chinese culture which emphasized the teachings of Confucius and the traditions of Taoism through many historic folk religions, known sometimes as Chinese Universalism.

Buddhism's magnificent growth lasted about 1200 years, from BC 500 to AD 700. It was another non-Christian faith that halted the spread of Buddhism—Islam. Islam's expansion across central Asia and into India had devastating effects on Buddhism in that region. Buddhism's heartland is today in Southeast Asia. In China, it is emerging from decades of official suppression. Nevertheless, the golden age of Buddhist expansion is long gone. While Buddhism is one of the "big three" missionary religions, there is little reason to think Buddhism will become a global presence on the scale of Christianity or Islam in the foreseeable future. Buddhism has lost considerable ground in its role as a major world religion today, claiming only 6% of the world's inhabitants. The Buddhist faith is diligently preserved in the monasteries and homes of Thailand, Cambodia, Myanmar, Laos, Vietnam, Sri Lanka, China (particularly in Tibet), Japan, South Korea, and other Asian nations. Buddhism does exist outside of Asia, but only as a tiny minority.

The Spread of Dar al-Islam

The spread of Islam is one of the most remarkable stories in the history of religion. Out of the Arabian Desert in the 600s, there emerged a movement that spread wide and fast, and over time it conquered most of the Christian world. In fact, had Charles Martel—known to medieval Christians as "the Hammer"—not defeated Islamic forces at the Battle of Tours in the year AD 732, the Western world might today be speaking Arabic. This is because historically Islamic leaders required their subjects to learn this language. Muslims believe that God revealed his will in Arabic. The scriptures of Islam are known as the Quran—God's uncorrupted revelation to humankind revealed to a man named Muhammad in the country we know today as Saudi Arabia.

Islam began when Muhammad claimed he had received revelations in the Arabic language from the archangel Gabriel. He then memorized these words and spoke them to scribes who in turn wrote them down. During his lifetime, Muhammad reasoned that the various Arabian tribes were fractured and should come together. He urged Arabs to unite and believe in only one God—known in Arabic as Allah—rather than the polytheism which was so common at the time. Muhammad believed polytheism to be wrongheaded and immoral. Muslims claim Muhammad was staunchly opposed to the worship of idols—a teaching he inherited from Judaism. There are stories of Muhammad purging places of worship, smashing idols and warning people to stop buying idols from the craftsmen. In fact, Muhammad's ideas were fiercely challenged during his lifetime because his policies threatened the livelihood of people who made a living out of creating and selling statues and other works of art that he dismissed as idols. For this reason, depictions of humans and animals are a very touchy issue in Islam. Most Muslims are uncomfortable with art that depicts people and animals; they fear a person may be lured to unintentionally participate in idolatry. Arabia was not purely polytheistic prior to the rise of Islam, however; Muhammad was very acquainted with Jews and Christians.

Typically, Muslims understand the term monotheist to include Jews, Christians and Muslims, although Muhammad fiercely opposed the Christian notion of the Trinity. Muhammad believed Jews and Christians should be treated more humanely than polytheists since they were also "people of the book." What Muhammad actually meant by this was that Jews and Christians indeed have much of God's revelation in the form of the Holy Bible. However, he argued, the Bible had become corrupted in time because of the many scribes who made mistakes when they copied the texts. In his view, centuries of copying the Bible by hand led to the point that it was no longer reliable. To this day most Muslims argue this, claiming that pure, unadulterated scripture from God is found only in the *Quran*.

Another important point emerges here: Muslims believe strongly that only the Arabic version of the *Quran* is the trusted source for authority. This is one big reason most Muslims are expected to learn at least some Arabic. It is thought people need to be able to hear God's revelations in the original tongue. This is very different from Christianity. Christians believe the scriptures can be translated without compromising the message. In other words, when a Christian reads a Bible in his or her own language, he or she is genuinely reading God's word for humankind. There is nothing more holy about the languages of the Bible—Hebrew, Aramaic, and Greek—than other languages. The point is that one should understand the message, regardless of the language. Muslims, however, believe that if the *Quran* is translated into another language, one is no longer reading the *Quran*. One is simply reading a translation of the meanings of the *Quran*. This would be like saying the Christian Bible is only authoritative in Hebrew and Greek and all translations compromise the authority of the text at least to some degree. In general, Christians consider the Bible in their own languages to be authoritative in their lives.

Muslims are those who accept Muhammad's teachings, which he claimed came straight from Allah. Muslims revere their text. They memorize large sections of it. They write it on their buildings in calligraphic form. *Quranic* calligraphy is one of the most popular art forms for Muslims. Muslims have a term for a person who memorizes the *Quran*: that person is deemed a *Hafiz*, which means "guardian" of the Islamic scriptures. Considering the fact that the *Quran* is about the same length as the Christian New Testament, this is a remarkable accomplishment indeed.

Muhammad lived from AD 570 to 632. His teachings come largely from the Bible, both Old and New Testaments, thus they are essentially a continuation of Judeo-Christian themes. In fact, Muslims consider Islam to be a "part 3" in many ways. First was Judaism, then Christianity, and now Islam is the final revelation of God's will to humans. Muslims firmly believe Islam to be the fulfillment of the truth that was first revealed to the prophets of the Hebrew Bible, then to the New Testament figures, and ultimately to Muhammad. Muslims argue that Muhammad was the last prophet. They certainly recognize the legitimacy of Jesus and the other prophets of the Bible. In fact Muslims revere Jesus. However, they staunchly deny the notion that Jesus could somehow be divine. They outright reject the Trinity—the idea that God is comprised of three: Father, Son, and Holy Spirit. In Islam, God is absolutely one. Saying that God begat Jesus or that God is comprised of three essences is a serious doctrinal error.

The most central teachings of the Islamic faith are called "the five pillars." The first pillar is the *Shahada* or, the confession of faith: "There is no God but God and Muhammad is God's prophet." The second pillar is *Salah*, meaning prayer. Muslims are required to pray five times a day at appointed hours. The third pillar is *Zakat*, or, giving alms to the poor. This is essentially the Muslim notion of charity. Muslims who have something to give are expected to give to those who have not. The fourth pillar is called *Sawm*, which is the Islamic fast. Muslims must fast during the Islamic month of Ramadan, which occurs during the ninth month of the 12-month Islamic calendar. Ramadan occurs roughly in September and October in Western calendars. During the fasting period, Muslims do not eat or drink from dawn to sundown. The fifth pillar is the *Hajj*, or, the pilgrimage to Mecca in Saudi Arabia. Mecca is the heartland of Islam, and it is the site of the *Ka'aba*, the most sacred structure in Islam. If possible, Muslims are expected to travel to Saudi Arabia at least once in their lifetime and participate in several rituals that show their solidarity as Muslims and their devotion to Allah.

Like Christianity, Islam had fantastic growth in its early years. By the time of Muhammad's death in 632, most of the tribal leaders in the Arabian Peninsula were in support of his teachings and had rallied behind him as the political and spiritual leader of the region. The first great period of Islamic expansion occurred between AD 632 and 732; this 100-year period is considered remarkable by devout Muslims and religion scholars alike. During that period, Islam had conquered huge chunks of the Christian world, and had converted hundreds of thousands of people. The Byzantine Empire, also known as the Eastern Roman Empire, suffered catastrophically as Arabs triumphed all over the Middle East, Iraq, Iran, central Asia, all across North Africa, Spain and Portugal and even parts of southern France. It was one of the most astounding religious conversions in history. Millions of people who were Christian or Zoroastrian or some tribal religion converted to Islam in the years following these highly successful conquests. The old Christian heartlands were decimated. Three of the great centers of Christianity were conquered in the name of Islam: Jerusalem, Antioch, and Alexandria. Damascus, once an esteemed center of Christian learning, became something of an Islamic capital. Egypt, the center of Christian monasticism, fell to the Arabs during this period. The same fate came upon the vast region of Algeria in North Africa, which had been strongly Christian prior to the period of Arab conquest.

In time, Islam deepened its roots in these lands, expanding in all directions. In the 900s, it spread into Anatolia, or modern-day Turkey, which was at the very heart of the Byzantine Empire. For centuries, Muslim warriors battled away at that once-thoroughly Christianized superpower until the capital city—Constantinople—finally fell in the year 1453. In time, Central Asia, consisting of the modern-day countries that end with the word "-stan" (Persian for "land"), became vastly Islamic nations: Uzbekistan, Afghanistan, Tajikistan, Turkmenistan, Kyrgyzstan, and Pakistan. Kazakhstan is exceptional here, as the population is split in half between Christianity and Islam.[6] By the early 1200s Islam had conquered northern India, and the region contains many Muslims today. In the 1300s and 1400s Islam spread to what we know as Indonesia and Malaysia, both fiercely Islamic states to the present. Many scholars consider Indonesia to contain more Muslims than any other country in the world.[7] Surprisingly, India contains one of the largest Islamic populations in the world. While only 13% of the population is Islamic, in a country of well over a billion people, it adds up fast.

Today, Islam continues to grow, but mainly through fertility rates. The great expansion of Islam symbolically came to a halt in 1492—the precise year that Columbus set sail. During that year, the Christian rulers King Ferdinand and Queen Isabella accomplished the "Reconquista," wherein they unified Spain and drove out the final remnants of Islamic rule in the Iberian Peninsula; they also drove out or coerced into conversion many of the remaining Muslims and Jews.[8] The year 1492 also famously marks the year that Isabella commissioned Christopher Columbus to sail West-ward, opening up a vast land known simply as "the New World."

The Islamic world is centered in Saudi Arabia and radiates outwardly from there. It is the primary religion of North Africa, the Middle East including Turkey, parts of the Balkans, much of Central Asia including patches in

Western China, parts of India and greater south Asia such as Pakistan and Bangladesh, and finally the archipelago of Indonesia and Malaysia. Some scholars refer to this region as the "Islamic Crescent," an apt term to use for two reasons:

1. the crescent moon has come to symbolize Islam—for example on the international flags of several Islamic nations; and

2. looking at a map, the Islamic world takes the geographical shape of a crescent. Muslims refer to this region of the world as Dar al-Islam, or, the house of Islam.

Christianity: A Religion That Is "Moving South"

Christianity's center of gravity has shifted in recent years. This phenomenon has caused a splash in the academic study of religion. Rarely does a person get to be a part of a paradigm shift in a particular field of study, however, that is precisely what is happening in the study of Christianity. The changes are astonishing. Christianity—by far the largest religion in the world today—has "moved south." No longer is Christianity primarily a "Northern" or "Western" faith. The majority of Christians today live in the "global South."

What is meant by that expression the "global South?" What scholars usually have in mind are Africa, Asia, Latin America, and Oceania (the South Pacific). Historically, other expressions have been used such as the "third world," the "two-thirds world," or the "developing world." The preferred term today is the "global South." The previous expressions are rather antiquated and somewhat biased. Nevertheless, the point here is that Christianity's demographics have radically changed, and few scholars were aware of the massive implications of these changes until quite recently. The watershed moment took place approximately in 1980 as Christianity "moved south" around that year. For many centuries prior to 1980 over half of the world's Christians lived in Europe and North America. After 1980 the majority of the world's Christians lived in Africa, Asia, Latin America, and Oceania.[9]

Several statistics emphasize the global demographic changes that the last 200 years have revealed.[10] In the year 1800, Christianity was the religion of about 23% of the world's population. By 1900, this number had increased to around 33%, where it has remained for over a century. On the surface, this does not sound terribly surprising; especially considering this was the time when Britain was embarking on its massive colonial project. During the nineteenth and early twentieth centuries, Britain rose to become the unrivaled superpower in the world, on land and on sea, and it opened up many opportunities for British missionaries: safe travel, military protection, an

English-language infrastructure, and rather unfettered access to the peoples of these lands who were considered British subjects.

Another key statistic illustrates Christianity's move to the global South.[11] In 1900, 82% of the world's Christians lived in Europe or North America; only 18% of the world's Christians were outside the Euro-North American block. In the year 2005, only 39% of the world's Christians lived in Europe or North America. During that 105 year period, Christianity's heartland moved south to the point that over 60% of the world's Christians now live in Asia, Africa, or Latin America.

How did this shift to the global South happen? This is a complicated question, but there are answers. The most obvious answer is Christian missions. In modern times, there were two great waves of Christian missions: the Catholic wave in the 1500s and the Protestant wave in the 1800s. During these periods, Christian missionaries from the West launched out on massive, expensive, and focused campaigns to take the gospel to non-Western nations. Millions of people accepted the Christian gospel and themselves became missionaries to their own peoples. Herein lays one of the great misconceptions of Christian missions. It is all too easy to think that the Western missionaries "won" entire continents over to Jesus Christ. Without minimizing the heroic deeds of these Euro-North American missionaries, the people who received them and worked with them deserve every bit as much credit for spreading the faith. The mass movements that occurred during the great expansion of Christianity could not have happened without indigenous agents. After all, what good could a missionary do without the benevolence and assistance of native peoples? How could a missionary even communicate with people of different cultures unless someone accepted him, protected him, fed him, taught him the language, and introduced him to others?

Western missionaries often arrived to these lands with few language skills, thus local people had to help them in the very basics of survival. Upon arriving to these foreign shores, Europeans and North Americans needed guidance on how to survive: which plants could be eaten, how to find fresh water, with whom to trade, how to act appropriately, how not to offend people, and the list goes on. What is more important for religious purposes is that the local peoples were the ones who "accepted" Jesus Christ. These converted locals gave rise to a burgeoning Christianity in their own region of the world. Once Christianity took root, it indigenized, moving away from the cultural assumptions of the missionaries who had originally brought the faith. Naturally, it began to reflect many of the local social and cultural norms. The mission churches were often very different than the churches back home in the USA or in Europe. Nevertheless, they were clearly Christian churches. Thus, in many ways, we could say that the missionaries to the global South were successful. They planted Christianity and the locals made the faith their own, resulting in thriving churches comprised of hundreds of millions of people all over the global South.

Perhaps as important as Christianity's historic, geographical shift is the changing Christian ethos—the way the world's Christians prefer to live out their faith. If present trends continue, the world's Christians will continue to embrace Pentecostal, charismatic forms of the faith. Pentecostal Christianity is growing apace in the world right now. One influential scholar, Paul Freston, writes:

> Within a couple of decades, half of the world's Christians will be in Africa and Latin America. By 2050, on current trends, there will be as many Pentecostals in the world as there are Hindus, and twice as many Pentecostals as Buddhists."[12]

Indeed, Pentecostal Christianity is one of the fastest growing religious movements in modern times.

Another question may be in order here: Why are we just now hearing about Christianity moving south? Again, this is a complicated question, but there are answers. One answer to this question has to do with academic bias. Simply put, the study of the growth of Christianity sounds more like theology than social-scientific research. "Church growth" and "Christian missions" have, until recently, been topics confined to seminaries (for training Christian clergy), Bible colleges, and other church-related institutions. As this bias dissipates, academics of all types—Christians or otherwise—are taking notice of the fact that the world's largest religion is certainly worth studying. As a result, many of the previous notions about this faith are being overhauled. For example, many Christians in the Western world still tend to think that Christianity is almost exclusively a Western religion. They are often stunned to learn that over the last few generations, Christianity has become largely irrelevant in the lives of most Europeans, and is becoming increasingly associated with the global South.

If Western academics are just realizing the changing face of Christianity, then who has brought it to their attention? The short answer to that question has to do with the field of missiology—the study of Christian missions. In the last half-century or so, there have been a handful of scholars who have taken notice of this changing of the guard. Kenneth Scott Latourette, Stephen Neill, and Andrew Walls were probably the most important Western scholars who emphasized these changes throughout the twentieth century.

Kenneth Scott Latourette (1884-1968) was an historian who enjoyed a long, distinguished career at Yale University. Between 1937 and 1945, he produced an important seven-volume study of the history of Christian expansion. Throughout his career, he took special notice of Christianity in the Far East, partly because he began his teaching career in China.

Stephen Neill (1900–1984) was a British scholar who served as a missionary to India and eventually became one of the chief historians of Christianity in South Asia. His career was a global one as he traveled extensively while working for the Swiss-based World Council of Churches. He was a religion professor in India, England, Germany, and Africa at various times in his life. Like Latourette, Neill began to see that as Christianity receded from Europe, it was thriving in various parts of the global South. Neill authored 70 books, and most of them dealt with global Christianity.[13]

Andrew Walls (1928–) was recently labeled "the most important person you don't know" in the journal *Christian History and Biography*.[14] Like Latourette and Neill, Walls spent the early part of his career teaching in the global South—in his case Sierra Leone and Nigeria. During his time teaching there, Walls began to see that he was living in the midst of a tremendous shift in history—and he compared it to early Christianity. Just as the Mediterranean region of the world became Christian during the first three centuries from the time of Christ, Walls was watching Africa become Christian in the 1950s. The missionaries had planted the seeds many years prior, but it was Africans who were really taking the faith as their own, creating Christian movements and institutions that were authentically African, not simply transplanted European forms of the faith. After moving back to Britain, Walls eventually founded the Centre for the Study of Christianity in the Non-Western World at the University of Edinburgh.[15]

Latourette, Neill, and Walls were three of the most significant Western thinkers who began to take notice of the epochal shifts in Christian demographics—and all three of them were former missionaries. Since then, a second generation of historians has arisen, but they are not necessarily coming at the topic from the background of Christian missions. Two of the leading thinkers in the field today—Lamin Sanneh of Yale University and Philip Jenkins of Penn State University—came to the field of world Christianity from Islamic studies (Sanneh) and the history of English criminal law (Jenkins). However, both of these towering scholars began to see that something very interesting was unfolding right before their eyes—in the words of Jenkins, the "Next Christendom" is in the global South.[16] Lamin Sanneh prefers to describe the phenomenon as "The Changing Face of Christianity."[17]

The Future of Christianity

Clearly, some major changes are going on in Christianity today—changes that will impact the future of this religion forever. This is not altogether surprising. Christianity has always morphed, reformed itself, and spread to new places. In all likelihood these trends will continue. Christianity, as we understand it now, is quite different from Christianity at other times and in other places. Christianity in Norway in the 1300s was very different than Christianity in Zambia in 2010. While the Christians in those places in those times held to many of the same principles—such as Christ's being sent by God and the resurrection—they vary considerably in how to practice the faith and how to interpret various texts of the Bible. Perhaps the genius of Christianity is its adaptability. It is always changing: geographically, theologically, liturgically, and socially.

Religions are never stagnant; like cultures they defy rigid categories and definitions. While Christianity was primarily a Middle Eastern faith in the year AD 200, it is now transcontinental, with the two pillars of Christian adherence being increasingly situated in sub-Saharan Africa and Latin America. The United States of America is still a bastion of Christian faith; this is significant because the USA is the third most populated nation in the world. However, if Americans resemble anything like their Western European counterparts in the coming decades, they may secularize. Europeans largely consider themselves nominally Christian, but comparatively few actually participate in church life. Amidst the epochal shifts and theological changes however, one thing is certain: Christianity will continue to reinvent itself, shifting from region to region, gaining converts in some places while losing members in others.

Today, the notion of Christianity moving south is attracting more scholarly attention because the implications are huge. Christianity is today the religion of one-third of the human race, about 33% of the planet's inhabitants.[18] The likelihood of this changing anytime soon is small because of higher fertility rates in the global South. Many Western nations have fertility rates that are in decline or soon will be such as Germany, Denmark, the U.K., France, and Italy.[19] Eastern European nations are in steep decline—the governments of Russia, Bulgaria, Romania, and Ukraine have launched national baby making programs that reward mothers of multiple children.

It might be natural for Westerners to think that the future of Christianity is dire due to these once strongly Christian nations becoming less populated. However, the statistic that is rarely given attention is that Christianity is growing rapidly in other places—and many of them have relatively high birth rates. Most Latin American countries easily replace themselves. African birth rates are the highest in the world. It is not uncommon for African women to have six children on average, which is indeed the case in several African nations such as the Democratic Republic of the Congo, Ethiopia, and Angola. Overall, because the high fertility of the global South offsets the low fertility of the global North, Christianity will continue to remain the largest religion in the world.

If current fertility trends continue, Islam and Christianity will continue to grow all over the world. Hinduism and Buddhism and other religions will continue to shrink in terms of global percentage. While Hindus constitute 13% and Buddhists 6% of the global population, these numbers will almost inevitably decline. Conversely, Christianity and Islam will continue to make small gains in percentage in the foreseeable future.

Some scholars comment that Islam is growing much more rapidly than Christianity; however, this conclusion is premature. There is little reason to assume the Islamic nations will have higher fertility rates than the Christian nations in the global South. Many of the theories which claim Islam is rapidly gaining ground on Christianity neglect the paradigm shifts outlined in this chapter. All things considered, it appears Christianity will continue to be the religion of about one-third of the human race well into the twenty-first century.

While Buddhism, Christianity, and Islam are "missionary" religions, they grow mainly because of fertility. It is significant to point out, however, that there *have* been watershed moments in history when entire people-groups converted to one religion or another, but they are exceptional. How will this play out in the future? Nobody knows. There is no crystal ball to show whether there will be another phenomenally successful period of religious expansion anytime soon. What is known is that in the history of religion there have been surprises that nobody could have foreseen. Religious growth is uncontrollable and unpredictable; the history of Christianity showcases this remarkably well. Only in retrospect can we actually discern these pivotal moments.

Christianity grew like a wildfire in the first three centuries after Jesus' death. Throughout history there were some highly significant episodes of mass conversions to Christianity. We can home in on four dates that proved epochal in four different parts of the world:

- In 313 the Roman Empire legalized Christianity;
- In 988 Russia adopted Christianity;
- In 1492 Latin America began to become Christianized; and
- In 1807 the Slave Trade Act was passed in England.

First, the year 312 marks Constantine's victorious Battle at the Milvian Bridge in Rome which he accredited to Christ. Shortly thereafter, Constantine began to show favor for this previously illegal religion, issuing the Edict of Milan in the year 313. That Edict represented a pivot in the history of Christianity— from illegal to legal status. Second, the year 988 was when Prince Vladimir of Kiev converted to Christianity and began to Christianize the people of the great Russian land mass. Third, 1492 marks the year Columbus' discoveries had the effect of initiating a massive campaign to Christianize the people of

The Middle East

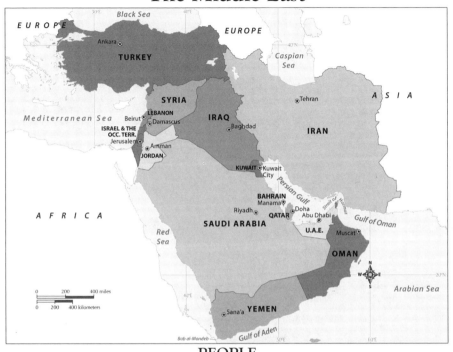

PEOPLE

Total Population:	270,398,623
Total Median Age:	24.7 years
Life Expectancy:	71.9 years
Fertility Rate:	2.88 children born/woman

RELIGION

Top Religion Percentages:	Muslim (93.20%)
	Christian (2.45%)
	Jewish (2.08)
Number of Christians:	6,611,769
Major Christian Groupings:	Catholic (58%)
	Orthodox (29%)
	Protestant/Independent (13%)

CHAPTER TWO

MIDDLE EASTERN CHRISTIANITY

C hristianity began in the city of Jerusalem. It is important to note that virtually all of the earliest followers of Jesus were Middle Eastern. Jesus Christ was Middle Eastern as were all of the apostles. While Christianity is obviously a global religion, it was first a Middle Eastern religion. This point is quite important because many people who travel from the Western world to the Middle East are often struck by the sheer foreignness of Christianity there: huge crowds taking pilgrimages, Christians parading around church buildings, bearded Orthodox men performing ancient liturgies that have scarcely changed over the course of hundreds of years. However foreign Christianity may appear in the Middle East, the fact remains that this is where it all began: this is where Jesus was born, died, and was resurrected; this is where the early church began; and this is where Christianity's most ancient roots lie.

What Is the Middle East?

The Middle East, like any other cultural block, is difficult to define. For the purposes of this book, the Middle East includes 14 countries.[1] Some scholars prefer to use cultural factors such as religion, language, and ethnicity as the primary attributes of a people group. Others prefer geography to determine precise border definitions. Any comprehensive, global attempt to understand the world's geography and culture must borrow from both approaches. For example, some parts of North Africa have much in common with the Middle East; therefore, many scholars prefer to include certain North African countries as part of the Middle East. Algeria, Libya, and Egypt are considered Arab countries due to centuries of Arab settlement, Islamic religion, and the fact that they mostly speak the Arabic language. However, North Africa in a geographical sense is obviously part of Africa. In this book, North African countries are discussed within the context of Africa. The Middle East, then, is that region stretching from Turkey in the west to Iran in the east, and from the

Turkey/Iran border in the north to Yemen and Oman in the south part of the Arabian Peninsula.

This region is not as monolithic as one might think. While Islam is certainly the majority religion for the people, there are many forms of Islam in the region. Israel and the Occupied Territories have a slight Jewish majority, making it the only country in the Middle East that does not have an Islamic majority. Islam in the Middle East has several variations that emphasize certain leaders or different approaches to being Islamic. Generally speaking, there are three large sects of Islam: Sunni (by far the largest), Shia (majority in Iraq, Iran, Bahrain, and Azerbaijan), and Sufi (the mystical forms of Islam). There are many other factions as well, primarily within Shia Islam, such as the Zaydis, the Ismailis, and the Ithna Ashari. The Middle East also features quite diverse ethnicities: Arabic, Turkish, Kurdish, and Persian may be the largest people-groups, but there are many others such as the Jewish and Uyghur peoples, and various sub-groups. Languages also vary, depending on the country. Various Arabic and Persian dialects are featured most prominently, but English, French, Syriac, Hebrew, and Urdu are among the many languages spoken in the region.

Looking at the numbers, the Middle East is strongly Islamic. Over 93% of the population explicitly identifies Islam as its religion. Based on the fact that Muslims tend to have higher birth rates than non-Muslims in the region, this already high percentage will likely increase in the future.[2] The only other issue that could potentially offset the increased percentage of Islam would be immigrants who come to the Middle East to work, especially in the oil industry. Considering the fact that religious apostasy is deeply resented in Islam—often punishable by death—mass conversion by Muslims to other religions is extremely unlikely. For obvious reasons, Muslims have very high retention rates when it comes to religion.

Westerners tend to know little about the Islamic world. One writer put it this way, "The Middle East is perhaps the most difficult region of the world for Westerners to comprehend."[3] Indeed, this assertion may be true for several reasons. First and perhaps most obviously is the fact that Westerners are generally warned by their governments not to travel to several nations in the Middle East; thus they rarely go except for official business. The U.S. Department of State's "current travel warnings" page almost always includes several Middle Eastern nations on the list. Saudi Arabia is a mainstay on the list, but Syria, Israel/Palestine, Yemen, Iran, Lebanon, and Iraq are frequently on the list as well. At one time Iran was a favorite travel spot for Westerners because of the rich history of the Persian Empire, but travel there has all but ceased since the Islamic Revolution in 1979 that rejected secular government in favor of a strongly religious government that follows Sharia Law. Iraq is not conducive for Western tourists due to recent wars. Historically, Israel has been an important country for Christians to visit because it is Christianity's birthplace. However, Israeli/Palestinian clashes have caused many organizations to stop traveling there. Some countries in the Middle East discourage Westerners to travel to their lands, except for business—primarily oil business. The U.S. Department of State warns: "Travel to Makkah (Mecca) and Medina, the cities where the two holiest mosques of Islam are located, is forbidden to non-Muslims."[4]

A second possible reason why Westerners may have a difficult time understanding the dynamics of the Middle East is political differences. Several Middle Eastern countries practice strict Sharia Law, such as Iran, Saudi Arabia, the United Arab Emirates (UAE), and Yemen. Many of them incorporate aspects of Islamic law into their legal systems, especially when it comes to domestic and family laws. Turkey, Lebanon, and Israel are different; they are strongly democratic, based mainly upon European models. Saudi Arabia, UAE, and Oman are monarchies and have certain restrictions on voting. For example, there is virtually no suffrage in the UAE and only men can vote in Saudi Arabia.[5]

Overall, Western nations have a difficult relationship with several of the Middle Eastern countries today. This is largely because of wars and political disputes in the region over the last several decades, but it is also because of long-standing rivalries between a nominally Christian West and a nominally Islamic Middle East. Perhaps the most volatile political issue is the existence of the state of Israel. In the late 1800s, Theodor Herzl (1860–1904), a Jew from the Austro-Hungarian Empire, led a mass immigration effort to the biblical land of Palestine. This movement became known as Zionism. It was a multicultural, large-scale movement for Jews around the world to immigrate to the Palestine region and become recognized as an independent Jewish state. Herzl's success in this regard culminated in 1948 with the founding of the modern nation-state of Israel. Zionists, mainly from Europe, established a European-style state in an Arab land, causing deep and lasting tensions that remain to the present day. Muslims tend to resent the existence of the state of Israel. They consider it an infringement on the rights of the Palestinians of the region who never agreed to the political arrangement. This problem is at the root of many other Middle-Eastern tensions today.

The third and perhaps most complex set of reasons why Westerners misunderstand the Middle East has to do with religion. Because the Middle East is the Islamic heartland of the world, any study of Christianity in the Middle East must include a serious study of Islam. Islam was born in the cities of Mecca and Medina, and these cities continue to be revered by Muslims worldwide. Westerners however have inherited a centuries-long history based largely on Christian theology, Christian texts, and Christian understandings. Christianity has been the religion of the Western world for a very long time. This is not the case in the Middle East, though. While Christianity had a significant presence there in the first several centuries of the faith, Islam's rise eventually curtailed that trend. Christianity's numbers have been on the decline for centuries in the Middle East. Today, the Middle East is an Islamic culture, quite different from Western civilization. For all of the similarities between Christianity and Islam—they worship the same God, revere many of the same prophets, and share many common beliefs and practices—the Christian West and the Islamic Middle East are two very different societies. The Middle East is Muslim. That does not sound terribly difficult to comprehend on the surface, but when one explores the implications of what it means to be a part of a Muslim culture as opposed to a Western culture, the differences are profound.

Muslims do not by and large conceive of their religion as something separate from the state. Europe used to have a strong marriage between religion and politics in the Medieval Ages, but today Western nations tend not to mix religion and politics nearly to the extent that is common in the Middle East. Many Western nations go to great lengths to ensure religion stays at arm's length from the state. In the Islamic Middle East, however, this is all very different. Muhammad, the prophet of Islam, believed the state should be under the authority of God. Christians can probably best understand this concept by looking at the Hebrew Bible, known to Christians as the Old Testament. The Jews did not have the "separation of church and state." Similarly, Muslims function with a fundamentally different view from Westerners. Muslims are often very proud of the fact that God is their ruler, and their religious teachers enforce God's laws in society. This approach protects the society from moral decadence. As in the Old Testament, God often punishes a society when it becomes unfaithful to the holy scriptures and the sacred traditions. Muslims often share this Old Testament mentality. Whereas in the Christian West the Bible is considered at best a historical influence on the country, in the Islamic Middle East the *Quran* continues to be the foundational document for most of the governments. As outlined above, there are exceptions to this dynamic, such as in Turkey and Lebanon. However, overall, most Islamic societies hold a deep suspicion for those who want to jettison the *Quran* from models of governance in favor of a Western-style secularism that works actively to make religious texts—whatever they may be—marginal in the governing affairs of women and men. A recent study by John Esposito and Dalia Mogahed concluded:

> While acknowledging and admiring many aspects of Western democracy, those [Islamic countries] surveyed do not favor wholesale adoption of Western models of democracy. Many appear to want their own democratic model that incorporates *Sharia*—and not one that is simply dependent on Western values.[6]

Nearly half of the American population can at least relate to this sentiment of blending religion and governance: "Forty-six percent of Americans say that the Bible should be "a" source, and 9% believe it should be the "only" source of legislation."[7]

The religion of Islam has teachings that are radically different from the New Testament. While these two religions indeed share much in common—most notably monotheism, a reverence for the Judeo-Christian prophets, and familiarity with the Old and New Testaments—there are areas where the two religions seem to have irreconcilable differences.[8] First and foremost, Muslims simply do not believe that Jesus is part of the Godhead. Christians believe Jesus is God in a unique way. Muslims reject this belief. Jesus, for them, is a prophet. In the Islamic mind, God is not comprised of three, such as in Trinitarian theology. Indeed Muslims strongly reject the notion of the Trinity.

Second, Muslims denounce the veneration of pictures, statues, and icons. One of the most important acts Muhammad ever committed was when he triumphantly cleansed the Kaaba—that structure in Mecca that Muslims pray towards—from all idols. Muslims believe it is entirely inappropriate to bow before pictures or statues. Muslims generally forbid even depicting humans and animals in art, so as not to lure someone into the sin of idolatry. Christians, in contrast, commonly incorporate icons and statues into their religious culture. In fact, Christians often have pictures of Jesus and the prophets in their Bibles, churches, and homes. Christianity has a long tradition of venerating artwork depicting biblical scenes and stories. To Muslims, the veneration of icons, statues, and religious artwork depicting people is heretical.

Third, and perhaps most significantly, Muslims and Christians are not on the same page. Literally, Muslims and Christians disagree on what constitutes Holy Scripture. For Muslims, the *Quran*—approximately the same size as the Christian New Testament—is the rule of faith. Christians, of course, believe the Bible—both Old and New Testaments—to be the Word of God. This is supremely important because the *Quran* and the Bible are very different books. While there is much crossover, there are some rather marked differences. For example, Muslims believe it was Ishmael, not Isaac, who was nearly sacrificed by Abraham. Muslims revere Ishmael and consider him an important prophet. Another major difference is that Muslims do not believe Jesus was crucified, whereas Christians consider the crucifixion of Jesus to be absolutely essential to the faith. Additionally, Muslims believe Muhammad to be crucial to the history of monotheism and to the story of God's unfolding revelation of his will to humankind. However, the Christian Bible was completed by around the year AD 100. The *Quran* was written down in the seventh century. Much of the *Quran* is utterly foreign to Christians as their scriptures know nothing of Muhammad. Thus, it is not surprising that Christians do not recognize Muhammad as a prophet. However, Muslims not only consider Muhammad as being important, he is the final prophet, what Muslims often call "the seal of the prophets." In the first pillar of Islam, the *Shahada* (profession of faith), it is declared by Muslims: "There is no god but Allah and Muhammad is the prophet of Allah."

For these reasons, and many more, Muslims view history through a lens that is very different from those of Christians. Muslims celebrate the rise of Islam and its expansion into what were formerly Christian lands. Muslims view Christianity as a faith inferior to Islam based on their belief that Muhammad is the final prophet, not Jesus. Consequently, Christians view Islam as fundamentally misguided, and Muslims view Christianity as incomplete. As a result, the two religions view history differently. Muslims believe that the Christian Scriptures are to some extent corrupted, resulting in a somewhat skewed belief system. Muslims believe Muhammad restored pure monotheism in Mecca 1400 years ago and Christianity was appropriately defeated in the resulting theological controversies that ensued during the expansion of Islam. Muslims celebrate the great, powerful days of the Islamic empires, ruled by the caliphs. They glory in the vast, contiguous empire that was created during Islamic expansion, connecting Spain to India under the banner of Islam. Muslims deeply resent the Christian crusades, a bloody attempt to reclaim land from Islam that had once been Christian. One of the great heroes in Islam is Saladin, a twelfth-century Muslim sultan who defeated the Christian crusaders in Palestine, virtually ending their hopes to reclaim that area for Christ. While Muslims treasure their glorious golden ages throughout history, they also have a very different take on the expansion of Christianity. Perhaps most conspicuously, Muslims deeply resent the era of European colonialism, when virtually the entire Islamic world fell under European, therefore Christian, dominance. Even today, many Muslims resent what they believe to be renewed imperial ambitions of the West in places such as Israel/Palestine, Iraq, and the oil rich regions of the Persian Gulf. Islam and Christianity, therefore, view history in extremely different ways. On the surface, the differences appear to be irreconcilable

Background: Christianity in the Middle East

While Christianity began in the Middle East, it has largely disappeared from that block of the world, at least in a statistically significant sense. As the overall numbers for the Middle East indicate, only about 2% of the population in this region is Christian. In some ways this circumstance is very surprising. The homeland of Jesus Christ is the least Christian cultural block in the world. What does this mean? Does this fact have any theological significance? If God indeed sent Jesus to the Middle East instead of, say, Latin America, then why did God allow Middle Easterners to abandon the faith? The near-extinction of Christianity in the Middle East causes many difficult questions for Christians.

Scrutinizing the overall numbers for Christianity in the Middle East, several trends can be witnessed. First of all, this is an overwhelmingly Muslim land. Islam became the dominant religion in the Middle East in the century following Muhammad's death in 632. Within one hundred years, by the year 732, Islam was the governing religion of the Middle East.[9] Scholars debate the conversion of the Middle East from Christianity to Islam, particularly regarding how quickly Islam became the religion of the majority of the people. Some theories hold that Islam became the religion of the common people rather quickly. Understanding the precise demographics is very difficult to do. For example, there is some scholarly ambiguity about how Christians and Muslims viewed one another. Did Christians consider Muslims a Christian sect? If so, at what point were Muslims viewed as a completely separate faith? These same questions permeate the early days of Christianity. At what point did Jews consider the Christian movement to be a completely different religion? These questions raise cautions when trying to estimate precisely when the Middle East became primarily Islamic. It is clear, though, that this land was predominantly Christian before the great Arab conquests. Turkey, for example, was quite possibly the most Christianized geographical region in the world at the beginning of the great jihads of early Islam; two of the five great Christian patriarchs were located there.

While the Islamic, Arab tribes had great success in their imperial ambitions, we also know that many Christians held onto their faith, even when being ruled by Muslims meant higher taxes, second-class status, and at times violent persecution. The spread of Islam was complex. While the Middle East became dominated politically by Islam within a hundred years of Muhammad's death in 632, certain people-groups often remained Christian for hundreds of years after that. The Middle East had a fairly significant Christian minority in several countries until the last hundred years or so, when Christianity all but died in the region. Wars, chaos, emigration, genocides, and various nationalisms have all had a part in the steady exodus of Christianity out of the Middle East. What exists now is only a tiny minority. Among the nearly 300 million people in the Middle East today, less than 7 million are Christians. Philip Jenkins has written about this steep decline:

> Reading an account of the Christian Middle East in the early twentieth century—of Smyrna or Trebizond or Diyarbakir—is to excavate a lost world. From the First World War onward, Christian communities were systematically eliminated across the Muslim world, and the Armenian horrors of 1915 are only the most glaring of a series of such atrocities that reached their peak between 1915 and 1925. Although these instances of massacre and persecution have no historical resonance for most Westerners today, they count among the worst examples of their kind.[10]

Christianity's exodus from the Middle East was both forced and voluntary. Looking at the mass emigrations of Christians to new lands, Davies and Conway write:

> ...A large number of Christians have been forced out or have emigrated to other Middle Eastern countries, to North America and Europe (and elsewhere) in order to provide better opportunities and circumstances for themselves and their families. This trend has continued into the twenty-first century...[11]

Christianity's recession from the Middle East seems to be the final chapter in a rich albeit turbulent history that has spanned twenty centuries.

There was a time when the Middle East was a well-spring for Christian theology and, despite existing under the banner of Islam, the Middle East contained a vast and important network of monasteries and schools. This heartland of Christianity produced prolific, sophisticated theologians whose names are virtually unknown to Western Christians today. Many Middle Eastern cities remained strongly Christian through the ages, and were often allowed to exist as enclaves within the Islamic realm of influence. Heroic chapters of Christian history take place in the Middle East, as many Christians died for their faith through the years, depending on the whims of Islamic rulers at any given time. Indeed, the martyrs are many in the Middle East, most of them unknown to history. History is usually written by the victors; in the Middle East, Christianity lost—and has in many ways become lost.

As Islam spread throughout the Middle East in the 600s, Christians found themselves in a position of having to learn Arabic, the vernacular tongue of their rulers.[12] Muslims revere the language of Arabic, arguing it is superior because it was selected as the medium by which humans would understand the intentions of God. According to Muslims, God revealed the *Quran* orally to Muhammad through the archangel Gabriel during the years 610 to 632. Muslims to this day have deep veneration for the language of Arabic, because of its association with God's chief revelation to Muhammad. Muslim art is dominated by Arabic calligraphy. Arabic poetry and Arabic recitations are a long tradition in the Islamic world, and when the Islamic imperial conquest began, it often meant the dominated culture would soon have to learn the language of its rulers. This process, known as Arabization, deeply affected Christian communities throughout the Middle East.[13] Many Christians were required to speak Arabic as their daily language. A group known as the Melkites was among the first Christian groups to adopt Arabic as their vernacular language. This community held fast to their Greek liturgy, but in their daily affairs and even in their Bible reading, they adopted Arabic. In the late 600s, the Melkites began translating the scriptures into Arabic and produced all kinds of scholarly texts in Arabic.[14] Their monasteries, located in Jerusalem, the Sinai region, and in Palestine all began relying rather exclusively on Arabic.

One important Arabic theologian named Abu Qurrah caused quite a stir when he began to use his pen to argue on behalf of Christianity. "Theodore Abu Qurrah is actually the first writer, whose name we know, who regularly wrote Christian theology in Arabic. He was a Melkite from Edessa in Syria."[15] Abu Qurrah was a bishop in Syria in the early 800s, but he also had many connections to monasteries in Jerusalem. He wrote in both Syriac and Arabic, but only his Arabic writings have survived. He knew how to speak Greek, but he did not seem to write in the language. Abu Qurrah received the ire of some of the Islamic theologians of the era. For example, one Muslim theologian wrote a tract entitled *Against Abu Qurrah, the Christian.*[16] Abu Qurrah is only one of many Christian theologians who wrote primarily in Arabic however. Sidney Griffith points out that while Arabic Christianity is a relatively underexplored field in the West, the Christians of the Middle East learned to adapt to the Arabic language quite well and produced ample theological writings in the language:

> Many well-informed westerners are still completely unaware of the fact that there is a large archive of texts in Arabic composed by Christians from as early as the eighth century of the Christian era and continuing right up to today. Arabic is often thought to be simply the language of the Muslims. ... It is almost as if in the western imagination the religious discourse and the intellectual concerns of Middle Eastern Christians were frozen in time, in the form they had at the time when the Islamic hegemony came over them in the seventh century. This unawareness of the continuing vitality of Christian life and culture in the world of Islam after the Islamic conquest is no doubt due in large part to the slow pace of the academic study of Christian Arabic in the West. It did not really become a going concern until the twentieth century.[17]

While Griffith bemoans the ignorance that most Westerners have of Arabic Christianity, he is also keenly aware that Christianity has precipitously declined to the point of "demographic insignificance in the Middle East."[18]

Iran, formerly Persia, is one important country in the Middle East that does not share the Arabic heritage that most of the rest of the region does. Iranians speak Persian, also known as "Farsi." The Persian language uses the Arabic script, but it is a completely different language with a history rooted in the Indo-European family of languages. Christianity in the Persian Empire has a long, at times flourishing, history.[19] Christians began establishing organized communities in Persia around the year AD 200. However, Christianity may well have been known to Persians at an even earlier date. Persian Christians are fond of pointing out that the three wise men who went to visit Jesus were from Persia. The gospel writer Luke is careful to point out that Persians were present at the very foundations of Christianity at Pentecost, including Parthians, Medes, and Elamites—all from modern-day Iran. Christianity rooted itself in Persia very early on in a little kingdom known as Osrhoene, on the Western border of Persia. The capital city of this kingdom was called Edessa, known today as Urfa in Turkey. Edessa became known to some simply as "Edessa the Blessed" due to its being one of the "... most significant early powerhouses of Christian expansion."[20] There is a long tradition that claims the king of Edessa may have corresponded with Jesus, although the veracity of the story is dubious. We do know that by the year AD 150, while Edessa was within the Parthian realm of influence (northeast Iran), Christianity had been embraced by many in the region. According to coin evidence, the king may have been baptized around the year 180; coins minted between 180 and 192 include a cross on the headdress of King Abqar VIII.[21] Edessa became one of the most important centers of early Christian scholarship, under the influence of the Patriarch of Antioch. Edessa became a Christian capital city, and a polyglot intellectual hub of Christianity. Greek, Aramaic, and Syriac were all widely used although the preferred language for literary purposes was Syriac.[22] One of the more important scholars to come out of Edessa was Tatian (born AD 150). Tatian wrote an extremely influential harmony of the gospels known as *The Diatessaron* which was for over two centuries "... the only Gospel known to the Eastern Christians and greatly revered."[23] The kingdom of Osrhoene "... was continuously involved in the wars between Rome and Parthia and later between Rome and the Persian Empire."[24] Thus, the influential school of Edessa was on the border of East and West and as a result became caught up in the political controversies that often spilled over into theology. For example, Tatian's *Diatessaron* was eventually declared heretical in the West, a decision likely motivated by political disputes rather than careful theological consideration.

When we stand back and attempt to understand this story of why Christianity has receded so dramatically in the Middle East, we are struck by several important considerations. While the most obvious reason for the decline in numbers relates to the growth and expansion of Islam, there are other reasons as well. First of all, Christians in the Middle East have always been heterogeneous. There are so many different types of Christianity there; it is mindboggling for the church historian, difficult to get a handle on. These are not primarily recent, Protestant developments, either. This fractured situation of the churches goes way back to the earliest forms of the faith. We have already witnessed how Christianity developed important schools of thought in the region very early on, such as at Edessa. Soon after, there developed competing schools of thought, generally centered on a monastery, a university, or a particularly influential theologian. Christianity has never been just one school of thought; Christians often disagree on many things, from the fundamental issues such as which texts should constitute the Bible to the more arbitrary matters such as how to decorate a Christian facility. Differing interpretations eventually lead to different institutions. Sometimes these institutions anathematize one another, which is precisely what happened in the Great Schism of 1054. We should point out here, however, that the Orthodox/Catholic split of 1054 and Luther's Protest of 1517 are but two of countless splits within Christianity through the years. The Middle East, being Christianity's homeland, saw many splits before the year 500. The dizzying arrays of churches we have today in the Middle East are a result of that tendency. What follows is a basic list of the major forms of Christianity that exist today in the Middle East[25]:

1. The Eastern Orthodox Family of Churches, which includes the following patriarchates:
   - Ecumenical Patriarch of Constantinople (Istanbul, Turkey)
   - Greek Orthodox Patriarchate of Jerusalem (Jerusalem, Israel)
   - Greek Orthodox Church of Antioch and All the East (Damascus, Syria)
2. The Oriental Orthodox Family of Churches, which includes the following patriarchates:
   - Armenian Catholicosate of Cilicia (Beirut, Lebanon)
   - Armenian Patriarchate of Constantinople (Istanbul, Turkey)
   - Armenian Patriarchate of Jerusalem (Jerusalem, Israel)
   - Syriac Orthodox Church of Antioch and All the East (Damascus, Syria)
3. The Catholic Family of Churches, which includes the following bodies:
   - Armenian Catholic Church of Cilicia (Beirut, Lebanon)
   - Chaldean Catholic Church of Babylon (Baghdad, Iraq)
   - Greek Melkite Catholic Patriarchate of Antioch, Alexandria, and Jerusalem (Damascus, Syria)
   - Latin Patriarchate of Jerusalem (Jerusalem, Israel)
   - Maronite Church of Antioch and All the East (Bkerke, Lebanon)
   - Syriac Catholic Church of Antioch (Beirut, Lebanon
4. The Assyrian Church of the East (Morton Grove, Illinois, USA).[26]
5. The Protestant and Evangelical Family of Churches, which includes numerous national and international denominations located all over the Middle East.

The heterogeneity of Christianity in the Middle East has had major implications historically. When Islam was growing at its most dramatic pace, Christians remained divided from one another. The Assyrian Church of the East—also known as the Nestorian Church—was deemed heretical as early as the Council of Ephesus in the year 431. Several major Middle Eastern Christian denominations were anathematized at the Council of Chalcedon in 451.

Many of the Christian divisions in those early centuries had to do with the nature of Christ—how exactly can one person be both human and divine? The consequences of these debates and declarations of heresy were a terribly fractured church.

When Islam came along, many Christians found the strong emphasis upon monotheism to be reassuring. Christians had long divided over how the Trinity could best be explained. Some argued that Christ was fully human and fully divine while others found that explanation to be less than fulfilling. How could something be "fully" two different things? Others tried to explain the Trinity through Greek categories of thinking: God is one essence but is made of three substances. Still others wanted to emphasize the singularly divine nature of Christ; they became known as monophysites ("one nature"). Muslims had no use for these confusing explanations. Many Christians who defected found it more reasonable to accept the staunch monotheism of Islam: God is one. The Muslim rejection of the Trinity offended many Christians, but some found it attractive.

Another consequence of Christian heterogeneity was that when Islam indeed came onto the scene, Christians often found themselves actually cheering for the Muslims. Muslim conquest could be violent, but at times it was peaceable. One thing was certain however: a united Christianity would have posed a greater defense than did a divided one. There were many Christians in the East who actually preferred being ruled by Muslims than being ruled by Byzantium. They found the Arabs to be quite accommodating, even accepting of their religion of Christianity. In contrast, though, many Christians in the East had been outright condemned by the Christians who attended the ecumenical councils. Thus, they were deeply hurt by fellow Christians. Various episodes in church history illustrate the oddity that Christians could often be their own worst enemies. The present-day situation in the Middle East is a result of those damaged relations through the years.

A second major reason for the recession of Christianity from the Middle East has to do with the crusades. Davies and Conway write: "Of all the events that have shaped the history and, especially, the religious history, of the Middle East, the medieval Crusades were of particular significance."[27] The Christian crusades were at their peak between the years 1095 and 1204. Whatever one thinks about the Islamic conquests and periods of great jihad, there can be no doubt that the crusades were equally as violent, barbaric, and damaging. Muslims were not the only victims of these Latin declarations of war; the Eastern Christians were as well. The crusader assault on the city of Constantinople in 1204 was as unexpected as it was unfair. The Christians of Constantinople had no idea these Latin Christians had come to destroy their city, as they were supposedly fellow Christians! In addition, the Muslims who came under crusader rule in Syria and Palestine were humiliated by Christian victory. This situation helps to explain the legendary, heroic status of Saladin in the Islamic world today.

A third reason for Christianity's decline in this region has to do with the final years of the Ottoman Empire, a world superpower that lasted from 1299 to 1923. This powerful, durable empire was built largely on the infrastructure of the Byzantine Empire, and at its peak encompassed Southeast Europe, the Middle East, and North Africa. For Christians, Ottoman rule meant they were generally considered second-class citizens, but at least they were allowed to exist. Muslims gave Christians and Jews a status known as *dhimmi*. Since Jews and Christians were considered "People of the Book," they were allowed to live, albeit with restrictions. The Ottoman Empire dealt with the dhimmi populations through the *millet* system. Under the millet system, the Ottomans recognized the religious leader of a particular region, for example, a Christian patriarch. This religious leader was allowed to govern his particular people, yet ultimately he was answerable to the Ottoman officials. "The millet system kept the various Christian groups apart from one another and reduced friction."[28] This system worked fairly well for some time—all the way into the 1800s in fact. However, "... matters deteriorated from the early nineteenth century as Muslim societies felt themselves under increasing threat from the Christian West."[29] In the early 1800s the system began to unravel to the point that Christians were persecuted heavily. One of the most horrific examples of this aggression was in 1821, on Easter morning, when "The patriarch of Constantinople was hanged outside his cathedral." Thus began what Philip Jenkins has termed the "Purging of Christians" that lasted all throughout the nineteenth century. The violence seemed to escalate unabated. The late 1800s witnessed tragedy upon tragedy: the Hamidian massacres (also known as Armenian massacres) of 1894 to 1896, the killing sprees in 1895 in Urfa (formerly Edessa) which included three thousand Christians burned alive in the cathedral, and ultimately the Armenian genocide that lasted from 1915 to 1924.[30] Estimates on how many Christians—Armenian, Greek, Assyrian, and Syrian—were killed in the genocide vary, but the figure is as high as 1.5 million people who were slaughtered for their faith during those years, in the final throes of the Ottoman Empire. It was in the late nineteenth and early twentieth century that the Middle East became, clearly, an almost completely Muslim part of the world. Writing on the calamities that befell the Christians during this period, Philip Jenkins writes the following:

> Across the Middle East, Christian communities vanished one after the other, like lights being switched off. Before 1914, Christian pockets were numerous and widespread, while by 1930, most had vanished or were in the process of disappearing.[31]

It is difficult to overemphasize the disastrous decline of Christianity in the Middle East in the early twentieth century. Despite terrible oppression throughout the nineteenth century, Christians still had a considerable presence there until the Armenian holocaust. For example, even in the year 1900 Muslims and Christians were almost equal in number in the Ottoman Empire: Christians comprised 46% and Muslims comprised about 51%.[32] What happened in the early twentieth century is just now being fully disclosed, although the nation of Turkey firmly opposes any attempt to characterize the events of that period as genocide. This has been an extremely sensitive topic in political affairs; the United States needs to be on friendly terms with Turkey. To this day, the United States federal government continues to withhold the label "genocide" from descriptions of the events that happened in those abominable years, although most of the individual states have used the term "genocide" to describe the massacres.

Middle Eastern Christianity Today

This section will highlight the current status of Christianity in various Middle Eastern countries. While space limitations do not allow the list to be comprehensive, the discussions here cover eight of the fourteen countries in the Middle East. An attempt has been made to represent the major trends in the region involving Christianity.

Iran

Iran is the second most populated country in the Middle East after Turkey. Iran's Christian community is less than one percent of the total population today. Most of the approximately 400,000 Christians who do live there are affiliated with the Orthodox families of churches. The largest group of Christians in Iran is the Armenian Christians; there are approximately 200,000 of them.[33] Protestant Christians are treated with suspicion in Iran. In 1990 an Evangelical pastor who converted to Christianity from Islam was "... charged with apostasy, sentenced to death, and executed."[34] This deplorable episode sent a strong and lasting message to Evangelical Christians thinking of proselytizing. According to the U.S. Department of State's International Religious Freedom Report 2008 (IRFR 2008), "Evangelical Church leaders are subject to pressure from authorities to sign pledges that they would not evangelize Muslims or allow Muslims to attend Church Services."[35] The IRFR 2008 also states, "The legal system discriminates against religious minorities." While Christians are discriminated against regularly, members of the Bahai Faith are worse off. According to the IRFR 2008, "Bahai blood ... can be spilled with impunity." The IRFR 2008 reported that during the year 2008 "Christians, particularly evangelicals, continued to be subject to harassment and close surveillance." Converts to Christianity run the risk of going to jail.

Iraq

Iraq's Christian population is in rapid decline due to the havoc caused by recent wars. There are about 500,000 Christians in Iraq today, around 2% of the total population. The largest Christian group is the Chaldean Catholics. Chaldean Catholics are Eastern Catholics who were formerly part of the Assyrian Church of the East (Nestorian) but joined with the Roman Catholic Church in the sixteenth century. The Chaldean Catholic Archbishop Paulos Faraj Rahho of Mosul was kidnapped and murdered in March of 2008 after leading congregational prayers. The BBC reported, "The archbishop ... was the latest in a long line of Chaldean clerics to be abducted in Iraq since the U.S.-led invasion in March 2003."[36] The Assyrian Church of the East used to be strong in Iraq, but during the persecutions of the late Ottoman Empire these Christians were significantly reduced in number. Many of the Assyrian Christians have immigrated to the Western world, a trend that continues apace today. The current Assyrian Catholicos-Patriarch, Mar Dinkha IV, lives in the United States because his homeland is far too dangerous. Christians have been targeted by various terrorist groups in Iraq in the aftermath of the 2003 American invasion, leading Christian Iraqis to emigrate out of their own country as refugees. Many Iraqi Christians have found a home in Syria, particularly in the city of Damascus where there is a large number of Christians.

Israel & the Occupied Territories

There are about 300,000 Christians in Israel and the Occupied Territories. Israel is a very unique country on several levels. It consists largely of immigrant families who settled there from Eastern and Western Europe in the last century or so; it is a Jewish country surrounded on all sides by Islamic nations; and it is believed to be a holy land in the minds of over half the world's population.[37] It is difficult to imagine how one small strip of land, through various historical circumstances, has come to be considered holy by most of the planet's people—leading to perhaps the world's most sensitive political issue. Israel is considered by Jews to be the "promised land"; it is considered by Christians to be the very birthplace of the Christian faith; and it is considered by Muslims to contain the third holiest site in the world—the Dome of the Rock shrine, quite possibly the oldest surviving Islamic structure in existence.

Israel has been ravaged by wars throughout the last century, particularly since it gained its status as a nation-state in 1948, much to the chagrin of Muslims in the region and worldwide. Israel is a Jewish-majority nation today, a fact which developed largely through Zionist immigration to Israel in the late nineteenth century and throughout the twentieth century. Today the Jewish population stands at around 72% of Israel and around 50% of the entire Israel and the Occupied Territories. The Islamic population is about 19% in Israel and about 42% of the entire Israel and the Occupied Territories. The Christian population is around 3% both in Israel as well as in the entire Israel and the Occupied Territories. Several Christian denominations house a patriarch in the capital city of Jerusalem. There are several important, old churches in Israel/Palestine such as the Church of the Annunciation in Nazareth, an Arab-majority city that is around 70% Islamic and 30% Christian. Other important churches are the Church of the Holy Sepulcher in the Old City of Jerusalem and the Church of the Nativity in Bethlehem, West Bank. Some of these churches are controversial sites. Access to the Holy Sepulcher Church, for example, is a volatile issue that has actually led to blows between monks of various Christian traditions.

The prospects for the future of Christianity in Israel and Palestine are bleak. Bailey and Bailey write,

> More than in other parts of the Middle East, the Christian community in the Holy Land clearly is endangered. The flight of refugees in 1948 and 1967 has been matched by recurring waves of emigration. A desperate economic situation, especially following the "closure" of the borders between the Palestinian territories and Jerusalem or Israel proper, has led many Christians to seek improved circumstances for themselves and their children. ...Land confiscation, the impact of settlement-building on the character of Jerusalem, the confiscation of identification cards, harsh occupation—all these have contributed to hopelessness and despair. At least 250,000 Palestinian Christians live in the diaspora, more than 60% of all Palestinian Christians worldwide. ...Within Israel proper, Christians in places like Nazareth live as second- or third-class citizens.[38]

Christians in Israel and Palestine find themselves in a dilemma: should they stay and continue to experience discrimination from both Jews and Muslims while trying to maintain a presence in the Christian heartland? Alternatively, should they emigrate out for better opportunities, leading to the demise of Christianity in the region? For many, the opportunity to leave is too tempting. Unfortunately, outbreaks of violence are common in Israel due to the unresolved political status of the West Bank and the Gaza Strip. Christians are often caught in the middle, making destinations like Europe, Australia, and Canada far more appealing for raising a family.

Jordan

Jordan has around six million people; approximately 200,000 (3%) of them are Christians. The majority of these Christians are Greek Orthodox. Jordan has proven to be a land of relative stability in the Middle East. Around two million Iraqis have immigrated to Jordan or Syria in the aftermath of the American invasion in 2003. Jordanian Christians tend to do fairly well in that country. They enjoy high levels of education and tend to be situated in the middle and upper classes. Christian schools and hospitals in Jordan are respected, causing many Jordanians to view them in a generally favorable light. Jordan has universal suffrage for all adults 18 years or older, and relations between Christians and the Sunni Islamic majority (93%) are good. The Jordanian government, like virtually all Islamic governments, views Christian proselytization unfavorably, and some foreign Christian missionaries have been deported in recent years. Perhaps somewhat ironically, several Orthodox and Catholic Christian communities have publicly denounced the Protestant Christians for attempting to evangelize Jordanians, according to the IRFR 2008.

Kuwait (and the Persian Gulf Region)

Kuwait is a country of around 2.6 million people, with a surprisingly high percentage of Christians—close to 10%. How can it be that such a high percentage of Christians are in a once-solidly Islamic country? As with other Persian Gulf nations, the Christians are not normally citizens but rather are foreign workers. Bailey and Bailey write:

> The great majority of the Christian population, however, is drawn from the foreign workers, who vastly outnumber the local populations in Kuwait, Qatar, and the United Arab Emirates and who represent more than a third of the total in Bahrain and Saudi Arabia. The majority of the workers come from Asia with the largest numbers coming from India and the Philippines. It is estimated that the total Christian population in the Gulf is between one and two million; of these, fewer than one thousand are indigenous people.[39]

While proselytization is forbidden, the governments of the region must come to terms with the implications of importing hundreds of thousands of foreigners for the oil industry. The forms of Christianity represented in these areas ranges a great deal. The largest are the Coptic and the various Eastern Catholic churches such as the Maronites (Middle Eastern Syriac Catholics), Armenian Catholics, and the Indian Catholic groups such as the Syro-Malabar and Syro-Malankara communities.

Lebanon

Lebanon is by far the most Christianized Middle Eastern nation. Of the four million people in Lebanon, around one-third of them are Christians. The Maronites are the largest Christian community in the country. Maronites are Eastern-Rite Catholics which means they are affiliated to the Roman Catholic Church. They have been affiliated with the Roman Catholic Church since the twelfth century yet developed a very different liturgy and traditions prior to joining. Arabic is the official language of Lebanon, but the Maronite liturgy is conducted in Syriac—a language closely associated to Aramaic. Lebanon's Christian population is diverse. While the Maronites are the largest Christian group, there are significant Greek Orthodox and Greek Catholic (known as Melkites) communities. There are other, smaller groups such as Armenian Orthodox and various Protestant groups. One important development in recent Lebanese demographics has been the declining percentage of Christians. Lebanon used to be majority Christian when it was established in 1943 after being granted independence from France. The President of Lebanon is required to be a Maronite Christian. However, Lebanon is a remarkably clear example of the significance of fertility rates. The IRFR 2008 states: "Over the past 60 years, there has been a steady decline in the number of Christians as compared to Muslims, mostly due to the emigration of large numbers of Maronite Christians and a higher than average birth rate among the Muslim population."

Lebanon is today 60% Islamic and that percentage will continue to increase if current fertility trends remain. Overall, Lebanon is an amicable place for Christians today, in spite of its violent past. The Middle East Council of Churches maintains its major offices in Beirut—the Lebanese capital city that is sometimes referred to as the "Paris of the East" due to French influence. Things are far from perfect in Lebanon, however. The country is home to one of the most virulently anti-Jewish groups in the world, known as Hezbollah. This organization claims the allegiance of large numbers of Lebanese people, and is very influential in the government. In 2006 Hezbollah launched a series of attacks on Israel that led to tit-for-tat violence between the two countries. The country's stability has been tested since then prompting Lebanon to appear on the United States Government's "Travel Warning List" frequently. While Lebanon seems to have passed through this difficult period, memories of the catastrophic Lebanese Civil War (1975–1990) still linger.

Syria

Syria has a population of around 20 million people. Around one million of them are Christians, coming primarily from the Orthodox and Catholic families. Syria has a long, rich history of Christianity. While only about 6% of Syria is Christian today, it is home to some of the oldest churches and monasteries in the world. In the "Christian Valley" (Wadi An-Nassara) of Syria there are still complete villages that have been Christian for well over 1500 years.[40] Portions of Syria were conquered by Christian crusaders in the twelfth century, and several monuments from that period stand today. Several ancient Christian denominations house their patriarch in Syria. Damascus, the capital city, has proven to be something of a city of refuge for Iraqi Christians who have fled their homeland en masse. Syria requires its Head of State to be Islamic, but overall the country has a long tradition of respecting all religions. Many Christian communities fleeing genocides and persecutions through the years have settled in Syria, making it a cornucopia for Christian variety. Christians are safe in Syria, and the government tends not to discriminate against them. For example, Christmas and Easter are both national holidays, and suffrage is universal for anyone 18 years or older. While it is technically illegal for Muslims to convert to Christianity in Syria, this offense is not enforced.[41] According to the IRFR 2008, the only incidents of religious persecution involved Muslims who were given lengthy prison sentences because they were found to be associated with international extremist groups.

Turkey

It is difficult to discuss Turkey without mentioning the genocides of the late nineteenth and early twentieth century that virtually extinguished Christianity in the country. Armenian, Assyrian, and Greek Christians were all mercilessly massacred during that dreadful period. As a result, there are very few Christians in the land that for many years was the heart of Christianity. Turkey was home to the important Christian city of Constantinople—New Rome—for centuries. The great city finally fell to the Ottoman Turks in 1453, ending the Byzantine Empire which lasted from 330 to 1453. The city of Constantinople was renamed Istanbul following national independence in 1923 under the leadership of Mustafa Kemal Ataturk. In many ways, the Ottoman Empire can be described as an Islamic Byzantine Empire. At its height in the early seventeenth century, it was comparable to the height of the Byzantine Empire in the tenth century.

Turkey is the most populous nation in the Middle East today with over 70 million people. It is almost fully Islamic (over 97%). Less than 1% of Turkey is Christian. There are only about 223,000 Christians in Turkey today. In spite of this drastic decline in Christian presence, one easily notices the vestiges of a former Christian heartland while visiting Turkey. The Hagia Sophia ("Holy Wisdom")—perhaps the most splendid church in the world—stands as a museum in Istanbul today. Churches and monasteries are scattered all over the land, hearkening back to the glory days of Orthodox Christianity. Clearly Islam in Turkey has incorporated a tremendous amount of Byzantine civilization, evinced in the architecture and culture. To some people, Turkish society feels more European than Middle Eastern. This is why many geographers prefer placing Turkey in the category of Europe. A different approach has been taken here due to the fact that Europe is better defined as a Christian civilization, and Turkey is so thoroughly Islamic, like the Middle East. However, in more ways than one, Turkey is a bridge between Europe and Asia, and Istanbul (Constantinople) represents the passageway from one continent to the other.

The Orthodox Church is the majority form of Christianity in Turkey, although clearly the numbers are tiny. At one time, however, Turkey was the very heart of the Orthodox world, and the patriarch of Constantinople was the highest authority in all of Christendom. Even today, the Patriarch of Constantinople enjoys a privileged status as being the spiritual head of the Eastern Orthodox Churches worldwide. Turkey is also home to Antioch, one of the five Patriarchs of the early and medieval church that comprised the pentarchy of Christendom. The old Cappadocia region of Turkey is also famous because of its many churches and monasteries carved into the volcanic, rugged terrain. Christians often fled to desolate areas like Cappadocia in order to escape various Islamic persecutions.[42] The region of Cappadocia is in central Turkey and is today known as the Nevsehir province. In early Christianity this region was known as Nyssa.

Turkey is a secular state and, at least officially, allows relative religious freedom, although cases of anti-Christian violence are common. The IRFR 2008 lists a whole host of violent offenses against Christians in 2007 and 2008, ranging from murders to kidnappings to widespread attacks on Christian institutions such as churches, monasteries, and radio stations. The IRFR 2008 states that Christians in Turkey face "societal suspicion and mistrust." Thus, while Turkey is officially secular, the nationalistic, Islamic ethos leads to less than ideal social conditions for Christians living there. Islamic extremism is present in Turkey and is cause for alarm for those in the European Union who continue to resist Turkey's endeavors to join.

Three Questions for Analysis

1. Why did Christianity die in the Middle East?

2. Why is so little known about Middle Eastern Christianity: its history, theologians, and eventual demise?

3. Is religion like evolution, where it is all a matter of "the survival of the fittest?"

Eastern Europe

PEOPLE

Total Population:	356,470,738
Total Median Age:	38.1 years
Life Expectancy:	70.15 years
Fertility Rate:	1.38 children born/woman

RELIGION

Top Religion Percentages:	Christian (79.76%)
	Muslim (9.33%)
	Nonreligious (8.46%)
	Atheist (1.81)
	Indigenous Religions (0.27%)
	Jewish (0.12%)
Number of Christians:	284,328,648
Major Christian Groupings:	Orthodox (67%)
	Catholic (23%)
	Protestant/Independent (10%)

CHAPTER THREE

EASTERN EUROPEAN CHRISTIANITY

C hristianity has been in Eastern Europe since the days of the apostles. According to the Bible, the apostle Paul traveled to Greece and Cyprus. The Eastern Orthodox tradition claims that the apostle Andrew traveled to the Ukraine in the 50s AD and tried to evangelize the region. There is a legend that Andrew proclaimed one day Kiev would be a great Christian city, which indeed occurred in the year 988, drastically changing the religious landscape of this massive swath of territory known to us as Eastern Europe. The year 988 is generally known as the beginning of the "conversion of the Slavs."

Of the eight regions of the world as defined in this book, Eastern Europe is the only place where the majority of the Christians are from the Orthodox traditions. Around 67% of Eastern European Christians are from the Orthodox families of churches. This percentage is far higher than anywhere else in the world. Middle Eastern Christians are 29% Orthodox. African Christianity is 10% Orthodox. The remaining five regions of the world have only tiny Orthodox communities, comprising 3% or less of the Christian population in those regions. Thus, a study of Eastern European Christianity is, more than anywhere else, a study of Orthodoxy. In many ways, Eastern European Christianity is a testament to the power and influence of the once-mighty Byzantine Empire, which lasted from 330 to 1453. When investigating Eastern European Christianity, this Byzantine legacy should be kept in mind.

What Is Eastern Europe?

Defining cultural blocks is a challenge, especially when it comes to Europe and Asia. Some scholars prefer to use the term *Eurasia* to encompass the three cultural regions of Western Europe, Eastern Europe, and Asia. Nevertheless, in this book, Eastern Europe is considered to be that region of the world that shares much with Western Europe but is in many ways distinct due to various episodes in history such as the Byzantine Empire and the Soviet Union (1922–1991).

Geographically, this region's land area is dominated by Russia. This fact, though, can be misleading because European Russia essentially ends at the Ural Mountains which stretch from the Kara Sea in the north down to the Caspian Sea in the south. The region of Siberia, the eastern side of Russia, is in some ways quite different from western Russia. Western Russia tends to share much with Western European culture. Siberia, however, is a vast, sparsely populated region with very few major cities, making it a rural culture. Spanning across eleven time zones, Russia is easily the largest country in the world in terms of sheer size, and that is due primarily to the Siberian land mass. Russia is also the most populated nation in Eastern Europe; over 140 million people live there. As a comparison, the second most populated nation in Eastern Europe is Ukraine, with about 46 million people. Ukraine and Russia share a tremendous amount in terms of history, culture, and especially religion. The other sizeable nations in Eastern Europe are Poland (39 million) and Romania (22 million). There are several Eastern European countries that have around 10 million people each: Belarus, Czech Republic, Greece, Hungary, and Serbia. The remaining countries in this cultural block range in population anywhere from several hundred thousand (Montenegro and Cyprus) to 8 million (Azerbaijan).

While Russia is easily the largest nation in Eastern Europe—both in terms of land as well as in population—it is only a part of this 25-country cultural block. Moving from north to south, this region's western edge is comprised of the following countries: Russia, Estonia, Latvia, Lithuania, Kaliningrad (part of Russia), Poland, the Czech Republic, Slovakia, Hungary, Croatia, Bosnia-Herzegovina, Montenegro, Albania, and Greece. With the exception of the landlocked countries of the Czech Republic, Slovakia, and Hungary, these countries touch either the Baltic Sea in the north or the Adriatic Sea in the south. All of these countries share a vast amount of culture and tradition with Western Europe. One of the primary differences, however, is that Western Europe is strongly Catholic and Protestant, whereas Eastern Europe is strongly Orthodox. For the purposes of this book, Georgia, Azerbaijan, and Armenia have also been included as a part of Eastern Europe. These three small countries are at the southern tip of Russia, occupying a small strip of land between the Black Sea and the Caspian Sea. While in some ways Cyprus should probably be considered part of the Middle East, it has been included here as a part of Eastern Europe due to its strong connections to Greece and its mainly Greek Orthodox population (around 80%). The remaining countries in this cultural block are Belarus, Ukraine, Moldova, Romania, Serbia, Kosovo, Bulgaria, and Macedonia. Geographically, Eastern Europe is surrounded by several important seas: the Barents, Baltic, Adriatic, Aegean, Black, and Caspian.

In terms of population, Eastern Europe ranks fifth among the eight cultural blocks of the world: just ahead of North America and just below Western

Europe. There are just over 350 million people in Eastern Europe today. However, the fertility rate for Eastern Europe is 1.38 children per woman, well below the world's average of 2.61 children per woman. Eastern Europe has the lowest fertility rate in the world. Of the world's eight cultural blocks, only Eastern and Western Europe are failing to replace themselves. However, Western Europe is an attractive destination for immigrants. Eastern Europe has to work harder to attract immigrants. Without factoring in immigration trends, any human society requires 2.1 women per children in order to maintain its current population.[1] Considering the fact that Eastern Europeans often emigrate away from Eastern Europe—usually in search of better jobs in Western Europe—the region's population will in all likelihood experience even more decline in the foreseeable future. Russia and other Eastern European countries have sponsored programs to try to offset this trend, and there are signs that some of these programs may be paying off. In 2006, Russian President Vladimir Putin declared low fertility to be "Russia's gravest problem." He claimed that Russia loses about 700,000 people each year.[2] In response, he created cash incentives for couples to have children.[3] Putin has also initiated a $300 million program to attract Russian people whose ancestors emigrated elsewhere through the centuries, often because of religious persecution.[4]

In addition to having low fertility rates and problematic immigration/emigration trends, Eastern Europe has a third problem: it is a relatively aged population. The median age in Eastern Europe is 38.1 years; only Western Europe (41.1) has an older population. Combined together, these demographic trends can lead to long-term problems. For example, what happens when there are not enough workers to support the aging population? What happens when the tax base becomes so small that major government programs have to be cut? Traditionally, the answer to these questions was immigration. However, the problem is that Eastern Europe's economy is not as strong as in Western Europe, and good jobs are harder to come by. Thus, many potential immigrants look elsewhere such as to Western Europe or North America. Additionally, Eastern Europeans are aware that with increased immigration, there are other problems that are introduced: cultural tensions, religious differences, and linguistic barriers. Mass immigration can certainly help a declining population, but there are often unforeseen downsides to immigration as well. In the case of Russia, that means it is worth the high cost to lure Russians back, rather than simply opening up the southeastern borders, where ample manpower exists. "Tens of millions of Chinese are just over the border, but Russia does not want to allow them in" because they do not speak Russian and their loyalty would never shift from Beijing to Moscow.[5]

Of the eight cultural blocks in the world, Christianity is the most popular religion in six of them: Africa, Eastern Europe, Latin America, North America, Oceania and Western Europe. Only in Asia and the Middle East is Christianity not the most popular religion. Eastern Europe is 80% Christian, 9% Muslim, and 9% Nonreligious. There are but few Atheists, Jews, and followers of Indigenous religions. Clearly, Eastern Europe is dominated by a Christian culture, at least nominally. Most of those Christians claim to be members of the Orthodox families of Christianity. There are significant Catholic and Protestant minorities, but make no mistake, this is an Orthodox land.

Of the 25 countries in this cultural block, 21 of them have a Christian majority. There are four Muslim-majority countries in Eastern Europe: Albania (64% Muslim), Azerbaijan (88% Muslim), Bosnia-Herzegovina (55% Muslim), and Kosovo (90% Muslim). Of these four Muslim-majority countries, Christianity is a significant minority in Albania (30%) and Bosnia-Herzegovina (39%).

While most Eastern European countries are dominated by Orthodox majorities, some of them are not. In addition to the Islamic countries, six of the Eastern European nations are primarily Catholic: Croatia, Czech Republic, Hungary, Lithuania, Poland, and Slovakia. Poland has one of the most thoroughly Catholic citizenships in the world; it produced the second longest pontificate in Roman Catholic history: Pope John Paul II (Pope 1978 to 2005). Estonia is an exceptional country in Eastern Europe; most of its Christians are Protestant or Independent.

While Eastern Europe has a significant Muslim minority (9%) and a fairly sizeable Roman Catholic population, it is largely an Orthodox region of the world. When it comes to politics, language, and ethnicity, however, it is a far more complicated—and controversial—picture. Eastern Europeans have historically struggled with issues surrounding ethnic identities. We have already discussed the Armenian genocides, and there are plenty of other examples of this kind of atrocity that has shaken Eastern Europe, particularly over the last century. The Balkans region has been particularly prone to political and social tensions in recent decades. The Balkans are usually considered to include Albania, Bosnia-Herzegovina, Bulgaria, Greece, Kosovo, Macedonia, Montenegro, Croatia, Serbia, and partly Slovenia, Romania, and the small European side of Turkey. This region is located between the Black Sea and the Adriatic Sea. The Balkans region is very diverse. Historically, it has been at the crossroads of Orthodox and Roman Catholic forms of Christianity, but it has also been a meeting point of sorts for Christianity and Islam. The Balkan region has been a volatile tinder box for a very long time. In the early twentieth century this region descended into all out war during what has been termed the Balkan Wars, lasting from 1912 to 1913. Much of the conflict had to do with former Ottoman states wanting their freedom. Historians consider the Balkan Wars as important precursors to the First World War which lasted from 1914 to 1918. In more recent decades, the Balkan region experienced a whole host of conflicts such as the Bosnian War and the Yugoslav Wars that have resulted in tiny nation-states based largely on ethnicity or religious affinity. Peace in this region seems all too elusive although in very recent times there have been glimmers of hope. For example, Kosovo's declaration of independence in 2008 has been recognized by dozens of countries including the USA, and Kosovo and Macedonia seem to have settled their boundary disputes.[6]

Probably the most significant conflict that wracked Eastern Europe in modern times was the Bolshevik Revolution and the subsequent creation of the Soviet Union, a vast, powerful institution lasting from 1922 to 1991. The Soviet Union, or, the USSR (Union of Soviet Socialist Republics), was a socialist state that covered much of Eastern Europe throughout the twentieth century. It was a system of government inspired largely by the writings of nineteenth-century philosopher Karl Marx. Marx was a long-time critic of competitive, capitalistic economies, predicting their eventual demise in favor of a socialist system. Essentially, Marx argued that social classes were deplorable for many reasons, and a more egalitarian society that shared property and profits was far more beneficial to people. Marx believed private ownership to be a fundamentally misguided idea. He reasoned that in capitalism, the vast proportion of goods become limited only to a wealthy, elite class—which he called the bourgeoisie. This leaves the masses—which he termed the proletariat—without access to most of the social benefits of their labor. The result is a huge chasm of polarization separating the rich from the poor. Marx's life-work was to convince his readers that socialism was superior to capitalist economies.

Karl Marx did not rise to international fame until after his death. Vladimir Lenin (1870–1924), leader of the Bolshevik Revolution in Russia in 1917, caused Marx to become a household name in the twentieth century. Lenin and his supporters and their rise to power touched off a series of events that led to the brutal Russian Civil War which lasted from 1917 to 1922. It was a horrific tragedy of mammoth proportions. Starvation was rampant, disease was rife, and various political factions were vying for power. It is generally held that when civilian casualties are included, over 10 million people died during the events of the Russian Civil War.[7] The Bolsheviks eventually won, overthrew the existing powers, and even executed the Tsar, Nicholas II, as well as his wife, Empress Alexandra, and their five children in 1918. Chaos ensued between various factions, but when the dust settled in 1922, Lenin and his Red Army had taken control of the government and had occupied the buildings.

It is important to bring out that Karl Marx's philosophies were essentially atheistic in character. Marx had no use for gods or religion and neither did the political leaders in the twentieth century who embraced his ideology. Marx believed religion to be the "opium of the masses," an indictment of Christianity that essentially charged religious faith with stifling the necessary socialist revolution. As a consequence, most Marxist lands became atheist lands. Vladimir Lenin, as well as his successors Joseph Stalin and Nikita Khrushchev, launched brutal attacks against the Orthodox Church. The Church, which had been so vital to the existence of Russia for hundreds of years, became severely crippled during the Soviet era, most conspicuously during Stalin's years (1922-1953), an era otherwise known as "Stalin's orgy of death." Even aged monks and priests were shot to death.[8] Khrushchev publicly spoke of his dream to display the last Russian priest on national television for all the country to see.[9]

The Soviet Union was a massive state that dominated Eastern Europe for nearly 70 years. Almost all of the countries included in our category "Eastern Europe" were connected to the Soviet Union at some point in time and were thus deeply affected by its approach to governance and economics, its cultural ethos, its dictatorial posture, and its strongly atheistic belief system. The only exceptions are Cyprus and Greece which both had political connections to Britain and the West throughout much of the twentieth century.[10] The majority of the Eastern European countries, however, became satellite states of the Soviet Union.

The Soviet Union characterized itself as an institution for the common people, thus the name "Soviet" which is the Russian word for "a council." The flag adopted by the Soviet Union was a red base with a hammer and sickle on it—representing the workers and peasant farmers. Over the hammer and sickle was a star, representing the Communist Party—which was the only legal political party during the Soviet era.

One of the ironic accomplishments of the Soviet government was how it managed to purge its lands of religion so effectively while at the same time declaring itself to be a revolution of the people. One would think that a popular revolution would tap into the religious heritage of Eastern Europe, a culture so enmeshed in religion that simply ripping religion out of it seemed impossible. Orchestrated assassinations, the destruction of churches, the imprisonment of priests, and the humiliation of clergy, however proved too much and, by and large, the Soviet Union by the 1980s had become quite irreligious—at least on the surface. What would happen if the oppression ceased? Would Eastern Europeans return to the religion of their forefathers and foremothers? The answers to these questions remain to be seen. The Soviet Union collapsed in 1991 and the fears and atheistic posture of this region of the world still has not had time to recover fully. Certainly there are signs that religion is making a comeback; however, it is unlikely that Eastern Europe will return to the extremely religious character of its pre-Soviet era anytime soon.

Background: Christianity in Eastern Europe

Let us take a snapshot of religion in Eastern Europe. Of the 25 countries in the Eastern European block,

- In fourteen of them Orthodoxy is the largest religious grouping: Armenia, Belarus, Bulgaria, Cyprus, Georgia, Greece, Latvia, Macedonia, Moldova, Montenegro, Romania, Russia, Serbia, and Ukraine.
- In six of them, the Roman Catholic Church is the largest religious institution: Croatia, Czech Republic, Hungary, Lithuania, Poland, and Slovakia.
- Four Eastern European countries are Islamic majority: Albania, Azerbaijan, Bosnia-Herzegovina, and Kosovo.
- In one Eastern European country, Protestant forms of Christianity comprise the largest religious grouping: Estonia.

Looking at the demographics of Eastern Europe, a few interesting trends can be seen. First, Eastern Europe is in freefall when it comes to population. All of the Christian majority Eastern European nations are in severe decline in terms of population. Some of the least fertile countries of the world are in Eastern Europe, especially Belarus, Bosnia-Herzegovina, Czech Republic, Latvia, Lithuania, Moldova, Poland, and Ukraine—all of which have fertility rates lower than 1.3! This is an alarming statistic for any country, but particularly so in countries that are trying to develop their economies. The term "autogenocide" seems appropriate for this situation. How can a developing country possibly achieve its goals when the workers are few and are forced to support an aging population who demand more and more health care? It is a quagmire for Eastern European countries. One interesting fact here that illustrates global trends: Muslims generally have more children than Christians. Of the 25 countries of Eastern Europe, only three of them are replacing themselves: Albania, Azerbaijan, and Kosovo. This is very significant. Only the Muslim countries of Eastern Europe are increasing their population through fertility. The rest of the region will have to rely on immigrants—an unlikely scenario due to the lack of jobs in most of Eastern Europe. These facts highlight why Vladimir Putin has declared this precise issue "Russia's gravest problem."

Christianity in Eastern Europe is ancient, steeped in tradition, and often linked to the political framework in any given region. Eastern Orthodoxy is generally organized according to nationalistic identities. While the Orthodox churches live in fellowship with each other, each national church is considered "autocephalous," a term that essentially means "self-governing." In other words, the head of an autocephalous church does not report to anyone. He is one of the highest officers in the Orthodox communion, and other religious leaders are not entitled to meddle in the affairs of his national church.

We should emphasize the pentarchy here, the five ancient Patriarchs: Jerusalem, Antioch, Alexandria, Rome, and Constantinople. Orthodox Christians believe Rome is living in schism, and should one day return. However, all of

the other four are located outside of Eastern Europe: three are in the Middle
East (Constantinople and Antioch are in Turkey, and Jerusalem is in Israel)
and one is in Africa (Alexandria, Egypt). In theory, all of the Patriarchs of the
ancient pentarchy share equal status. There is a special esteem given to the
Ecumenical Patriarch of Constantinople however. He resides in Turkey, but
even he is considered "first among equals" with an emphasis on "equal."
Rome used to enjoy that prestige. However, since living in schism—according
to the Orthodox mind—the Roman bishop no longer warrants that status. The
other leaders of these national churches are usually known as Patriarch, Archbishop, or Metropolitan, although clearly the ancient five command the highest respect. There are several important national churches in Eastern Europe
that stand out here:

- Patriarch of Russia: probably a little over 100 million members;
- Patriarch of Romania: around 22 million;
- Archbishop of Greece: around 10 million;
- Patriarch of Serbia: around 8 million;
- Patriarch of Bulgaria: 5 to 6 million;
- Catholicos-Patriarch of Georgia: around 4 million.

There is some controversy in the Orthodox churches regarding how autocephaly is determined. Some Orthodox Christians argue that autocephaly can be
granted by an autocephalous Patriarch. Others argue that a council, led by the
Ecumenical Patriarch of Constantinople, must be convened in order for autocephaly to be granted. This rule has led to some hard feelings among some
members of Orthodox churches, especially immigrant Orthodox communities
outside of the homeland. One example here is the Orthodox Church in America—a church with around one million members. It has been granted autocephaly by several national churches, but others have refrained from recognizing
it. David Melling, an Orthodox specialist, has written of the distinctions between autocephaly and autonomy:

> An autocephalous church is one which is independent of the authority of any other.
> ...An autonomous church is one which is independent in the conduct of its internal
> affairs, but requires the approval of its mother church for the appointment of its chief
> hierarch, and sometimes in other matters. The status of some churches is
> controverted, recognized by some as autocephalous but by other churches as only
> autonomous.[11]

Often, as is usual in the Orthodox families of churches, these matters take
time to sort out, usually centuries.

The Eastern European churches have much in common, although there
are some major differences. Some of the differences have to do with ethnic

identity and language. For example, Greece and Cyprus are Greek. However, the vast majority of Eastern Europeans are majority Slavic, such as in Czech Republic, Slovakia, Russia, Serbia, Bulgaria, Poland, Belarus, Croatia, Macedonia, Ukraine, and Montenegro. The languages vary a great deal, but liturgically speaking, many of them have some connection to the ancient Greek language of the New Testament. While clergy in Greece still conduct their liturgies in the old Koine (New Testament) Greek, the Slavic churches conduct their liturgies in their own vernacular languages. However, it is important to note the Slavic languages share many connections to the Greek language. The Slavic languages are based on the Cyrillic alphabet—a Greek-based alphabet inspired by the Bible translation work of Cyril and Methodius, the "apostles to the Slavs." Cyril and Methodius famously evangelized the Slavic peoples in the ninth century and created an alphabet so that they could become literate. They were brothers and are deeply venerated in all of the Eastern Orthodox Churches, considered on a par with the apostles themselves.

The conversion of the Slavs in the ninth century is a remarkable story. Cyril and Methodius were Byzantine Greeks from Thessaloniki. They realized that to the north and northwest of the Byzantine Empire lay several people-groups who had up to that time not received the gospel in a meaningful way: Moravians (modern-day Czech Republic and Slovakia), Bulgarians, Serbs, Ukrainians and Russians. Saint Photius was the Patriarch of Constantinople at the time who commissioned the two brothers to take the gospel to the Slavs. They began by creating a Slavic alphabet, which was unavailable at the time. The language they created for the Bible and for the liturgy is known as "Old Church Slavonic" and is still used today by the Russian Orthodox and other Slavic churches. This language issue would prove to be supremely important, for the people came to understand the Bible in their own languages thanks to the two brothers.

Throughout history, the Roman Catholic Church generally insisted that the liturgy be in Latin if at all possible. However, the tendency of the Orthodox Church has been to favor the vernacular of the people. The German Latin Catholics of the ninth century were as eager as the Byzantine-Greek churches to expand their mission projects, and they worked against Cyril and Methodius in the Czechoslovakian (Moravian) region. They even put Methodius in prison and expelled the Greeks from the land. In this case, the Latin Christians succeeded, and Moravia became Roman Catholic. Even today, the Czech Republic and Slovakia are strongly Catholic, with only a tiny Orthodox representation around 1%. In other words, it was not a great start for the brothers destined for missionary fame. Their work looked fruitless, but their disciples were motivated. Cyril and Methodius had created a group of followers, and these followers completed the Slavonic translations of the Bible and liturgy as well as many other religious texts. The literary legacy of Cyril and Methodius is probably their greatest achievement.

Driven from Moravia, the disciples of Cyril and Methodius turned to the region of Bulgaria in the late 800s, where they competed with the German Latin Catholics to win the allegiance of the people. Orthodoxy won this battle; the Bulgarian Church was awarded its own independent Archbishopric, and the people were able to use their own Slavonic language thanks to Cyril and Methodius and their followers. Serbia watched all of this play out and they knew they could go either Catholic or Orthodox. They chose to go Orthodox, mainly due to the language factor. The entire region that is on the border of Eastern-Western Europe is a fascinating study of Latin Catholic-Byzantine Greek Eastern relations. Some of the regions went Orthodox and some went Catholic. Some, however, were split. The region of Albania and Bosnia-Herzegovina is an example of people-groups that divided over religion. Even today the demographics of those two countries reflect centuries-old trends. Albania is 64% Muslim and 30% Christian; however, the Christians are divided about half and half between Catholic and Orthodox. Bosnia-Herzegovina is perhaps even more complicated. It is about 55% Islamic and nearly 40% Christian. The Christians, though, are divided between Orthodoxy (70%) and Catholic (30%). Various regions remain divided due to religion. Other regions, however, came together, uniting under the banner of one religion, as in Greece (Orthodox), Poland (Catholic), and Armenia (an autocephalous Orthodox Church).

Russia's Christianization is a highly important event in the history of Christianity because it contains the largest Orthodox Church in the world. The Byzantine Empire, led by Patriarch of Constantinople Photius, had orchestrated an attempt to convert the Slavs of Russia in the 860s. They had some success, but no Byzantine could have predicted how wonderfully their endeavors would pay off in the coming decades.

Various Byzantine missionaries worked in Russia—the land of the Rus' peoples—until the 950s, when Olga, a Russian Princess in the city of Kiev (today in Ukraine), converted to Christ. Her son did not follow her into Christianity, but her grandson did. This was a pivotal breakthrough. In the year 988, Olga's grandson, Vladimir—who was by then king—converted to Christianity. Vladimir reigned from 980 to 1015. He chose as his queen a woman named Anna—a member of the Byzantine royal family. This event marked the beginning of a formal relationship between the Byzantine Empire and the Russian Empire. Anna happened to be the sister of Basil II, a powerful Byzantine Emperor who reigned for over half a century, from 976 to 1025, and this relationship was the catalyst that turned Russia into the next major Christian empire. As the Byzantine Empire declined, the Russian Empire was on the rise. In time, Moscow became known as the "Third Rome" after Rome and

Constantinople. Due to these events, Orthodox Christianity became the official religion of the Russian people until the Bolsheviks took power in 1917 and began their systematic campaign to expel religion.

The conversion of Russia was rapid, thorough, exuberant, and extremely transformative—resembling the 300s with Constantine. In time, Russia began to gain confidence, seeing itself as the rightful heir to the declining Byzantine Empire, the Third Rome. Monasteries were erected all across the land, and they were almost always accompanied by laypeople that came along and built villages around them. The monastic movement is indelibly connected to the expansion of Russian territory. Vladimir and his successors embraced Christianity wholeheartedly, greatly expanding the Christian world.

The conversion of Russia continued into the small towns and outposts of the Russian Empire during succeeding generations. All seemed to be moving along quite well for Christianized Russia until around 1240, when the Mongols invaded. With their superior military skills they managed to sack Kiev—the capital of the Russian-influenced territories of the time, but now the capital of the Ukraine. While the city of Kiev itself was decimated by the Mongols' brutal methods, the church survived. The city of Moscow, located further north, gradually became the new heartland of the Rus' peoples, albeit a land subject to Mongolian Muslims for two and a half centuries—from 1240 to about 1480—when Russia finally broke free from the Islamic regime. The Russians referred to their Mongolian overlords as the Golden Horde. Russians do not think fondly of that long period of subjugation, calling it the "Mongol Tatar Yoke." Russia is not unique in this regard. "All Orthodox countries had been at one time or another under the domination of Islam."[12]

Russian missionaries continued to do their work throughout the Mongol era (1240–1480). Like Cyril and Methodius, they learned foreign languages—and there were plenty across the vast plains of Russia. They translated the Bible and liturgy into the local vernaculars and built monasteries that served as community rally-points.

The most important monk and Russian saint is Sergius of Radonezh (1314–1392); he is still the most respected figure in the Russian church. His baptized name was "Bartholomew" which is the name often used for him. Sergius was a hermit who gathered a group of disciples, culminating in a full-blown monastery. He tapped into the Russian zeitgeist with his affection towards the poor and his self-deprecating approach to life and faith. He dressed in shabby clothes and was often bypassed by visitors as a regular laborer in the garden or kitchen of the monastery due to his refusal to excuse himself from the work of a regular monk. Sergius was also a great force in the expansion of Russia as his mission work led to the development of remote monasteries which would be followed by surrounding townships. Sergius' followers continued to establish monasteries in his honor throughout the fourteenth and fifteenth centuries. Russia grew rapidly during this time, becoming a "vast network of religious houses," particularly in the north.[13] Sergius has been called the Builder of Russia. The Trinity Lavra of St. Sergius, founded by this revered Russian saint, is the most important Russian monastery and is today the heart of Russian Christianity. It is located about an hour's drive from Moscow and houses hundreds of monks. It is an important pilgrimage site for Russian Orthodox Christians.

For better or for worse, the Russian Orthodox Church became enmeshed with the state throughout its history. Serge Schmemann writes, "For centuries the Russian Orthodox Church had served as a handmaiden of the tsars."[14] This situation is not unique in the Orthodox family of churches. The precedent was set in 325 when Constantine presided over the Council of Nicea. Since then, most Orthodox churches are linked to the state. This church-state relationship has been known variously as "Caesaropapism" or "symphonia." However, at various times this idea played out in different ways. Sometimes the religious leaders had the upper hand, but more often, the political ruler was in charge, as in the case of Peter the Great—the dictatorial Emperor of Russian lands in the late seventeenth and early eighteenth centuries. Peter the Great (ruled 1682–1725) usurped all control over the church and essentially turned the church into an arm of the state. Bishop Timothy Ware writes, "Peter's religious reforms aroused considerable opposition in Russia, but it was ruthlessly silenced."[15] Thereafter, for well over two centuries—from approximately 1700 to 1917– the church effectively became part of the massive, complex bureaucracy of the empire, under the authority of the state. This Caesaropapist system had some benefits, but as evinced often throughout history, tremendous power and privilege threaten to corrupt. This reality was part of the problem that the Bolsheviks had with religion—it was essentially one and the same with the state. In other words, if a revolution was to overthrow the old political order, then the religion that justified and legitimized that same state must also go. The system of symphonia came to a screeching halt with the Bolshevik Revolution in 1917. Suddenly, the Russian Orthodox Church fell out of favor to a degree rarely seen in religious history. Thenceforth, the church was, in Marxist terms, a terrible drug that had to be eradicated from the Russian consciousness at all costs.

Religiously, the Soviet Union's official belief system was atheism. Although Soviet attempts to eradicate religion were largely successful—virtually eliminating Christian practice from the land—there was always a small remnant that remained faithful against all odds. Paul Mojzes argues that during Soviet times, it was largely the babushkas—the old grandmothers—who kept the faith alive during this dark time in Christian history.

> Astonishingly, even in the midst of Soviet persecution of the churches, there were times when the churches were packed with elderly people—mostly *babushkas* (grandmotherly women), sometimes holding their grandchildren in their arms, standing for hours devoutly transfigured by the holiness of the moment in contrast to the bleakness of their existence. ...One might say with a fair degree of justification that it was the *babushkas* who kept the faith alive.[16]

Mojzes goes on to argue that the elderly were the only segment of the population that did not need to fear the repercussions of practicing religion. If younger people practiced, they would, in the best case, lose their jobs and, in the worst case, they would be killed. *Babushkas* were less threatening to the authorities. Russian Orthodoxy owes a great debt to these elderly people, particularly the devoted, defiantly religious *babushkas*.

One of the greater developments in recent, former-Soviet history is that "People are no long afraid of punishment" when it comes to religion.[17] From 1922 to 1991, Russian Christians were under harsh persecution. The number of clergy murders is mindboggling. Just to put into perspective how widespread the persecution of Christian leadership was in Russia under Communism, let us take one example. Paul Mojzes, a Yugoslavian-American scholar of Orthodoxy, wrote the following:

> During the darkest days of the Stalinist *chistka* (purges), the hierarchy of the Russian Orthodox Church was reduced to four bishops in the entire land. It is estimated that between 1917 and 1943 nearly three hundred bishops and *forty-five thousand priests were martyred*. No one knows the exact number of active laypeople tortured and executed, but their number was in the hundreds of thousands, if not millions. ... It seemed that the Communists would succeed in eradicating religion.[18]

This number—45,000—is almost exactly the number of Catholic priests that are currently serving in the United States of America.[19] Let us keep this in perspective by pointing out that the USA has more Christians than any other country in the world, and the Roman Catholic Church is by far the largest denomination in the USA. Thus, the eradication of priests in Russia during the early years of Communism would be akin to eliminating the entire Roman Catholic clergy in the United States over the course of a quarter century. This is a breathtaking shift. The Russian people were cognizant of what was happening around them. As a result, a culture of fear enveloped Russian Christians. Most of those who practiced their faith in Soviet times did so in secret. It is thus a remarkable change that Christians in the former Soviet territories—which encompasses virtually all of Eastern Europe—seem finally to have shaken the fear of persecution, and are more or less free to practice their religion without fear. The residue of Soviet oppression of faith is like a cultural mist, however, and it does not evaporate instantaneously.

Eastern European Christianity Today

In this section we will highlight the current status of Christianity in various Eastern European countries. There are 25 countries in Eastern Europe, so the selection here is intended to represent some of the major trends in the region as they pertain to Christianity.

Albania

Albania was part of the Byzantine Empire, but then fell to the Ottomans. In the fourteenth century many Christians converted to Islam all over the Ottoman Empire and Albania followed that larger trend. Albania is a Balkan state and, like other nations in the Balkans, was at the crossroads of Orthodox Christianity, Roman Catholic Christianity, and Islam. Albania is a Muslim-majority nation, but has a strong (around 30%) Christian minority distributed almost equally between Catholics and Orthodox. Christianity in Albania was brutally suppressed during Soviet times. More than any other Soviet satellite nation, Albanian leaders, led by Enver Hoxha (led Albania from 1944 to 1985), bought into atheism wholesale. Part of the reason for this was the religious tensions due to a pluralistic society. Nevertheless, Albania's persecution of religion is infamous, particularly after 1967, when a Cultural Revolution similar to Mao Tse Tung's in China absolutely forbade religion. In the Constitution of 1976, Albania outlawed all forms of religious practice, whatever they may be.[20] Timothy Ware writes,

> Albania was now the first truly atheist state in the world: every place of worship had been closed and every visible expression of religious faith eliminated. Repression fell with equal severity on Orthodox, Roman Catholics and Muslims.[21]

When the Soviet Union disintegrated in 1991, it was learned that every single Orthodox bishop in Albania had died. A Greek bishop was appointed, Archbishop Anastasios Yannoulatos, and he has led a well-known revival among the Orthodox Christians now that religious freedom is the law of the land. One problem the Church of Albania has to contend with, however, is the number of emigrants that leave this former Soviet stronghold for better jobs in Greece.

Armenia

Armenia is famous for being the oldest national church in the world, established in the year 301. Armenian Christianity is also known for being a preserver of Byzantine Christianity, although it is part of the Oriental Orthodox rather than the larger Eastern Orthodox. Armenian Christians receive the respect of the worldwide church for a number of reasons:

- They are the oldest national church;
- Along with Georgia, they preserved the Christian faith despite centuries of Islamic persecutions, including the genocides of the late nineteenth and early twentieth century;
- They defied the Soviet Union in many ways, keeping their faith alive in spite of Soviet pressure for "atheization."[22]

For these reasons, many Eastern Orthodox Christians are working to heal the schism between themselves and the Oriental Orthodox Christians, a division that goes back to the Council of Chalcedon in 451. Thus, Oriental Orthodox Christians are often known as "non-Chalcedonian" Christians. Timothy Ware writes,

> When thinking about reunion, Eastern Orthodox look primarily not to the west but to their neighbours in the east, the Oriental Orthodox. ... Non-Chalcedonians stand closer to us ... than does any Christian confession in the west. Of all the current dialogues in which the Orthodox Church is engaged, it is that with the Non-Chalcedonians which is proving to be the most fruitful and by far the most likely to result in practical action within the immediate future.[23]

Orthodox Christians today tend to view the schisms of the fifth century at the Councils of Ephesus (431) and Chalcedon (451) as less about theology and probably more about politics. The dogged faithfulness of those Christians who were anathematized by the Catholic and Eastern Orthodox communities has caused Christians worldwide to stand in deep reverence toward their unflinching commitments to Christ.

Greece

The Greek Orthodox Church is one of the most famous national churches in the world. The Greek liturgy is esteemed largely because of language. Koine Greek was the language of the New Testament and is still the liturgical language of Greek Orthodox Christians. The term "Greek" can be misleading, since most of the Byzantine-influenced churches incorporated the Greek liturgy into their own. For example, the ancient Patriarchates of Constantinople, Alexandria, Antioch, and Jerusalem are often called "Greek Orthodox." In other words, when people speak of "Greek Orthodoxy," they generally have in mind "Eastern Orthodoxy"—which is of course a much, much larger entity than simply "the Church of Greece." This linguistic dependence on Greek does not mean that the other Greek-related churches are somehow dependent upon Greece or look to Greece as superior; rather, the autocephalous churches are self-governing, albeit with the recognition that the Patriarch of Constantinople is a "first among equals." The Church of Greece has produced some of the finest theologians throughout history, and their mystics and monks—famously scattered about Mount Athos which is located on a small peninsula in the north of Greece—are revered in Christian history for their deeply ascetic way of life. Christianity in Greece was fortunate in that it was not captured by the Soviet regime during the twentieth century; Greece and Cyprus were the only two countries of Eastern Europe that did not fall under the Soviet locus of power. However, it would be misleading to think that Greece did not have its own political turmoil throughout the twentieth century; Greece on several occasions became embattled over whether to follow Communism and Socialism or to live democratically. Greece was coveted by both Italy's fascist regime as well as by Nazi Germany—which occupied Greece between 1941 and 1944.[24] Only since the late 1970s has Greece become a relatively stable society along the lines of Western Europe. Today, Greece is a strongly Orthodox nation. Religious freedom is enshrined in the nation's laws, but there is no separation between church and state. The state pays clergy salaries and supports the Orthodox infrastructure such as education and church buildings. The state also offers financial assistance to some Muslim religious leaders who lead in an official capacity.[25]

Hungary

Hungary is one of the Catholic majority nations of Eastern Europe, along with Croatia, Czech Republic, Lithuania, Poland, and Slovakia. Hungary is a profoundly Christian nation, but the demographics are quite unique and diverse for an Eastern European nation. Hungary's Christians are 68% Catholic, 30% Protestant, and only 2% Orthodox. Hungary became Christian in the year 1000, under its first king, (Saint) Stephen, who adopted the Western Roman Catholic faith as the religion of his empire. Much of Hungary became Protestant in the sixteenth century due largely to its substantial Germanic minority in the region. Calvinism also made gains at that time. Yale historian Latourette believed Protestantism's rise in Hungary had everything to do with the clash of the Ottomans with the Hungarian kingdom. The Muslim Turks, who had defeated the Kingdom of Hungary in 1526,

> ...[T]ended to favor Protestants as against Roman Catholics, presumably because the former were less likely to support attempts by princes of the West, Roman Catholics, to reconquer the region.[26]

The Kingdom of Hungary enjoyed great prestige during the years of the power-ful Austro-Hungarian Habsburg Empire from 1867 to 1918, but it suddenly collapsed amidst the First World War and was humiliated by the international community when its land was reduced by more than two-thirds. The loss of land was to be expected due to Hungary's role in the outbreak of the Great War. "Hungary deserved punishment ... Of all the peoples in Austria-Hungary, they had been the most reluctant to surrender," writes historian Margaret Macmillan. She continues,

> Although Austria-Hungary bore as much responsibility as Germany for the fatal series of events that led to the outbreak of war in 1914, by 1918 even its enemies saw it as very much the junior partner, dragged along by and increasingly subordinate to an expansionist Germany hell-bent on the conquest of Europe.[27]

Hungary was further ravaged in the Second World War because of its dupli-citous dealings with Germany and Russia. Ultimately, its tentative alliance with Nazi Germany backfired. In 1945, after Nazi Germany collapsed, Hungary was taken over by the Soviet Union and remained a Soviet satellite state until 1991.[28] Today, Hungary identifies more with the West than with the East: it is a member of the North Atlantic Treaty Organization (since 1999) and the European Union (since 2004). Hungary allows freedom of religion and provides a leading example of how religious pluralism can work successful-ly in the region.

Poland

Like Hungary, Poland is one of six Catholic Eastern European nations, al-though Poland is almost entirely Catholic. With around 40 million people, Poland is the third most populated nation in Eastern Europe after Russia and Ukraine. It is a strongly Christian (96%) nation, and the Roman Catholic Church dominates statistically. In some ways this is unique, for Ukraine and Belarus just east of Poland are two strongly Orthodox nations. To the west is northern Germany with a Protestant majority. There is a swath of land, how-ever, including Poland, Lithuania, Czech Republic, Slovakia, and Austria that is strongly Roman Catholic. While firmly Catholic, Poland seems to be show-ing some secularization tendencies, as is the cultural trend in Western Europe right now. For example, the government of Poland recently began subsidizing in-vitro fertilization for barren couples—a move that contradicts the teachings of the Roman Catholic Church.[29] Furthermore, the Polish church has recently reported a 24% drop in vocations, and half of the priests in that country want to end the requirement of celibacy.[30] Nevertheless, the Polish church is strong and vibrant and is far from the level of secularization that has enveloped Western Europe. Perhaps the most famous Pole in all of history is Pope John

Paul II, a beloved figure in the national consciousness. At 27 years, John Paul II's reign (1978 to 2005) was the second longest in the history of the Roman Catholic Church. John Paul II was the only Polish Pope in history, and the first non-Italian since the early 1500s. He is credited by many with hastening the fall of Communism—an event of no small significance in Poland, a country under Soviet rule from 1945 to 1989.

Romania

While Albania was probably the harshest environment for Christians under Soviet rule, the Romanian Orthodox Church was perhaps the least suppressed during the period, albeit with sporadic and at times intense persecution. Timothy Ware writes, "Throughout the Communist period the number of clergy in Romania continued to rise, and many new churches were opened.... [T]here was also a striking monastic renewal."[31] However, we must not take this idea too far; this was the Soviet Union after all, and religion was by and large taboo. Pacurariu writes that the church was "a barely tolerated institution" under the dictatorial rule of Nicolae Ceausescu (ruled Romania 1965–1989). Faculties were closed, priests were sporadically arrested, and "Massive church demolishing began in Bucharest in the 1960s."[32] The church noticed the developing trend under Ceausescu's rule and, in many minds, began to compromise with the government in order to preserve itself. The end result was "...the Church's moral authority had been gravely impaired because of its cooperation with the hated regime."[33]

Romania is an interesting case study in the ambiguity of what constitutes "Eastern" or "Western" Europe. On the one hand, Romania's language is Latin-based, thus linguistically it identifies more with the Western part of Europe. On the other hand, the country is overwhelmingly Orthodox, connecting it to Eastern Europe. Romanian Christianity has ancient roots—possibly even prior to Constantine's Edict of Milan in 313. Romanians consider themselves, along with the Greeks, to be "...the earliest Christian people in south-east Europe.[34] For centuries Romania remained a largely imperial church, although historically there were various centers for Orthodoxy in the land: Moldova (or, Moldavia—known historically as Bessarabia—which is now its own country), Transylvania, and Wallachia. Along with Russia, Romania's Orthodox revival has been influenced greatly in recent years by a classic text in the Eastern Orthodox traditions known as the *Philokalia* ("love of the beautiful").[35] The *Philokalia* is a collection of readings from the mystical, hesychast tradition of Eastern Orthodoxy. The texts were composed over the course of a millennium between the fourth and fifteenth centuries by many different monks. "The *Philokalia*, more than any other text, reflects the Eastern Church's interpretation of the Bible's meaning."[36]

Russia

The Russian Orthodox Church's response to the rapidly changing conditions in post-Soviet society is important, for the Russian church in many ways is a guiding force to the Orthodox churches of the region.[37] The transition has been chaotic; prior to the period of *glasnost*, church activity was severely restricted and participation in it meant persecution such as the loss of a job, rejection from the university, or even imprisonment. *Glasnost* was Mikhail Gorbachev's (led Russia from 1985 to 1991) idea in the 1980s that Russia should become more open and transparent. When *glasnost* came, it was very disorienting for Russians who had been forced to live under oppressive, Marxist suspicion for seven decades. When the Soviet Union fell in 1991, there was a religious revival: churches were restored, priests ordained, hundreds of monasteries revived. It was a time for rediscovery. However, the change, in some ways, may have been too rapid:

> In 1987 there were only three monasteries in Russia; today there are 478. Then there were just two seminaries; now there are 25. Most striking is the explosion of churches, from about 2000 in Gorbachev's time to nearly 13,000 today. The Russian Orthodox Church has grown into a sprawling institution, with dozens of publishing houses and hundreds of thriving journals, newspapers, and websites.[38]

The new period of openness has been both a blessing and a curse for the Russian Orthodox Church. On the positive side, Russians are today rather free to practice their faith and a powerful force has been unleashed in the charitable sector: orphanages, various church outreach programs, youth works, hospital chaplaincies and prison ministries. However, in the minds of the Orthodox, there are new problems which will take time to address. For example, Protestant and Catholic missionaries flooded the land after the Soviet Union fell, a move the Orthodox Church deeply resents, and they established various non-Orthodox churches all across the region. Second, secularization—a ubiquitous trend in Western Europe—is prominent, and it is not altogether clear yet whether Russia will take the religious route or the secular route. While the majority of Russians call themselves Orthodox, church attendance is in the single digits, resembling that of Western Europe. A third problem is the old tendency of the Russian Church to enmesh itself within the state. Schmemann writes,

> ...[C]ritics argue that Alexy and other senior prelates have been all too happy to accept the trappings of a state church and have done little to resist the Kremlin's drift into authoritarianism. Although the Russian Constitution calls for the separation of church and state, Russia's three post-Soviet presidents—Boris Yeltsin, Vladimir Putin, and Dmitry Medvedev—have made regular, well-publicized appearances in church, and Orthodox bishops and priests are fixtures at state functions.[39]

It is not clear which direction the Russian clergy will direct the church, whether into a handmaiden of the state or an autonomous entity, free to challenge the state.

Serbia

One of the more volatile nations in Europe, Serbia has been racked by conflict in recent times. A former part of the now-defunct nation of Yugoslavia, Serbia's political turmoil has continued even since its declaration of independence in 2006. Kosovo, a strongly Islamic region, seceded from Christian Serbia in 2008 and its status is recognized by some nations but not by others. Serbia was a part of Yugoslavia and was thus connected to the Soviet Union during the Cold War. However, the leader of the Communist Party in Yugoslavia—President Josip Broz Tito (ruled 1945 to 1980)—consistently kept Moscow at arm's length. Nevertheless, when the Soviet Union began to crack apart, Yugoslavia erupted into violence—a horrific chapter known as the Yugoslav Wars. In the 1990s, Slobodan Milosevic (in power from 1989 to 2000) was president of a Serbian state and led a bloody campaign to recreate a Serbian empire in the tattered region by spearheading various assaults on non-Serbs. Milosevic was charged with crimes against humanity, including genocide, by the International Criminal Tribunal but died during the proceedings. Serbia is today an independent nation, although the sensitivities around the secessionist state of Kosovo keep tensions high.

The Serbian Church is autocephalous and has members all throughout the Balkans, prominently in Serbia, Montenegro, Bosnia and Herzegovina, Croatia, and Macedonia. Serbian identity is tied to the Eastern Orthodox Church. Serbs speak the same language of Croats and Bosnians, but they differ in religion: Croats tend to be Catholic and Bosnians tend to be Islamic. There are significant numbers of Serbs in Bosnia, however. In Serbia, "Love for the Church and loyalty to the nation are inextricably linked."[40] This leads to the tendency of nationalism being intertwined with the church. Serbs were on both sides of nationalistic, ethnic violence during the latter part of the twentieth century; however, they were persecuted terribly at the hands of Croatian fascists during the Second World War. Ware notes, "In Croatia half the Serbian population perished, and many Orthodox were forcibly 'converted' to Roman Catholicism at gunpoint."[41] This caused deep resentment towards Catholics by Serbians throughout the late twentieth century. The resentment was unleashed in the wars of the 1990s between Serbs and Croats.

The Serbian church today consists of over eight million members. It has centers of learning in Belgrade, Serbia's capital, as well as in the United States (Libertyville, Illinois) and in Bosnia and Herzegovina. One of the unique aspects of the Serbian church is the highly popular ritual celebration known as

Slava—a family festival that commemorates the family's saint day, when the family was baptized into the Christian faith out of its pagan background a millennium ago. This day is supremely important to Serbians for the preservation of their culture, primarily against the threat of Islam. Perhaps more than others, Serbians realize what was pointed out earlier: "All Orthodox countries had been at one time or another under the domination of Islam."[42]

Ukraine

Ukraine has the second largest population in Eastern Europe, and one of the most complicated religious histories in all of Europe. At one time the Russian Empire was based in Kiev, the capital and largest city of Ukraine. Thus, Ukraine became Orthodox in 988 when Vladimir of Kiev converted to the faith and expected the same of his people. Like much of Russia, Kievan Rus fell to the Mongol invasions in the thirteenth century. In the fourteenth century, Poland and Lithuania defeated the Mongols and brought with them Roman Catholic Christianity. This forced a difficult decision upon Ukraine. In 1596, at the famous Council of Brest-Litovsk (also known as the Union of Brest), the leadership of the Ukrainian Church allied itself with Rome. Many of the members and clergy disapproved, however, leading to a rebellion that fractured the Christians of Ukraine. The Roman Church was in the midst of the Counter-Reformation and thus attempted to make up for lost lands in northern Europe. Jesuit schools were established to train the people in the ways of Rome. A power struggle ensued. "[T]he Union of Brest has embittered relations between Orthodoxy and Rome from 1596 until the present day."[43] In time, the Orthodox tradition managed to win the devotion of the majority of the people; however, many others remained Roman Catholic. These Christians are known as "Ukrainian Greek Catholic." They are Orthodox (Greek) in virtually every way with the exception that they honor the Roman pope as supreme. Even their liturgy is Orthodox and their priests are allowed to marry. During Ukraine's Soviet years, the Roman Church was outlawed, representing "...perhaps the darkest chapter in the story of the Moscow Patriarchate's collusion with Communism."[44] Today, tensions between Catholic and Orthodox Christians in Ukraine remain. "Eastern Catholics" in Ukraine are often derided as "Uniates"—a pejorative term that is still a bone of contention. Of the many Eastern Catholic churches in the world, the Ukrainian Greek Catholic is the largest, with over four million members.[45]

One of the latest developments of Christianity in Ukraine has been the growth of Protestant and Independent churches. One of the more important examples is the Embassy of the Blessed Kingdom of God founded by Nigerian-born Sunday Adelaja in the early 1990s. Philip Jenkins writes, "The church offers a charismatic and supernatural-oriented message, as followers claim to have been cured of cancer, AIDS, and to have been raised from the dead."[46] Pastor Adelaja claims his church is the largest congregation in Europe. At well over 25,000 members in the city of Kiev alone, his claim may well be accurate.[47]

Three Questions for Analysis

1. Does socialism seem to be better for people than religion?

2. Is Christianity healthier when it emphasizes the ancient traditions (as in Orthodoxy) or when it always tries to reform (as in Protestantism)?

3. Eastern Europe's population is in steep decline. Is having fewer babies, or no babies, perhaps the most responsible thing to do from an environmental perspective?

Western Europe

PEOPLE

Total Population:	389,846,133
Total Median Age:	41.1 years
Life Expectancy:	79.6 years
Fertility Rate:	1.56 children born/woman

RELIGION

Top Religion Percentages:	Christian (78.09%)
	Nonreligious (14.21%)
	Muslim (3.86%)
	Atheist (2.73)
	Jewish (0.31%)
	Hindu (0.16%)
Number of Christians:	304,430,845
Major Christian Groupings:	Catholic (63.22%)
	Protestant/Independent (36.00%)
	Orthodox (0.78%)

• C H A P T E R   F O U R •

WESTERN EUROPEAN CHRISTIANITY

I n 2002, Philip Jenkins's enormously popular book *The Next Christendom* began with this line: "Europe is the Faith."[1] Jenkins was quoting a well-known French-born writer named Joseph Hilaire Belloc who lived from 1870 to 1953. As wrong-headed as it seems today, at the time, Belloc was spot on. Europe was indeed the faith. In the year 1900, well over two-thirds of the world's Christians lived in Europe.[2] Europe in 1900 was basically divided into three segments: Eastern Europe was mainly Orthodox, while Western Europe was either Protestant or Catholic. Northern Europe was largely Protestant while southern Europe was solidly Catholic.

To illustrate the European face of Christianity in recent history, another statistic will be helpful. In 1900, eight of the world's top ten Christian-populated countries were in Europe: Britain, Germany, France, Spain, Italy, Russia, Poland, and Ukraine, although the latter three are in Eastern Europe.[3] The two non-European countries that made it into this top-ten list were the USA and Brazil, both former colonies of Western European nations and were thus, respectively, strongly Protestant and Catholic. There was little doubt: Europe, clearly, was the faith.

Today, the situation is completely different. In 2005, Germany was the lone Western European nation still on that list.[4] Christianity now is a global faith. The world's top ten Christian-populated countries today are the USA, Mexico, Brazil, Germany, Russia, India, China, Philippines, Nigeria, and the Democratic Republic of the Congo. To further complicate matters, Western Europeans do not attend church much anymore. In 2006, Pope Benedict went to his native Germany—a country where less than 15% of the population attends Mass anymore—and warned "[W]e are no longer able to hear God ... God strikes us as pre-scientific, no longer suited for our age."[5] Perhaps Philip Jenkins said it best:

> Europe is demonstrably *not* the Faith. The era of Western Christianity has passed within our lifetimes, and the day of Southern Christianity is dawning. The fact of change itself if undeniable: it has happened, and will continue to happen.[6]

Why did this occur? Why did Western Europe, apparently, get up and walk away from faith? This is a big question, and many historians, theologians, and social scientists are still trying to make sense of it.

What Is Western Europe?

Many scholars prefer to speak of a united "Europe" rather than splitting it into two. Others prefer to cast the net wider still and refer to "Eurasia." Culturally, however, Europe and Asia have different tendencies, different religions that are prominent, many different customs, and a different history. Similarly, we can apply the same argument to Europe; Eastern Europe and Western Europe have much in common, but there are striking differences in the cultures. While it is difficult to articulate, there are two different forms of ethos at work in Western and in Eastern Europe. To continue this thought, northwest Europe—being Protestant—is quite different from southwest Europe—being Catholic. This argument could go on ad infinitum. However, for the purposes here, Western Europe consists of 30 countries and territories, and all of them are at least nominally Christian-majority.

Western Europe has striking parallels to Eastern Europe: their populations are the oldest among the eight cultural blocks of the world—indicating an aging population; they both have the lowest fertility rates in the world, and they have about the same number and percentage of Christians. The major differences of course come in the forms of politics and economics. During the late twentieth century, Eastern Europe was communist while most of Western Europe was democratic. Economically, Western Europe developed more rapidly than did its Eastern counterpart—perhaps explaining why Western Europe's life expectancy (79.6) is much higher than Eastern Europe's (70.15). Western Europe, in fact, has the highest life expectancy in the world. Europeans may be giving up on organized religion, but in terms of health, Western Europeans are doing very well as a cultural block, considering they live longer than anyone else on earth, perhaps longer than any other humans in history. Western Europe's longevity points to a healthy and prosperous society. However, with a declining population, this high standard of living may become compromised in the future.

Western Europe ranks as the fourth most populated cultural block in the world, after Asia, Africa, and Latin America. The highly populated nations of Western Europe are Germany (82 million), France (62 million), United Kingdom (61 million), Italy (58 million), and Spain (40 million). The other nations that have at least nine million people are the Netherlands, Belgium, Portugal, and Sweden. Austria and Switzerland fall just short of nine million. The major Scandinavian nations in northern Europe—Denmark, Finland, and Norway—

each have around five million people, as does Ireland. The rest of the nations and territories have comparatively low populations: Andorra, Channel Islands, Faeroe Islands, Gibraltar, Greenland, Holy See (Vatican City), Iceland, Isle of Man, Liechtenstein, Luxembourg, Malta, Monaco, San Marino, Slovenia, and Svalbard.

While Western Europe ranks fourth in population, this fact may change in the near future due to a declining fertility rate. While Eastern Europe is less fertile than Western Europe, neither of them are replacing themselves, a phenomenon that Philip Jenkins has labeled "The Birth Dearth ... a self-destructive social experiment unprecedented in human history ... [a] slow-motion autogenocide."[7] Western Europe's fertility rate is today an abysmal 1.56, hardly enough to keep its population in the future without turning to immigration. Western Europe also reflects an aging population, spelling problems for the future. The cost-heavy socialized medical systems in Europe are being paid for by fewer and fewer workers. In recent history, the countries of Western Europe have been known as welfare states, looking after the needs of their lowest socio-economic segments of the population. However, this approach costs money. Many immigrants come with health problems not typically seen these days in the West, such as "... vitamin deficiencies, intestinal parasites and infectious diseases like tuberculosis, for instance—and unusually high levels of emotional trauma and stress," due to tragedies such as war, extreme poverty, and political or religious persecution, even genocide—witness the large numbers of Armenian, Sudanese, and Vietnamese immigrants all over the Western world.[8] Unless trends change soon, all of Western Europe will experience a major crunch in the not-too-distant future.

Western Europe's median age is easily the highest in the world, at 41.1 years. For the time being, Western Europe is relying on immigration to stay in the black financially. However, this poses some cultural dilemmas for this cultural block. Immigrants come to new lands with their own culture, religion, and expectations. Some immigrants prefer the lifestyle of their home countries, and the only reason they or their ancestors moved to Western Europe in the first place was to find good employment. However, as time goes on, those people stay, and begin to affect the culture around them. People begin to see their historical cultures preferable to their new, adopted home. They begin to want to change their new context so that it will become more like what they used to experience back where they came from. This is one reason the Archbishop of Canterbury, the head of the Anglican Communion of churches, suggested some Islamic communities in Britain might best be served if the British government implemented aspects of Sharia Law.[9] Sharia Law is a massive and complex system of law many Islamic countries use in all matters ranging from punishment for crime to how best to proceed when a couple wants a divorce. Archbishop Williams has argued that the United Kingdom must "face up to the fact" that Muslims do not relate well to the British system.[10] Many of them are practicing Sharia Law anyway because they look to their clergy as leaders—essentially disregarding the laws of the land in favor of abiding by the Quran and its trusted interpreters. Rowan Williams has argued that his suggestions are nothing new—there is already flexibility in place in British legislation regarding other religions, including Jews. In *The Times* of London, it was pointed out amidst the row:

> Orthodox Jews already operate a well established network of religious courts, the beth din, to decide matters of divorce and to settle disputes. They are based on ancient Jewish law and run under the authority of the Chief Rabbi. However, the courts are entirely voluntary and subordinate to the British legal system.[11]

Thus, in Williams's view, the same rights and nuances in legislation that are afforded to British Jews should also be explored for Muslims. Perhaps not unexpectedly, this suggestion caused a major outcry. Williams has been trenchantly criticized for this view, no doubt because of recent clashes involving the Islamic world and Western Europe such as the Madrid and London bombings of 2004 and 2005 as well as the Iraq and Afghanistan wars—wars that saw Britain take a leading part. Nevertheless, the point here is that mass immigration leads to cultural problems that would otherwise not come up. However, there is no turning back at this point. Immigration is a fact that is changing the cultural landscape of Western Europe. At this point, it does not really matter how strict the laws become, how high the fences are built, or how much Westerners long for the old days when immigrant populations were small and silent. Western Europe has a changing face; that trend is here to stay.

Religiously, Western Europe was for centuries the homeland for Western Christianity—first for the Latin Roman Catholic Church and after 1517 the various Protestants forms of faith. Western Europe was indeed coterminous with Western, Latin-based Christianity for many centuries. Secularization has destroyed that link—at least for the time being—but still, in many ways even today, Western Europe seems bathed in Latin, Roman Christianity.

Statistically, Western Europe is Christian. In every single Western European nation, Christianity is the majority religion. Overall, Western European Christians are 63% Catholic, 36% Protestant, and less than 1% Orthodox. This statistic demonstrates precisely why Eastern Europe should be placed in a different category than Western Europe. Eastern Europe, an Orthodox land, comes to an end at some point in central Europe. There are very few Orthodox Christians in Western Europe when we look at the overall numbers. In spite of seeing Byzantine churches sporadically in Western Europe, the statistics for Orthodox Christianity are tiny, only .78% of the Christian population. To put this tiny number into perspective, there are three groups that are larger than Orthodox Christianity in Western Europe: Nonreligious (14%), Muslim

(4%), and Atheist (3%). In other words, as cultural blocks, it is clear that Eastern and Western Europe can scarcely be placed into the same category due to their vastly different historical and cultural developments.

Of the 30 countries of Western Europe, 18 are Roman Catholic and 12 are Protestant. Virtually all of the Protestant nations are in the northern part of Western Europe: Denmark, Finland, Greenland, Iceland, Norway, Sweden, and the United Kingdom, for example. It is striking just how Protestant these countries are. In Western Europe, a nation is either Catholic or Protestant, and the statistics are almost always overwhelming. This dynamic has largely to do with an old Western European treaty that declared "*cuius regio, eius religio*," or, "whose realm, (use) his religion." This treaty, the all-important Treaty of Westphalia, essentially set the stage for what we know as either Catholic or Protestant Europe. The conclusion of that treaty meant that if a person's ruler was Protestant, the person was expected to be Protestant. If he was Catholic, he remained faithful to Rome. As a result, in Western Europe, Protestant nations are usually very Protestant and Catholic nations are very Catholic. There are only a few nations in Western Europe that are split. Germany is an excellent case study for looking at this topic. After the Reformation, Germany—where the Protestant Reformation began—became rent into two: a Protestant north and a Roman Catholic south. To this day, that essential character continues. Of the Christians in Germany today—which constitute 72% of the entire population—a little over half are Protestant (54%) and a little under half are Roman Catholic (44%). Another similar example is Holland, or, the Netherlands, where 57% of the Christians are Catholic and 43% of them are Protestant. It should be pointed out, however, that Holland is today only 66% Christian—very surprising for a land that used to be the soul of Protestantism in mainland Europe. Switzerland is the other example of a roughly half/half population, where slightly more than half are Roman Catholic. Germany, Holland, and Switzerland today still reflect the fractures that came about in the Protestant Reformation of the sixteenth century. However, with these exceptions, Western European nations are either strongly Catholic or Protestant.[12] In many of the thirty nations and territories of Western Europe we see Catholic or Protestant percentages over 90% among the Christians. In Denmark, Finland, Greenland, Iceland, and Norway the Christians are 98%, or more, Protestant. In several countries, the Christians are at least 95% Catholic: Andorra, Holy See (of course!), Ireland, Italy, Luxembourg, Malta, Monaco, Portugal, San Marino, Slovenia, and Spain. In other words, Western European nations are not very diverse when it comes to religious composition. Every country is majority Christian, and in the vast majority of cases the majority form of Christianity is rather dominant.

One of the most striking changes in Western Europe during the twentieth century was its move toward being a secular society. The numbers do not really bear this out, since most people simply declare themselves to be Christian without really practicing the faith. However, the statistics are beginning to show some cracks in this once unmistakably Christian land. Many people in Western Europe are beginning to declare themselves "nonreligious." The Western European nations that have significant nonreligious populations are: Austria (13%), Belgium (10%), France (16%), Italy (13%), Netherlands (whopping 24%), Sweden (18%), Switzerland (11%), and the UK (13%).

Another interesting trend is the rise of Islam in Western Europe. During the era of colonial expansion (roughly 1500 to 1950), Western Europe ruled much of the world. Many connections were made between civilizations, and these connections remain. This is why one can find so many Caribbean people in the UK and so many Algerians in France. These colonial powers created an exchange of population that has led to what many are calling "reverse immigration." It used to be the case that Western Europeans moved to their colonial lands in order to start a new society overseas. Some of these colonies were successful, such as in North America, Latin America, and Australia. These three colonial projects rooted themselves in these new lands, and today these lands are very European in many ways. However, in some lands, such as in China, India, the Middle East, and most of Africa, the colonial enterprise essentially did not work. In those cases, the Europeans went home once the nations declared themselves to be independent. We can still find a few bizarre examples—such as a few British-stock farmers in Zimbabwe or a tiny French Pied-Noir community in Algeria. These are the scattered remnants of Western European rule, but the vast majority of Western European settlers went home after these lands gained their independence. One of the most striking examples was the flight from India that occurred in 1947. India was at one time home to a large number of Western Europeans—mainly British but also Americans, French, and Portuguese. However, after Gandhi and Nehru successfully, although peacefully, revolted, the Europeans quickly returned to Europe.

Thus, the "reverse immigration" phenomenon is a residual effect of sorts. The relationship—that was initiated by Western Europeans—has in some ways backfired. While Western Europeans may have left these lands, the people from those areas followed their retreating colonial rulers, a situation some have fittingly referred to as "The Empire Strikes Back."[13] These former imperial strongholds, armed with language skills, Western learning, and residual connections to Western Europe, are today moving to the lands of their former masters. In some cases, this trend provides peculiar demographic trends. Today, several Western European nations have significant Islamic enclaves of nearly 5%, for example in Austria, Belgium, Denmark, Germany, and Switzerland. A few Western European nations are over 5% Islamic: France (8%), Liechtenstein (6%), and the Netherlands (6%). Overall, Western Europe today is approximately 4% Muslim, and this number will in all likelihood climb much higher due to birth rates and immigration. It should be noted that it is far easier to immigrate to a land when there are familial connections; these family members can serve as sponsors for those who wish to move to the superior economies of Western Europe. Once a person immigrates to Western Europe, potential floodgates are opened. If one person is successful in his or her immigration attempts, s/he is then capable of sponsoring family members, and they can in turn sponsor their family members, and so on. Familial connections make immigration attractive. When a person from Algeria immigrates to France, it is natural to want to be joined by family, and to help other relations achieve a better life. Some countries of the world are in political turmoil, and many of these immigrants are able to make their move to Western Europe fairly seamless by declaring refugee status. Again, why would a person refuse this offer? If one's homeland is dangerous, it is perfectly natural to try to move out of that volatile context. In turn, it is perfectly normal to want better conditions for one's family as well.

We must point out here that as of right now, it is not at all clear that Islam will be the dominant religion in Western Europe in the ages to come. For every Islamic immigrant going to Western Europe from North Africa, there is a Christian immigrant from sub-Saharan Africa or the Caribbean. Nevertheless, in the meantime, one thing is obvious—Islam is growing as a percentage in Western Europe. In 2004, the eminent historian of Islam, Princeton's Bernard Lewis, famously predicted that according to current trends, Western Europe will be Islamic-majority by the end of the current century.[14] This is a startling prediction. Could this possibly be true? The problem with guessing that far into the future is that there are many variables complicating Lewis's forecast. For one, nobody knows if Muslims will continue to have high fertility rates in Europe, perhaps they may become Europeanized in this regard. Secondly, nobody knows how loose Western European immigration laws will remain in the future; for the time being, Europe has no other choice but to sponsor immigrants who will work and provide a financial base for the aging population. Third, there is the matter of Christian immigrants moving into Europe. These Christians sometimes have fertility rates as high as or higher than Muslim populations. As Philip Jenkins remarked,

> Accounts of the collapse of Christianity fail to take notice of the enormously significant growth of immigrant churches among Africans, Chinese, Filipinos, Koreans, and Latin Americans. Even if we accept the grimmest view of the fate of Christianity among ethnic Europeans, then these new churches represent an exciting new planting, even a re-evangelization of Europe. Already in London, half the Christians attending church on any given Sunday are of African or Afro-Caribbean ethnicity. Rome is home to at least fifty thousand Filipinos, most of whom are fervently loyal Catholics, and similar populations are reshaping Christian life across the continent.15

Nevertheless, for the time being, ubiquitous conferences, books, and scholarly articles abound, pronouncing the demise of Christianity in Western Europe. A 2007 conference entitled "The De-Christianization of Europe" is not at all unique.[16]

Background: Christianity in Western Europe

In the previous section, we unpacked some of the basic statistics, highlighting that Western Europe is strongly Catholic (18 nations) and Protestant (12 nations). In this section, we will provide a brief overview Western European Christianity; however, our focus will turn to recent times, when this cultural block began to secularize. What happened? More importantly why did it happen? Why is it that Europeans are so irreligious in comparison with most cultures of the world? What were the factors involved? China became atheistic because Mao Tse Tung forced Marxism onto the people. Likewise, the Soviet Union became de-Christianized by coercion; it was not a choice consciously made by the masses. Western Europe is different. Western Europeans stopped going to Church *on their own accord*. Why?

Christianity has deep roots in Western Europe. The apostle Paul went to Rome and apparently died there, as did the apostle Peter. Christianity took root very early on. Slowly but surely, beginning in the south, Christianity worked itself up the continent through missions, immigration, and population reversals, such as Goths and Franks who overpowered the Romans and became rulers of the land. In many cases these soldiers and settlers from the north held onto the Christian faith of their conquered subjects. While Rome might have "fallen" according to Edward Gibbon, the Roman Catholic faith was graciously accepted by the fierce warrior peoples of Europe. Starting from the Mediterranean south of Europe, missionaries made their way north. It took centuries, but eventually this entire block of the world became Christian. Some of the individual stories are fascinating.

The brilliant linguist and biblical scholar Jerome (lived 347–420) translated the Bible into Latin, ultimately paving the way for what became a distinct Western Christianity, freeing itself from the hegemony of the Greek churches in the East. Jerome's translation of the Bible into Latin was trailblazing, enabling the educated literates of the Western Roman Empire to have the Bible in their own tongue—the "common" or "vulgar" version—which was what the people spoke. This masterpiece of biblical scholarship came to be known as the Latin "Vulgate,"—a translation that stood the test of time, serving as the authoritative Roman Catholic translation from the early 400s to the Second

Vatican Council in the 1960s. Some conservative Catholics pine for the halcyon days when the Latin text and liturgy were revered.

The famous Welch Saint Patrick (lived 390–460) was captured as a slave in the early 400s and worked in Ireland for six years before escaping. Ultimately he returned to Ireland and initiated what would become one of the most completely Christianized lands in all of Western Europe.

The Italian Saint Benedict of Nursia (lived 480–547) founded what we know as Western monasticism in the early 500s, establishing several monasteries that spawned a massive Western European movement of piety that shaped the medieval world and consciousness. Monasteries became the hospitals, the travel lodges, the centers of learning, and much, much more. Benedict authored one of the most famous texts in all of human literature—the *Benedictine Rule*. Though based on the writings of the Eastern mystic John Cassian (360–435), the *Benedictine Rule* became perhaps the most influential text in Western Europe for a millennium, paving the way for a ubiquitous monastic culture that thrived in the medieval West.

The Irish Gaelic Saint Columba (lived 521–597) evangelized the Picts of modern-day Scotland in the sixth century, centering himself at the famous monastery of Iona, which served as a beacon of monasticism throughout the medieval world. The monks of Iona and their counterparts in Ireland became famous for their exquisite illuminated manuscripts—hand-copies of religious texts. The *Book of Kells* and the *Lindisfarne Gospels* are but two shining examples of the exquisite scholarship and cultured artistic abilities of the monks of this region.

Saint Boniface (lived 672–754) is often called the Apostle to the Germans. Courageously trekking his way through Germany's dense forests in the eighth century, he challenged pagan religions. Legend has it that he would chop down the holy oak trees dedicated to the local gods such as Thor. Boniface set the stage for the Christianization of west-central Europe, a fact that picked up speed shortly after Charlemagne, the great Frankish medieval emperor, allied himself to Christianity on Christmas Day in the year 800—beginning the long rivalry between the two lungs of European Christendom: the Roman Catholic West and the Greek (or Byzantine) Orthodox East.

Scandinavia (Norway, Finland, Sweden, Iceland, Denmark, and other Nordic territories) was evangelized later. Regarding the Christianization of that land—one of the least understood chapters of Christian expansion in Western Europe—Irvin and Sunquist write:

> In Scandinavia Viking raiders unintentionally helped introduce Christianity into their homelands. Christians taken captive and brought back as slaves quickly introduced the practice of their faith there. By the time churches to the south sent missionary bishops to Scandinavia, there was already some familiarity among the inhabitants

regarding Christianity's teachings and practices. Christianity proved attractive to the northern inhabitants.[17]

The missionary who often gets the credit here is Saint Ansgar (lived 801–865), the Apostle of the North. Ansgar labored as a missionary in the Nordic lands until eventually he was ordained as the first bishop of Denmark and Sweden. Shortly thereafter, the royal houses of the scattered kingdoms in the north began adopting Christianity. In the year 1000, the last Scandinavian outpost, Iceland, formally adopted Christianity, making a very "... convenient marker to assess the state of the Christian movement at the end of its first millennium."[18]

Christendom was precisely the result of missionary endeavors like the ones mentioned above. However, innumerable other stories were involved in Latin Christianity's rise to dominance in Western Europe such as trade, immigration, wars, intermarriage, and so on.

While the stories are endless, one thing is clear: a culture was being formed. A self-conscious community was arising.

> ... [A] larger civilization was being stitched together. Entry into the western community ... meant entry into Christendom, a word that first appeared in Anglo-Saxon England around this period. Traditional ... boundaries were no longer clear, in either language or geography. The traditional local histories of national warrior heroes and gods were being superseded by a longer history, that of the Roman Christian past. What was emerging was a common civilization. While a host of local cultures, economies, vernacular tongues, and political institutions covered the land, it was held together by a fairly unified ecclesiastical structure, led by a class of educated leaders and clerics who spoke a common language (Latin) in their liturgy and theology.[19]

This was Christendom—the kingdom of Christ on earth. And the pope, the bishop of Rome, was the vicar.

Western European Christendom survived as a fairly united cultural block for another half-millennium. While Christianity had become the religion of most of the rulers by AD 1000, there was much instruction that had to be done. The masses were largely illiterate; thus for information about Christianity they were reliant on the magnificent art and architecture that bejeweled the entire land mass. Stain-glass windows depicted local stories of local saints—stories that people could relate to. In Western European churches, local saints depicted in the art and architecture are some of the most important sources for communal identity in a particular region. However, the larger narratives are ample and pervasive as well. During medieval Christendom, a pilgrim traveling from Leeds in Britain to Rome in Italy could stop and rest at hospitality inns, worship at local churches, and pray with Christians in monasteries—all along his journey. While difficult and arduous, many did this. In a world where healing was linked to relics and basilicas, the holy cities were thought to be sacred, offering tangible benefits to the faithful soul who came to receive succor from the hands of the church.

While Medieval Christendom was indeed an unmistakably Christian society, it would be misguided to think these people were uniquely holy in the history of humankind. The sins and scandals are as prominent as the acts of charity. Oftentimes, as in life, the dual forces of virtue and vice could become wrapped into one, as in the case of many priests and popes—men who dutifully served their church, yet duplicitously carried on illicit love affairs, power-grabbed the highest offices of the church, or watched as so-called heretics writhed in pain at the stake. One of the most human accounts occurred in the twelfth century and involved an important French abbess named Heloise and her famous theologian-lover Peter Abelard; it is one of the best known stories of forbidden love in the West. These two towering intellects fall in love, passionately make love, and are overcome with love—all under the pretense of Abelard tutoring Heloise in the things of God: theology. They had a child, which caused them great damage, especially Abelard—he was castrated by Heloise's uncle as an act of revenge. Both of them were ostracized, but their intellectual gifts were too powerful, enabling both of them to become leaders—in Abelard's case in the university and in Heloise's case in the convent. They remained in written communication to the end of Abelard's life. Although he eventually renounced the relationship as sinful, Heloise seemed forever devoted to Abelard, and to the memory of their passionate love sessions. Heloise's powerful love for Abelard burdened her to the end of her life:

> In my case the pleasures of lovers that we shared have been too sweet—they can never displease me, and can scarcely be banished from my thoughts. ... Even during the celebration of the Mass, when our prayers should be purest, lewd visions of the pleasures we shared take such a hold upon my unhappy soul that my thoughts are on their wantonness instead of on my prayers. Everything we did, and also the times and places, are stamped on my heart along with your image, so that I live through it all again with you.[20]

Heloise never fully rebounded from the impact of their brief yet powerful trysts:

> God is my witness that if Augustus, emperor of the whole world, thought fit to honor me with marriage and conferred all the earth on me forever it would be sweeter and more honorable to me to be, not his empress, but your whore.[21]

The story of Heloise and Abelard is one of the great medieval stories. Medieval life-writing tends towards the extreme: heroes and villains. It is illuminating to read the story of something far more typical—people, with struggles, doing their best to navigate a holy life amidst a world of temptation.

In the fourteenth century, something new began happening in Europe. Scholars have struggled to articulate what precisely happened, referring to it as a "rebirth," or "renaissance." Beginning in Italy, a cultural ethos began to emerge that was somewhat different from the previous. New ideas began to emerge across the various disciplines: art, architecture, historical studies, mathematics, astronomy, and philosophy. Michelangelo and Leonardo da Vinci were only two products of something occurring on a much wider level. Copernicus (1473-1543) had the audacity to challenge the long-held assumptions of the church that the earth was the center of the universe. Copernicus, a committed Catholic, was challenging much more than the ordering of the celestial spheres—he was challenging the authority of the church. Galileo (1564-1642) did not inaugurate the idea of a heliocentric universe; rather, he confirmed it with the development of his telescope. What was at issue? Science was not necessarily the issue—that had been going on since the days of Aristotle. What was new was the approach to authority. People tended not to question authority prior to this cultural mood we know as the Renaissance.

Martin Luther (1483-1546), therefore, was not alone in his awareness that authority could be challenged. Luther was simply applying to theology a method that was being applied to scientific knowledge. It is a very curious fact that Luther and Copernicus were almost exact contemporaries. Both of them, at almost exactly the same time, were doing something very similar— challenging long-held assumptions about authority. Luther's major contribution to knowledge was his interpretive principle of *sola scriptura*, or, "only scripture." In other words, the pope is not necessarily correct. It depends on how he measures up in light of the scriptures: if he says something that has no warrant in scripture, then he must be challenged. This suggestion is precisely why Luther began to question indulgences, purgatory, and the entire church hierarchy altogether. He thought the pursuit of truth had become compromised. Luther believed truth could be found if one simply cared to look carefully enough at the text—and the text proved him correct, in his mind.

While this is not the place to unpack how the medieval world transitioned into the modern, it will suffice for us to point out that this new approach to information, this new doubting posture toward authority, became somewhat common after Luther. We can say this: before Luther, it was terrifically difficult to challenge the authoritative framework of the medieval world and its power structures. After Luther, it was not uncommon to do so.

Terrible wars broke out all across Western Europe due to Luther's protest, an event we know today as the Protestant Reformation. While Luther was indeed protesting against many teachings in his church, it must not be forgotten that he was working for reform. His fundamental motive was to help, not split, his church. In time, however, Luther, a son of the Church, became anathematized, cast out, and cut off. He was deemed a heretic. Thus were the beginnings of the Protestant Reformation and thus was the beginning of the wars of religion that split Western Europe into two: a Protestant north and a Roman Catholic south.

One of the most important consequences of the Reformation was the rise of national identities. Luther had the effect of paving the way towards "nation-states." This began to happen at what is known as the Treaty of Westphalia, in 1648. It was essentially a truce that was intended to bring peace to a warring Western Europe. In many ways it was successful. The Treaty of Westphalia solved the crisis with the dictum: *cuius regio, eius religio*, "whose realm, (use) his religion."

The Treaty of Westphalia represents the beginning of a phenomenon that became more apparent in the twentieth century: secularization. Secularization is essentially a cultural movement wherein religion becomes marginalized to the periphery. Today, it is common for Western Europeans to know very little about Christianity. Secularization challenges the assumption that religion is good for society. Like the Treaty of Westphalia, secularization is essentially a living argument that religions need to back off in order for society to be free and peaceful. Perhaps more than anything else, secularization is an erasure of the distinction between the sacred and the profane. Religious holidays become downplayed, sacred places lose their religious quality, the influence of the clergy becomes drastically reduced. It is common today to visit Western Europe and see churches turned into pubs, stores, warehouses, even mosques.

Why did this happen? There are many answers. Let us highlight only the most prominent reasons for the secularization of Western Europe:

- Nationalism: the nation-state supplanted the role of the pope, formerly known as the Supreme Pontiff. People began to identify with the land due to *cuius regio, eius religio*;
- Modernization: people moved to the cities. There was a breakdown in the old agrarian structure of society;
- Individualism: Luther's legacy persists—a deep questioning and a need to return to the sources (in Latin, *ad fontes*) for anything to become truly authenticated as true;
- Scientific advance: experimentation took precedence to religious tradition. As a result, there was an erosion of confidence in the religious texts, clergy, and institutions. Rational coherence was determined by experimentation, not by conformity to social codes or religious norms; and
- Religious pluralism: the Italian circumnavigators began to encounter people from vastly different cultures in Latin America, Africa, India, and China. These people did not have Christianity, and they seemed to be doing just fine without it.

These are some of the larger, contextual pieces of a puzzle that still confounds historians and social scientists. However, it is far from a complete picture. For example, Peter Berger, in his brilliant classic *The Homeless Mind: Modernization and Consciousness*, persuasively argues that humans in the West are discontent because of mass bureaucratization. He writes that humans no longer feel connected to their families due to migratory trends. Humans who change contexts are in many ways socially homeless, living a confused existence, "A world in which everything is in constant motion."[22] What is the net result? The result is that religion in the Western world may well be in a serious crisis. "The age-old function of religion—to provide ultimate certainty amid the exigencies of the human condition—has been severely shaken." Berger provides a label for this predicament: "social homelessness."[23]

Perhaps the three Western European thinkers most responsible for the shift towards secularization are Marx, Darwin, and Freud. Karl Marx and Charles Darwin both lived their entire lives in the nineteenth century, while Freud is more recent—he died in 1939. As discussed at length in the previous chapter, Marx impacted the economic climate of twentieth century Europe a great deal. Darwin affected the way people viewed people. Do humans come from God, or are we the product of blind, natural evolution? If the book of Genesis is based on myths, then is anything in the Bible trustworthy? Freud, more than the previous two, was hostile towards religion. Marx thought religion was truly unhealthy for society, but he did not want to see a widespread persecution of religion—which is precisely what happened in the name of Marxism. Darwin seemed rather disinterested in religion, preoccupied with the natural world. He certainly struggled with faith-related matters, but a zealous antagonist of religion he was not. Freud was different. Freud believed religion was harmful, like an illness. He thought it wise to actually reprogram his patients, removing religious belief from their minds as completely as possible. Freud scathingly referred to religion as "an illusion." Considering he was a Jew living in a Catholic (Austria) context, his suspicion of religion is perhaps not too surprising. Freud's trenchant indictments and pejorative putdowns of religion are well-known. He refers to religious ideas as "illusions," "historical residues," and "neurotic relics."[24] Perhaps most indicting, Freud defines it thus: "Religion would thus be the universal obsessional neurosis of humanity; like the obsessional neurosis of children, it arose out of the Oedipus complex."[25] Freud's conclusion was that religion must be ripped out of the mind by psychoanalysis, "... an impartial instrument, like the infinitesimal calculus."[26] Freud's conviction was that humans must grow up:

Men cannot remain children forever; they must in the end go out into 'hostile life'. We may call this 'education to reality'. Need I confess to you that the sole purpose of my book is to point out the necessity of this forward step?[27]

Perhaps Western Europe bought into this to some extent.

The reality of the basic premise of the secularization thesis is undeniable—Western Europeans do not go to church anything like they used to. However, what does this mean? Scholars do not really seem to know why Western Europe turned so secular in the twentieth century. Are Western Europeans actually less religious, or are they simply avoiding the institutional structures of religion? Every single Western European nation has secularized, if by that we mean church participation has fallen precipitously. There are several other key indicators to illustrate the secularization thesis:

- Policy making takes place separate and apart from the churches;
- Schools are no longer in the hands of the clergy;
- Charitable, benevolent welfare is largely in the hands of the state;
- Hospitals are not controlled by the churches;
- Church attendance is, in most cases, under 10% of the population in Western Europe.[28]

The question persists however: Why? Some scholars tend to think in terms of economic growth. In Marxist terms, when the needs of the people are met, religion will simply wither away—there will be no need for it. There is credibility to this view. However, there are so many counterexamples, such as the USA which remains a vibrantly religious culture.

The long decline of religion in Western Europe continues today; it is evidently a cultural juggernaut. Attendance rates are at their lowest in history, and there is little evidence to indicate a turnaround. In the late twentieth century, about 40% of Western Europeans claimed they "never" attended church.[29] Grace Davie, a noted scholar of secularization in Western Europe, wrote, "An ignorance of even the basic understandings of Christian teaching is the norm in modern Europe, especially among young people."[30]

There are some creative theories however, such as Graeme Smith's, which call the secularization thesis into question. Smith argues a fascinating idea—that secularization is simply Christianity in disguise:

[S]ecularism is not the end of Christianity, nor is it a sign of the godless nature of the West. Rather, we should think of secularism as the latest expression of the Christian religion. ... Secularism is Christian ethics shorn of its doctrine. It is the ongoing commitment to do good, understood in traditional Christian terms, without a concern for the technicalities of the teachings of the Church. ... In Western secular society we talk about good deeds, and on the whole we are charitable to our neighbours and those in need. But in public we do not talk much about Christianity.

> ... Secularism in the West is a new manifestation of Christianity, but one that is not immediately obvious because it lacks the usual scaffolding we associate with the Christian religion.[31]

Graeme Smith is not alone in this. Distinguished anthropologist Jonathan Benthall argues a highly nuanced thesis that says, essentially, religion never went away. For all this talk about Europe secularizing, the propensity for religiosity is universal, pan-human, and nothing has supplanted that. Humanitarian movements, strikingly similar to Christianity's prophetic voice of justice, are clearly a modern outworking of religious tendencies. In other words, religion is not receding in Western Europe. Rather, it is being reinvented.

In a highly creative analysis, Benthall argues that religion is very difficult to define. If we define religion as Christianity, Judaism, or Islam, then sure, religion seems to be less prominent in Western Europe. However, if the definition of religion is opened up to include concepts such as social justice, environmental activism, charity, and civility, then religion in Western Europe has merely adapted itself to suit a scientifically advanced context created by modernization and scientific methods. While miracles may have been expelled in this worldview, the longing to heal people through medicine certainly has not. Both of these approaches are rooted in a deep and abiding human orientation towards religion.[32] Grace Davie is another who argues that while Western Europeans tend not to belong to a church, they still believe.[33] Her idea has become known as the "believing without belonging" thesis.[33]

One of the greatest European Protestant theologians of the twentieth century, Dietrich Bonhoeffer (1906–1945), while awaiting execution in a Nazi prison, famously wrote about the future of Christianity in Europe. Bonhoeffer foresaw a secular future for Europe. He was partially reacting to how his fellow countrymen could have possibly allowed Hitler's rise to power—in a supposedly Christianized Germany. Bonhoeffer conspired with others to assassinate Hitler, but their plot failed. In his theological musings, Bonhoeffer struggled with the meaning of Christianity as a religion. In his view, the future of Christianity in Europe was a "religion-less" Christianity.[34] He envisioned a Christianity that was a lifestyle more than it was an institution. He wrote of Christianity "coming of age," of the world no longer needing God in an intellectual sense. Some believe Bonhoeffer may have been correct. Perhaps, indeed, Christianity as an organized religion in Western Europe would cease to exist. Perhaps the Christianity of the future would be a Christ-like ethic, a very humane treatment of other people, and compassionate social institutions, without the rituals, clergy, and buildings. Perhaps the future of Christianity would be kindness, love, and justice, lived out in the lives of the people in a natural way, without the constant prodding of the church? To many, Bonhoeffer may have been speaking about Western Europe as it exists today. To some, Bonhoeffer's vision of the future of Western European Christianity was correct.

While Western Europe has indeed secularized, and continues to do so, we would be remiss if we did not point out that there are faithful remnants scattered about the land, bearing a witness for a somewhat ghostly Christian past. In addition, reverse immigration has led to some new churches that are bursting at the seams. London has several megachurches, and most of them are either African or Caribbean. There are thriving traditional churches as well such as Holy Trinity Brompton, where Nicky Gumbel transformed the "Alpha Course" into a worldwide phenomenon for introducing the Christian faith to non-Christians—kind of ironic in a historically Christian city like London. Indeed, Gumbel recognized that his fellow Londoners had almost no idea about even the very basics of the Christian faith.

Western Europe is today no valley of dry bones. While the vast majority of people do not attend church, there are still bastions of Christian witness. For example, the World Council of Churches, based in Geneva, Switzerland, is the hub for the largest Christian network in the world and the flagship for the interdenominational ecumenical movement. Pentecostal churches are popping up all over the region, as in virtually all corners of the world. Immigrant churches (and mosques) are full and growing, with little signs of becoming secular like their native counterparts. Thus, in many ways the ancient Christian faith is still very much alive in former Christendom. Nevertheless, there is no way to predict what will happen in Western Europe. For all the talk about the rise of Christianity in the global South, it is perhaps just as likely that Christianity may, one day, rise up again in Western Europe, perhaps only in a different guise.

Western European Christianity Today

We will now highlight a smattering of examples of Christianity in Western Europe today. There are 30 countries and territories in Western Europe; choices have been strategically made, intended to illustrate larger trends in the region.

France

France has a modern legacy of being somewhat hostile toward religion. David Martin writes, "Stretching back to 1789, France had oscillated violently between being eldest daughter of the Church and first beacon of enlightenment."[35] The French Revolution is seen today as a "convenient boundary post" for a discussion of the origin of modern atheism.[36] The French Revolution (1789 to 1799) was a period of upheaval for the Roman Catholic Church in France. The church was implicated in many of the social ills leading up to the storming of the Bastille in 1789, and thus paid a heavy price. Many of the eighteenth century philosophers in France were hostile to what they perceived was a corrupt, anti-intellectual, authoritarian church. Diderot, Rousseau, and Voltaire did not quite live to see the Revolution, but they certainly set the stage for what would eventually become popular disdain for the church in the land that was, in fourteenth century Avignon, home to the Supreme Pontiff. For many years, the French Republic and the institution of the Catholic Church in France, have had a tumultuous relationship. Religion in France is a volatile issue. "Anyone preaching a religious message in France awakens all these contradictory echoes, along with sophisticated disaffection with the very idea of religion."[37] While France is today a majority-Catholic nation, the people are largely secular. As immigration continues however, this could change—in favor of Islam. France is today about 8% Islamic, but "...by 2050 France's Muslim minority could be approaching 25 percent of the population."[38] France is one of the most secular countries in Europe. Around 60% of the people "never" attend church.[39] Some scholars have argued that France may indeed still be religious, citing the phenomenally popular pilgrimages going on these days.[40] For instance, the small town of Lourdes near the Spanish border is perhaps the greatest pilgrimage site in all of Western Europe, hosting millions of Christians each year who make their way to the church in hopes of obtaining some of the healing water. Lourdes was the site of several Marian apparitions in 1858 and has ever since been purported to offer miraculous healings to visiting pilgrims. Taize, near Poitiers and Tours, is another important pilgrimage site in France, attracting tens of thousands of young people each year for large, ecumenically oriented devotional gatherings. The Taize Community is actually an ecumenical monastic group but has turned into a prayer center for Europe's youth. It was founded by "Brother Roger" in 1940 and has impacted hundreds of thousands of young Europeans since. There was an outpouring of love and shock when in 2005 Brother Roger was stabbed to death during an evening prayer service by a mentally disturbed woman.

Germany

Germany is considered to be a mixed nation when it comes to religion. The numbers are slightly in favor of Protestant Christians, but there is a sizeable Catholic minority. The current Pope Benedict XVI—Joseph Ratzinger—is German. To illustrate the secularizing trends in Germany, we need to look no further than Benedict's papacy since he took office. Profoundly concerned with secularization, the pope has spoken on several occasions against the secularizing tendencies of Western Europe. As in the case of France, the people do not attend church much anymore, but they still show signs of spiritual fervor. In 2006 Pope Benedict was greeted by an audience of 250,000 people assembled to partake of the Mass. Ironically, however, the topic of his sermon that day was secularization.[41] Recent reports, however, show signs of life in Germany. While over 20% of Germany's citizens declare themselves to be non-religious, an outright majority declare themselves to be religious. According to the U.S. Department of State's *International Religious Freedom Report 2008*, Germany is no longer drifting in the direction of secularization. The IRFR 2008 cites an important study in Germany,

> ... [W]hich failed to confirm the commonly held belief that the country was becoming more secular. Fully 70 percent of adult respondents said they were religious, and of those, 18 percent said they were "deeply religious" and regularly attend worship services.[42]

Germany has an illustrious history when it comes to Christianity. Linked to the Holy Roman Empire for centuries, Germany is probably best known today for being the homeland of Martin Luther, the father of the sixteenth century Protestant Reformation—which, truly, changed the world. While Germany gears up for the 500th anniversary of Luther's *95 Theses* in 2017, the focus these days is on ecumenical cooperation. Several Protestant denominations are currently reaching out to each other, trying to patch up longstanding theological divisions.[43] From north to south, German Protestant denominations are in the process of creating a united Protestant Church in Germany, illustrating perhaps financial difficulties, but also a willingness to put historical conflicts aside in favor of Christian fellowship. Germany is today the largest financial contributor to the World Council of Churches, the most important institution of the ecumenical movement. Overall, however, Germany is today a religiously ambivalent nation. There continues to be a cloud of suspicion hovering over the state-affiliated churches of Germany, both Protestants and Catholic, for their shameful role in not sufficiently denouncing the rise of Nazism in the twentieth century. Perhaps this helps to explain why "Young Germans [are] failing to respond to Pope Benedict."[44]

Ireland

Ireland is the land of the longest-standing Protestant-Catholic rivalry in Western Europe. The island was rent into two in the twentieth century, divided largely on religious lines: a Catholic south—"Ireland"—and a Protestant northeast known today as British "Northern Ireland." Ireland however is an independent nation-state. For many years, Ireland and Northern Ireland were thought to be the last remnants of an actively Christian Europe—spawning the hypothesis that religious competition between Catholics and Protestants essentially worked in favor of religiosity. In the last couple of decades, however,

Ireland, too, has begun a serious decline in religious participation. As of 2005, according to Catholic Church records, there is still a majority (60%) who attend mass once a week; however, this number is expected to decline due to massive retirements among the aging clergy.[45] The Belfast Agreement–also known as the Good Friday Agreement–of 1998 was a monumental and largely successful peace accord aimed at easing tensions between the Catholics and Protestants. The entire situation in Ireland is a case study of Western European Christianity: the evangelization by Patrick in the 400s, the Romanization of the island in subsequent centuries, the marvelously sophisticated monastic tradition of medieval times, the impact of the Protestant Reformation, and finally, the secularization of the land in recent years.

Italy

Italy is strongly Catholic, but like other Western European nations, has become largely secular–only 20% of Italians regularly participate in their faith.[46] Perhaps more than any other nation besides Vatican City–merely a neighborhood in Rome with less than a thousand residents–Italy is identified with the Roman Catholic Church. Italy has an illustrious history. Its capital city, Rome, was once the center of the Western world. Italy is the heartland of the Roman Catholic Church, by far the largest denomination in Christianity. In the thirteenth century Italy was the birthplace of the Renaissance–an intellectual movement that profoundly shaped the Western world. Until recent times, the Roman Catholic Church was indistinguishable from the political structure of Italy. In the late nineteenth century, Italy's secularization process began in earnest, leading to a radically diminished role for the Church. The Papal States, a group of territories in Italy governed by the pope since the sixth century, ceased to exist in 1870–during the First Vatican Council of 1869-1870. The only remnant of a politically involved papacy is the tiny nation of the Holy See, or, Vatican City, which came into being in 1929. As in the case with many other Western European nations, there continues to be suspicion toward the Roman Catholic Church due to its equivocal relationship with Nazi Germany in World War Two. While Italy is not quite as secular as France or Spain, the future appears rather grim. Philip Jenkins argues that "Residual Christianity" simply does not hang on in the long run: "Contemporary churches are surviving on accumulated capital, which is evaporating at an alarming rate."[47] David Martin points to Italy's 1975 vote for the legalization of divorce as a significant monument in the secularization of Italy; it showcased for all to see how a defiant church could easily be overpowered in public policy.[48]

Spain

Spain was the world's superpower in the sixteenth and seventeenth centuries. It is often cited as the home of the Spanish Inquisition—a blight in Christian history that created a culture of religious fear in Spain from the fifteenth to the nineteenth centuries.[49] Today its empire has been reduced to the Canary Islands off the coast of Morocco and Spanish North Africa—basically two tiny territories on the Mediterranean coast of Morocco. Spain is strongly Catholic, although in practice it is very secular. Well over half of Spain's citizens "never" attend mass.[50] Spain was ruled by a dictator, Francisco Franco, from 1936 to 1975. The dictatorship of Franco had a major role to play in the secularization of Spain, largely because Franco cast himself as a conservative Catholic, fighting against the atheist, communist world. Once Spain democratized after the death of Franco, the larger trends of Western Europe began to become evident. Before caricaturing Spain as secular, however, we must take caution, as with other Western European nations. Spain, like Italy and France, is a heartland of Christian pilgrimage: Avila—home to St. Teresa; Santiago de Compostela—and old pilgrimage site in honor of St. James the patron saint of Spain; and Montserrat—home to a monastery associated with the Black Madonna (La Moreneta). These three pilgrimage sites attract millions, especially youths, every year. While Islam does not have a statistically large presence in Spain, there are still some Muslims who remember Spain was at one time firmly under Islamic rule. In 1492, Monarchs Ferdinand and Isabella drove out the final remnants of an Islamic Empire in the Iberian Peninsula. This event was the culmination of the *Reconquista*, or, "Reconquest" of the region in the name of Christianity and has remained a cause for resentment among many Muslims worldwide. Tensions related to the *Reconquista* remain, however. In 2004 Muslim extremists in Madrid targeted the commuter train system, killing nearly 200 people and wounding nearly 20,000.

Sweden

Sweden is one of the happiest, and most secular, places on the planet. Even for Western Europe it is considered among the most secular. I have heard Swedes say "In Sweden we don't believe in God, we believe in people." Sweden's tendencies are reflected in the practices of other Scandinavian nations as well. Scandinavians are simply not religious anymore, at least in the traditional sense of being religious. In addition, they are regularly cited as being among the happiest, most satisfied people on the face of the earth.[51] Skeptic Phil Zuckerman argues,

> Denmark and Sweden … are probably the least religious countries in the world, and possibly in the history of the world. … Most people are nonreligious and don't

worship Jesus or Vishnu, don't revere sacred texts, don't pray, and don't give much credence to the essential dogmas of the world's great faiths. In clean and green Scandinavia, few people speak of God, few people spend much time thinking about theological matters ... Society without God is not only possible, but can be quite civil and pleasant. ... Denmark and Sweden are remarkably strong, safe, healthy, moral, and prosperous societies. ... It is crucial for people to know that it is actually quite possible for a society to lose its religious beliefs and still be well-functioning.[52]

The secularization trends in Scandinavian nations are well documented. Sweden separated its church and state in the year 2000, severing a connection that went back to the Protestant Reformation. Now, however, Sweden seems to celebrate its atheistic aura. Sweden's English newspaper recently proclaimed:

It seems the ubiquitous Holy Spirit has met its match in Sweden. ... Quite simply, the majority of Swedes don't think the big man exists. That's according to a European Commission report from 2005 which states just 23 percent of Swedes believe there is a God. ... Contrast this with the United States, where a Harris poll from 2005 showed that 82 percent of Americans believe in the Big G. Swedes ... have abandoned religion altogether. ... Echoes of hallelujah are becoming harder to hear and you can count the heads in most congregations on two hands. "It's probably only around one percent of the population that regularly attend church services," admits Brunne [Priest and assistant to the Bishop of Stockholm].[53]

The U.S. Department of State has caught on to the Scandinavian trends, citing that people opt out of the church because unless they do so they have to pay a tax on their income that is used to pay the clergy. It is still fairly common for Swedes to baptize their babies and ask for a church funeral, however. The Church of Sweden baptized 65% of all children born in the country in 2006; however, that number is in decline.[54]

United Kingdom

The UK holds the record for being, at one time, the largest empire in the history of humankind—pretty remarkable for a country slightly smaller than Oregon. In its heyday, the British Empire was in charge of about a quarter of the world's population. One of the most remarkable accomplishments of Britain was its ability to convert large people groups to the Christian faith. British missionaries such as David Livingstone (Africa), Hudson Taylor (China), and William Carey (India) spawned missions that grew exponentially through the years. The British legacy is evinced in language and in faith, notably in the worldwide Anglican communion of churches, which is vibrant and growing in the global south. Therefore, it is perhaps with some surprise to hear that Britain has gone secular. While statistics may still indicate the UK is largely religious, the active participation of the people tells a different story:

Attendance at religious services was significantly different from the number of adherents. According to a report released on May 8, 2008, by Religious Trends, only 4 million Christians attend services on a regular basis (defined as at least once a month) in the country. ... [M]ore than 50 percent of Muslims regularly worship at mosques.[55]

As in all of Western Europe, predictions for the future of Christianity in the UK are very difficult. There are far too many variables. Will the rise of Islam incite a competitive religious environment between Muslims and Christians, thus increasing Christian participation in the faith? Will immigrants from the global South actually reverse the trends evident today? How will fertility rates affect the future of Christianity in the UK? Whether or not Christianity makes a comeback in the UK—or in Western Europe for that matter—one thing is clear, the twentieth century was "hardly a success story."[56]

Three Questions for Analysis

1. Is secularization, perhaps, the fulfillment of Christianity?

2. The pope and many others have argued that Western Europe is a Christian society. This is one reason why Turkey has not yet been allowed entrance into the European Union. What kind of problems might arise if Turkey—a nation that is 97% Islamic—was allowed to join the E.U.?

3. Some have argued that Western Europe always leads the world in cultural shifts. In other words, since Western Europe has secularized, the rest of the world inevitably will follow. Do you agree with this idea? Why or why not?

Latin America and The Caribbean

PEOPLE

Total Population:	580,413,248
Total Median Age:	26.9 years
Life Expectancy:	73.14 years
Fertility Rate:	2.42 children born/woman

RELIGION

Top Religion Percentages:	Christian (92.62%)
	Indigenous Religions (2.91%)
	Nonreligious (2.88%)
	Atheist (2.73%)
Number of Christians:	537,579,955
Major Christian Groupings:	Catholic (82.60%)
	Protestant (17.17%)
	Orthodox (0.23%)

LATIN AMERICAN AND CARIBBEAN CHRISTIANITY

C hristianity in Latin America and the Caribbean is of particular interest because it has been recorded meticulously and much of the history has been preserved and documented. Christianity's arrival to the New World can be dated to October 12, 1492, when Christopher Columbus (1451–1506) landed on an island the Western European explorers named Hispaniola, or, modern-day Dominican Republic and Haiti.[1] Looking back with the privilege of over 500 years of history, we cannot help but laugh when we hear that Columbus thought he had reached a group of islands somewhere off the coast of India. In retrospect, we realize just how important this new "discovery" by a Western European was. Obviously Columbus did not discover the Americas; people had lived there for thousands of years before him. Siberians had crossed the Bering Strait into Alaska around 12,000 B.C.[2] They established myriad settlements from the Aleutian Islands to Patagonia—the southernmost tip of South America.

1492 is a monumental year in history, marking a turning point in the history of humankind. Prior to Columbus, world maps simply did not have the new world. Looking at a world map today, it is discernable what Columbus was thinking. He thought he had sailed from Spain, heading west, crossed the Atlantic, and had run into the "Indies"—what Europeans called the lands of South and Southeast Asia such as India, Indonesia, Thailand, Malaysia, the Philippines, and so on. Imagine a world map without North or South America—this was Columbus' map. The gargantuan proportions of the two huge continents he had just sailed into did not register with him. Because he thought he had reached India, he named the inhabitants of this new place "Indians"—the word by which they are still mistakenly known. There were many civilizations in this New World. It has been estimated that there were 57 million people living in the Americas when Columbus arrived, which would have been around one-eighth of the world's population.[3]

In his mind, he was "sailing west to get to the East."[4] Columbus's stature as an explorer cannot be overstated. He is perhaps the greatest explorer the world has known, certainly at the very top of a very short list. However, what he began was a cataclysmic epoch in world history—a series of genocides that crippled and extinguished entire civilizations. [5] Columbus recognized the beginnings of what was to be an utter massacre. He realized his own culture's technological superiority. He also saw glaring vulnerabilities in the masses of people he was encountering, as he pointed out to his Queen Isabella in 1492:

> They have no iron. ... They are very gentle and do not know what evil is; nor do they kill others, nor steal; and they are without weapons and so timid that a hundred of them flee from one of our men even if our men are teasing them. And they are credulous and aware that there is a God in heaven and convinced that we come from the heavens. ... Your Highness ought to resolve to make them Christians: for I believe that if you begin, in a short time you will end up having converted to our Holy Faith a multitude of peoples and acquiring large dominions and great riches and all of their peoples for Spain. Because without doubt there is in these lands a very great quantity of gold.[6]

It is uncanny how accurate Christopher Columbus would be proven to be, and in a very short period of time. The brutal chapters of history that were touched off by this early encounter set the stage for the Latin American and Caribbean experience of Christianity. In many ways the story is a sad one. Latin America, even its name, bears all the hallmarks of a subjugated land: "It was discovered, colonized, evangelized, exploited, developed, and debated. ... In most of these chapters of its history, Latin America played a passive role."[7] On the other hand, it was probably the greatest act of evangelism the history of Christianity has ever known. The data speaks for itself: Latin America and the Caribbean, by far, have the most Christianized populations in the world (93%), and they have more Christians than any other cultural block in the world (almost 550 million). Unmistakably, Latin America is a Christian heartland of the world today.

What are Latin America and the Caribbean?

Latin America and the Caribbean are included here as one major cultural block, although as the case with any cultural block, there are innate ambiguities. The two most obvious difficulties are whether Mexico is part of "North America," and whether we can possibly refer to Latin America and the Caribbean as similar in any meaningful sense. There are arguments for and against both of these proposals. First, Mexico appears to be part of North America when looking at a map. In addition, there are some political justifications for including Mexico as part of North America such as NAFTA—the North American Free Trade Agreement between the United States, Canada, and Mexico. However, Latinos often refer to Americans as *norteamericanos*, recognizing distinctions that, historically, have been based on language, religion, political allegiance, and culture. North Americans have been largely influenced by Britain, and to a lesser extent France, since these were the principle powers that colonized the region. English prevails as the primary language of communication in North America whereas Spanish, Portuguese, and Creole languages have been predominant in Latin America and much of the Caribbean. In addition, Protestantism has historically been the religion of most North Americans, particularly in the United States, whereas Latin America has been strongly Roman Catholic throughout its post-Columbian history. In terms of politics and culture, social scientists have often discussed the "Protestant ethic" that characterized the northwest parts of Europe that seem to have given birth to modern-day capitalism as we know it today. This ethos survived in North America to a large degree. North America developed much faster economically than did Latin America. Politically, North America has been functioning as a liberal democracy for well over two centuries whereas Latin America has a very different, much more complex history in its political development. Most Latin American nations are only recently moving to democratic systems of government. In much of the 1970s and 1980s, several Latin American nations were dominated by military regimes. Only in the 1990s did we witness constitutional democracy as the favored system of government in many of the region's countries.

Latin America and the Caribbean contain 47 countries and territories. The majority of these are tiny islands in the Caribbean that are excellent case studies in what European colonialism used to look like. Studying a map of the Caribbean, we can see the plentiful parentheses that demonstrate the European presence. Many of these islands, however, have declared independence, particularly in the 1960s when the European super empires were falling apart during an age of revolution and independence. Nevertheless, there are still ample examples of colonial hangover: Aruba and the Netherlands Antilles are still part of the Netherlands; Guadeloupe and Martinique are still part of France; Cayman Islands, British Virgin Islands, Turks and Caicos Islands, Anguilla, and Montserrat are still British; Puerto Rico is part of the United States. These regions are old colonial strongholds, and some of them switched hands more than once during the heyday of colonialism. Most of these islands are sparsely populated, although some are fairly substantial such as Cuba (11 million), Haiti (9 million), Dominican Republic (10 million), Puerto Rico (4 million) and Jamaica (3 million). Anguilla, Antigua and Barbuda, British Virgin Islands, Cayman Islands, Dominica, Grenada, Montserrat, and Saint Kitts and Nevis all have less than 100,000 people.

Defining the Caribbean region can become confusing. The Caribbean Sea is a useful point of reference, as it is the body of water around which Central America, the Caribbean Islands, and the northern part of South America are organized. The western wall of the Caribbean Sea is Central America: Yucatan

Peninsula (Mexico), Belize, Guatemala, Honduras, Nicaragua, Costa Rica, and Panama. The southern rim of the Caribbean is the northernmost edge of South America: Colombia, Venezuela, Guyana, Suriname, and French Guiana. The northern border of the Caribbean Sea is a broken wall comprised of the comparatively substantial islands of Cuba, Jamaica, Haiti, Dominican Republic, and Puerto Rico—a region geographers call the Greater Antilles. The Eastern side of the Caribbean Sea is often known as the Lesser Antilles, and is comprised of many small islands. These islands are often subdivided into the Leeward Islands and the Windward Islands.[8] The entire region goes by many names. Columbus called them the Indies, which is why they are often referred to as the West Indies. Some geographers use very specific names for various regions of the area. The word that seems to have caught on for the region, however, is the Caribbean, although it is in no sense a precise word. There are over 7,000 islands in the region, scattered about, making it difficult to make precise geographical definitions. In addition, the cultural diversity of the Caribbean—a legacy of European and American colonialism—also complicates attempts to categorize the region into clear cut people-groups.

The other major body of water in the region is the Gulf of Mexico; however the Gulf of Mexico is northwest of the Caribbean Sea, occupying a central point around which Mexico, the southeastern United States, and Cuba form a distinct border. The Gulf of Mexico is essentially a large pool with an international rim: Mexico, Mexico's Yucatan Peninsula, Texas, Louisiana, Mississippi, Alabama, Florida, and Cuba.

South America is a little easier to define. There are 12 countries and one territory in South America: Colombia, Venezuela, Guyana, Suriname, French Guiana (a territory of France), Brazil, Ecuador, Peru, Bolivia, Chile, Paraguay, Argentina, and Uruguay. Chile and Argentina are long countries, stretching for vast distances from Bolivia—in the central part of the continent—down nearly to Antarctica.

The cultural block of Latin America is usually conceived of as that great land mass south of California, Arizona, New Mexico, and Texas. This area was settled largely by Spanish and Portuguese citizens. While the vast majority of these countries used to be part of Spain, the huge country of Brazil belonged to the Portuguese during colonial times. Much of the Caribbean was settled by the Spanish, such as Cuba, the Dominican Republic, and Puerto Rico; however, some of these places were conquered by other imperial powers. Guyana was Dutch and later British and, although it reached independence in 1966, is still an English-speaking nation. Suriname was Spanish, then English, then Dutch, and finally achieved independence in 1975. The Caribbean nations get even more confusing. Many of the Caribbean nations speak English and some speak French.

During the high tide of European colonialism, the entire region of Latin America and the Caribbean offered copious resources that bolstered European economies for centuries. Overall, however, we can say with some reservation that this entire region—Latin America and the Caribbean—share a cultural history of colonization, (mainly) Roman Catholic Christianity, and an ethos defined largely by three major people-groups: Iberian settlers from Spain and Portugal, indigenous peoples whose presence in the region pre-date the European-stock by thousands of years, and black Africans who were imported to provide labor for the massively expanding commercial enterprises that dominated the sixteenth through the twentieth century. There are many other groups that a survey like this has to overlook such as the many Indians (from India) who went to Guyana, Suriname, and Trinidad and Tobago to work the farms in the aftermath of the abolition of slavery. All three of those nations have sizeable Hindu minorities: Guyana is 33% Hindu; Suriname is 17% Hindu; and Trinidad and Tobago is 24% Hindu.

While there are dozens of tiny republics in the Caribbean, Central America, and northern South America, there are two highly populated countries in Latin America: Brazil and Mexico. Brazil has around 200 million citizens, making it the fifth most populated country in the world. Mexico has around 110 million citizens, making it one of the larger nations in the world as well. The other significant countries in terms of population are Colombia (45 million), Argentina (40 million), Peru (29 million), and Venezuela (26 million). While many people today herald the rise of Protestantism—especially Pentecostal forms—in Latin America, the Catholic Church is still a strong majority in the region. To put this into perspective, there are 13 countries in Latin America that contain over 9 million inhabitants each, and in all of them Roman Catholic Christianity dominates. Indeed the Roman Catholic Church's heartland is in Latin America. Easily the largest national Catholic populations in the world are Brazil (130 million) and Mexico (95 million).

The region of Latin America and the Caribbean is one of the most highly populated places in the world—it is ranked third (out of eight) with nearly 600 million people. Only Asia and Africa have more people. The fertility of Latin America and the Caribbean is comparatively high, at 2.42 children born per woman. Only Africa and the Middle East have higher fertility. In terms of economic development, Latin America is a mixed bag. There are millions of people who are without basic resources, yet there are cities that are as developed as European and North American cities. Visitors to Latin America are often struck by the economic disparity—there may be a large *barrio* or slum-neighborhood located next to a high-rise American hotel used for international business and conferences. The economic situation in Latin America reflects this polarization, and is today one of the great problems in the region. The wealth is concentrated into the hands of a few; however, the poor are really poor and to a large extent neglected. Millions of people in Latin America and the Caribbean (especially Haiti) lack access to clean water and decent sanitation technology. Latin America is just now beginning to make inroads into this issue, which revolves largely around an old system of caste purity, dating back to the Spanish and Portuguese.

When Columbus arrived in 1492, he encountered indigenous peoples that he mistakenly thought were inhabitants of islands off the coast of India. These Amerindian peoples were many and various, organized along tribal lines. Columbus first encountered a tribe called the Tainos, who spoke the language of Arawak. However, there were many other people-groups that were soon encountered by the Spanish—Caribs, Guanajatebeys, and Ciboneys to name but a few. As the conquistadors moved inland, they discovered many other tribes, but were particularly awed by two highly organized and sophisticated empires—one based in Mexico, on the site of modern-day Mexico City, and the other based in Peru. The first was an Aztec Empire with its headquarters at Tenochtitlan; the second was the Empire of the Incas based at Cuzco, Peru. The Europeans were astonished by these advanced civilizations and urban settings. One conquistador described the Aztec Empire thus,

> ... [W]e saw so many cities and villages built in the water and other great towns on dry land and that straight and level causeway going towards Mexico, we were amazed and said that it was like the enchantments they tell of in the legend of *Amadis*, on account of the great towers and buildings rising from the water, and all built of masonry. And some of the soldiers even asked whether the things that we saw were not a dream.[9]

Upon entering the Aztec capital, this Spanish sergeant declared:

> How spacious and well built they were, of beautiful stone work and cedar wood ... with great rooms and courts, wonderful to behold, covered with awnings of cotton cloth. ... When we had looked at all of this, we went to the orchard and garden, which was such a wonderful thing to see and walk in, that I was never tired of looking. ... [T]he great canoes were able to pass into the garden from the lake through an opening that had been made so that there was no need for their occupants to land. And all was cemented and very splendid with many kinds of stone monuments with pictures on them.[10]

It was almost too much to behold. This Spanish soldier was utterly overwhelmed by the New World:

> I say again that I stood looking at it and thought that never in the world would there be discovered other lands such as these, for at that time there was no Peru, nor any thought of it. Of all these wonders that I then beheld today all is overthrown and lost, nothing left standing.[11]

Everything was toppled in one of the most complete destructions of a civilization on record.

The conquistadors, "... a gang of adventurers, mostly men quite insignificant at home," annihilated, gutted, and utterly subjugated the peoples whom they had at first so admired. They turned them into slaves under the *encomienda* system whereby they would "protect" the Indians whom they defeated by working them on their own plantations. The conquistadors tolerated no opposition from rebel forces, and took, at will, many of the defeated women as their concubines.[12] The children of these unions were, in Latino eyes, racially inferior to pure blooded Europeans, a stigma that in many ways continues today. The Spanish had all kinds of identification techniques that appear absurd to modern sensibilities. The Spanish who were born in Spain were called *peninsulares*; these individuals were the highest on the scale of racial purity. Next came the *criollos* who were pure-blooded Spaniards but were born outside of Spain; their parents could be *peninsulares* or *criollos*, or a mixture of the two. After that was a dizzying array of *mestizo* (mixed blood) categories, purity directly linked to the percentage of Spanish blood. Since the conquistadors were men, the effect of *mestizo* offspring was immediate. The Spanish came up with meticulously organized understandings for how pure a person's European blood was. There was the *castizo*—a person three-fourths European and one-quarter Amerindian. This was the result of a child born to a full-blooded European and a *mestizo* who was half European and half Amerindian. *Cholos* were persons with mixed race, but were generally considered impure because the Amerindian percentage was too high. Miscegenation occurred at all levels and became even more complex when Africans were introduced to the New World to work as slaves. *Mulattoes* were those from European and African unions. *Zambos* were the unions of African slaves and Amerindians—many slaves managed to escape and were often welcomed into Amerindian communities. It all became rather complicated and racial "purity" could be disguised or, on occasion, even purchased with good connections.

While discussing the miscegenation of Latin America and the Caribbean, it is important to point out that most of the indigenous peoples were not lucky enough to survive; the slaves who were brought in later fared even worse. The Amerindian peoples were often victims of European-born diseases such as small-pox. In this contact, UCLA physiology professor Jared Diamond has pointed out:

> Far more Native Americans died in bed from Eurasian germs than on the battlefield from European guns and swords. Those germs undermined Indian resistance by killing most Indians and their leaders and by sapping the survivors' morale. ... What gave the Spaniards a decisive advantage was smallpox, which reached Mexico in 1520 with one infected slave arriving from Spanish Cuba. The resulting epidemic proceeded to kill nearly half of the Aztecs, including Emperor Cuitlahuac. Aztec

survivors were demoralized by the mysterious illness that killed Indians and spared Spaniards, as if advertising the Spaniards' invincibility. By 1618, Mexico's initial population of about 20 million had plummeted to about 1.6 million.[13]

The Spanish victories were so widespread, one-sided, and complete that all who witnessed the events were amazed. Hispaniola was conquered almost immediately after Columbus. The conquest of Cuba dates to 1515. Cortes' genocidal successes over the Aztecs in Mexico date to around 1520. The other major superpower in the Americas was the Inca civilization which brutally fell to Francisco Pizarro in 1532. Overcoming unbelievable odds—less than 200 Spanish soldiers to 80,000 Incas—Pizarro consolidated the western side of Latin America for the Spanish Empire. Jared Diamond argues that the reasons for Spanish success were obvious: guns, horses, and European-born germs. These combined to mark a ferocious invasion whereby small Spanish army bands would regularly obliterate cities and towns, overpowering indigenous armies 500 times their size.[14] By the mid-sixteenth century, the vast triangular region from the Dominican Republic to Mexico City to Lima, Peru was firmly in Spanish hands. There were only a few tribal strongholds, but they were in retreat, and unnecessary for that matter. The Europeans had firmly established their rule, and Roman Catholic Christianity became, automatically, the religion of the Americas. There was no such thing as separation of church and state in those early years; that did not develop until much, much later.

Historian Adrian Hastings writes, "Seldom has genocide, actually in no way intended, been so rapid or so complete."[15] In fact, the sudden decline of indigenous inhabitants is precisely what spawned the era of slavery in the region—the pool of workers had been deeply impacted, stymieing the search for gold and other natural resources so vital to Spanish economical development. Times were good for the Spaniards; they were granted large tracts of land; they had cheap labor; they were in charge; they were increasingly wealthy; and they were fulfilling their call to colonize, civilize, and Christianize the lands that were, truly, now "Latin American." The only problem was the increasing shortage of labor:

> Almost everywhere the Indian population rapidly and steadily declined ... It seems most likely that the Indian population of Spanish-ruled America by the late sixteenth century was less than a quarter of what it had been a hundred years earlier, and it continued to be reduced by the enforced labour which became all the worse as total numbers declined.[16]

Natives had to be replaced, and slavery was introduced into the New World around 1517—the year the Protestant Reformation was breaking out in Europe.[17] The Spaniards, the Portuguese, and later the British, the French, and the Dutch—all of them "imported" millions of African slaves through the years to work the mines, farms, and sugar plantations that were becoming normative in Latin America and the Caribbean. Slaves would occasionally escape and run miles and miles into the bushes or above the upper reaches of river rapids so that they could manage to start a new life, sometimes with Natives, other times alone in their own colonies—as in the case of the "Bush Negroes" of Dutch Guiana and the "Maroons" of Jamaica who "... escaped from the Spanish during the British capture of the Island and settled in inaccessible mountain country from which they conducted raids on nearby plantations."[18] Slavery in Latin America is a long and egregious story that only came to an official end in 1888 when Brazil finally abolished the practice, although, unofficially, it continues. As recently as July 2007 a sugar plantation was raided by the Brazilian government and over 1,000 slaves were set free. Since 1995, the Labour Ministry of Brazil claims to have set free over 21,000 slaves.[19]

Thus were the chaotic, violent, dangerous, and unsavory beginnings of a society perpetually linked to subjugation and human injustice. Matters have improved, but far too many things have remained the same. Injustices were indeed perpetuated, but there were almost always Christians outraged by the atrocities. To this day, Latin America is described as Janus-faced. Gonzalez writes:

> Almost from its very outset, the church in Latin America had two faces. The dominant face was the one that justified what was being done in the name of evangelization. ... Conversely, we will also encounter those who protested against injustice—and particularly against injustice in the name of Christianity. This is the other face of Latin American Christianity.[20]

Gonzalez goes on to describe how Latin American Christianity has always exhibited both faces: a cruel and institutional form of the faith that seems blind to oppression, often conspiring against the good of the people, but also a voice of protest, a prophetic vision of justice, a fiery anger at the inhumanity evinced all around. Gonzalez claims:

> While it is true that ... British colonization of North America was generally accomplished with less cruelty to the native population than its Spanish and Portuguese counterparts, it is also true that there have always been in Latin American Catholicism voices of prophetic protest that were seldom matched in the British colonies.[21]

Latin America and the Caribbean have groans in the soil. It is a land that has been under siege since Columbus and his brother began taking indigenous slaves on the island of Hispaniola. Native Americans had no recourse in the face of superior weaponry and stronger European immune systems. Many natives saw little future in a life of forced labor and thus committed mass suicide.

Many women aborted their children or killed them in order to avoid contact with these brutal conquerors, the conquistadors.[22] The lands of Latin America and the Caribbean have been racked with conflict over the course of 500 years—numerous revolutions, military dictatorships, economic collapses, regular changes in governance, and a culture of victimization—little surprise given the history. While many of the nations of Latin America and the Caribbean achieved independence in the early nineteenth century, it remained a culture of injustice. In most cases, lighter skin meant more opportunity. The region maintained a European-heritage dominance that has remained in effect. Native Americans and African-descent peoples continue to battle against a culture of injustice, although there are exceptions to this rather bleak stereotype.

The perplexing question that immediately comes to mind, however, is how has the religion of Christianity managed to fare so well in a culture that, seemingly, should have been extremely wary of this religion? Why did indigenous peoples and Africans in Latin America and the Caribbean adopt the religion of their masters and destroyers? Why does Christianity continue to be such a vital part of the Latin American landscape, more than in any other cultural block of the world?

Today, Latin America and the Caribbean have more Christians than any place on earth. This region is about 93% Christian, making it the most thoroughly Christianized cultural block. In the next section, we will try to provide some contextualization for this rather astonishing development. How has Christianity managed to enmesh itself so deeply into the terrain of this land? The evidence seems to defy the results. Western Europe has secularized; the people hardly bother to attend a mass anymore. However, Latin America, the land that was conquered by Western Europeans, has emerged to replace Western Europe as a modern heartland of the Christian faith. A torch seems to have passed from one culture to the next.

Background: Christianity in Latin America and the Caribbean

Eminent theologian Harvey Cox described the conquest of Latin America and the Caribbean:

> It was Cortes who said, "We have come here to gather souls into the true church, and to *get much gold*." And I think the second part of his motivation was at least as important as the first.[23]

As should be well-established at this point in the chapter, the Spanish and Portuguese brought their Roman Catholic faith, but the way they evangelized the natives and later the Africans was, to say the least, unorthodox. In the minds of the Spanish and Portuguese, they were accomplishing a great thing. However, we cannot help but to sympathize with peoples whose lives were cut short, their civilizations pillaged, their women taken against their will, mandatory slave labor, and cultural vandalism rarely seen in history. Mass despair must have settled over this once proud region of the world. The Europeans were not content to only destroy the buildings and eliminate all resistance; it was a systematic campaign to purge the New World even of the memory of the pre-Columbian past. Jared Diamond writes of a bishop, Diego de Landa, who lived in the Yucatan Peninsula between 1549 and 1578:

> In one of history's worst acts of cultural vandalism, he burned all Maya manuscripts that he could locate in his effort to eliminate "paganism," so that only four survive today.[24]

This is one reason Native American religions are so very foreign to Westerners. There are certainly scholarly books written on the topic, but the documentary source material could have been far more abundant had this cultural destruction not taken place.

We have to keep in mind, however, that at the time of colonization, Spain was truly a great power. It was probably the foremost power in the world at the time, highly advanced in technology, and riding a vast wave of confidence. It is a very important point that 1492–the precise year Columbus set sail–happens to be the year that Spain, after hundreds of years of battle with the Muslim Moors, finally achieved victory. Al-Andalus was the name given to Islamic Spain by the Moors, and they ruled over much of Spain between their initial conquest in 711 all the way until 1492–when Ferdinand and Isabella finally succeeded in forcing Muhammad XII of Granada to surrender unconditionally. Christopher Columbus claimed to have been there on that day when Spain was declared fully under the banner of Christendom. It was a *cause célèbre* for all Christians as well as Muslims. The great age of Islam seemed to be on the decline. Christianity was, for the time being, triumphant. Europe was once again fully Christian in the minds of many; Muslims, no doubt, realized the devastating loss, and had to come to terms with the fact that their longstanding hegemony in the Mediterranean region would soon be challenged. Indeed that is what happened as the European powers continued to climb and expand, circling the world with their circumnavigators, planting colonies from east to west, and, eventually, demonstrating–for the entire world to see–that Islam was no longer the preeminent cultural force in the world. The center of gravity of global power had shifted. Europe's time had come.

Christianity developed swiftly in Latin America and the Caribbean. Columbus did not stay in the New World very long after that first voyage. Only a few months later, in early 1493, he returned to Spain, leaving a few dozen men in Haiti to create a settlement. In September of 1493 he sailed back to the Caribbean, this time with hundreds of men, including several missionaries, largely from monastic backgrounds such as Franciscans and Dominicans. Christianity went hand in hand with conquest. It was a unique blending of cross and crown, epitomized in the concept of *patronato real*, or, royal patronage. *Patronato real* was a decision granted by the pope to give the Spanish crown all authority in the New World—authority to make decisions, authority for appointing clergy, and authority in all matters related to trade and colonial settlement. Eventually, Portugal became outraged by this apparent *carte blanche* and took steps to intercede in hopes of having some of the New World as its own. Their protests paid handsome dividends for them, as the pope granted Portugal the other half of the "New World"—as it was known at the time. This decision occurred at the famous Treaty of Tordesillas in 1494, and illustrates the absurd confidence of Western Europe during the rising tide of colonialism. This absurdity is well-illustrated by the pope simply cutting Latin America in half, declaring one half for Spain and the other half for Portugal, with no regard for the people who had lived there for thousands of years.

We must say a word here about *what kind* of Christianity was introduced into the New World. For people in the twenty-first century, it is nearly impossible to fully understand the implications of a church-state relationship like that seen in Medieval Europe and into the early modern era. This form of Christianity was tied to the state. It was virtually impossible to understand one without the other. In other words, there was no place where Christianity ended and the state began. The two were enmeshed. Combined with this was the unique context of Spain in 1492 and after. Adrian Hastings adeptly described this unique confluence of trends:

> God had called the New World into existence to put right the mishaps of the Old. ...
> God had ... demonstrated almost incontrovertibly the entirely special role that Spain
> was called upon to play in sacred and human history. The development of the history
> of Christianity in Latin America was shaped, in consequence, not just by Catholicism,
> of a mixed medieval and Counter-Reformation sort, not just by its being part of a
> large colonial empire, but by a very special sort of sacred imperialism, a conviction of
> the hand of providence, of manifest destiny, which is foundational to the thinking of
> almost everyone upon the Spanish side.[25]

Everything seemed so perfect and providential. Spain discovered these lands. God had led the Spanish to the New World. God had delivered the indigenous peoples into Christian hands against overwhelming, biblical proportions. As a result, God would see them through. Islam and Judaism were being forced out of Europe in the *reconquista*, Protestants were to be driven north, Eastern Orthodoxy had suffered catastrophic defeat in 1453—demonstrating

God's wrath, and newly encountered pagans in the Americas were to be brought into the Roman Catholic fold.

Of course there were other questions of a more material nature going on as well such as: How much gold is there in the New World? It did not take long before colonial settlers began to see the vast natural resources of Latin America and the Caribbean, a land teeming with new spices, women, abundant food and water, gold and silver, human resources for labour—there was no end to it. The New World was a land of opportunity. Perhaps more than anything else, however, at least in the minds of Indians, the Europeans were intoxicated by gold. If there ever was a gold rush, this was it. One Aztec account goes like this:

> When they were given these presents (gold, quetzal feathers, golden necklaces), the Spaniards burst into smiles; their eyes shone with pleasure; they were delighted by them. They picked up the gold and fingered it like monkeys; they seemed to be transported by joy, as if their hearts were illumined and made new. The truth is that they longed and lusted for gold. Their bodies swelled with greed, and their hunger was ravenous. They hungered like pigs for the gold . . . They were like one who speaks a barbarous tongue: everything they said was in a barbarous tongue.[26]

Then as now, money makes monkeys of men. Gold, for Spanish settlers, meant a better life. Gold in those days was purchasing power.

Not all Spaniards were as brazen as Cortes in their unbridled mission for conquest. Questions of a humanitarian nature began to be asked such as: What is a human being? Must the Indians be respected? Is it permissible to capture and enslave other humans? If so, then who can be enslaved? Indians? Africans? Mixed? If mixed, then what blood percentage must not be enslaved? The dividing line between a full-fledged human and an inferior being was blurry. Europeans assumed the natives to be naturally inferior. *How* inferior was the question. Some thought Indians to be halfway between beasts and humans. A few tried to paint the picture of a Noble Savage—a people who were pristine, uncorrupted, and pure. Still others invented that highly graduated, systematized racial hierarchy based on blood "purity." Of course purity meant European purity.

In 1550, under Holy Roman Emperor Charles V, there came a council at Valladolid, Spain, to determine whether it was lawful to wage war on Indians before preaching Christianity to them. This has come to be known as "The Great Debate" and it focussed on two questions:

1. What is the true nature of the Indian?
2. Can Europeans use violence to eliminate Indian religions and instil Christianity?

Juan Gines de Sepulveda argued in a 500-page treatise that the Natives were inferior ... "as monkeys to men."[27] Therefore, the natural position of the natives was slavery. The other side of the debate was represented by Bartolomé de las Casas, a Dominican priest who had served as a bishop in the Mayan communities. He defended the natives extensively. He argued that the natives were already practicing a "wild" form of Christianity, thus there was no need to use violence. He even argued that the Indians were superior to the Spanish in some ways.

Bartolomé de Las Casas (1484–1566) is perhaps "the supreme figure of the religious history of Spanish America."[28] He was a Spanish priest who had been involved in the conquering of Cuba and reaped a bountiful harvest of land and serfs. The entire situation of the plight of the Natives began to wear on his conscience and he freed his slaves, pledging to fight for them. Eventually he came to oppose African slavery as well, and dedicated his life's work to challenging the inhumanity of the colonial enterprise in the Americas. He rose to become bishop of Guatemala and denied the forgiveness of sins to those who held on to their slaves. His legacy is profound and his writings are revered, but his legacy would not reach fruition for many generations. Las Casas's *Short Account of the Destruction of the Indies* is a shocking record, a "... numbing round of killings, beatings, rapes and enslavements."[29] Las Casas's writings were way ahead of their time. His voice was that of an activist, holding up a mirror to horrors going on around him so that those who participated could realize the atrocious nature of their behaviors and crimes. His life purpose was described in the preamble of his will:

> I have had no other interests but this: to liberate [the Indians] from the violent deaths which they have suffered and suffer ... through compassion at seeing so many multitudes of people who are rational, docile, humble, gentle and simple, who are so well equipped to receive our Holy Catholic Faith and every moral doctrine ... God is my witness.[30]

Las Casas was no opponent of his country, rather only of what he perceived to be wrong. He believed his culture was in grave danger, and had committed moral sin:

> I do not wish to see my country destroyed as a divine punishment for sins against the honour of God and the true Faith.[31]

Las Casas was certainly not alone in his thirst for justice in a culture that, in his view, had abandoned it in favor of its lust for gold. Las Casas was a lone voice crying in the wilderness, but eventually his critique and his perspective would be embraced by many—unfortunately that did not occur for hundreds of years.

Las Casas was certainly not alone in his condemnation of what was happening in Latin America and the Caribbean. One extraordinary account comes from the pen of a Peruvian Indian named Guaman Poma de Ayala (1550–1616). Poma authored an amazing, thoughtful document of 1190 pages and 496 illustrations, written in Spanish and Quechua. Poma's book, entitled *The First Chronicle and Good Government*, is a defense of the morality and goodness of Indian civilization prior to the Spanish presence. He argued that the Indians were actually Christian due to their high standards of morality and justice; they were just in need of the light of Christ. Poma criticized the Spanish onslaught amongst his peoples in the Andes, but perhaps the greatest contribution of the work is its fusion of Indian beliefs with the Christian narrative. He believed his people's destiny was also a part of God's unfolding plan. His work weaves Peruvian beliefs together with biblical ideals in order to present a more humane history and interpretation of his people's past—a history that had been demonized by Europeans as barbaric and heathenish. Poma's work went unacknowledged by the Spanish; by sheer chance it was discovered in a library archive in Copenhagen, Denmark of all places in 1895—adding insult to injury.[32]

A third voice that serves as something of a counterpoint to the rampant exploitation that has characterized much of Latin American history is the delightfully mysterious figure of Juan Diego—the embodiment of religious syncretism in Latin American Christianity. Juan Diego represents not only the pristine faith of an Indian in a climate of powerlessness, but he also represents something of a surreptitious voice of protest. Juan Diego saw a vision of the Virgin Mary in 1531. He claimed she wanted him to have a chapel built for her at Tepeyac, which, interestingly, was the home of one of the most important gods in the region—the goddess Tonantzin, the Mother of the Gods, who had been worshiped there for ages. Juan Diego went to the bishop of the region, named Zumarraga, and asked him if he would build the chapel. Zumarraga refused, but doggedly, Juan Diego kept returning until one day he brought with him a bouquet of flowers wrapped in his cape. He opened the cape for the bishop and out came the flowers. The bishop was impressed because it was wintertime and flowers were not in bloom. Furthermore, the flowers had stained the cape—forming the shape of a woman. That cape is now on display in Mexico City and is the most important pilgrimage site for all of Latin America, known as the Virgin of Guadalupe. This has been a supremely important story in Latin American history, particularly in Mexico where in 1746 the Virgin was declared to be their universal patron. The image of the Virgin has been holy for Mexican Catholics ever since, most notably when Catholic Priest Father Hidalgo led a peasant uprising in 1810 that eventually led to Mexican independence from Spain. In the uprising his troops battled under the banner of the Virgin. It was a tactic adopted by several others at various places throughout the region during the 1800s as Latin American nations, one by one, declared their independence.

One of the sad truths of Latin American history is the plight of the African slave. Men and women from Africa often failed to live to see their new home in the Americas as they died of disease in cramped, unsanitary conditions while being shipped across the Atlantic Ocean. Even as independence was being achieved, and the rights of the Indian were being recognized, the situation of the slave was far slower to improve. The year 1807 is often hailed as a triumphant victory, which it was, but to many slaves it did not matter. 1807 may have been the year that the British abolished slavery, but it continued apace in many other contexts such as in the French Empire until the 1830s and in the Spanish and Portuguese areas of influence throughout the 1870s and 1880s.

It is intriguing to realize that many slaves arrived to the New World as Christians. West Africa had been under the influence of Islam for a very long time, and thus would have known something of Christianity, but during the slave trade, there were mission projects going on all along the west coast of Africa.[33] There is good evidence to indicate that many Congolese slaves had been Christian since the fifteenth century because the King of Kongo had been baptized by Portuguese Catholics in 1491.[34] In other words, the Portuguese were in all likelihood capturing, enslaving, and trading some Catholics.

Christianity in Latin America has been deeply impacted by all parties involved in this story. While this is a largely Catholic cultural block, there is tremendous influence of indigenous religions, both Native American and African, that continue. The Virgin of Guadalupe—perhaps originally the goddess Tonantzin in disguise—is a testament, as is the practice of Voodoo in Haiti, where 95% of the population is Christian but nearly everybody incorporates Voodoo to some extent.[35] Rastafarianism is another good example of the fusion of Christianity and African themes, particularly in Jamaica where Bob Marley became a famous convert to the syncretistic faith.

Growing up in New Mexico, I witnessed this syncretism first hand. For example, there is a little church in the mountains of my home state called *El Santuario de Chimayo* which is famous for its dirt, which, it is claimed, has healing properties. There is a hole in the ground containing soil that pilgrims from afar rub on their knees, eyes, or even on their head. Thousands of pilgrims visit this tiny town each year to partake of the healing properties, prompting the New Mexico Office of the State Historian's claim that the *Santuario* is "... no doubt the most important Catholic pilgrimage center in the United States. As many as 300,000 pilgrims visit the shrine every year, approximately 30,000 during Holy Week alone."[36] Prospects for healing have always drawn believers into the fold, since the earliest days of Christianity. Philip Jenkins writes,

> Healing is the key element that has allowed Christianity to compete so successfully with its rivals outside the Christian tradition, with traditional religion in Africa, with various animist and spiritist movements of African origin in Brazil, with shamanism in Korea.[37]

The tradition of healing is alive and well in Latin American and Caribbean Christianity, particularly among Catholics. Amanda Porterfield, in her remarkable book *Healing in the History of Christianity* writes:

> Catholic and Protestant missionaries urged separation between Christian practice and heathen superstition, but Catholics tended to be more willing to accommodate native beliefs and practices and build on them toward Catholic ends.[38]

The mixture of Roman Catholic Christianity with local indigenous religion or African customs is readily on display in virtually any church in Latin America and the Caribbean.

Religion scholars and social scientists use a variety of terms to describe the act of mixing one culture's religion with another: inculturation, acculturation, syncretism, or cultural adaptation. These words are attempts at giving a name to a very complex process whereby one person convincingly shares aspects of his or her faith with another. However, the result is often that both interlocutors are changed somewhat. This is a very important point because, often, people assume that Christianity was successfully superimposed upon a passive people. This is true—but to a limited extent. The process is probably better explained as Christianity being woven into the fabric of a larger framework—a larger culture—resulting in an intercultural tapestry. Thus, Christianity is indeed adopted, but many of the practices existent prior to Christianity's impact are upheld.

In some cases, however, Christianity was superimposed. In these cases, the analogy would probably be better characterized as a palimpsest. A palimpsest is a manuscript, usually made of animal-skin parchment, which was used in ancient times. A good piece of parchment was prized, and thus there were occasions where two or three layers of writing accumulated on a parchment. When somebody wanted to write something on this used parchment, they simply erased the words, and wrote anew on the newly scraped surface. Scholars can now use ultraviolet technology to reveal layers of text on top of each other. In other words, the layer that is evident to the naked eye may only be the top layer of a textual stratification. Underneath are languages and concepts and teachings that only the trained scholar can decipher. Similarly, when Christianity encountered Latin American and Caribbean societies, there were times when the Christian faith was superimposed. However, the previous religions often did not disappear. Trained scholars can see the pre-existent religion underneath. These two examples—the tapestry and the palimpsest—are but two of many examples of how religions intermix and cross-pollinate.

Latin America has inherited a legacy that has endured from the early days of colonial rule. This is what Gonzalez means by the "two faces" of Latin American Christianity. Latin America was exploited, conflicted, and torn into pieces during colonial rule. This legacy of victimization is certainly present. However, that was not the complete picture. Most Latin American countries achieved independence in the early 1800s, although it was overwhelmingly European peoples who were in positions of governance. All through the years, however, there was dissonance, revolts, and reactionary movements that pulsated throughout the history of the region. Slave rebellions, controversies between Jesuits and the European crowns, independence from Europe, Marxist-style revolutions in the twentieth century, cries for social justice, birth pangs leading to democracy—Latin America's history is one of contrasts. Christianity has had a central role in virtually all of these episodes.

Latin American and Caribbean Christianity Today

Latin American Christianity today is vibrant and indigenous. Certainly the Roman Catholic Church is the prominent religion of Latin America, but this has become far more nuanced in recent times, particularly since the advent of Pentecostal Christianity in the early 1900s. A century ago, it would have been unthinkable to imagine any Latin American country with Spanish or Portuguese roots becoming Protestant. However, since Pentecostalism arrived by way of two Swedish missionaries in the early twentieth century, its growth has been explosive.[39] As one source puts it, "Latin America is currently experiencing a dramatic period of change in its associational life that we are only beginning to understand."[40] Already in Latin America and the Caribbean, 16 countries or territories are Protestant majority. This statistic does not explain the whole story; most of these were under British or Dutch rule, and have therefore been Protestant for some time. Some of these places contain fairly substantial populations such as the Bahamas, Barbados, Guyana, Jamaica, and Trinidad and Tobago. However, in the overall scheme of things, these are rather small nations and territories in comparison with the major nations of the mainland. Nevertheless, there are nations in Central and South America that are showing signs of eventually—very possibly—becoming Protestant. Considering Protestantism had only a tiny presence on the mainland in 1900, it is perhaps surprising to see that Brazil, easily Latin America's largest country in both size and population, is now almost 30% Protestant. Chile and Guatemala are both pushing 30% *Evangelico*—the word used for Evangelicals, Protestants, and Pentecostals in Latin America. Even in conservative Bolivia we see a significant

Evangelico minority of 15%. Mexico, Peru, and Venezuela are all around 10% Protestant.

We have to use caution here because, clearly, Latin America is not going to have a Protestant majority anytime soon; however, these trends should continue in the foreseeable future. In time, a Protestant Latin America is not out of the question. That's quite spectacular for a country where "... you are Catholic just by breathing the air."[41] Nevertheless, for the time being, we are here talking about the heart of the Roman Church.

Many people have made much of a Latin American theological phenomenon that emerged in the 1970s known as Liberation Theology. This movement achieved fame when a Peruvian priest named Gustavo Gutierrez published his bombshell book, *The Theology of Liberation* which essentially argued that God had a "preferential option for the poor." This now-famous phrase was adopted by CELAM, the Conference of Latin American bishops, during its meeting in 1968 at Medellin, Colombia. That conference was a turning point in Latin American Christianity.

> ...[The Conference] has been described as a kind of declaration of independence. Borrowing extensively from Marxist terminology, the assembled bishops condemned neocolonialism, exploitation, and the institutionalized violence of capitalist society, and demanded fundamental economic and social reforms.[42]

This quickly became an important catch-phrase in Latin American Christianity due to the masses of poor people throughout the continent. The movement even spread to other continents and served as a socialist-leaning theology of correction—God did not prefer the wealthy, the elite, and powerful. Rather, God had a "preferential option for the poor," so clearly evinced in the teachings of Jesus. This movement inspired many through its grassroots approach; they organized small groups known as Christian Base Communities that continue to be an important force in Latin America, particularly in Brazil. These groups emphasize social teachings, have Bible study and prayer times, but most importantly they empower laity since Latin America has an alarming shortage of priests.

The "theology of liberation" became a hallmark of Latin American Christianity in the aftermath of the Second Vatican Council in the 1960s. Some even lost their lives as martyrs while preaching this teaching. One famous martyr during this turbulent time, Archbishop Oscar Romero, was shot in the heart in 1980 while leading a mass. Archbishop Romero is a beloved figure in Latin American theology and his "preferential option for the poor" was evident in his teachings near the end of his life.

The liberation theology movement caught on in the Catholic Church—albeit with resistance—but it did not have the direct impact that Pentecostal Christianity has had. Some have argued that while liberation theology had a preferential option for the poor, the poor, apparently, took a preferential option for Pentecostalism.[43] Why has Pentecostalism grown so much in Latin America? Some of the older theories are that American influence in the region has promoted this form of Protestant faith, although that theory has been largely abandoned in scholarly circles.[44] This newfound faith is certainly not hurt by American influence, but that is too limited an explanation that does not account for the millions of Pentecostal Christians who have few connections to North America. Truly Pentecostal Christianity in Latin America is its own movement. There are certainly large Pentecostal denominations that have churches both in Latin America and in North America, but the leadership is almost always Latino. Besides, there are millions of Pentecostals who are fiercely independent, completely disconnected from any larger denominational framework—this has been a hallmark of Pentecostal Christianity that plays out all over the world. One intriguing point that could be argued here is that the Christian Base Community movement—originally a Catholic movement—actually strengthened the Pentecostal movement because of the emphasis on the leading role of laypeople. Lay Catholics got a taste of leadership, recognized they were being ignored by the overly hierarchical Catholic Church, and began organizing their own Christian movements.

Pentecostal Christianity has proven to be such a rising force in the region that they have frequently been demonized by Catholic hierarchs as "sects" and their members compared to "ravenous wolves" by Pope John Paul II due to their sheep-stealing from the Catholic fold.[45] Pentecostals, though, have never been known for their ecumenicity with Catholics and frequently argue that the Roman Catholic Church is corrupt beyond repair. Protestant-Catholic controversies have a long history in the Western world, but it is a fairly recent development in Latin America. Certainly nothing the likes of the Thirty Years War will arise out of this situation—as happened in seventeenth century Europe—but nevertheless Catholic-Protestant tensions are high at times. Europe's bloody era of religious conflict will not be repeated because Latin American governments are far more pluralistic when it comes to religion, and democratic—something rather unfamiliar to Western Europeans in the post-Reformation era. Besides, Pentecostal Christians—particularly in Latin America—tend to have disdain towards politics, and want no part in governance other than to be left alone:

> Pentecostal churches historically have avoided engaging the political realm, in part, because "the world" is viewed as corrupt and, furthermore, Christ is returning soon, so why should one devote time to transforming social and political structures? The more urgent mandate is to "save souls" so they will not suffer eternal damnation.[46]

Another argues the following:

[A] common theme in Pentecostal messages is that politics is "dirty" and therefore to be avoided. Association with political groups, movements, or tendencies is frowned upon in many Pentecostal circles.[47]

Pentecostals are no longer on the margins of society in Latin America. They are still a rising demographic according to the numbers. They have several factors on their side, too, that bode well for their future:

- Pentecostals do not have a bureaucratic path to becoming a pastor; many Pentecostals are untrained in the academic sense;
- Pentecostals do not have the baggage of history like the Catholic Church does, particularly when it comes to collusion with the government;
- The Pentecostal churches often operate on a budget a fraction the size of a Catholic parish—empowering leaders to plant new churches at a relatively low expense;
- Pentecostals are increasingly fitting the mold of the "Protestant ethic" thesis which has proven true in many cases—people who turn their lives around and commit to God often end up in a much better socioeconomic situation than when they were living with various social vices.

Argentina

Argentina, ranked fourth in population in Latin America and the Caribbean, is strongly Catholic. There are about the same number of Muslims as there are *Evangelicos*.[48] While the so-called "mainline" Protestant churches have been in Argentina for some time, they tend not to convert those around them—they are more organized along the lines of ideological enclaves. Pentecostal Christians tend to convert others in Latin America, and Pentecostalism got a late start in Argentina. While there is no guarantee that Pentecostalism will grow in Argentina like it has in other parts of Latin America, there can be little doubt that it will expand in the future. The U.S. Department of State notes that Protestant, particularly "newer evangelical churches" have been growing recently.[49] Perhaps the most important event in recent Argentine history is the *Guerra Sucia*, or, the "Dirty War" that took place in the late 1970s and early 1980s. It was a horrific period in Argentine history. Thousands of people—particularly police officers and military personnel—vanished and were likely murdered by the militant junta that was in power during the period. These have become known as the *vuelos de la muerte*, or, the death flights that were coterminous with the Dirty War. It is believed many of the vanished were dropped by aircraft into the Atlantic Ocean. Argentina allows for religious freedom today, although the Constitution makes an explicit preference for the Roman Catholic faith. The government provides tax-exempt subsidies to the

Catholic clergy and extends privileges to the Catholic Church in education and other areas.[50]

Brazil

Brazil occupies roughly half of the continent of South America, making it the largest country in the region. It is also the most populated country in Latin America. Brazil is a fascinating country when it comes to religion; it is extremely diverse. After the USA, Brazil has the second largest population of Christians in the world, and should retain that ranking for the foreseeable future. Brazilians can make a very significant claim at this moment in history: within its borders is the largest Catholic population in the world *as well as* the largest Pentecostal population in the world. There are many communities of mainline Protestants in Brazil, but historically they came as immigrants and are small in comparison with the flourishing indigenous Pentecostal groups. The entire Protestant population is around 27% of the country and Pentecostals account for around 85% of that number.[51] Pentecostals in Brazil are strong and growing, and are increasingly impacting the country's social fiber.[52] Already, the Brazilian Assemblies of God claim over 21 million members, whereas the homeland of that denomination, the USA, has only around 3 million members.[53] Pentecostals tend to be suspicious of participating in politics, but there is one notable exception to that: the controversial Brazilian-based Pentecostal denomination called the *Igreja Universal do Reino de Deus* (often known as IURD; in English it is known as the Universal Church of the Kingdom of God, or UCKG). Founded in 1977, this denomination claims to have six million members in dozens of countries. They are very influential in Brazil; they own one of the largest media conglomerations in the country and have seen several of their members reach very high levels of government in Brazil, including the senator Marcello Crivella, known widely to be a member of the IURD.[54] The IURD has been involved in several high-profile scandals that may have affected their once-spectacular growth. They are vehemently opposed to the veneration of icons and statues, putting them at odds with Roman Catholics in heated debates. The most famous was the "Kicking of the Saint" incident in 1995 when an IURD bishop stomped on an image of the Virgin Mary on national television in order to prove its impotence. These tensions continue in Brazil today.

Chile

Chile is nearly one-third Pentecostal, although it is perhaps surprising that it only began to separate the Catholic Church from the state in 1996. Chile was the last Latin American country to legalize divorce, which occurred in 2004.[55]

Chile does not allow abortion, either, although this is the common stance of most Latin American countries. The Catholic Church still retains tremendous power and influence in Chile. However, Pentecostalism has indigenous roots there, making it appear less of an outside religion and more of an authentically Chilean expression of faith. There was a major Pentecostal revival in 1909 in a Methodist Church in the city of Valparaiso.[56] Chilean Pentecostal churches were the first Pentecostal denominations to formally join the World Council of Churches, in 1961, illustrating Chile's unique blend of Pentecostalism with ecumenism.[57]

In 1973, Augusto Pinochet led a military coup that was supported by the CIA in the United States. It was originally intended to overthrow socialist rule due to the anxiety of the Cold War which was at its peak. Chileans had elected an overt Socialist named Salvador Allende to be their president in 1970, touching off a turbulent series of events in Latin America pitting socialist revolutionaries against military dictatorships. Pinochet's U.S. backed military junta overthrew the government and he remained dictator until democracy was restored in 1990. It was a brutal time in Chile's history as thousands were forced into exiled, hundreds were assassinated, and countless others were incarcerated and tortured if found even slightly out of line with the military junta. Pinochet's group established a rogue government that banned all other political parties and suspended the Constitution for the first several years of his dictatorship. Pinochet was heavy-handed with the Catholic Church and in some cases began to build formal bridges with Protestants and Pentecostals. Pinochet died in 2006 and his legacy is a mixed one in Chile; some revere his legacy and others despise him as a criminal and murderer. There are efforts to implement ecumenical relations in Chile, but overall, relations remain strained. Jeffrey Gros writes, "Anti-Protestant sentiments and anti-Catholic prejudices go deep in Chilean culture."[58] Perhaps some of the tension derives from the breakup of the Catholic monopoly on religion in the country. One important Latino scholar claims that the Pentecostal churches now claim the allegiance of 36% of the population.[59]

Cuba

Cuba's relatively low percentage of Christian affiliation (58%) is conspicuous, although likely misleading. Marxist influence has a long history of leading many to publicly declare themselves non-religious while perhaps practicing their faith clandestinely. Fidel Castro rose to power in 1959 and ruled until 2008, when he appointed his brother Raul as president. Cuba was at the vanguard of spreading communism and Marxist ideas throughout Latin America during the second half of the twentieth century. Fidel Castro and Che Guevara (1928–1967) were probably the two most recognized leaders of the socialist cause in Latin America during the Cold War. Following Guevara's death, Castro became the undisputed hero of the socialist agenda in the region, accompanied with the typically Marxist-atheistic belief system, although Castro was not nearly as harsh on Christianity as most other revolutionaries in the century. Suppression of Christianity in Cuba was ideological and not generally violent. Overt Christians were prohibited from getting jobs in education, psychology, and government as late as 1991. Since then, the situation for Christians has relaxed somewhat. Castro even allowed Pope John Paul II to visit in 1998, a carefully watched development amongst Christians. Cuba—like Haiti, Jamaica, and Brazil—has a large African influence, a remnant of the African slave trade. This plays out in a variety of indigenous religions primarily impacted by African indigenous traditions. In Cuba, these African movements are fairly common, particularly the religion of Santeria which is something of a synthesis of Nigerian (Yoruba) religion, Roman Catholic Christianity, and Native American religion. Christianity in Cuba is one of the most interesting stories in the region; as Fidel Castro backs off and his brother implements his own ideas, it may well be that Christianity will get a new lease of life.

El Salvador

It is impossible to talk about El Salvador without mentioning Archbishop Oscar Romero (1917–1980), probably the most heroic and celebrated Christian figure in Latin American and Caribbean Christianity today. Romero was a conservative, status-quo Catholic, but began to move towards a liberationist perspective when his Jesuit friend, Rutilio Grande, was murdered in 1977. Romero became an outspoken activist for the poor thereafter, critiquing the elite and condemning the death squads that regularly terrorized villages and targeted individuals for assassinations. The archbishop knew he would soon be killed. "His opponents circulated leaflets with a simple message: 'Be a patriot. Kill a priest.'"[60] Romero escaped a plot to blow up the altar in the cathedral while he presided, but he was not as fortunate on March 24, 1980, while administering Mass, he was shot in the heart by a member of the death squads. His final words, in the midst of the homily of that mass, were prophetic:

> Those who give themselves up in service to others for love of Christ, they will live. Just as the grain of wheat seems to die, but does not. ... There is a harvest because it dies, because it allows itself to be sacrificed in the soil. ... May this broken body and this blood, shed for humankind, nourish us, so that we too may give up our bodies and our blood to suffering and to pain, like Christ—not for ourselves, but to bring forth visions of justice and of peace for our people.[61]

A loud shot rang out in the church at that moment. Romero had been martyred while holding up the elements of the Eucharist—the bread and the cup.

His blood spilled onto the altar. Undoubtedly, Romero will one day become a saint in the Roman Church. Romero was one of many priests, monks, nuns, and other faithful Catholics "... killed by government death squads and American bombs" during this violent period.[62] One might think this would strengthen the Catholic Church in El Salvador; however, El Salvadorans are joining the Pentecostal and Evangelical churches en masse. While statistics vary, some recent claims are that over 30% of El Salvadorans are *Evangelicos*. "Some three-quarters of these Evangelical converts belong to the tongues-speaking, faith-healing and boisterous Pentecostal traditions."[63] El Salvador's capital, San Salvador, is now home to over a dozen Pentecostal mega-churches whose memberships are in the thousands.

Guatemala

Guatemala is a fascinating case-study in how Protestants were linked to the militaristic, U.S.-backed governments in the 1960s and 1970s. Guatemala experienced a horrific civil war that lasted 36 years, ending in 1996. Over 100,000 people were killed, making it one of Latin America's most violent conflicts. One of the most brutal military leaders was Efrain Rios Montt, who led the military in the 1980s. Montt was supposedly a born-again Christian bent on eliminating left-wing leaders who were more often than not Catholic. Philip Jenkins describes the linkage of Protestants to the U.S.-backed forces during the period:

> In Guatemala and El Salvador, insurgencies were suppressed by extreme official violence, accompanied by massacre and torture, and it was in the midst of these dirty wars that Protestant and Pentecostal churches made their greatest advances. According to common allegations made at the time, military authorities were exasperated with Catholic radicalism and explicitly decided to foster more amenable Pentecostal churches, which would preach unquestioning obedience to the government. Pentecostal preachers were "better than gunships," not to mention cheaper.[64]

Evangelicos in Guatemala are strong, and involved in politics. In 1991, Jorge Antonio Serrano Elias became "... the first Protestant to be democratically elected president of a Latin American nation."[65]

Guyana

Guyana is a unique Latin American country for several reasons: it is the one country on the mainland continent of South America where English is the official language; it was a British colony; and Christianity only represents about half of the population today. The vast majority of the Christians are

Protestants. Interestingly, about one-third of Guyana is Hindu, as Indians were brought to the region in the 1800s after the slave trade was abolished by the British in 1807. This also accounts for the relatively high percentage (8%) of Muslims. Unfortunately, Guyana is almost inevitably linked to the cult leader Jim Jones (1931–1978), an American pastor who forced members of his "Peoples Temple" cult to move there in the 1970s and found "Jonestown." The experiment ended in disaster as over 900 people were forced by Jones to drink cyanide poison on November 17, 1978. Earlier that day, Jones had authorized the murder of a U.S. Congressman, Leo Ryan, who had come to investigate the cult. It was the worst massacre of U.S. civilians until September 11, 2001.

Haiti

Haiti has the reputation of being the poorest country in the western hemisphere. Originally settled by Columbus' men, it quickly became a Spanish stronghold in the New World. The native Taino people of the island of Hispaniola—modern day Haiti/Dominican Republic—were virtually destroyed during those early years of occupation. In 1697, Spain ceded Haiti to the French, who imported masses of African slaves. Haiti became a highly productive colony for France, and one of the wealthiest in the Caribbean. Haiti is famous for its early revolution which occurred in 1804, becoming the first black republic to do so. The country has been racked with high unemployment, poverty, terribly difficult living conditions, and an unstable government ever since. While almost entirely Christian—mainly Catholic—Haiti is also coterminous with voodoo, or, African-based spiritualism. Haitians mix voodoo (also known as vodun) with Catholic Christianity to form a unique blend of polytheism, ancestor veneration, and the communion of the Catholic saints. Virtually all Catholics are regular practitioners of voodoo in Haiti. In recent years Haiti has seen explosive growth of Protestant communities who often decry voodoo as unchristian.

Jamaica

Jamaica is strongly Christian, but elicits some intriguing trends. While initially colonized by Spain and then England in 1655, neither Catholicism nor Anglicanism is strong in the country today. Jamaica is only about 4% Roman Catholic and 4% Anglican. This is odd because generally an independent colony retains the religion of the former colonizers. In this case, however, Jamaica proves to be an exception. The Church of God, a Pentecostal denomination, claims about a quarter of Jamaica's population. Seventh-Day Adventists claim about 11%. There are a range of other denominations such as Jehovah's Witnesses, Moravian, Methodists, and others who claim 1-2% of the people.[66] Pentecostalism is strong and growing in Jamaica.

Mexico

Mexico has a large population and is strongly Catholic. Protestants and Independents have begun to make inroads in Mexico, but it remains around 90% Catholic. Mexico has almost 100 million Catholics, making it the second largest Catholic population in the world after Brazil. There was a time in Mexico's history when secularism seemed to be on the rise, beginning in the mid-nineteenth century; it became particularly conspicuous during the Mexican Revolution in 1910 when revolutionaries regularly spoke out against the church. Perhaps the most important Mexican general of the Revolution was Francisco "Pancho" Villa (1878–1923), an ardent critic of the Catholic Church. Mexico remained a rather anti-cleric state until the 1970s when President Luis Echevarria visited Pope Paul VI at Vatican City and renewed ties between Mexico and the Catholic Church. In 1979, Pope John Paul II made a famous visit to Mexico, becoming the first pope to visit the nation. He recognized the oversight the church had made, and he returned several times during his pontificate. John Paul II was a frequent critic of North America's neglect of Mexico and Latin America in general, arguing that Latin America is like Lazarus in the gospel of Luke (16:19–31), begging at the gates, covered with sores, longing to eat what fell from the rich man's (North America) table. In the story, the rich man goes to hell. With poignant but indicting imagery, the pope was warning the richer nations, particularly North Americans, not to neglect their neighbors to the south.[67]

Mexico today fully allows for religious freedom, although the southern state of Chiapas has witnessed atrocities against indigenous Protestants since the early 1990s.[68] One of the important Pentecostal denominations in Mexico is the *La Luz del Mundo* (the Light of the World). It has a famous pyramidal-shaped church building in the city of Guadalajara that claims to be the largest non-Catholic church building in all Latin America. We would be remiss if we did not, once again, mention Our Lady of Guadalupe, the ubiquitous symbol of Mexican Catholicism that is increasingly seen in North American cities with strong Mexican populations. The image of Our Lady is imprinted on the hearts of all Mexican Catholics and the Basilica in Mexico City is quite possibly the most visited shrine in all of Christianity.

Peru

Peru was one of the great empires of the Americas when the Spanish arrived. Francisco Pizarro conquered the Inca Empire in 1532, a feat that came as a shock even to him due to the advanced nature and sheer numbers of people in the Incan civilization. Pizarro conquered the capital, Cusco, and built a new empire for Spain in the city of Lima. Peru has been strongly influenced by Roman Catholic Christianity ever since, although it is another one of the nations reporting a spike in Protestant growth. The U.S. Department of State reported that *Evangelicos* may have increased from 2% to 15% in just the last two decades. This trend may pick up steam because dictator Alberto Fujimori, President of Peru from 1990 to 2000, was notoriously hard on Protestants. His attitude was surprising to many because many Protestants banded together to get him elected in the first place. Fujimori, a Catholic, was convicted in 2009 for human rights violations such as massacres and kidnappings; he will likely spend the remainder of his life in jail unless his daughter Keiko, who happens to be a highly popular politician in Peru, manages to exonerate her father—which she intends to do if elected in 2011. Fujimori was known to be very close to Opus Dei, a conservative Catholic organization that is strong and influential in Peru. The city of Lima has become somewhat famous in modern Christianity due to its being the city where the document "Baptism, Eucharist and Ministry" was adopted by the World Council of Churches in 1982. It is often known as "the Lima Document," or "BEM." It is probably the most significant ecumenical document of the twentieth century, as it explores fundamental areas of church life across the denominational spectrum. This document is generally required reading in ecumenical studies.

Puerto Rico

Puerto Rico and its archipelago came under Spanish rule during Columbus' life. It became a possession of the USA in 1898 after the Americans defeated Spain in the Spanish-American War and remains in that status to the present. Puerto Ricans have U.S. citizenship but also have internal self government. Puerto Rico is a densely populated island of around 4 million people. Spanish is the primary language, although English is studied in school. It is strongly Christian with a Catholic majority, although at 27%, Protestants are a strong minority. When the American government took control of Puerto Rico, Protestant denominations were formally encouraged to do work there. Essentially, the U.S. government split the territory up into various jurisdictions, allowing different Protestant groups to evangelize the main island. The main groups involved were Presbyterians, Methodists, Baptists, Congregationalists, and Disciples of Christ. These denominations took a leading role in various aspects of Puerto Rican society. Pentecostal movements are active in Puerto Rico today and have strong connections to the Latino populations in the U.S. A couple of these movements are rather infamous. For example, one group, founded by Juana Garcia, the *la diosa Mita* (the goddess Mita), ministered mainly to the poor and expanded on the principle that all believers shared everything in common, "Believers would give all their possessions and salaries to Mita, and this was invested so as to benefit the body of believers."[69] A more infamous movement known as *Creciendo en Gracia* (Growing in Grace) has been heavily criticized largely because of its being so well-covered in the media. The American television show ABC Primetime featured a documentary called "Jesus of Suburbia" on the movement, founded by ex-criminal Jose Luis de Jesus Miranda, from Puerto Rico. The documentary showed bizarre clips such as followers tattooing 666 onto their skin and claiming Miranda to be Jesus Christ incarnate. Miranda has established a multi-million dollar empire and claims the allegiance of thousands of people. His teaching is that, in essence, there is no such thing as sin. Perhaps this doctrine allows him to have his cake and eat it too.

Three Questions for Analysis

1. Describe how the "two faces" of Latin American Christianity have manifested themselves throughout history?

2. Why did indigenous peoples and Africans in Latin America and the Caribbean adopt the religion of their oppressors?

3. Is it morally wrong for Pentecostals to evangelize Catholic lands? Why or why not?

North America

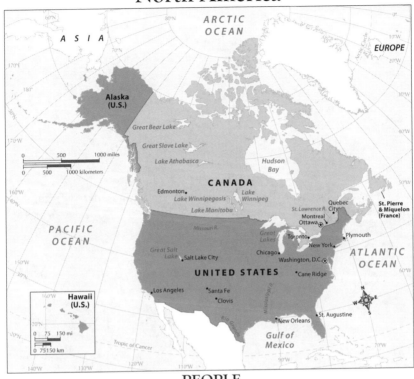

PEOPLE

Total Population:	337,044,380
Total Median Age:	37 years
Life Expectancy:	78.44 years
Fertility Rate:	2.05 children born/woman

RELIGION

Top Religion Percentages:	Christian (81.44%)
	Nonreligious (11.47%)
	Jewish (1.73%)
	Muslim (1.59%)
	Buddhist (0.85%)
Number of Christians:	274,505,073
Major Christian Groupings:	Protestant/Independent (63%),
	Catholic (35%),
	Orthodox (2%)

• C H A P T E R   S I X •

NORTH AMERICAN CHRISTIANITY

The United States of America has more Christians than any other nation on earth. Historically, the religious freedom enjoyed by Americans is very different from religious freedom in Europe. The United States has been described as giddy with religious freedom. For example, there are dozens of Baptist denominations, tens of millions of practicing Roman Catholics, many and various immigrant groups coming to America with great religious vitality, and the explosive growth of the modern Pentecostal movement—which in fact originated in America. Indeed, in America there is a certain pride attached to the bewildering diversity of Christianity. While Europe is secularizing, America remains highly religious. Canada is somewhere in between; Canadians tend to be more religious than Europeans, but not as religious as Americans.

Added together, there are around 300 million Christians in North America, and religious participation is high compared with Europe. North Americans defy the secularization thesis, at least for the time being. This circumstance has proven to be quite a conundrum for some scholars, considering the fact that North America's history for nearly 500 years has been so enmeshed with Europe's. Will North America continue to be relatively religious in the foreseeable future? Of course there is no way to know. Some scholars, such as Harvey Cox and Peter Berger, argued in the 1960s and 1970s that Americans would probably secularize along the lines of the European model.[1] This prediction has not materialized. However, that does not mean it will not happen. Conversely, there is some indication that Europeans may not be as secular as once thought. Additionally, immigration and fertility trends may result in Europeans becoming more religious in the future. Similarly, North America is an immigrant land, and immigrants often have the effect of revitalizing religion. Thus, it is balderdash to think that North America—or Europe for that matter—is inevitably drifting toward secularization, and religion's fate is sealed as agnosticism erodes all grounds for religious belief. One could argue that precisely the opposite is going on.

This entire discussion was brought to a head in April of 2009 when *Newsweek* magazine featured an ominously black cover with the words, arranged in a cruciform shape, "The Decline and Fall of Christian America." This image and corresponding article created a flurry of opinions in the media ranging from the expected "good riddance" perspective to the more common views that: First of all, Christianity is not declining in America; second, it is high time for another revival. The featured article of that issue, "The End of Christian America," by Jon Meacham, was intended to demonstrate that based on a recent survey Americans are abandoning the faith. However, the article seemed to only impassion preachers and believers with greater fervor, enlivening a type of spirituality in America that is characteristically revivalist in nature. Americans are experienced revivalists, and they should be, as Christianity in North America has been nurtured by fiery sermons, altar calls, and passionate testimonials for centuries. The unique combination of Christianity and marketplace pluralism has led to a Christianity that is consumer-driven. Churches that cannot compete will die. Historically, this situation is unique to America. Europeans had state churches. Thus, American churches have always had to grapple with how to get the consumer excited, how to keep the faith relevant, and how to instill brand loyalty when the alternatives are so ... tempting.

North America's importance in world Christianity is huge, particularly in the last century, known to some as *The Century of the Holy Spirit*. Indeed, this was the title of an important study of the global Pentecostal movement, perhaps the most important development in the history of Christianity in the last 500 years.[2] The famous 1906 Azusa Street Revival in Los Angeles continues to reverberate, radically reshaping Christianity all over the world. The implications and effects of the Azusa Street Revival continue to be processed by scholars and charismatic Christians alike, but one could reasonably argue that the importance of that gathering is as significant as Martin Luther's reforms in the sixteenth century. What was originally a little gathering of pious, charismatic Christians in Los Angeles has morphed into the new and preferred style of Christianity. Rote, foreign liturgies with highly regimented orders of worship are increasingly being jettisoned in favor of drums, dancing, emotional and ecstatic worship services, and the unleashing of the Holy Spirit with a fiery passion. Unmistakably, Christianity is becoming more and more Pentecostal. This movement is profoundly impacting world Christianity, world cultures, and even global politics.

In this chapter alone, the author speaks as an insider. As a dual citizen of the USA and Canada, I am a part of this story. Visiting Europe, studying in Asia, or worshipping in Latin America is naturally very helpful for the scholar's task. However, living in a place, understanding the ethos, speaking the vernacular, hearing the stories over the course of decades, being nurtured within—these are experiences one can only fully comprehend by being deeply rooted somewhere, bathed as it were in the traditions and culture. Even so, when it comes to North American Christianity, I do not speak as an authority; rather, I speak as a participant. No individual can master Christianity in North America, in all of its colorful guises and divergent forms.

What Is North America?

In contrast to the other cultural blocks in this study, North America is easy to define, as it consists of the USA and Canada.[3] Some might argue that Mexico is part of North America; however, Mexico is linguistically, politically, and culturally much more Latin American than it is North American. In fact, most Mexicans refer to American citizens as *los norteamericanos*.

Saint Augustine, Florida, is the oldest continuously occupied city in America that was founded by Europeans—in this case the Spanish. It was founded in 1565 but was ceded to the USA in the early 1800s, along with the rest of Florida. Indeed, the territory of the United States of America grew rapidly in the 1800s under the banner of "manifest destiny"—a catch phrase to emphasize the idea that America was to be a nation spanning coast to coast. Through a series of wars, acquisitions, treaties, and purchases, the United States expanded exponentially during the nineteenth century. Beginning with the declaration of independence by the thirteen original colonies in the late eighteenth century, America expanded vastly throughout the nineteenth as they gained leverage over their former British rulers as well as over the Spanish and French Empires which had vast imperial holdings in what is today U.S. land.

The Louisiana Purchase of 1803 added far more than simply Louisiana to the burgeoning nation; rather, fourteen of today's United States were gained from Napoleon's France for a breathtakingly cheap sum. The swath of land from Louisiana to Montana today forms the heart of the USA; the original deal included nearly a million square miles of pristine land. The expansion to California was inevitable.

Mexico, an independent nation since the early 1800s, ceded a massive amount of land to the U.S. in 1848. This huge chunk of land—known today as the American Southwest—is some of the most important land in the USA, consisting of California, Arizona, Nevada, Utah, parts of New Mexico and Colorado. California, America's most populous state, was at one time a series of coastal missions established by the Spanish Franciscan missionary Junipero Serra, hence the Spanish names of virtually all cities in that state. California is an interesting case study in Christian missions, as Russian Orthodox missionaries came across the Bering Strait and established missions and settlements in Alaska and down the coast until they met the Spanish Catholics in northern California. The Oregon Territory, including Idaho and Washington, was ceded to the U.S. by the British in the year 1846. Russia ceded the largest state in the USA, Alaska, in 1867. Hawaii was annexed by the U.S. in 1898, thus completing what is included today in the nation's 50 states.

Canada has an entirely different history, remaining far more linked to Britain and France, and for a much longer time. Even today, Canada's currency features the British Queen and, at least theoretically, Canada's head of state is the British monarch. The Governor General of Canada is the representative of the British Crown on Canadian soil. However, for all intents and purposes, Canada is a sovereign nation. Beginning in the Confederation of 1867 and culminating in the Canada Act of 1982, Canada's dependence on the British government is virtually non-existent today.

Perhaps surprisingly, it is not the Spanish, French, or British who can lay claim to being the first Europeans in the New World—that honor belongs to Leif Ericson, the Norse explorer from Iceland who established a settlement in Newfoundland, Canada, around the year 1000. While the historical evidence is vague, the scholarly consensus at this point in history is that Ericson, or at least some of his people, made settlements in modern-day Greenland and continued on to establish Vinland, "... a short-lived settlement at L'Anse aux Meadows in Newfoundland."[4] Ericson may have been Christian due to his connection to Norway, which was being Christianized at that very time. Stephen Neill, the distinguished historian of Christian missions, wrote:

> Erik the Red's son Leif had been baptized in Norway in the time of Olaf Tryggvesson (969–1000) [Viking Christian King of Norway], and brought back a priest with him [to the Greenland settlement of Brattalid].[5]

In other words, it could well be the case that Leif Ericson was the first Christian to ever touch North American soil. For whatever reason, the Norse settlements did not continue.

The French began exploring what became the St. Lawrence River in Canada as early as 1534 when Jacques Cartier suspected he had found a Northwest Passage to China.[6] Cartier was obviously wrong, highlighted in his naming a town in Quebec "Lachine," a town that still exists today. Cartier is also believed to have given the name "Canada" to New France, based on his understanding of an Iroquois word. In the 1560s, some French Protestants, known as Huguenots, established a settlement at Fort Caroline—modern day Jacksonville, Florida. It was short-lived however. The Protestant-Catholic rivalry was intense at this stage in history. Spanish Catholics discovered a Protestant settlement on land they were eager to claim for Spain, and the result was catastrophic; hundreds of Huguenots were slaughtered and the settlement collapsed. The French were unable to successfully establish a continuous settlement until 1603, the year Samuel de Champlain arrived. In 1608 he raised the French flag over a place he called Quebec City.

Generally, after an initial expedition of discovery, missionaries were recruited to plant the traditional European models of religion into the minds and hearts of the native populations. Missionaries were an important part of the second wave of Europeans arriving in the Americas, both in the North as well as in Central and South America. We must keep in mind that much of what is today North America was once part of Latin America. Thus, the missionaries whom Columbus brought with him on successive journeys have a major role to play in the North American story, since many of those missionaries ended up in places like Florida, New Mexico, Texas, and California—places more associated with North America today.

Many French Catholic missions were established around the Great Lakes, particularly in what is now Quebec, known then as "New France." The Jesuits took the leading role here in the mid-seventeenth century, notably through the efforts of a brilliant polyglot—Jacques Marquette—the young Jesuit who continued his explorations and mission work southward on the Mississippi River, nearly to the Gulf of Mexico. The French developed overall good relations with the natives and had success in converting them to Roman Catholic Christianity. Many Iroquois were among the peoples who converted quickly. The Jesuits proved to be geniuses at assimilating Christianity to the local context—frequently incorporating aspects of indigenous belief and ritual into a larger Christian framework. French settlements continued southward along the Saint Lawrence and down the Mississippi all the way to the Gulf of Mexico. New Orleans was founded in 1718, named after the French city of Orleans.

North America was on its way to becoming Europeanized and Christianized with the seemingly endless waves of Europeans coming ashore—Portuguese, Spanish, French, Dutch and English—all throughout the sixteenth, seventeenth, and eighteenth centuries. All of them brought their faith with them and established national churches affiliated to their empires back in Europe.

- Jamestown was established by Anglicans in 1607 and became Virginia, named after Elizabeth I, the supposedly "Virgin Queen" because she never married.
- In 1608 Quebec became the center of a strongly Roman Catholic New France.
- 1608 was also the year that Santa Fe—the capital of New Mexico—was founded, although Spanish settlers had been there for several years prior.
- 1620 is an important year in American history. This is the year a group of "Puritans"—English Calvinists—arrived to Massachusetts on a ship called the Mayflower. These "Pilgrims" were committed to a purer form

of Christianity than what was being offered in Europe at the time and thus journeyed westward to the New World for religious purposes. They were fiercely independent and established autonomous churches, known later as Congregationalist churches.

- In the 1620s New Amsterdam was established as a Dutch settlement; these colonists were Dutch Reformed Christians.
- The colony of Maryland was established by Lord Baltimore (Cecil Calvert) in 1632 by persecuted English Catholics as well as English convicts who had been relocated as a form of exile.
- Germans began migrating to the New World en masse in the 1680s, leading to many and various forms of Christianity taking root in North America such as Mennonites, Moravians, Pietists, Lutherans, and German Catholics.
- William Penn converted to Quakerism and championed religious toleration in the state that bears his name, Pennsylvania, founding it in 1681. Penn is often sited with Roger Williams of Rhode Island as the shapers of religious pluralism in America.
- Beginning in 1769, Spanish Franciscans led by Junipero Serra founded several missions on the coast of California.
- Upper Canada—modern-day southern Ontario—was formerly French land but was ceded to the British after the Seven Years' War (French and Indian War) ended in 1763. The Treaty of Paris ended both the Seven Years' War as well as French colonial ambitions in North America.[7] In 1791 Upper Canada was officially founded as a British colony, thus establishing an important Anglican foothold on the north side of the Great Lakes.
- In the 1790s Russian Orthodox priests, led by Saint Herman, began to have success converting the Aleutian peoples of Alaska after establishing a base at Kodiak Island.
- The industrial revolution of the late eighteenth and early nineteenth centuries led to vast immigrant populations from Ireland and Italy who relocated to the New World to make a better life. Italians and Irish are generally Catholic; as a result of that period of influx the Roman Catholic Church is today the largest single denomination in both Canada and the USA. The catastrophic Irish potato famines of the 1840s and 1850s reduced that country's population by as much as a quarter, and many of them ended up in North America, paving the way for later waves of immigration.

Thus it is clear that what was once a sparsely populated wilderness, completely devoid of Europeans, within a relatively short time became a concoction of European narratives all thrown together to form a proverbial "melting pot."

Canadians, it should be pointed out, dislike this analogy, preferring "mosaic" instead. Nevertheless, whether melting pot or mosaic, there was within a couple hundred years from Columbus a continent vastly largely than anybody suspected, populated mainly by Europeans, speaking European languages, worshiping in European ways, following European customs, and struggling to make non-Europeans conform to this model. Religiously, it is important to keep in mind that these Europeans were strongly influenced by church polity and structure in Europe. Many of these people simply assumed that each New World colony should have its own distinct religion—as was largely the case throughout European history. However, it increasingly became clear that Christianity in North America was going to be fundamentally different than Christianity in Europe in one critical way: the state church idea was simply not viable; there was far too much diversity.

All of this brings up two classes of people that are often scraped over in a rapid-fire historical presentation such as this: indigenous and slaves. In the Europeanization of America, indigenous rights were rarely honored, as pointed out in the Latin American chapter. Slaves, both African and indigenous, were treated even worse. African-imported slavery was introduced by the colonists of Virginia in 1619, about a decade after Jamestown was established. Enslavement of indigenous peoples began much earlier, just shortly after Columbus' arrival.

For Natives and Africans alike, life was hard and unjust. It seems odd today that indentured servitude and slavery went rather unopposed until the nineteenth century, and then it took America's bloodiest battle to finally eradicate the land of that appalling business. It should be pointed out that there were, from early on, prophets amongst the European-Americans who opposed the inhumane institutions that assumed people were valid forms of property:

> Quakers and German Mennonites in Pennsylvania, who in 1688 asked the pointed question, "Have these poor negers not as much right to fight for their freedom as you have to keep them slaves?" But such protests were very rare. ... [S]laves and the smaller number of free African Americans originally found Christianity as alien as other aspects of European culture. A combination of masters unwilling to provide religious instruction and slaves alienated from those who did try to preach to them meant that it was not until the early eighteenth century that a few African Americans began to respond positively to the Christian message. ... Not until the coming of evangelical revivalism in the 1730s would an appreciable number of African Americans be drawn into the churches.[8]

The issue of slavery eventually rent the United States of America into two, leading to the Civil War which lasted from 1861 to 1865. It remains probably the most sensitive national topic in the history of Christianity in America, perhaps rivaled only by the treatment of the original inhabitants of this vast frontier land.

The Native American meta-narrative is far from monolithic. Human origins in the Americas are estimated to date between 14,000 and 35,000 years ago.[9] The famous archaeological site near Clovis, New Mexico, provides key evidence to the colonization by the first human beings in the New World:

> ... Clovis sites, named after the type site near the town of Clovis, New Mexico, where their characteristic large stone spearpoints were first recognized.[10] Hundreds of Clovis sites are now known, blanketing all 48 of the lower U.S. states south into Mexico. Unquestioned evidence of human presence appears soon thereafter in Amazonia and in Patagonia. These facts suggest the interpretation that Clovis sites document the America's first colonization by people, who quickly multiplied, expanded, and filled the two continents.[11]

European peoples found the Native Americans to be highly religious. Generally, they were shamanistic, meaning there was a medicine man or healer who could be consulted for understanding the spirit realm. There was a fundamentally animistic worldview—the belief that spirits animate virtually everything. There were many taboos, such as which animals could or could not be killed for food, which places were sacred and thus could not be violated, and what behavior or activity was forbidden. However, the evidence indicates that while there were some grounds for having an overall religious framework for understanding indigenous North American religiosity, the distinctions between tribal forms of faith were pronounced indeed. One writer put it this way, "In such a picture of manyness, it seems fair to ask if there were as many Native American religions as there were Native American languages and cultures."[12]

There are three major people groups in the early history of Canada and the United States: Natives, Europeans, and Africans. Polynesians, Asians, and Middle Easterners are parts of the story that can only be mentioned: Hawaii was a Polynesian kingdom prior to annexation by America. Asians have been a part of North America since at least the mid-eighteenth century when some Filipinos arrived on Spanish ships, and later Chinese and Japanese immigrants played a huge role in building the American and Canadian transcontinental railroads in the 1800s. Middle Easterners were represented by Sephardic Jews, albeit living as "Conversos," (nominal converts to Christianity because of the Spanish Inquisition) who arrived to the New World with Columbus on his very first journey. One of these Jews, Rodrigo de Triana, was probably the first from Columbus' crew to site America.[13]

North America is today a diverse population teeming with many different cultures and people groups. In both the USA and Canada, "white" can mean many different things, as can "Black" or "Asian" or whatever. For example, U.S. President Barak Obama is generally thought of as a Black man; however,

his mother was white. There comes a point in race analysis when language de-
volves into oblivion. Many "white" people have Amerindian blood and many
"Black" people have "white" blood and many "Natives" have several European
bloodlines. It is at the point today that the U.S. Census Bureau has jettisoned
the listing for "Hispanic":

> A separate listing for Hispanic ethnicity is not included because the US Census
> Bureau considers Hispanic to mean a person of Latin American descent (including
> persons of Cuban, Mexican, or Puerto Rican origin) living in the US who may be of
> any race or ethnic group (white, Black, Asian, etc.).[14]

Racial categorization is increasingly difficult, especially in a melting pot like
the U.S. Nevertheless, the government statistics for the racial demographics in
the U.S. are as follows: non-Hispanic white: 65%; Hispanic: 15%; Black: 13%;
Asian 4%; Amerindian: 1%.[15]

While the United States is the third most populated country in the world,
and will be for some time, the North American block as a whole is rather
sparsely populated, ranking sixth out of eight cultural blocks. Only the Middle
East and Oceania are less populated. North American fertility rates are comparatively low, ranking sixth out of the eight cultural blocks. Only Eastern and
Western Europe have lower fertility rates. Nevertheless, at 2.05 children per
woman, North America is nearing the safe zone in terms of population stability. This is also due to immigration. Immigration to North America is highly
popular at this moment in history, and there is every reason to believe the
North American population will continue to grow steadily in the future. Canada is heavily reliant upon immigration due to a low fertility rate, at 1.57
children per woman. However, Canada is a highly desirable place to live as is
evident in the large number of immigration applications each year.[16] North
America continues to attract immigrants of all kinds, most prominently from
the Latin American neighbors to the south. Latinos are responsible for the
lion's share of North American immigrants, particularly in the U.S. It is predicted by the year 2050 the Hispanic population will account for one-third of
the U.S. population. According to a Pew Research Center report in 2008,
American demographics will be quite different in 2050:

> The Latin population, already the nation's largest minority group, will triple in size
> and will account for most of the nation's population growth from 2005 through
> 2050. Hispanics will make up 29% of the U.S. population in 2050, compared with
> 14% in 2005.[17]

Based on these rates, by 2100, America may be more aptly described as a part
of Latin America if these race-based predictions continue. However, as pointed

out, it is very difficult to categorize people racially in America; there comes a point where racial differentiations make little sense.

North America contains a relatively old population, ranking as the third oldest cultural block after Eastern and Western Europe. The median age of North Americans is around 37 years. North America and Europe are quite unique in this respect. The rest of the world's cultural blocks range between Africa's astonishingly young median age of 19 years to Oceania's 33 years. Life expectancy in North America is high. North Americans outlive everybody in the world with the lone exception of Western Europe. North Americans live to be 78 years old on average. Canada in particular boasts one of the highest life expectancies in the world, at 81 years! It is a very short list of countries that have a life expectancy over 80 years; only about ten nations in the world can make that claim.

Background: Christianity in North America

North America today is a Christian land. Anyone who travels internationally will quickly get the sense that people all over the world understand this. It is difficult to even comprehend the development of post-Columbian North America without constantly referring to Christianity. While there are more overall Christians in Latin America, Africa, Asia, Western Europe, and Eastern Europe than there are in North America, there is a high percentage of Christians in North America, at 81%. Even then, Latin America's percentage of Christians is far higher at 93%. Nevertheless, when one travels abroad, it is common to encounter the stereotype that Christianity and America are closely related.

Religiously, America is not as diverse as one might think. Yes, the diversity within American Christianity is vast, but it is nonetheless strongly Christian— to the point that non-Christian religions may adopt Christian aspects, such as can be encountered with the curious experience of noticing a "Buddhist church". To be a non-Christian in America puts one outside of the mainstream cultural zeitgeist in some ways. Muslims, Hindus, atheists, and Taoists have religious freedom in America, to be sure. Americans are a very, very tolerant people according to social scientists.[18] Despite their tolerance, however, they are overall very Christian. Furthermore, Americans are a lot more active in their faith than their European counterparts. Americans tend to be involved with their churches, evinced in the stadium-like worship services taking place every Sunday in the many cities scattered across the region. Some theologians and pastors react to this caricature—that America is a strongly Christian nation. For example, Pastor Gregory Boyd's 2006 book *The Myth of a Christian Nation* argues that Jesus' preaching has little to do with the political order; Jesus was preaching a kingdom not of this world. However, to argue that America is not a Christian nation, or was not intended to be a Christian nation, or somehow is moving towards being a non-Christian nation, is to miss the elephant in the room. American history is a story of revival, a struggle for religious freedom, and an exercise in applying Christian theology in new contexts. American history is laden with biblical imagery and language: the conversion of the Native, the emancipation of the slave, manifest destiny, the struggle for freedom for all, the equality of women, the ethics, the courtrooms, the political jockeying at each presidential election—these are almost always enmeshed within the larger context of a Christian meta-narrative.

It did not have to be this way. In fact, it was almost a story of Islam. Martin Marty, one of the greatest American church historians, in his ingenious way, captures a glimpse of what might have been:

> ... Had discovery, exploration, and settlement occurred a century or two earlier than it did, there might have been less point in analyzing the fortunes of Protestants and Catholics in North America. Islamic cultures and societies instead had been expanding. No one can know what the Muslim armies could have done, but we do see much that they did set out to achieve against Christendom. Muslims possessed the armies, the ambition to match, the imperial designs, the resources, and the hunger for more, to drive the Indians west. Then, fortuitously or providentially, as the North American Protestants would say, Islamdom was pushed back from Spain in and before 1492, and it was Christendom that was able to produce the effective military forces. Many of these Protestants also argued that God had hidden their favored "virginal" continent until the Catholic Church had been countered, compromised,[19] and checked in the northern European nations by the Protestant Reformation.

In other words, had Ferdinand and Isabella fallen short of their goal of a Christianized Iberian Peninsula, North America surely would have been colonized by Muslims. Moorish Spain came to a screeching halt in 1492—which happened to be the year of a massive leap forward in Christian expansion.

When Europeans arrived to North America, they discovered a vast land teeming with game, ample freshwater, infinite resources, breathtaking mountains, endless forests, and people—people they knew nothing about. Mistakenly, they thought they were somewhere in Asia. Jacques Cartier's error of thinking he was in China and Columbus's error of thinking he was in India were not unique. However, these two incidents drive home two important points: first, Europeans had no idea where they were; second, Europeans simply could not comprehend the scale of the New World they had encountered. In time, these explorers, missionaries, and colonists began to learn things about these people. As in the Latin American context, the collision of cultures proved catastrophic to the indigenous peoples, particularly anything that might resemble an empire—these had to be toppled. In the case of North America, we witness a similar story, a tragic one. Native communities contracted European diseases and died by the tens of thousands. They were en-slaved. They were driven to reservations in order to get out of the way of the white peoples. Martin Marty paints a bleak picture:

> ... There was virtually no attempt to understand or to do anything but destroy all traces of native religion. ... The treatment of the native people by the government and by agents, often supported by the churches, is now universally regarded as disgraceful. The government broke treaty after treaty and inhibited or prohibited Indian sacred rites, while non-Indian American majorities forced the native people onto usually barren reservations, without resources or status.[20]

However, Marty goes on to point out that there was a small class of people who did attempt to learn something about indigenous ways: the missionaries.

This observation raises an important issue: why are so many Native Americans Christian today? To most indigenous peoples, "The white person's God was repugnant."[21] However, why did they eventually adopt that God as their own? Was it forced upon them? Are Native Americans today the gullible legacy of a people who are still afraid to return to their pre-Christian religions?

This matter is very complicated. However, what we can be sure of is this: there were always missionaries who critiqued the deplorable treatment of Native peoples. Moreover, many missionaries gave their very lives to Native communities, serving until death. When we ask the question of why so many Native peoples are largely Christian today, we have to keep two facts in mind: First, some missionaries were good to them and peacefully persuaded them to accept Christ and the Bible; second, Natives often assimilated Christianity into their own worldviews. In other words, Natives tended to fuse European Christianity with many of their own beliefs, leading to a syncretism that exists today. Native American Christians, like all Christians throughout history, had to sift Christianity from culture. They discarded what they perceived to be erroneous, abominable, or questionable, and held on to the things they found to be true: the gospel—chiefly a man who came to earth, who was victimized by the powerful rulers of the day, and who died so that they might eventually unite with the Great Spirit and with the ancestors. The heart of the Christian gospel made perfect sense, leading to a unique Native American spirituality that freely borrows from both the Bible and ancestral spirituality. Nevertheless, after all of the atrocities committed by Europeans against the indigenous, we have to wonder, with Mark Noll, why "... *any* of the Indians took the Christian message for themselves."[22]

My sister-in-law was born in a tiny town near Gallup, New Mexico, called Rehoboth, located in the northwest part of the state off the old Route 66 which connected Chicago to Los Angeles. That famed highway more or less pulled together the vast western frontier, opening up a new world for Americans in the twentieth century. Rehoboth is a Navajo community, the largest

Native American nation in North America. My wife's parents were once missionaries there in the 1960s; however, mission work had been going on there since "The Long Walk" when in 1864 thousands of Navajos were forcibly resettled to Fort Sumner.[23] The Rehoboth cemetery tells an important story: missionaries often gave their lives to the people they were trying to evangelize. Today, it is common for people to go on one-week mission trips, or perhaps someone will spend a summer at a mission point during college. However, in former times, missionaries were commonly expected to go somewhere to stay, and to be buried among the people they came to know as their own. In that cemetery lies a six year old—the daughter of a missionary. There's a group of headstones belonging to the Musket family, who worked among the Navajos for four generations. Marie Davis is buried there—she worked as a cook at the Rehoboth school for many years. There they are, faithful missionaries buried side by side with some of the famous "Code Talkers"—those Navajo heroes from World War Two whose language protected confidential American battle tactics from being compromised by Japanese cryptographers.

The missionaries at Rehoboth bring out an ambivalent response in me. On one hand, how can they be criticized? While the American government ran these people from place to place in various "Trail of Tears" tragedies, the missionaries often planted themselves in Native contexts, relying on Native help through the winters, teaching Natives how to deal with the white man's world that was inevitably coming. Nevertheless, from my context today, these missionaries could be terribly bigoted. One missionary at Rehoboth wrote that his objective was to take an Indian and make him white in all but skin color: "Kill the Indian in him, and save the man."[24] This was not altogether different from the catch-phrase associated with David Livingstone's mission-cry to Africa, to "civilize and Christianize" the heathen.

While a distinguished historian such as Mark Noll can describe the Native American missions as "more destructive than constructive," not all missionaries deserve the role of villain.[25] Missions were not all the same. Virtually all European colonies sponsored mission work of some sort. It is difficult business to judge people in the past. No doubt our own inadequacies and biases will be judged by those who will stand on our own shoulders one day. Nonetheless, it is a bit perplexing how chauvinistic and ethnocentric the European peoples could be. They genuinely believed that the Indians needed to accept Christ. This is admirable enough when we look at it theologically. Why in the world would not somebody try to change somebody else's belief system if he or she truly believed in heaven and hell? Muslims, Christians, and Buddhists of all sorts continue to try to convert people to their own belief system. At least missionaries were trying to prevent others from the torments of hell. These days, it is common for people in the West to either, first, deny the existence of hell; or, second, operate by the assumption that all people—or virtually all people—

will go to heaven anyway. In other words, the very basis for mission work is to-day undermined by cultural assumptions. If somebody thinks hell does not exist, then why try to convert somebody? If everyone is destined to go to heaven, then what is the use trying to get somebody to believe something different about God, faith, or afterlife?

In many ways, Western pluralism has trumped the whole rational for mission work. North American pluralism—the mentality that reasons the one thing a person must never do to another is to say his or her "truth" is wrong or incomplete—seems to be the philosophical champion for now. Nowadays, it is common for people to try to meet physical needs without meddling in the spiritual realm. For example, Westerners regularly travel great distances to do medical mission work, or humanitarian work such as rebuilding a house or helping a community to access fresh water. However, it is not altogether common for a Westerner to go to a genuinely non-Christian place such as Islamic Africa, Buddhist and Hindu Asia, or Jewish Israel—and proactively try to convert these people, convincing them to accept Christianity as truth. We must remember that in colonial times, the missionaries did both. They brought the gospel, but they also brought schools, hospitals, technology, and other forms of real physical aid.

Rehoboth is but one of many examples of white Americans attempting to help people spiritually as well as physically. We can criticize their endeavors as much as we like, but perhaps it is more difficult to point out the other side of the story. Glib dismissal of missionaries as zealous brainwashers is no different from dismissing Indians as viciously untamed savages. To fall into the trap of completely condemning a people group is to abandon the whole purpose of historical thinking: to understand the complexity. History is never simple. One-sided accounts of any person, event or activity are fundamentally unhistorical. While the treatment of Natives by European peoples was always riddled with paternalism and discord, the fact is that many missionaries spent their entire lives working for the betterment of indigenous communities. Touching examples of European mission work such as the Huron Carol—an old Canadian hymn written by Jesuits to teach the Huron Indians about the Christian faith—are manifold. However, the dark side of European missions is an ever present force, such as in the case of the residential school debacle—where Native Americans were taken from their homes and forced into the church-led schools for an overhaul of their worldview. Canada in particular has had to deal with this hurtful epoch to the present day.

One of the most significant books that deals with this tragic chapter of American history is called *Ishi: In Two Worlds: A Biography of the Last Wild Indian in North America*, by Theodora Kroeber.[26] It is an excruciating story. Ishi, the last member of the Yahi tribe—and possibly the last Indian to live the majority of his life outside of Western culture before entering the Euro-American world—stumbled out of the woods of northern California in 1911. He was desperate, hungry, and fearing for his life. His people had all been massacred. Ishi was essentially adopted by a concerned anthropology professor from the University of California who studied him carefully. Almost immediately, the California Museum of Anthropology created an exhibit based on Ishi, including the opportunity for visitors to watch Ishi make arrows and create fire. Before Ishi's death to tuberculosis in 1916 he was able to speak several hundred English words, which greatly aided researchers in their reconstruction of Yahi culture.[27]

Another people group that was constantly marginalized throughout North American history was the African. It is a history of atrocity after atrocity. Again, though, not all slave-holders were merciless and violent. Some were rather decent. For well over two centuries in America, slavery was simply part of life, like it was in the Greco-Roman world of the New Testament. Slavery is still a highly contested issue in Islam today, particularly in North Africa and the Middle East. While Saudi Arabia abolished slavery in 1962, modern renditions of the institutions have been consistently condemned by the U.S. government to little avail.[28] Slavery has been a universal tendency throughout history, regardless of the color of one's skin, and it continues today in various forms. A cursory glance at human trafficking, human payments, child marriage, sexual slavery, and other deplorable manifestations of slavery today will force one to realize it is a complicated institution that continues, albeit in new and equally sinister guises. While slavery was a horrific era in North American history, it would be wrong to consider it exclusively a historical phenomenon.

African slaves were transported to Spanish territory in the early years of the sixteenth century. The first recorded account of slaves in the British colonies was in 1619, a year before the Mayflower arrived to Plymouth. Recent discoveries have produced some fascinating information about these Africans; first and foremost, they were probably Christians.[29] The first slaves to British America came on two British ships called the Treasurer and the White Lion. They were from the modern-day nations of Angola and the Congo. They were originally a group of 350 slaves captured by the Portuguese, bound for Veracruz, Mexico, when they were intercepted by two British pirate ships flying the Dutch flag. The British pirates took a total of around 60 of the slaves before allowing the rest to continue on to Veracruz. This event began a new era in the northern Americas. These Africans spoke Bantu languages but their homeland, the Kingdom of Ndongo (in modern day Angola and Congo), had been conquered by the Portuguese in the 1500s. Earlier however, in 1490, their king converted to Roman Catholic Christianity and had his people baptized as well. These Africans were literate and the British colonists eventually awarded them their freedom from indentured servant hood—a category of human servitude in North America that was not attached to race until the early eighteenth century.

Slavery's history in North America is rooted in the notion of indentured servitude. This was a system of labor enforced upon Indians, Africans, and Europeans alike. It preceded the racist-linked chattel slavery idea. In essence indentured servitude offered a way out: work hard enough or long enough and you'll eventually become a landowner, with up to 50 acres. Many white indentured servants came to America for a variety of reasons: they had been convicted of a crime, they sold themselves just to survive, they wanted to make the passage to the New World but had no money, or perhaps they were in great debt. An indentured servant would go into debt when he crossed the Atlantic by ship. However, he could pay off his travel debts as well as any other debts he owed once employed as an indentured servant in the New World. After a period of time—usually around five years or so—the "freedom dues" would be paid, allowing the servant to obtain a land grant and start a new life of his own. In the 1700s this labor system began to take on racial overtones, against Blacks and indigenous Americans. The way the law was set up was that non-Christians could be indentured indefinitely. Most slaves were Black, due to the fact that most of the Natives died out because of smallpox or else moved further west. However, there were some white slaves and some Native American slaves. In contrast, there were also some Native Americans and freed Blacks who held slaves. The institution of slavery consisted in many forms throughout America, most notably in the plantations of the South, who held onto the institution several decades longer than in the North. The Civil War, from 1861 to 1865, was largely fought over the issue of whether slavery should continue. The census of 1860 is particularly significant as it was the last major census held before the Civil War.[30] In 1860, America's population was 31 million, with around four million slaves. Slaves made up about 13 percent of the population. Around 400,000 Americans were slaveholders, meaning about 8% of American families were slaveholders.

Again, the question emerges: Why did slaves by and large adopt Christianity? First of all, as pointed out, some of the slaves were already Christians. Perhaps their Christian faith was inchoate—as happens sometimes when a king converts, but the people do not thoroughly understand the new religion. Alternatively, perhaps the slave owners knew it was to their advantage if they did not give occasion for slaves to explain their Christian faith. A third scenario would be that slaves were essentially forced into Christianity. These more skeptical theories, however, leave little room for the interpretation that maybe many slaves truly believed Christ was their Lord and Savior. It would be irresponsible to claim that all Blacks in America were duped into Christianity or were forced into it. Slaves, like Native Americans, often realized the stark difference between Christianity and culture. Christianity—the gospel, the Creator

God, the Holy Spirit, the parables, the story of redemption of humans through Christ, the anti-establishment teachings of Jesus—no doubt these things made perfect sense. Historian Martin Marty asks "What kind of God ... would grant privilege to persons with white skin who wielded whips, condemning those from Africa to a world of unending servitude and misery?"[31] The answer for Africans was that this whip-wielding God did not exist. God must be something else. Indeed, that is where African Americans have profoundly shaped theology, depictions of Christ, the nature of the church, and the overall Christian ethos in America. Yes, most Africans became Christian, but not exactly with the same worldview of the European stock. Africans related better to stories of freedom in the Old Testament—for example Moses leading the people out of bondage. Negro spirituals developed, often becoming a code-language of sorts, rallying Black believers to a time when enslavement would be no more— even if that meant on the other side of the Jordan, in heaven. Perhaps most significantly, African-American churches began to produce leaders of their own. Empowerment came with Black assembly. Leaders would rise to the top and occasionally, aided by sympathetic whites, would learn to read and write and most importantly ... to critique. Such was the case of Frederick Douglass, the famed Black abolitionist whose freedom was bought by some British supporters of his ideas. Perhaps less well known is the fact that Douglass was an ordained minister in the African Methodist Episcopal Church, a denomination founded in 1816 by Rev. Richard Allen in order to provide a forum for Black worship and preaching without interference from Whites. This was the first African-American denomination in the United States, and it was hugely successful. Critiques of the institution of slavery, coming from both Blacks and Whites, led to an impasse: either slavery must stay or go. The Civil War made the decision for Americans and the institution was declared illegal, although equal rights were not to be introduced for another century.

African Americans were not simply "freed" by the Civil War; they contributed enormously themselves. Rev. Richard Allen became involved in the illegal freeing of slaves, as did many of his churches. Harriet Tubman, who lived from 1822 to 1913, was another of the big names here. She escaped from slavery and ended up freeing countless others through the Underground Railroad—a network of safe houses for escaped slaves on the run to the northern part of the U.S. The northern states abolished the institution of slavery in 1807 along with the British. Abolition in Britain, led by the indefatigable efforts of the evangelical Christian William Wilberforce, spread quickly all over Europe and the European-influenced world. We must reiterate, however, that it still goes on. While much of the Islamic world abolished slavery in the 1960s, as pointed out, it continues in ways less conspicuous. Slavery always has been a secretive business. The abolition of slavery was a complicated affair in America, and many people were involved in making it happen. Credit is due to many people such as Harriet Beecher Stowe, whose novel *Uncle Tom's Cabin* (1852) became the most important anti-slavery book in America. Stowe was a devout Christian, ardent abolitionist, and a hero to many. President Lincoln praised her, knowing full well that her novel on the cruelty of slavery persuaded hundreds of thousands of Americans that it was an institution that had to be abolished once and for all. We should also point to the Quakers, that pacifist, peace-tradition that was speaking out against slavery in the 1600s, well before Thomas Jefferson and George Washington bought their own slaves.

Christianity in North America has always had a very different ethos from Christianity in Europe. There has always been an activist bent to it, as well as a mechanism for adaptation built within. While the early Puritanism of the 1600s became notorious for its rigidity, there were always innovations that came along, shaking up the religious landscape. This has been part and parcel of the story of Christian America. Historically, Christianity has been so enmeshed into the fiber of the land that virtually every movement shapes and is shaped by Christian innovation. Perhaps the most conspicuous innovations in the history of American Christianity have come in the form of revivals. America has had three major periods of revival: the First and Second Great Awakenings of the eighteenth and nineteenth centuries, and the Pentecostal Revival of the twentieth century.

The First Great Awakening was a revival movement led largely by the preaching of American Puritan theologian Jonathan Edwards (1703–1758). Edwards lived in Connecticut and Massachusetts and never witnessed the American break with Britain. Today, Edwards is often caricatured as the author of the vehement and frightening sermon "Sinners in the Hands of an Angry God," with all of its descriptions of the horrors of hell, with, apparently, the intent to scare people away from sin and the devil. In this sermon, his description of "wicked men" must have made many congregants shift in their pews:

> They [wicked men] deserve to be cast into hell ... justice calls aloud for an infinite punishment of their sins. ... The sword of divine justice is every moment brandished over their heads ... Every unconverted man properly belongs to hell; that is his place. ... They are now the objects of that very same anger and wrath of God, that is expressed in the torments of hell. ... Yea, God is a great deal more angry with great numbers that are now on earth: yea, doubtless, with many that are now *in this congregation*, who it may be are at ease, than he is with many of those who are now in the flames of hell. ... The devil stands ready to fall upon them, and seize them as his own. ... They belong to him; he has their souls in his possession. ... The old serpent is gaping for them; hell opens its mouth wide to receive them.[32]

Obviously this sort of thing does not preach well today, but in those days it yielded a great harvest. Edwards had a rebirth experience and believed all humans had to repent in order to be saved. Some scholars declare that religion was actually on the decline in America at that time, which would have prompted a voice like Edwards to shake them from their slumbers. This picture of Edwards is only half true. There was another side to him. He was an admired intellectual, serving as Princeton's president for a short time. His writings continue to be studied in American seminaries. He also conducted mission work to the Mohican Indians later in his life, evincing a genuine concern for the souls of all—that they may come to know Christ as he had.

There was a second major figure in the First Great Awakening, however, who had more of an impact on the common people. George Whitefield (1714-1770) was a celebrity in America in his day. He was an itinerant preacher who had been a member of John Wesley's inner circle at Oxford, making him part of the Methodist movement. He took America by storm, entertaining tens of thousands with his theatrical sermons, his experiential-based Christianity that urged people to love God from the heart, and his emotional pleas for Americans to get right with God. Whitefield's sermons were extraordinarily successful. His revivals resulted in thousands recommitting their lives to Christ—not just to a particular denominational affiliation—but to Christ. Mark Noll theorizes that Whitefield may have been heard by half of the inhabitants of the seven American colonies he visited during his initial 10-week tour.[33] Whitefield set the stage for what has become known as evangelicalism. He is one of the most significant figures in the history and development of that form of American piety that is so common today in the churches. At the very core of Whitefield's teachings was the conviction that each person must have a born-again experience. He or she will often experience a "warming of the heart," to borrow a phrase from his friend John Wesley. A strong, self-sacrificing commitment to Christ as Lord was the only qualifier in the salvation of a human being. In other words, humans do not become saved because of works, denominational affiliation, ritual, or anything else. Christ died to save sinners. And that is how sinners get back to God—via Christ. Perhaps most importantly, Whitefield set the stage for what would become a very ecumenical form of Christianity in America. Whitefield was an Anglican, yet in no sense did he believe Anglicanism was the only way to God:

> I saw regenerate souls among the Baptists, among the Presbyterians, among the Independents, and among the Church [i.e., Anglican] folks—all children of God, and yet all born again in a different way of worship: and who can tell which is the most evangelical?[34]

Christianity in the Western world is entering a post-denominational phase. Established denominations are by and large losing out. The non-denominational and interdenominational churches are thriving. Whitefield's pioneering efforts are reaping a harvest worldwide as Christians less and less affiliate to established denominations, preferring instead simple Christ-follower status.

The Second Great Awakening was different from the first. Scholars struggle to assign dates to the awakenings. The general consensus is that the First Great Awakening occurred in the 1730s and lasted through the 1750s. The Second Great Awakening began about a half century later, in the aftermath of the Declaration of Independence from England. The young nation of the USA had decided early on, in 1791, that it needed an amendment to the U.S. Constitution that explicitly disestablished religion from the state, resulting in that very important sentence that often raises its head in American politics:

> Congress shall make no law respecting an establishment of religion, or prohibiting the free exercise thereof.

Whether this (apparently) "secularization clause" impacted the religiosity of America can be debated, but one thing is for sure—a revival soon ensued that in some ways has remained in America ever since.

One of the most important revivals in American history was the Cane Ridge Revival of 1801 that took place in Kentucky and attracted more than 25,000 people.[35] Considered the high point of the Second Great Awakening, it was a jubilant affair full of enthusiastic preaching and "emotional excesses," leading to "... a significant transformation in American religious life."[36] By our standards today, the Cane Ridge gathering looks strongly akin to the Pentecostal movement. Eyewitnesses described people spontaneously singing, barking like dogs, running around making ecstatic noises, expressing joy with shouts to God, jerking on the ground after falling down in repentance of sin, shaking, and spontaneously preaching on tree stumps. It was fantastic for revivalists that saw this as the work of God. It was shocking for the more established Christians of the mainline groups such as Catholics and high-church Anglicans.

Just when it appeared the fires of the Second Great Awakening might be cooling, a revivalist came on the scene the likes of which had not been seen since George Whitefield. His name was Charles Grandison Finney (1792–1875) and he stoked the fires of revival yet again—extending that awakening another generation or even two. Finney was a home-grown American farmer who understood the American soul perhaps better than anyone before Billy Graham. Finney was a Presbyterian, but in the Second Great Awakening there was an American ethos that was far less concerned with denominational affiliation than with the status of one's soul. In some ways, this is the great innovation in American Christianity that Europe never has been able to fully obtain. American Christianity is highly ecumenical. Denominational loyalty is fickle. In fact, Ellison Research released findings in 2009 that showed American

Protestants are more likely to remain faithful to a brand of toothpaste or even to a particular toilet paper than to their denomination![37] This would be an unspeakable horror (or hysterically laughable) in the European context. Charles Finney had a lot to do with this. Finney and the other revivalists in the Second Great Awakening simply did not focus on denominational affiliation; rather they were concerned with the individual having a born again experience. Finney's "anxious bench"—wherein people would sit on a special pew for prayer or potential conversion to Christ—became one of many "new measures" geared to break the heart of the sinner, allowing Christ to enter in. The culmination of these events would be a conversion experience which meant baptism, public testimony, or confession wherein the new convert would die to the old life and begin afresh, in Christ. This approach to the Christian experience is still very much alive in evangelical forms of Christianity.

Perhaps the greatest beneficiaries of the revivals were the Methodists. People joined up with them in great numbers, especially after Cane Ridge:

> By the 1840s there were more Methodist Churches in the United States than there were federal post offices![38]

Other transplanted British denominations grew markedly such as Baptists and Presbyterians. Perhaps the most conspicuous changes on the American religious landscape, however, were the rising number of new denominations. Religion was everywhere. People were joining new religions, inventing new movements, and prophesying all sorts of things. As we pointed out earlier, America was "giddy" with religion in this environment of vast freedom on the frontier. Many American denominations that are still with us today find their origins in the Second Great Awakening:

- ■ *The Disciples of Christ.* Barton Stone and the father-son team of Thomas and Alexander Campbell established this movement shortly after the Cane Ridge Revival. They were originally Presbyterians, but they became put off by all of the different Christian sects and denominations. They refused to label themselves "Methodists" or "Presbyterians" or "Anglicans" or "Congregationalists." They simply wanted to be called "Christians." Thus, they called their movement the "Christian Church" or "The Disciples of Christ." Ironically, the movement turned into another denomination, although it has had two major splits through the years, and now there are three major arteries of this movement: the mainline Protestant "Disciples of Christ," the evangelical "Christian Church," and the "Churches of Christ" which are in most cases non-instrumental (a cappella). Several millions of Christians in the world identify with this movement, including myself.

- *The Seventh-Day Adventists.* This denomination was begun in the 1830s and 1840s by a Baptist minister named William Miller. His followers were originally called "Millerites." He taught that the second coming of Christ was imminent. Many believed him and followed his predictions from the book of Daniel that Jesus would come in 1844. It did not happen, so he predicted again ... and again ... and nothing happened. Eventually a new, female leader emerged in the movement. Ellen White was a charismatic leader who claimed to have special spiritual abilities. She became widely respected in the Millerite movement, particularly because of her emphasis on healing. She established healing centers and wrote copious amounts of material pertaining to spiritual warfare, Christian healing, and prophecy. In the wake of her emphasis on healing, this movement sent medical missionaries all over the globe, leading to a global expansion of the faith. Adventism continues today and is a worldwide denomination consisting of 15 million members in over 200 countries. Only a small percentage of the movement is today in the U.S. One of their unique characteristics is that they claim that the Jewish Sabbath was never meant to be changed from Saturday to Sunday. Thus, they continue to meet on the "Seventh Day".

- *Jehovah Witnesses.* Many North Americans have had these missionary-minded people knock on the door at some point. This American movement was founded in the 1870s by Charles Taze Russell. Like Adventism, it, too, claimed the end of the world was imminent. This movement has made many predictions for the end of days, even as late as 1975. Their journals *The Watchtower* and *Awake!* are published in many countries all over the world. Jehovah's witnesses meet in buildings which they call "Kingdom Halls." There is tension between the Jehovah's Witnesses and the state; they refrain from saying pledges to flags, singing patriotic hymns, serving in the military, recognizing holidays and festivals, and even celebrating birthdays. They do not recognize the Trinity, and they reject the idea of eternal torment in hell. They believe that only 144,000 people will go to heaven to reign with Christ, but the remainder of the saved will actually live on a renewed, paradise-like earth. Jehovah's Witnesses are occasionally in the news because of their rejection of blood transfusions. Like most Christian groups, they are also experiencing vast growth in the southern hemisphere. They have around seven million active members worldwide. There are over 200,000 "publishers" (active members) in each of the following countries: U.S., Brazil, Japan, Italy, Mexico, and Nigeria.

- *Church of Christ, Scientist.* This movement was begun in Boston in the 1870s by a woman named Mary Baker Eddy who has a fascinating story. She married at a young age but her husband died the next year. Later she married again, but her husband had an affair, so she divorced him after 20 years of marriage. A few years after the divorce she married Asa Eddy, who died only five years after marrying her. Eddy believed the Bible had healed her injured spine, without the use of any medicines. She believed the New Testament held the answers to not only spiritual health, but physical as well. She wrote a book about this entitled *Science and Health* which is a sacred text in this movement. The movement also inspired the well-respected *Christian Science Monitor* which is read widely in print and on the internet as a trusted source for world news. Their membership is in decline and sits somewhere around 100,000 today.

- *Mormons.* The Church of Jesus Christ of Latter Day Saints was begun by New Yorker Joseph Smith in the 1820s. He claimed God called him to become the leader of the true church. He was a visionary, believing God communicated with him in a variety of ways. He published the *Book of Mormon* which he said came from Egyptian gold plates he found in the countryside. The premise of Smith's teachings is that Jesus went to the Americas after his crucifixion in Jerusalem in order to inaugurate a new church among the Natives. Smith later authored two other books: *The Pearl of Great Price* and *Doctrine and Covenants*. Along with the Bible, these texts serve as their religious canon. Smith's movement began in New York but moved to Ohio, then Missouri, then Illinois, and eventually to Salt Lake City, Utah, where they are headquartered today. In its early history the movement was often persecuted—usually over the issue of polygamy, which Smith and the early leading men practiced. Smith's life is a highly intriguing one, making for fascinating reading. He had many wives, a practice that was abolished by most Mormons around the year 1900. One peculiar teaching of Smith's is vicarious baptism—that a person can be baptized for someone else who was already dead. This has given rise to excellent genealogical collections by the Mormons because they believe they can actually achieve salvation for people through this act. Smith ran an unsuccessful bid for the U.S. presidency in the 1840s. He died a violent death in 1844 during an escape from jail where he was involved in a gun battle that saw several people killed, including himself, after which he fell from the jail's second-floor window. The Mormon movement survived and the leadership was taken over by Brigham Young (1801–1877). They relocated to Utah where Young declared polygamy to be official church doctrine. The U.S. government pressured them and after Young died, a large section of the church dropped this practice. Some Mormon factions still hold to the teaching which makes news from time to time.

For example Warren Jeffs was on the FBI's Top Ten Most Wanted List for some time before being apprehended in 2006. Winston Blackmore has openly defied the Canadian government by declaring on CNN's "Larry King Live" that he had married several girls under 16 years of age.[39] He was finally arrested in early 2009. Mormon beliefs include no consumption of tea or coffee, although they can drink Coca Cola. The issue is not really about caffeine, but some Mormons do place the emphasis on caffeine as a mind-altering substance, thus leading them to avoid caffeine altogether. They cannot take tobacco or alcohol either. The LDS church has around 13 million members and about half are in the U.S. Other large populations are in Mexico, Brazil, Central American nations, the U.K., and Canada. Mormons are well known for their door to door style of evangelism by sending two young adults to mission points all over the world. Mormons are encouraged to do this after high school for a period of two years, known as their mission. Over a million young people have gone on a mission.[40]

The few examples here are but a tip of the iceberg created by the Second Great Awakening. The diversity and innovation of Christianity in the U.S. is staggering. There are many more examples that we could have discussed. However, for all the talk about Protestant proliferation, innovation, and religious pluralism, the greatest impact of the Second Great Awakening did not come to pass until the early twentieth century, with the spectacularly complex modern Pentecostal revival.

Much ink has been spent trying to figure out what happened all over the Christian world in the early years of the twentieth century, but one thing that is unmistakable: the revival continues to grow larger and larger, transforming world Christianity in ways we can only dimly understand at the present. Christian worship and practice have taken on renewed vitality. There is today a renewed supernaturalism and a fervor that was rather unexpected. While some may argue philosophically—that the new supernatural emphasis in Christianity is the result of a postmodern reaction—the Pentecostals like to think they have simply resurrected the ethos displayed in early Christianity. In the New Testament, miracles were common, demons were confronted, faith-healings were entirely normal, Satan was a constant threat, and persecution was to be expected.

Pentecostal Christianity has its roots in John Wesley's teaching in the 1700s, but the emphasis on the supernatural power of the Holy Spirit was not central to Wesley. This came later in the various "apostolic" and "holiness" movements in the aftermath of Methodist revivalism. As pointed out earlier, there was an embryonic form of Pentecostal Christianity present at the Cane Ridge Revival in Kentucky in 1801. However, the full-blown Pentecostal emphasis on miracles, tongue-speaking, and baptism in the Holy Spirit did not emerge until the early 1900s. It is difficult to point to one precise event that got the ball rolling, as there were several things going on all over the world at that time that qualify as beginning points:

- Agnes Ozman of Topeka, Kansas spoke in tongues on December 31, 1900.
- The Welsh Revival of 1904 "... first set all Wales ablaze, then London and then all of England, until people from all over the world were coming to see if this was the new Pentecost."[41]
- There was a charismatic revival in 1905 led by an Anglican woman named Pandita Ramabi at her Mukti Mission in Pune, India.
- Korea witnessed the Pyongyang Revival in 1907, which spread into mainland China.
- American John Graham Lake went to South Africa in 1908 to spread the Pentecostal message—it was phenomenally successful there.
- The Chilean Revival began in 1909, touching of a powerful Pentecostal movement in Latin America.

Nonetheless, there was something special about the 1906 Azusa Street Revival in Los Angeles, led by William Seymour, a son of freed slaves. Perhaps Los Angeles is the most fitting context for a revival of world Christianity. It is a land of prosperity; it is a city of dreams; it is the "city of angels"; it is a city that represents the future of America—a largely Latino one; it is America's second-largest city; it is a city of diversity—of many, many tongues. Some Pentecostals might view Los Angeles as the divinely appointed place of renewal. Whatever the case, something special happened there, in that city, in 1906. For many reasons, scholars consider it the real impetus that led to the situation we have now: Christianity, the world over, is becoming charismatic and Pentecostal.

American Christianity is messy; it is more complicated than European Christianity chiefly because of the disestablishment of religion from the state, but it also has a lot to do with the great periods of revival. What Europeans might view as improper, Americans revel in: the ability to invent a new deno- mination, the ability of the individual to live a religious life completely di- vorced from the government, the extemporaneous nature of faith, and the full- throttle individualism that leads people to attend a church based on the latest fad or the greatest preacher. American Christians are consumers, and they want their religion to be relevant, irrespective of brands. As for toilet paper and toothpaste? Well that is another story.

In many ways, we can say that MartinLuther's novel philosophy of religion reached its zenith in the United States of America. Luther did not intend for this to happen. He could not have imagined the extent to which Protestant proliferation would occur because of his vision. While Luther did see signs of an intractable situation, he would be utterly amazed at just how differently people read the Bible in their own contexts. *Sola Scriptura* means something very different in America than it did in Germany in the sixteenth century. Americans think, "You have your interpretation, I have mine. So let's see who's right." Luther did not think this way at all. Luther did not condone new denominations. Luther wanted religion to be individual, from the heart, justification from God—not from the parish priest. However, once you open that can of worms and tell people the authority is not really the authority, a revolution becomes inevitable. And this is what continues to happen on the American scene and the world over.

North American Christianity Today

It is helpful to point out the differences between American and Canadian trends in religion today, although the ethos of Christianity in these two countries is not as stark as the statistics might suggest.

Canada

Since Canada was a part of the British crown for so long, there was more restraint in religion historically. This is beginning to break down, however. Perhaps the most conspicuous difference, though, can be seen in the statistics for this chapter. American Christianity is 66% Protestant and 32% Catholic. Canadian Christianity is essentially the opposite of that, 68% Catholic and 28% Protestant. While the number of Canadian Catholics is much larger than that for Protestants, it should be kept in mind that Catholicism is often an identity more than it is a regular part of one's weekly routine. Quebecois Christianity, for example, looks staunchly Catholic, but in fact took a sudden and highly unanticipated nose dive in the 1950s and 1960s. The so-called Quiet Revolution in Quebec saw the church's influence plummet. Throughout Canadian history, the Francophone Catholics of Quebec were well-known for their deeply Catholic, ultramontanist (extreme loyalty to the Roman pope), and conservative ways. This all changed between 1950 and 1980. One scholar described the "... spectacular drop in religious practice after the 1970s" and the Quiet Revolution's impact on Catholic Christianity in Quebec as being "quite brutal."[42] During that period, the political power in French Canada suddenly, and remarkably, slipped right out of the hands of the church.

While Canadian Christianity is indeed secularizing, according to one researcher it is not nearly as secular as Europe. The foremost scholar of Canadian Christianity today is probably Reginald Bibby; he has been following

Canadian Christian trends since the early 1980s. Bibby points out several important trends about Canadian Christians. First of all, in direct contradiction to Americans, Canadians tend to remain far more loyal to their respective denominations:

> For reasons known only to the gods, Canadians have shown little inclination to abandon the dominant groups—even when those groups have frequently given up on them. Psychologically and emotionally, people across the country continue to cling, sometimes perilously, to the religious traditions of their youth.[43]

Bibby has also been a champion of the post-secularization thesis—that while Canada seemed to be turning secular a few decades ago, the reality today is a much more nuanced understanding. Bibby has argued that while the statistics seem to support a decline in church attendance, Canadians obviously have not abandoned the notion of faith, or, in his words, "latent spirituality." Canadians today continue to have a "... fascination with mystery, the search for meaning, and religious memory."[44] Bibby analyzes the innate need for spirituality in Canada as apparently part of the human condition, a need that manifests itself at times of crises such as September 11, 2001—an event that touched a nerve in Canada not only because of proximity but because many of the American planes that day ended up landing on Canadian tarmacs.

Canadian Christianity today is fairly strong. About three-fourths of Canadians explicitly declare themselves Christian. The Catholic Church is by far the strongest denomination. Protestantism in Canada is led by the United Church of Canada which has the allegiance of about 10% of Canadians. Anglicanism is the second largest Protestant church with around 7%, followed by Baptists and Lutherans who each claim less than 3% of the Canadian population. There are about the same number of Muslims as there are Lutherans in Canada. Canadian evangelicals have a small but significant-and-growing voice. YC Alberta, a massive Christian youth rally held annually in Edmonton, Alberta, attracts around 16,000 young people each spring. This activity is one of several major evangelical initiatives in Canada today. Canadian evangelicals are apparent in politics as well. A recent Prime Minister of Canada, Stephen Harper, is a conservative evangelical. Overall, Canada, like America, is strongly Christian. Only about 6% of Canadians claim to be members of non-Christian religions.[45]

United States

American Christianity is so vast and unorganized that there is no way to neatly explain it. We can point out a few general tendencies that may be helpful, but the truth of the matter is that pretty much any type of Christianity is available in this land of the most Christians.

Perhaps the loudest Christian movements in America are the evangelical and fundamentalist movements. Both of these have roots in Europe, and both have been influenced a great deal by American revivalism—but they are not the same. Fundamentalism is a movement that was shaped largely by anti-modernist Christians in the early twentieth century. An influential series of pamphlets known as *The Fundamentals* was published between the years of 1910 and 1915, essentially forcing American clergymen to choose whether they were going to accept the authority of the Bible or not. Many scholars in that era had been strongly influenced by German higher criticism—a university movement that encouraged academics to study the Bible in a scientific frame-work, dismissing the miracles as only functional for faith, not scientifically ac-curate. The higher criticism movement was fiercely opposed by some American Christians. This conservative segment of the American population often refers to the Bible as "infallible" and "inerrant"—meaning the Bible is without error or contradiction. America's most famous trial, the "Monkey Trial," also known as the "Scope's Trial," illustrates the dichotomy that took place in American Christianity in the twentieth century. It took place in Tennessee in 1925 and dealt with the issue of whether Darwinian evolution should be taught in the public schools. While the core decision had to do with who gets to choose the school curriculum—the people or the government—the underlying question of that trial was something quite different: is the Bible true or not? It is a conver-sation that every American adult, almost without exception, has participated in at some level.

The evangelical ethos in America is clearly an outworking of the longstanding revivalist tendencies of the nation. American revivalism has deep roots and shows no signs of dissipating. Americans love a good sermon, an in-spiring social movement, or the latest Christian bestseller. Martin LutherKing, Jr.'s speeches tapped into this artery. The civil rights movement was in some ways a revival; it was a recognition that Christianity had grown crusty, dilapi-dated, and gravely incompatible with God's will. King was able to incite crowds in the thousands to share his view that Christianity must change. King was a Baptist preacher and he was fully aware of the influence a revival could have on the landscape of America.

All the great preachers in twentieth century America recognized this social need for reform through the pulpit—Aimee Semple McPherson, Billy Graham, and Oral Roberts are at the top of the list. All three of them preached a born-again style gospel that resonated deeply with the American need for conti-nuous moral reform. All of them emphasized a highly individualistic Chris-tianity—where Jesus is met personally, almost face to face. Billy Graham became famous for his altar calls; millions of people responded to his message. He was probably heard by more people than any other preacher in history due to his massive crusades as well as his use of modern technology and mass communication techniques. Audiences were mesmerized by his riveting, powerful approach to preaching the gospel. He had a quality that few preachers ever attain: fearlessness. Billy Graham preached the gospel with great courage, to the point that the listener felt inclined to make a choice for Christ—yes or no—for there was no middle ground.

American Christianity today is changing yet again. There is another round of revival going on that is difficult to define at this stage in history. Some people call it "emerging Christianity." Others call it "the emergent church." In all reality, it is at its heart another round of revival spreading across the land—almost as if American Christianity feeds itself on revival. Writers such as Dan Kimball, Brian McLaren, and Rob Bell are at the top of a short list of what could be described as spokesmen for this movement. All three of these leaders are arguing that Christianity must change if it is to be relevant to Americans today and in the future. Undeniably, the emerging church movement is transforming the contours of American Christianity today. Kimball's claim "they like Jesus but not the church"—which happens to be the title of his 2007 book—resonates deeply with university students. McLaren's book *Everything Must Change* has a revolutionary ring to it, tapping into the cultural zeitgeist of 1960s America—a magnetic and fascinating period in the consciousness of young Americans today. Young Christians have the sense that they are the future of the church, and they need to change the church to make it succeed. This has been one of the great strokes of genius of the evangelical movement since its earliest days.[46] Evangelical churches focus on youths. Space is made for young leaders through mentoring programs, youth-led events, and youth empowerment. Often, the youth-led activities look more like a rock and roll concert than a traditional worship service. Even the sermon topics are unabashedly aimed at youth culture. Rob Bell's "Sex God Tour" was wildly popular amongst emerging church Christians, as he explored "the endless connections between sexuality and spirituality."[47]

Teaching religion in the university setting has given me insight into this emerging movement. Many young Christians today are conceiving Christianity in a very different way. At times, it is difficult to even comprehend how this form of Christianity works. Allow me to provide a few snapshots of emerging Christians and what I have learned from them in my own context:

- When asked about the church he attended, one young Christian simply stated, "I don't attend a church per se, I just hang out with Jesus."
- One of my students started a ministry on the beach, where they basically sit around and wait for the Holy Spirit to bring someone to them, so they can share Jesus with them.
- "Mosaic" is a Los Angeles emerging church that meets at a night club. Often the congregants can smell the sweat from the steamy dancing the

night before. They do not have a membership; people are just invited to show up whenever.

- When I asked one of my students how he understands Christ, he said, "I think of Christ as a homeless man standing in line at the homeless shelter, waiting for soup. That's what Christ is to me."
- Several of my students have argued that Christianity makes room for people from other religions. There is the sense that only God can judge, therefore Muslims and Buddhists have insights into religion that Christians need.

Clearly, we are not talking Billy Graham here; this is a new paradigm.

However, these voices are only representative of a part of the new forms of Christianity in America today. There are others that are more traditional, more conservative, and even more indicting than those of the recent past. One author, Michael Horton, has referred to American Christianity as "Christless Christianity." His thesis is that Christianity in America has become theologically suspect. On his Web site, he is congratulated for helping Christians to recognize "the train wreck that is so much of popular Christianity."[48] A central argument is that mega-church pastors in America are leaving Christ out of their sermons. They are preaching therapeutic mumbo jumbo that is much more about positive thinking and social justice than about the historic teachings of Christ and the apostles. Horton targets the mega-church pastors, such as Joel Osteen, pastor of America's largest congregation, the Lakewood Church in Houston Texas, which averages well over 40,000 people a week. Horton also has a bone to pick with Rick Warren, pastor of the Saddleback mega-church in California. Horton argues that Warren's call to "Deeds, Not Creeds" is very different from the gospel: "If this is the good news, then we are all in trouble."[49] Horton's scathing critiques are reminiscent of John Calvin, who happens to be one of his great mentors.

We close this chapter on American Christianity with a few statistics and a few anecdotes. First, while it is true that the Roman Catholic Church is the largest denomination in America, it accounts for only about a quarter of the country's population. Additionally, we have to keep in mind that Catholicism is often enmeshed into one's identity, rather than a clear sign of active church participation. The second largest group in America is the Baptists, claiming about 16% of the American population. Third, at around 7%, are the Methodist churches, followed by small numbers of Presbyterians and Anglicans.[50] The problem with these statistics is that they fail to consider the number of Pentecostals and charismatic Christians, who often do not associate with formal denominations, but which have been estimated to comprise nearly a quarter of America's Christians.[51]

When we move beyond the statistics we will see a few trends going on in American Christianity today:

Americans are free agents when it comes to religion. Brand loyalty is becoming obsolete. Increasingly Americans are opting not to join mainline denominations—a trend that has been going on for some time.[52]

American mega-churches may be the object of scorn for some, but they are fantastically successful at bringing in the sheaves. It is not at all uncommon for Americans to place their membership in a congregation with over a thousand members.

American Christianity is often segregated. Martin Luther King, Jr.'s statement that Sunday morning at 11:00 am is America's "most segregated hour" still has relevance.[53] Many American denominations are organized along racial or ethnic lines, as in the case of immigrants and "Black churches" such as the African Methodist Episcopal Church and the Church of God in Christ.

Women are increasingly entering ordained ministry. The *New York Times* reported in 2006, "Women now make up 51% of the students in divinity school."[54] Indeed, women are increasingly finding the top spot in American denominations, as in the case of Sharon Watkins of the Christian Church (Disciples of Christ) and Katharine Schori of the Episcopal Church.

More than any other issue, perhaps with the exception of abortion, American Christians are split over homosexuality. In the words of sociologist Alan Wolfe, "Here is indeed the ultimate test of American tolerance."[55] According to a 2009 survey from Pew Research, most (56%) American mainline Protestants believe homosexuality should be accepted; however, only 39% of Black Protestant churches and 26% of Evangelical Protestants thought homosexuality should be accepted.[56] This issue continues to touch nerves on both sides.

Finally, we must come back to the defining feature of American Christianity—its freedom. Early on in the chapter we pointed out how Americans appear "giddy" with religious freedom. Perhaps only in America can one attend the "Hell Yeah" church or listen to a pastor who cusses during his sermons, preaching on topics such as "Biblical Oral Sex."[57]

Three Questions for Analysis

1. Does the USA seem to be secularizing? Why or why not?

2. Should missionaries be criticized or admired for their attempts to convert the Native peoples?

3. Why do you think revivalism in America has become such a vital part of the fabric of the country?

Asia

PEOPLE

Total Population:	3,767,141,703
Total Median Age:	28.9 years
Life Expectancy:	70.67 years
Fertility Rate:	2.35 children born/woman

RELIGION

Top Religion Percentages:	Hindu (23.35%)
	Muslim (19.34%)
	Nonreligious (16.05%)
	Chinese Universalist (10.16%)
	Buddhism (10.06%),
	Christian (9.25%)
	Atheist (3.20%)
Number of Christians:	348,299,020
Major Christian Groupings:	Protestant/Independent (65%)
	Catholic (33%),
	Orthodox (2%)

CHAPTER SEVEN

ASIAN CHRISTIANITY

Asia is where the people are. The world's population is around seven billion and Asia accounts for around four billion—well over half. The combined populations of India and China are over two and a half billion—well over one-third of the entire population of humanity. These numbers are staggering.

Asia's influence in world affairs is increasing rapidly. Few predicted the rise of Asia, especially China, to superpower status. This ascension caught almost everyone off-guard, including intelligence specialists. The swiftness of Asia's rise has been, in a word, unprecedented. In the context of discussing why Chinese communism has had economic success while Soviet communism seems to have failed, Robert Strayer writes:

> Growth rates averaging 10% a year, sustained for more than two decades, represent the most impressive record of economic performance of modern world history. Rising standards of living, improved incomes, better diets, declining poverty, lower mortality rates, and a diminished rural-urban gap—all of this surely contributed to the legitimacy of the communist regime.

In the last few years, China has leapfrogged over France, Russia, the UK, Germany, and Japan to become the second largest economy in the world. There can be little doubt that the future of world economics will see China only increase its market share in nearly every way. It has become a leviathan in global economics. In addition, if China has become a leviathan, then India is a juggernaut. India's Gross Domestic Product (GDP) is now in the world's top five, making it a member of the very short list of true power players in the world's economy. In fact, whether one looks at the International Monetary Fund, the World Bank, or the CIA, three of the top five GDPs in the world are in Asia: China, Japan, and India. This massively dense population of the world is coming into its own, and these developments were rather unthinkable just a half-century ago. Who knows how much Asia will continue to grow? The CIA predicts that by 2015 China's GDP will have surpassed the entire GDP of all of the European Union countries combined, and will have nearly caught the United States. The U.S. government's predictions are as quizzical as anyone else's: "Estimates of developments in China over the next 15 years are fraught with unknowables."[2]

In the study of global Christianity, Asia represents even more unknowables. Some have predicted that Christianity in Asia may undergo a demographic boom in the very near future. The sheer thought that Christianity and Buddhism in Asia are about equal seems perplexing. Who could have foreseen this situation?

Caution is necessary when talking about the possibility that Asia may witness mass conversions to Christianity in the twenty-first century. Very rarely in world religion do large people-groups convert to another faith. John Hick has written:

> Consider a very obvious fact, so obvious that it is often not noticed, and hardly ever taken into account by theologians. This is that in the vast majority of cases, probably 98 or 99%, the religion to which anyone adheres depends upon where they are born.[3]

While South Korea has certainly proven to be exceptional in this regard—that country has experienced a major movement toward Christianity in the last century—the truth is that Christianity in Asia is a small presence. About nine percent of Asians are Christians. That is a low number. Looking at the world rankings for the eight cultural blocks of the world, only the Middle East has a smaller percentage of Christians—and Christianity is an endangered species in that region.

What Is Asia?

Asia has been defined in a multitude of ways through the ages. Many people consider the Middle East to be part of Asia. In some ways it is, particularly when we figure that much of the Middle East used to be called Asia Minor. In this study, however, the Middle East is its own culture. This decision was made largely on religious grounds, although there are other reasons. A good argument can also be made to include eastern Russia—Siberia—as a part of Asia. However, this inclusion would trigger political complexities. While many Siberian people-groups may be culturally closer to Asians, a sizeable number of them are in fact Slavic, or at least partly so. Another difficulty here is whether to consider the countries of Central Asia as being Eastern European, Middle Eastern, or Asian. Some might even be inclined to include Australasia—including Australia, New Zealand, and Papua New Guinea—as a part of Asia. Many arguments can be made in various directions, and the nomenclature is far from consistent today.

For the purposes of this book, Asia consists of 33 countries and territories. The northern border of Asia is Kazakhstan, China, and Mongolia—the three nations that rest just under the border of central and eastern Russia. The western border of Asia includes Kazakhstan, Turkmenistan, Afghanistan, and Pakistan. Asia's southern border consists of various archipelagos: Maldives, British Indian Ocean Territory, Cocos Islands, Christmas Island, Indonesia, Timor-Leste, and others. The term South Asia is usually identified with India and those cultures that have been shaped by Indian ways of life: Bangladesh, Bhutan, Nepal, Pakistan, and Sri Lanka. When speaking of Southeast Asia, scholars generally have in mind Myanmar, Cambodia, Laos, Thailand, Vietnam, Malaysia, Philippines, and Indonesia. The eastern border of Asia consists of Japan, Taiwan, and the Philippines, which are archipelagos, but the mainland's eastern border is North and South Korea, China, and Vietnam.

For the Westerner, Asia seems stunningly crowded. Westerners have a different sense of space than Asians. I will never forget my first time in Asia. I stepped off the plane into Kolkata (formerly Calcutta), India, a metropolis of 15 million people, surely too many for the surveyors to count. I felt barraged by a sea of people. What is surprising is that Kolkata is only the third largest metropolitan area in India, after Mumbai (Bombay) and Delhi![4] When combined, these three cities alone have a population approaching the United Kingdom's. Six of the world's ten most populated countries are in Asia: China, India, Indonesia, Pakistan, Bangladesh, and Japan. Asia claims 13 of the top 20 most populated cities in the world: Tokyo, Seoul, Delhi, Mumbai, Manila, Shanghai, Osaka, Kolkata, Karachi, Canton, Jakarta, Beijing, and Dhaka.[5]

India is on pace to become the most populated country in the world fairly soon due to its fertility rate of 2.76 children per woman, compared with China's 1.77. The fertility rates in Asia have declined quite a bit in recent years. China's one child policy, introduced in 1979, has had a lot to do with that—although the policy is directed mainly at urban populations which constitute only a third of the Chinese population.[6] It is perhaps surprising that the fertility rate in Asia is not as high as one might imagine. The overall fertility rate for this cultural block is 2.35, making it the fourth most fertile region of the world—slightly higher than Oceania and slightly lower than Latin America/Caribbean. It is significantly less than Africa's 4.72 fertility rate.

While Asia's fertility rate has abated in recent years, the life expectancy is rising. Asians today live to be nearly 71 years old, although the disparity is huge. Asia has some of the longest-living people in the world. The Japanese are known to live to very ripe ages (82 years), and they tend to remain in good health in their old age. The same is true in Singapore, South Korea, and Taiwan. There are many other countries, however, which have conspicuously low life expectancies such as Laos (56), Nepal (61), Pakistan (64), and worst of all

Afghanistan (44)—where violence and disease have caused one of the lowest life expectancies in the world, even lower than in Africa.

We are dealing here with a highly diverse part of the world, more diverse than any other—evinced in the religious demographics. Asia is the land of Buddhism, Hinduism, Taoism, Confucianism, Shinto, and is home to the world's largest Islamic communities (Indonesia, Pakistan, India, and Bangladesh). While Hinduism is the largest religion of Asia, it is limited mainly to India and Nepal. Islam is actually the religion that can claim more countries in Asia than any other religion. Thirteen out of 33 Asian nations/territories have an Islamic majority: Afghanistan (99%), Bangladesh (89%), Brunei, Cocos Islands, Indonesia, Kazakhstan, Kyrgyzstan, Malaysia, Maldives (98%), Pakistan (96%), Tajikistan, Turkmenistan (99%), and Uzbekistan. As seen in the percentages, several of these are almost completely Islamic.

Marxism led many Asians throughout the twentieth century to think of themselves as nonreligious; however, this term is highly ambiguous. An example of this is North Korea, where on paper the majority declare themselves to be nonreligious, but in reality there is a Marxist cult linked to the totalitarian state, particularly the "Dear Leader" Kim Jong-Il. Marxist personality cults were common in Asia in the mid-to-late twentieth century. Generally they were linked to communist and fascist dictators in Europe such as Hitler, Stalin, Mussolini, and Romania's Ceausescu; however, Asia too had its share of these hostile and narcissistic egomaniacs: Chairman Mao Tse Tung (Mao Zedong) of China was the best known, but there were others such as Ho Chi Minh in Vietnam and Ferdinand Marcos in the Philippines.

The fourth largest religious demographic in China is "Chinese Universalist"—a catch-all term that essentially encompasses Confucianism, Taoism, and local, indigenous Chinese religions. It is often called the folk religion of China, as it was easily the majority worldview prior to Marxism's persecution of all religions. It revolves largely around ancestor veneration, but includes a vast array of local religious beliefs, deities, and practices. Buddhism, the majority religion for eight Asian nations—Bhutan, Cambodia, Japan, Laos, Myanmar, Sri Lanka, Thailand, and Vietnam—actually ranks only fifth in Asia. However, the Buddhist influences in Asia are considerable. Many Asians assume teachings that are common in Buddhism, particularly in China and Japan. Buddhist influences on afterlife understandings in Asia are far more significant than the number of Buddhists would seem to indicate.

Asian diversity is evident in many other ways as well. Peter Phan, an expert on Christianity in Asia, points to three important overall characteristics of Asia: extreme poverty, cultural diversity, and religious pluralism.[7] Religion is only one of the lenses that can be used to explore this most fascinatingly complex part of the world. Language could be used, but it would quickly spin out of control due to the breathtaking variety; Indonesia alone has 742 "living languages" right now![8] Politics—as in the case of the former Soviet Union or in democratic Western Europe—could be used, but it is too diverse: India is the world's largest democracy, China is the world's largest autocracy, and Japan is the world's oldest monarchy (although entirely symbolic). Economically, Asia has some of the world's wealthiest people: Mukesh Ambani and Lakshmi Mittal are in the top 10, and they are both from India—a country that is home to some of the poorest of the poor.[9]

India is comprised of nearly 20% Dalits—people considered "untouchable" by most Indians. Dalits—a Marathi word meaning "ground down, crushed underfoot"—are some of the most disenfranchised, systemically oppressed people in the world. The Dalits are a huge class of people:

> There are more Dalits in India than there are people in Brazil, marginally more. If taken as a national population they would be the fifth largest in the world after China, India, the U.S., and Indonesia.[10]

Dalits are perhaps more "crushed" than any people-group in the world today, a situation blamed largely on the ancient caste mindset in India:

> The Dalit issue today is one of the worst examples of discrimination ... This discrimination persists despite government efforts to improve the situation through affirmative action ... Of course, we cannot discount the fact that some upward mobility has occurred for Dalits ... but ... it is untouchability more than anything else that is responsible for the denial of human rights to this group of people. In fact untouchability is central to caste. ... To call it a social evil is to trivialize it enormously. It is and has been for a very long time an extremely sophisticated economic and political strategy for ensuring a perpetual pool of demoralized, cheap labor that has no sense of its bargaining power. This forced labor or free labor is not accounted for in the gross domestic product of the Indian economy.[11]

The situation is even worse for women Dalits, in a country where boys are more highly valued than girls:

> India's food is produced primarily by Dalit women. They are the lowest paid section of agrarian society. Therefore, it is a triple burden: a burden of class, caste and gender.[12]

While the caste system is unique to India and Indian-influenced societies such as Pakistan, Bangladesh, and Nepal, the concept of a desperately poor agrarian class with little influence, little education, and virtually no way to reverse the trend is common in Asia. It is a dismaying situation, but the solutions will not come from the West; they will have to come from within. Post-colonial resentment has not completely receded from Asia. It was not too long ago that the West, politically, ruled most of the world, and Asia was no exception.

This fact leads our discussion into the realm of colonialism—a complicated, controversial, and at times volatile topic that essentially deals with the nature of power, racism, classism, and world civilizations. Over the last few centuries in particular, Asia's history has been enmeshed with the West's. During the heyday of colonialism, vast swaths of "the Orient"—as Asia was called—came under the rule of Western European powers. However, by no means were Western nations the only ones prone to control and colonize another society—Russia, China, and Japan have all been colonial powers at various stages. Nevertheless, during the nineteenth and twentieth centuries in particular, much of Asia came under Western hegemony. It was the culmination of centuries of attempts. Successful control of most of Asia lasted until 1947, when greater India—which included Pakistan, Bangladesh, Burma (Myanmar), the Himalayan Kingdoms, and Sri Lanka—declared its independence from Britain as a result of mass protests. Mohandas Gandhi and Jawaharlal Nehru were the leading voices in a revolution that spelled the end of British rule in South Asia. The British were far from alone during European dominance of Asia. Beginning in 1498 with the landing of the Portuguese explorer Vasco da Gama on the southwest coast of India, over the course of centuries, the various Western empires annexed more and more land, especially the ports. They established lucrative trading companies that served to build massive wealth in the Western world. This is only a smattering of the vastness of European colonialism in Asia:

- The Portuguese held parts of India (Goa), China (Macau), Japan (Nagasaki), Malaysia (Malacca), and much of Indonesia;
- The French held large parts of the Eastern side of India, notably Pondicherry (Puducherry), the "French concessions" of southeast China (including Shanghai), Cambodia, Laos, Vietnam, part of Thailand;
- Denmark had the important Indian port of Tranquebar;
- Spain was in control of the Philippines and parts of Taiwan;
- The Dutch Empire was strong in Indonesia, Sri Lanka, Malaysia (Malacca region), Macau (in China), and various ports in India;
- The British Empire was the largest of the European empires. It included India—"the jewel of the crown" with all of the various regions included; several Chinese ports (notably Hong Kong), Malaysia, Singapore, and others;
- Although not European, from 1899 to 1946 the United States took charge of the Philippines.

This long season of foreign rule began unraveling shortly after World War II, as the colonies continued to slide out of the grip of the Western world. When

China reclaimed Macao from the Portuguese in 1999, it was the end of an era. The *New York Times* included an article on the unheralded event:

> Five hundred years of European colonialism in Asia sputters to a close here this weekend ... At the stroke of midnight on Sunday, China will reclaim this tiny enclave from Portugal, raising its red flag over another patch of Chinese soil ... Unlike Britain's handover of nearby Hong Kong two years ago, which was heralded by years of Chinese anticipation and British angst, this is not the reluctant surrender of a prized possession. ... Since then, the Portuguese administration has presided over Macao's steady deterioration into a disreputable, vaguely sinister gambling destination for weekend wagerers from Hong Kong ... The economy has withered and Macao has become ever more hooked on casinos.[13]

Thus, European hegemony in Asia was ended. Vasco da Gama's arrival began in 1498 with a bang; da Gama's successors left with a whimper—like a dog with his tail tucked between his legs.

Who could have thought that Christianity in Asia would experience more growth once the Christian Westerners left? Few could have predicted this phenomenon; however, this sentiment seems to resonate much of the time. When Christianity is allowed to indigenize, becoming assimilated into the language and customs of the local context, it becomes healthier and far more natural. Christianity has always had the ability to settle into a culture—transforming it and being transformed by it—in a constant dance of give and take. Many were surprised by Christianity's resilience in the postcolonial era:

> Throughout the 1950s and 1960s leading scholars and other observers ... predicted with breathtaking confidence and uniformity that Christianity in Asia and Africa would collapse once the coercive pressures of Western colonialism were removed. As it happens, Christianity and especially Protestantism saw continuing expansion, not contraction, in the last decades of the twentieth century. ... In other words, Christianity's *postcolonial* growth in both Asia and Africa was at least as dramatic as its colonial growth.[14]

In the last part of the twentieth century, Christians in Asia, regardless of their view of the colonial system, found themselves without the missionaries, and the Christians adapted marvelously well. More specifically, in 1900, 4% of the world's Christians lived in Asia. In 2005, 17% of the world's Christians lived in Asia.[15] There are already far more Christians in Asia than in North America.

Background: Christianity in Asia

It is perhaps unfortunate that most Asians came to see Christianity as a Western religion. Peter Phan has commented eloquently on this fact:

> With regard to Asian Christianity, one of the bitter ironies of history is that though born in (West) Asia, Christianity returned to its birthplace as a foreign religion and is still widely regarded as such by Asians.[16]

Why did this happen? How did this happen? There are several answers to these questions, depending upon the country in question. One of the obvious reasons Christianity became associated with the Western world was because of missionaries. This could play out in ways for the better or for worse. Cynics perceived Christian missions to be the van of European expansion. Lumsdaine writes:

> ... The perception that Christians and especially evangelicals are "foreign," "anti-national," and U.S.-backed "neo-imperialists" is probably more entrenched and pervasive in Asia than in Africa or even Latin America.[17]

Philip Jenkins brought to a larger audience just how volatile this situation can be, even in very recent times, in various parts of Asia:[18]

- In Pakistan in the 1980s a series of laws were passed with excruciating results for Christians, including the death penalty or life imprisonment for anyone who evangelizes a Muslim—which is already nearly 100% of the population.
- Indonesia has been a tinderbox for Christian-Muslim conflict. In the year 2000, "Thousands of Christians were forced to convert to Islam in public ceremonies, some of which included circumcision for both men and women. Hundreds of Christians were killed for refusing to convert." It was "... a successful act of ethnic/religious cleansing that was largely ignored by Western governments and media."[19]
- In southern Philippines, in the Islamic strongholds, there have been high profile murders against Christians, including a Catholic bishop murdered right outside his cathedral in 1997. Kidnappings of Christians are not uncommon.

There are countless examples similar to these across Asia. In India, outbursts of Hindu fundamentalist violence scarcely attract the attention of Western media. In the West, Hindus have the reputation for "live and let live" when it comes to religion, but this is far from accurate at certain times in certain places—most famously in Orissa in late 2008 when even the Western world became aware of the atrocities. Dozens of Christians were killed during the mob violence; the total is still not altogether clear since so many of the victims were among the very, very poor. It has been estimated that 50,000 people were left homeless and at least 13 educational institutions were destroyed.[20] This case was probably the most widely publicized persecution of Christians in India since the death of Australian missionary Graham Staines and his two young sons in 1999. In that case, Staines, who had been working with leprosy patients, was sleeping in his station wagon with his boys when a Hindu mob lit it on fire and refused to let them out.[21]

However, much of the anti-Western reaction by Asians during the twentieth century had less to do with religion than with politics. Nation after nation began declaring independence from the West, asserting autonomy and in many cases emphasizing a totally new epoch of self-reliance, as happened in China under Chairman Mao. The Cold War set the stage for a fractured Asia. Several nations aligned with the democratic West (the "first world"), several aligned more with Russian-led communism (Soviet "second world"), and still others became part of the "third world"—which originally meant they were non-aligned and thus neutral.

It is unwise to paint with too large a brush because Asian responses to a postcolonial world were highly variegated, defying any uniform understanding. For example, after the Second World War, Japan and the four "Asian Tigers"—South Korea, Taiwan, Hong Kong, and Singapore—based their governments and economies on Western models and modernized rapidly throughout the century; they are today every bit as developed, if not more so, than the West. Nevertheless, by far the more common trajectory was for Asian nations to assert their independence, even through armed revolt. The result was, too often, Civil War and profound violence on a catastrophic scale. A few examples will suffice:

- China's casualties under Mao Tse Tung are almost unbelievable, estimated to be 65 million in the *Black Book of Communism*.[22] This would make Mao responsible for far more deaths than any individual in the history of humankind.
- When the British left India in 1947, India split into India and the Islamic Republic of Pakistan (which included Bangladesh). Millions of Hindus and Sikhs fled to India while millions of Muslims migrated to Pakistan. Half a million people were killed in what may have been the largest mass migration of people in history.[23]
- The Vietnam War was a series of violent clashes spread out between 1959 and 1975. While American casualties were in the tens of thousands, Vietnamese casualties were in the hundreds of thousands.

- Cambodia's communist Khmer Rouge is responsible for perhaps two million deaths through war, intense persecution of dissenters, and failed economic policies that led to mass starvation. Pol Pot and his crew were Marxists, fiercely opposed to Western capitalism.
- Korea's split into North and South occurred in the aftermath of World War Two, splitting the country into a Soviet-influenced north and an American-influenced south. Heightened Cold War animosities resulted in the Korean War in the early 1950s, a conflict that led to hundreds of thousands of deaths when civilians are included.
- Afghanistan has been a disastrous war zone for decades. The Soviets were at war with Afghanistan from 1979 to 1988. The United States entered Afghanistan shortly after the events of September 11, 2001.
- Japan became the first Asian power in modern times to defeat a European power in the Russo-Japanese War from 1904 to 1905. Japan became a colonial power with territory that included Taiwan, Korea, Manchuria (Northeast China), and continued to expand into Southeast Asia until the bombings of Hiroshima and Nagasaki in 1945 by the U.S.
- The Philippines were granted independence from the U.S. in 1946, but their modern history was fraught with violence. A former Spanish colony, the Americans took control of the islands after the Spanish-American War of 1898. The Philippines resisted however, leading to the Philippine-American War that lasted until 1902. Hundreds of thousands of Filipino civilians were killed.

As we can see, Asia has grounds for being wary of Western ideas (Marxism), Western politics (many wars), and Western motives (colonialism). While many Asians are grateful to the West, there is certainly a suspicion—a postcolonial caution—that is typically encountered by Westerners who visit Asia. Since Christianity is so integrally linked to the Western world, it is no surprise that Asians might be prone to a lengthy pause before considering this faith as their own. This is unfortunate in many ways, chiefly two: First, Communism proved far more devastating than Christianity or any other ideology in the history of humankind—around 100 million people lost their lives during the twentieth century due to this sordid philosophy; second, because Christianity gets, albeit uncritically, rolled into one with Western politics and Western wars; it is easy to forget the founder of Christianity was probably a pacifist. In other words, Christianity should not be on trial when Asians condemn "the West," rather, Western political ideologies. Of course the two cannot be cleanly separated, as there is credence to the notion that Christianity may foster the conditions for reprehensible, distorted philosophies. At its core, though, Christianity is very different from what was exhibited by the Western world—Marxism, World Wars, nuclear armaments, colonial domination—during the last two centuries.

While Asians do tend to identify Christianity with the arrival of Westerners during the age of exploration in the fifteenth century and after—certainly a reasonable thing to do—by all means this is not the complete story. Christianity has been in Asia from very early on. The Christians of India, known as the Thomas Christians, claim Christianity was established there in the year AD 52. While some Western scholars doubt this claim due to a lack of hard evidence, there is no doubt that Christianity is very old there, at least 1700 years old.[24] These Orthodox Christians are in the Syriac family—meaning their liturgies are performed in a tongue closely related to Aramaic, the language of Jesus. Regardless of what Westerners might think, the tradition is unequivocal—Thomas, the initially doubtful apostle of Christ—came to India and established Christianity in seven towns.

Christianity entered Asia in four waves:

1. The early, relatively undocumented missions that were often linked to Judaism;
2. The Nestorian missions;
3. The Roman Catholic, mainly southern European missions;
4. The Protestant period, linked mainly with northern Europe and later with North American missions.[25]

Early Missions

The fall of the Temple in AD 70 was devastating to Jews in Jerusalem and the surrounding region. However, the Jewish diaspora would prove favorable for Christian growth. As earliest Christians were by and large Jewish, the belief that Jesus was the Jewish messiah spread far and wide along these routes. Paul, probably the greatest missionary of early Christianity, is mentioned in the book of Acts as normally attending the synagogues first when entering a new town. However, he and Peter and the other early leaders of Christianity began to conceptualize a faith open to Gentiles. This is when Christianity began to move west, well beyond the Semitic sphere. A point of caution is in order here, however: we must not de-emphasize the Semitic character of many early Christians, particularly east of the Roman Empire. While Paul and Peter worked their way west, there is another story, not told in the book of Acts, of missionaries who worked their way east. As one scholar put it,

The foundation tradition of Eastern churches, beginning in the last decades of the first century, was formed amongst Aramaic- and Syriac-speaking Jewish communities in Syria and Mesopotamia.[26]

Thus, Semitic Christianity is as important as or more important than Hellenistic Christianity in terms of growth. Arabic, Aramaic, Syriac, Hebrew, and Amharic (spoken in Ethiopia) were the languages that served as a Semitic framework for the Christians who worked their way east of the Holy Land in order to spread the Christian faith. These Semitic Christians were very successful in their missionary endeavors, establishing churches, monasteries, and centers of learning all over the Middle East, the eastern frontier of the Roman Empire, the Sassanid Persian Empire (226–651), southern Arabia and the Persian Gulf, around the north rim of the Arabian Sea—a route well-established—and into India.

The Nestorian Missions

Christians in Persia had a sophisticated, well-connected infrastructure centered in the city of Edessa by the year 200. Moffett writes, "Sometime before the year 200 the Christians of Edessa came out of the shadows."[27] The king of that city, Abgar VIII (the Great), probably converted to Christianity during his reign: from AD 177 to 212. Edessa served as a hub for Christian learning and missions that spread across northern Iran and into Merv, a city in modern-day Turkmenistan, in the 300s. Only God knows the pursuits of these Nestorian Christian missionaries from the Church of the East. Without doubt they were mission-minded. Thus looking at a map, the Nestorian advance, by the 400s, extended from Eastern Turkmenistan to Sri Lanka. As a side note, the Armenians—who had converted to Christianity in 301—also established churches all over the Black Sea and Caspian Sea areas. While Armenia is a very small country today, vestiges of the old Armenian network of churches remain in Iran, Turkey, and many other places across the Middle East. Nevertheless, when it comes to Asia, the Nestorians began to make breathtaking progress in the 400s, launching several mission campaigns still further east. Following the well-traveled "Silk Road" trading routes, the Nestorians would have been amply supplied with Asian audiences for their preaching.

The high point of the Nestorian missionary period was from about 650 to 850, perhaps most importantly from 780 to 823, when the most famous Nestorian Patriarch, Timothy, was Catholicos of "Perhaps a quarter of the world's Christians."[28] Based in Seleucia, in modern-day Iraq, Patriarch Timothy sponsored hugely ambitious missionary endeavors, all the way into Tibet. It was not on Timothy's watch, however, that Christianity entered China. Rather, in 635, a Persian Nestorian monk named Alopen arrived to the Chinese capital, modern-day Xian, and established a monastery there.[29] There is a famous "Nestorian Stele" that commemorates these missionaries of the "Religion of Light" on display at the Beilin Museum in Xian, China. This tablet reveals all kinds of wonderful information about the Nestorians. It lays out their belief that Jesus died on the cross in order to save people in all four directions, and that Jesus illuminates the old religions by casting new light on them. The tablet shows their belief in Satan, the Trinity, the Incarnation, and the Virgin Birth. It tells us that the missionaries gathered at 7:00 am for the salvation of everyone. The tablet is also significant in its weaving of Taoist understandings with Christian beliefs. There is a clear attempt to uphold the integrity of local Chinese beliefs and customs without compromising Christian truth.[30] It is a lasting testament to the success of Nestorian Christianity in East Asia.

In all likelihood, Nestorian missionaries reached Korea, in the Far East, before the year 987.[31] The year 987 is significant, for that is when a Nestorian monk living in Baghdad wrote, "There is not a single Christian left in China."[32] The Nestorian church as a whole began a period of decline in the tenth century, under heavy-handed policies and violent persecutions. Their struggle, on all fronts, was against the odds. In the East, a politically destabilized and newly xenophobic China proved challenging for further Christian advance. In Central Asia and the Middle East, Islam had risen to the fore. The Western world had long since written off the churches of the East as heretical. All combined, it was a disaster, and Nestorian Christianity's period of expansion stopped abruptly.

Under the Mongols in the thirteenth century, especially the fifth Great Khan Kublai, Nestorian Christianity witnessed a period of protection, and actually began to flourish again. In fact, Kublai came to know two forms of Christianity when the Venetian explorer East Marco Polo (1254–1324) visited him and they apparently developed a friendly acquaintance. Marco Polo probably would have at least introduced Roman Catholic Christianity to the Khan. However, when the Mongol empires began converting to Islam in the fourteenth century, the final straw came down. In that century,

...the religious tolerance of Mongol imperial rule gave way to a new destructive wave of widespread Mongolian ferocities fueled by conquering Muslim zeal, and the shattered remnants of Asian Christianity were left isolated in ever small pockets of desperation.[33]

After that, Islam reigned supreme in Central Asia and the candles of the Nestorian Churches were abruptly put out ... one by one. The Nestorian Church—known officially as the Assyrian Church of the East—is estimated to have less than half a million members now. Due to recent pillaging in their homeland of Iraq, the future of this church's existence is precarious.[34]

The Roman Catholic Missions

The Roman Catholic missions took root during the age of exploration. Anywhere the European explorers landed, the priests were sure to follow. The

Spanish and Portuguese were the world's superpowers at the time, and as a result their ships were free to roam the seas in a period of magnificent discovery.

India: Vasco da Gama was the first European to sail directly from Europe to India, which he accomplished in 1498. It is fascinating to note that when the Portuguese arrived at India, some of the first people they contacted were Christians—the Thomas Christians. What seemed to be fortuitous ended up disastrous. The Roman Catholics believed the Thomas Christians to be living in heresy, so they went about converting them to Roman-style Christianity. However, the Orthodox Christians were aghast at some of the practices of the Catholics, resulting in considerable misunderstandings. Serious conflicts broke out as a result and the scars remain today. The Thomas Christians of South India are depressingly fractured into myriad forms, harboring resentment toward each other for what happened in the 1500s. Other Roman Catholic missionaries continued the mission work in India alongside colonial developments by the Portuguese. Spanish priest Francis Xavier went to India in 1542. By that time, Portugal had secured some of the ports and was carrying on significant trade with the Indians. Xavier—one of the founders of the Jesuits—based himself at Goa on the west coast. He was a tireless missionary; his candle burned bright but fast as he died at the age of 46. He is considered one of the greatest evangelists in history and is the patron saint of Roman Catholic missionaries.

Japan: Japan is an interesting case study, mainly because of what once appeared to be an awesome opportunity for Jesuit missionaries all but vanished to the point that today the Christians in Japan are a tiny minority. Japan is one context where persecution succeeded. It is often the case that persecution leads to growth; however, in the case of Japan the persecutions largely snuffed out the candles of a once-burgeoning Christian presence. Xavier had phenomenal success in Japan during his three years there. Philip Jenkins writes,

> For decades, success followed success, so that by about 1600, it seemed that Japan would soon be a Catholic nation. Nagasaki became a bishopric in 1596, and the first ordinations of Japanese priests followed in 1601. Hundreds of thousands of Japanese were baptized.[35]

By 1615, there were a half-million Christians in Japan, mainly around Nagasaki. A disastrous surprise occurred, however, when the Tokugawa Shoguns began to have serious misgivings with this foreign religion, and suppressed it brutally. Hundreds of missionaries and Japanese Catholics were tortured, burned, crucified, and beheaded. The Christians who continued to practice their faith clandestinely have become famous. Known as the Kakure Kirishitan community, they preserved the Catholic faith in secret. Part of their fame in recent years stems from the important novel *Silence* by Japanese Christian author Shusaku Endo.[36]

China: The Jesuits arrived to China in the late 1500s. The most notable of the Jesuits in China was Matteo Ricci (1552–1610). Ricci is considered one of the great Catholic missionaries of all time because of his ability to assimilate Christianity into another culture. He amazed the Chinese with his memorization abilities, clock-making skills, cartography and astronomy knowledge, and math prowess. He moved around to several places in China and ended up in Peking (Beijing), making it his mission to get on the good side of the ruling authorities. Dressing like a Confucian scholar and learning the customs and languages, Ricci was more than anything a missionary and he enjoyed great success in this. It is estimated he led more than 2000 Chinese to Christianity.[37]

The Franciscans, Dominicans, and Augustinians followed the Jesuits into China, but were highly critical of some of their methods, leading to an episode known as "the Chinese rites controversies." It was essentially a series of theological disputes over the issues of ancestor veneration, theological concepts, how to translate important Christian terms into Chinese languages, and the blurry line of religious assimilation and syncretism in general. What began as a theological disagreement blew out of proportion and the pope dissolved the Jesuits from 1773 to 1814. The rulers of China took note of the strange events. They had profound respect for the Jesuits. Those sent to replace the Jesuits were not up to the task. By 1793 the Chinese Emperor Ch'ien-lung considered the Europeans to be "barbarians of the west" and dismissed Western pleas for the opportunity to conduct trade with them.[38] These and other problems led to a severe lack of credibility for the Roman Church. Catholic Christianity began to be formally suppressed. How did the Catholic Church allow this to unravel? Looking back, the timing could not have been worse. Moffett writes,

At a time when the population of the [Chinese] empire was exploding, from 116 million in 1710 to 275 million in 1796, Christian missions and the Chinese church were disintegrating. ... In the year 1700 the Roman Catholic missions in China had reported about three hundred thousand Christians in China. A hundred years later, around 1800, there were probably only half as many.[39]

Indeed, Asia was proving to be the lost opportunity in the history of Christianity—and many of the losses were self-inflicted.

The Chinese rites controversy is often used as a case study in how deeply Christians may disagree on the extent of assimilation in the transplanting of faith. Assimilation was an issue with which all missionaries had to deal. Should missionaries become "like them"? Alternatively, should they force "them" to by and large become "like us"—speaking our language, emulating our customs, believing the things we believe. In other words, to what extent must a Christian compromise his own culture in order to win people for Christ? Jesuits were known to assimilate deeply into the culture they were missionizing. Other orders, such as the Franciscans and Dominicans, resisted. Major debates came out of this, related to, for example, the worship of ancestors. Another example is that the Jesuits used Chinese words in their theology, to the horror of the other orders. The Dominicans were aghast when they found out that the Jesuits honored Confucius, declaring he was not in hell—obviously where the Dominicans believed he was. The entire episode so offended the Chinese imperials that they eventually became hostile towards this dissentious faith that they were once so attracted to. As a result, Christianity floundered in all Asia during the age of European expansion, with perhaps one exception, the Philippines. Moffett writes:

> The rites controversy also became an ominous impediment to the progress of Catholic missions in other parts of Asia. It not only set the Catholic mission orders against each other, it frustrated the pope's efforts toward Catholic unity.[40]

The Chinese rites controversy had huge ramifications. Catholic Christianity was stymied in Asia at a time when the Protestants were gaining a foothold.

Philippines: It would be misguided to paint a picture that Catholic Christianity was a failure all over Asia during the age of expansion. The Philippines is a very significant exception, due to the high population and high fertility rate of the country. The Philippines fell under Spanish control around 1570. Drawing from their enormous success in Central and South America, the Spanish learned that if they could convert the leader, they could likely win them all. The Spanish priests were able to accomplish the baptism of several important chiefs in the Philippines, most notably in Manila, where the chief allowed unimpeded propagation of the Christian faith.[41] One theory on why Christianity fit so well into Filipino culture is because "Christian practices were vaguely akin to indigenous rituals."[42] The Catholic emphases on ritual, holy water, saints, amulets, beads, and other talismans worked supremely well in a shamanistic, magic-oriented society. The Catholic system of praying to saints meshed perfectly with a context of spirit worship and ancestor veneration. "In this way a kind of folk Catholicism was enabled to take firm root in the northern part of the Philippines."[43] It spread south from there, although Islam has remained fairly strong in the southern regions, around 6 to 7% of the national population.

The Protestant Period

Protestant missions got a late start in Asia. They began in India in 1706 with the work of an extraordinarily gifted German named Bartholomaeus Ziegenbalg, who established several churches in the southeast part of India, known as the Tamil region. Protestant European countries had been trading with India for some time, and they were outright opposed to the missionaries for fear that they would disrupt trade. Ziegenbalg was thrown into jail by the Danish governor of south India at the time. His challenges were fairly representative during the era of early Protestant missions in India. Missionaries were deeply resented by European businessmen who needed peace. Converting people to another faith would prove divisive and could be highly resented by the locals. However, it was the colonial administrators and the European trading companies—such as the Dutch East Indian Company and the British East India Company—who resented the missionaries the most.

Probably the most famous missionary to India was William Carey, often called the father of modern missions. Carey conducted mission work in Serampore, near Calcutta, beginning in 1793. His mission work focused largely on Bible translation. Carey, the son of a Baptist shoemaker, was linguistically gifted, overseeing the translation of the Bible into several Indian languages. His approach to missions was that if the Bible can be read by the people, then the people will eventually understand and turn to Christ. It is a pattern still followed by many Protestant missionary organizations.

Scottish missionary Robert Morrison entered China in 1807, the first Protestant to do so. His chief contribution was to translate the Old and New Testaments into Mandarin, a herculean task. The problem for Morrison, as well as with the other Protestants who would follow in his path, was that Christian missionaries by this time were associated with the other European businessmen who were involved in the opium-trade. Some missionaries traveled with ships that were involved with importing Indian-grown opium into China—and many Chinese people became addicted. The problem was that the Chinese government prohibited this trade; and the Europeans defiantly continued the practice. The Europeans, primarily the British and Portuguese, got rich and bought Chinese products with the opium money. The missionaries however got lumped in with the opium trade. The Opium Wars of the 1830s and 1850s led to a suspicion of all things Western by the Chinese government.

The Taiping Rebellion (1850–1864) did not help the cause of Christianity, either, as over 20 million Chinese people died during this bizarre chapter of history. The rebellion began when a delusional Christian convert named Hong Xiuquan claimed to be the brother of Jesus Christ. Hong was joined by another radical named Yang Xiuqing who claimed to speak on behalf of God and eventually organized a militia that grew to the point that it rivaled the Chinese government. Initially, the missionaries sided with these men, rooting for them, since they were Christians. However, in time the Westerners began to realize the extraordinary theological claims of the revolutionaries. Eventually, the Chinese Empire, with the help of Western military forces, stamped out the rebellion, but the loss of life was massive—well into the millions.[44] The Chinese people made a link between Christianity and this event. It was the most severe blow to Christianity in Chinese history; the residual effects are incalculable. Moffett writes:

> Ever since the disastrous Taiping Rebellion, most Chinese found it difficult to distinguish the semi-Christianity of the Taiping rebels from the faith of the missionaries, and as a result lived with the perception that Christianity was the handmaiden of rebellion. ... It is not surprising, therefore, to find that fast though the church might be growing in China, it was faced and sometimes outpaced[45] by a rising storm of Chinese protest against all things foreign, including Christianity.

After the Taiping Rebellion, only a miracle could restore credibility to Christianity in China. The reverberations from the events continue today.

Hudson Taylor is probably the best known Protestant Christian missionary to China. He lived from 1832 to 1905 and served 51 years in China, founding the China Inland Mission (CIM)—known today as the Overseas Missionary Fellowship (OMF). Like the Jesuits he took on the customs and dress of the Chinese. Unlike the Jesuits, he preferred to minister to the poor villagers rather than the aristocracy. His methods were novel for his day in age: the missionaries did not have to be ordained, they could be women, they did not have to be from any particular denomination, and they were not promised regular income—only free will offerings from the churches. Taylor's missions grew rapidly in the late 1800s and had some success in changing Christianity's image. The success, however, was short-lived due to yet another violent clash between East and West, the Boxer Rebellion.

The Boxer Rebellion (1899–1901) was an anti-foreign, anti-Christian movement in China and Mongolia that wiped out tens of thousands of Chinese Christians, as well as several hundred missionaries—from Protestant, Catholic, and even Orthodox backgrounds. It was a devastating blow for Christian progress in China and Mongolia. Missionaries were burned to death, cut to pieces, many infants and children were brutally murdered, and missionaries who had devoted years to medical work and education were ruthlessly dragged out of their homes and slaughtered in public. The Chinese Christians who had grown so close to the missionaries were massacred as traitors. The stories from this persecution are particularly gruesome: one Chinese Christian woman—Mrs. Chiang—who had a son in the local Christian college, could not run due to the ancient foot-binding custom for women in that country. She was discovered crawling in search of food, was caught and "literally minced" by swordsmen.[46]

The Boxer's Rebellion, as awful as it was, was a Chinese call for independence, for justice, and for empowerment in a land that was quickly being overrun by Europeans and Japanese. Mark Galli writes that the uprising was in all actuality an explosion of resentment toward foreign powers and policies that were less than fair:

> The causes of the uprising were many and complex, but the arrogance of the foreigners is as good a summation as any. Since the 1840s, foreigners had forced China's hand in treaty after treaty, gaining control of large parts of the country. The English, Americans, French, Dutch, Spanish, Germany, and the largest group, Japanese, had divided up the country as if they were playing the board game *Risk*. Foreigners sometimes owned whole cities. Worse, they swaggered through China knowing they could not be arrested for any crime. ... Missionary pride and Chinese anger shot up in 1899 when the Chinese government conferred official status on missionaries, making a bishop or superintendent the equal of a provincial governor, and any foreigner the equivalent of district magistrates. ... Many missionaries publicly ridiculed sacred Chinese beliefs—ancestor worship and Confucian precepts. Some charged into temples while Chinese were worshiping and denounced them for bowing to idols.[47]

The Boxer Rebellion was eventually crushed by an eight-nation alliance including the U.S., U.K., Russia, Japan, Italy, France, Austria-Hungary, and Germany. They all had to coordinate their militaries and ground troops to try to stop the Boxers' highly charged attacks on all things Western. This conflict created a fracture in China, which eventually collapsed the weakened Qing Dynasty (Manchu Dynasty) and led to the Chinese civil wars in the 1920s, 1930s, and 1940s between the Soviet-supported communists and the Western-supported Nationalists. The Nationalist Party, known as the KMT or Republic of China, eventually lost the wars and was forced to migrate to the island of Formosa (Taiwan).

The Second Sino-Japanese War was fought between China and Japan between 1937 and 1945. The Japanese government's incessant encroachments into China finally ceased as a result of the American bombs that crippled the Japanese war efforts. With the Japanese vanquished from China, the Chinese Civil War began again and lasted until 1950. When the dust settled in 1950, the communists, led by Mao Tse Tung (1893–1976), had consolidated power. Virtually all missionaries were forced out of China.

In 1900, out of a population of 472 million people in China, less than two million Christians existed there, or, less than one-half of one percent.[48] It was around this time that many Chinese Christians began to recognize the need to disassociate themselves from the Western churches. In the first half of the twentieth century Chinese Christianity began to indigenize. Several preachers rose up during this period and are still revered in China today. John Sung (Song Shangjie, 1901–1944) was one of these. Son of a Methodist pastor, Sung went to Ohio State University and earned a doctorate in chemistry, dazzling his teachers by his abilities. He eventually enrolled in Union Theological Seminary in New York. One night in 1927 Sung happened to attend a Baptist church in Harlem and heard a black female preacher who left a major impression on him. He radically changed—to the point people thought he was insane and locked him in an asylum for 189 days. After his release he went back to China and became "the Billy Graham of Asia." Sung travelled tirelessly, establishing evangelistic bands and sending out disciples. His life was cut short but his legacy is powerful.[49]

Sung was one of a growing crop of home-grown evangelists who did not bring the baggage of a foreigner. Throughout the early decades of the twentieth century, several other Christian movements sprouted into being, emphasizing the indigenous aspect: the Pentecostal True Jesus Church, the Assembly Hall, the Spiritual Gifts Church, and the Jesus Family.[50] Yu Guozhen, Zhang Boliang, Jing Dianying, and Wang Mingdao were some of the more prominent evangelists who called for a more indigenous Chinese Christianity. These Christians, and their descendants in the house-church movement, are responsible for the magnificent and ambitious growth that has occurred in Chinese Christianity in spite of decades of oppression. In the early part of the twentieth century these Christians marked out a plan, known as the "Back to Jerusalem" movement.[51] Essentially, their long-term goal was to spread Christianity across Asia and the Islamic world, and right back into the heart of the Middle East: Jerusalem. The extraordinary journey of the indigenous Chinese Christian movement, as well as its contemporary expansion, was documented in the film "The Cross—Jesus in China." It is a powerful testimony to Christian perseverance in the face of persecution.[52]

One of the most prolific evangelists in Chinese Christian history was Watchman Nee (1903–1972), known in China as Ni Tuosheng. He led the Assembly Hall, also known as the Little Flock. Watchman Nee was one of the few twentieth century Chinese leaders even known by Western Christians. A self-educated man, Nee wrote dozens of books that are widely regarded by Christians worldwide. He was strongly in favor of a church that was authentically Chinese, without any foreign influence. His group has become known for its strongly evangelistic nature. Nee was imprisoned due to Mao's crackdowns on religion and he spent the last two decades of his life incarcerated. Through his friend and fellow evangelist Witness Lee, the movement made significant gains in Taiwan. The Little Flock has become an international movement known today by the name "Local Churches," and is based primarily in Taipei, Taiwan, and Anaheim, California.[53]

Watchman Nee was one of many Asian Christian leaders whose ministries were cut short during their prime in the mid-twentieth century. The atheist policies of the communist government threatened to snuff out Chinese Christianity altogether during the brutal years of Mao Tse Tung (ruled 1949-1976). Mao's rise to power and subsequent attacks on religion were a pivotal time in the history of Christianity in China. Mao became a war hero in the aftermath of chaos, and he was able to work his way into the hearts and minds of the Chinese nation. He represented victory, independence, freedom from foreign rule, resistance to Japanese and Western imperialism, and forward thinking. While his ironfisted rule and dictatorial approach indeed gained stability and independence for China, it came at a staggering cost of millions upon millions of lives—through xenophobic policies, brutal suppression of resistance, failed agricultural experiments, and his militaristic rise to power.

As far as religion is concerned, Mao Tse Tung considered it poisonous. Within a few years of his taking power, all missionaries were gone. Mao recognized that an atheistic society was impossible and thus he began to regulate all religious activity through a special office dedicated to this purpose, beginning in 1951.[54] Offices were established to regulate Catholics, Protestants, Muslims, Buddhists, and Taoists. Not all Christians were opposed to the communist takeover, indeed many, especially Protestants, welcomed the development. The Protestant Three-Self Patriotic Movement (TSPM) is strongly loyal to the Chinese state, although there are many "underground" Christians who believe the TSPM is illegitimate due to their allegiance to an officially atheistic government. This has led to a great fissure in Chinese Christianity. There are official churches registered with the state, but there are many unregistered churches—both Catholic and Protestant—known by various names: the underground church, the illegal Christians, unrecognized Christians, or the unaffiliated churches.

During the years 1966-1969, Mao implemented the "Great Proletarian Cultural Revolution." The Cultural Revolution impacted every stratum of Chinese society, and the religious were in no way spared; indeed, they were blamed as being part of the "Four Olds"—according to Mao these were things that needed to change in order for China to progress: old customs, old culture, old habits, and old ideas. All religious leaders were severely restricted; many were put to death. It was a period of social chaos as all intellectuals, particularly those with significant religious commitments, were disgraced and usually sent to the countryside for manual labor. Christianity in China was on the brink of ruin, or so it seemed. Out of the ashes however was a network of underground churches. Tiedemann, a specialist on China, writes:

> Since then [late 1970s] an explosive growth of Christianity has occurred in many parts of the country. This so-called 'Christianity fever' has been particularly prevalent in Chinese Protestantism. Exact figures are difficult to establish, since many Christians do not wish to register with the TSPM because of the latter's close collaboration with the government. Similar problems exist between the 'official' Catholic Church regulated by the CCPA [Chinese Catholic Patriotic Association] and the 'pro-Rome' underground movement led by the so-called 'little black priests'. Yet in spite of these divisions, the tight control exercised by the Religious Affairs Bureau and sporadic bouts of harassment, the Catholic and Protestant Churches continue to grow.[55]

Some scholars predict that China is experiencing widespread Christian growth. Others are more skeptical. It might take years before anyone really knows just how much Christianity is growing in China. Right now it is clear that Christianity has made substantial gains since 1900, when less than one percent was Christian. Today, it is estimated China may be eight or nine percent Christian.

While Protestants have had limited successes in China, the more obvious cases of Protestant success have been in South Korea—which may soon be Christian majority— and Northeast India—which has three states that are majority Christian: Nagaland, Mizoram, and Meghalaya. Occasionally one hears of Christian revival movements in Indonesia, Vietnam, Nepal, and perhaps a growing movement in North Korea, but these are often overstated. In some cases there is such a paucity of solid information on religious demographics in Asian nations that any conclusion beyond an educated guess remains dubious. Islamic nations in Asia, for example, are notorious for skewing the statistics. Charges of distorted religious demographics in China and India are commonplace.

Overall, however, Christianity in Asia has not progressed in the fantastical ways that it has in other regions of the global south such as Africa, Latin America, and Oceania. Indeed some even refer to "The 'failure' of Christianity in Asia."[56]

Asian Christianity Today

The status of Asian Christianity today can be summarized with the following statistics:

- Asia is estimated to be 9.25% Christian, which means nearly 350 million Christians live there;

- Out of 33 countries and territories, Christianity is the most practiced religion in four: British Indian Ocean Territory (BIOT—which is statistically insignificant), Philippines, South Korea, and Timore-Leste;
- Christian allegiance is over 10% in ten of Asia's countries and territories: BIOT, Brunei, Christmas Island, Cocos Islands, Indonesia, Kazakhstan, Philippines, Singapore, South Korea, and Timor-Leste;
- Protestant/Independent Christianity is by far the largest form of Christianity in Asia, with 65% of the market share. The Roman Catholic Church claims 33% and Orthodoxy claims a mere 2%—chiefly in India with the ancient Thomas Christians, and the Central Asian nations (Kazakhstan, Kyrgyzstan, Tajikistan, Turkmenistan, Uzbekistan), which are historically within the sphere of Orthodox influence;
- Christianity is growing in Asia—from less than 1% in 1900 to nearly 10% a century later.

Afghanistan

Afghanistan is over 99% Islamic. It is not alone in Asian nations in this regard. The Maldives, Pakistan, and Turkmenistan are almost entirely Islamic nations in Asia as well. Bangladesh is about 90% Islamic. Afghanistan has descended into an abyss of violence and despair over the last few decades. From 1979 to 1988 the country was engaged in a protracted conflict with the Soviet Union. Some argue this proved pivotal in bringing down the USSR and transforming the world order. It is estimated that over a million Afghanis died during that conflict.[57] Afghanistan was ripped to shreds, left to pick up the pieces, and subsequently descended into chaos as warlords battled over various parts of the country. The Taliban government—an ultraconservative form of Islamic Sharia rule—ruled the country from 1996 to 2001 when the U.S.-led coalition invaded in order to break up Islamic fundamentalism in the country. It was believed by the U.S. government that the attacks of September 11, 2001, were essentially mapped out and orchestrated from Taliban members in Afghanistan. To date, the mastermind of the 9/11 attacks, Osama bin Laden, has yet to be found and is believed to be on the border in the mountains between Pakistan and Afghanistan. Bin Laden has been on the FBIs Most Wanted List ever since, with a reward of $25 million for anyone who can provide information leading to his arrest. The U.S. government claims there is one Christian church in Afghanistan.[58] Afghanistan is an extremely conservative Islamic nation. As recently as 2006 converts to Christianity were arrested, and those who leave the Islamic faith run the risk of losing their lives. Missionaries who are discovered to be proselytizing are promptly deported. Converts to Christianity bring tremendous shame on families in this fiercely Islamic society; when it does happen, they are often murdered without any legal repercussions.[59]

China

Christianity claims the allegiance of less than 10% of the nation, but it is doubtlessly growing in China. There is no way to know how fast this is happening, however. The Chinese government has proven to be much more tolerant in recent years and some are envisioning a day when even the underground churches are able to meet without any harassment. In recent years some Chinese economists have theorized that Christianity leads to economic prosperity, and thus may be very good for society.[60] It is not uncommon to see journalists becoming mesmerized by China's embrace of Christianity in their reporting. For example, in 2004, Geoffrey York of Canada's *Globe and Mail* wrote an article while in Beijing entitled: "Jesus challenging Marx for soul of China," with the claim that "Millions are turning to Christianity" and "China is in the process of becoming Christianized."[61] One scholar argues that Christianity is beginning to compete with the Communist Party in the villages, and is significantly shaping local politics in the Chinese countryside. The government takes issue with this and is attempting to curb the trend, however.[62] Sociologist David Martin has argued that as Chinese people move to the cities and as communism is leaving an ideological vacuum, Pentecostal Christianity seems to be filling a void.[63] The revitalization of Chinese Christianity can be summarized:

> Anyone who has worshiped with Christians in China cannot fail to be impressed by their vibrancy and faithful witness. Every week millions of believers eager to hear God's word flock to city and country churches alike. The vitality of the church in China is confirmed by sanctuaries so packed that countless worshipers sit on stools in makeshift courtyards listening by loudspeaker. In some urban churches, video equipment transmits the service to overflow rooms for those arriving too late to find seats in the sanctuary. It is not unusual for rural Christians to travel several hours to attend a worship service. They are disappointed when the sermon is less than an hour![64]

As China continues to open itself up to new ideologies and to loosen its grip on religion, there is little doubt that Christianity will continue to make inroads.

India

Christianity in India is primarily a religion for the very, very poor. Dalit Christians often find Christianity a useful alternative to existing as outcastes in a society that rigidly upholds the pollution-based caste system. However, those who convert out of Hinduism are often harassed, as happened in 2008 and 2009. While the percentage of Indian Christianity is in the single digits, estimates range wildly. I was once told by an Indian Christian leader that if all of the Dalits were counted, then the percentage of Christians in India could be perhaps 20%. This estimate seems far too high, but it suggests two points: first, the majority of Christians in India are of very low castes and they often go overlooked in statistical compilations; and, second, there is a confidence in the Indian churches that they are not a fringe faith with a questionable future. Rather, they are growing, vibrant, and see no signs of decline. The famous St. Thomas Christians of South India are in many ways accepted by the Hindu majority, largely because of their ancient heritage. It is the recent converts who attract the negative attention. Evangelism is a difficult topic in India. Like in most Asian societies, there is a strong social stigma when a person converts out of the religion of their ancestors and family and joins up with a new group. The Thomas Christians hold little threat because they are seen as almost a caste and are not involved in winning converts as the independent churches are. In India, there is the added difficulty that Protestant and Catholic forms of Christianity are associated with Western, imperial rule and are thus foreigner faiths. Protestant/Independent Christianity, particularly in the charismatic forms, are definitely growing in India, but it is difficult to ascertain whether Christianity's market share is growing. If the Hindutva movement—Hindu nationalism—continues to attract Indians, then Christianity's future does not look bright. Hindutva has repercussions that go far and wide: economic discrimination, equal opportunity discrimination, social stigma that claims Christianity is not truly Indian, and outright persecution at various times—including martyrdom in extreme cases.

Indonesia

Indonesia is the fourth most populated country in the world, with around 250 million people. Well over half of the people are Islamic in the traditional sense, making it one of the largest national Islamic nations in the world. There is also a "neoreligionist" movement that is defined by David Barrett as "... syncretizing traditional animism with, firstly, Hinduism and Buddhism and later Islam.... From one point of view they may be described as Islamized new religions."[65] If these neoreligionists were included in the overall numbers for Islam, then the percentage of Muslims in Indonesia would be much higher. Philip Jenkins has discussed the concept of "statistical chicanery" which is conspicuous in Indonesia, although there are historical explanations:

> Let us for instance take the nation of Indonesia, purportedly the world's most populous Muslim country. While most people would agree that Islam is very strong in Indonesia, political factors partly explained the enormous growth of self-described Muslims in that nation from the mid-1960s on. At a time of homicidal official anticommunism, failure to acknowledge any religion on official identity papers immediately raised suspicions about a person's possible seditious attitudes, and as a

result, millions were now inspired to declare themselves Muslim. Memories of this era may explain why Indonesia appears to have a vast Muslim population, 85% of the whole, or some 180 million strong.[66]

Christianity in Indonesia is historically linked to the Roman Catholic Portuguese or the Dutch Protestant traders, although independence was achieved from the Dutch in 1949. Being so closely identified with colonial rule does not exactly bid well for the future of Christianity in a postcolonial context. In recent years there has been an increasing amount of violence against Christians in Indonesia, prompting human rights groups to speak out. While freedom of religion is, in theory, on the books in Indonesia, various forms of Sharia Law are recognized in half of Indonesia's 32 provinces because of the Regional Autonomy Law of 2000 which allows local governments to pass Islamic Law.[67] The U.S. Department of State reports several incidents of the closure of churches as well as the prevention of the construction of new churches.[68] The future of Christianity in Indonesia is altogether unclear. In this archipelago of over 17,000 islands—6,000 of which are inhabited—and over 700 languages, it is impossible to know which people-groups will form religious alliances with whom. In the currently delicate context of Indonesian religion, the possibilities of mass conversions to Christianity are unlikely due to the reprisals that have—and inevitably would—ensue. Islamist terrorist groups such as the *Jemaah Islamiyah* inflicted tremendous harm in the late 1990s and early 2000s. Memories of beheadings, bombed churches, ethnic cleansings, and forcible conversions are still fresh; Christians invite disaster when they launch revivals or evangelistic projects.[69]

Japan

Japan is a "graying" nation. It is the only nation in Asia to have a median age in the 40s. If current trends continue, such as Japan's extremely low fertility rate (1.22 children born per woman), it is possible the median age will reach 50 years old in the near future! Christianity's heyday has come and gone. Led by the Catholic Church, notably Francis Xavier in the 1500s, the country seemed to be turning Christian. It was however almost completely wiped out through an intense persecution in the 1600s—one of the more horrific mass martyrdoms in Christian history. Japan was forcibly opened to the West when Commodore Matthew Perry's "black ships" arrived to its shores in 1854. Protestants followed up with a brief evangelization effort in the late 1800s, but it fizzled as Japanese nationalism and imperialism reached new heights. Christianity in Japan is statistically insignificant today, around two percent. Japan is generally considered, like most Western European nations, to be a country that is secularizing. One would think there is little reason for hope that Christianity might resurge. However, Leroy Seat, a Western scholar who lived in Japan for nearly forty years, wrote:

> I am very optimistic about the future of Christianity in that country ... Part of my optimism for Japan is based on the continued presence of Christian schools in Japan. Among Protestants alone, there are over one hundred Christian institutions affiliated with the Education Association of Christians Schools in Japan, and these include some of the largest and most prestigious private universities in the country.[70]

He goes on to discuss a national survey that seemed to indicate a preference amongst the Japanese youth for Christianity if they were required to choose a religion. He also cites the fact that many weddings in Japan are conducted in Christian ceremonies, often with Christian counseling taking place beforehand. His view is that Japanese have high regard for Christianity, and a mass movement may be waiting in the wings, similar to what happened in South Korea during the twentieth century.

Kazakhstan

Along with several other Central Asian nations—Kyrgyzstan, Tajikistan, Turkmenistan, Uzbekistan—Kazakhstan was for a time within the Orthodox world. However, Islam is today the religion of choice in the region. The Central Asian nations contain some of the most thoroughly Muslim populations in the world. Kazakhstan is somewhat exceptional here, as only about half of the population is Muslim. The second largest group is the nonreligious (26%), who are a vestige of Soviet rule in the country—from 1936 to 1991. Christians account for around 14% of the population and are primarily Russian Orthodox. The country, however, seems destined to move more in the direction of Islam in the foreseeable future as Saudi Arabia has sponsored a wealth of programs geared towards Islamization of the former Soviet satellite: paid trips to Mecca for the hajj, a massive mosque-building campaign, newly constructed Islamic colleges, Arabic language programs, over a million copies of the Quran—accompanied by paid teachers to explain it, and a UAE-sponsored project to erect a mosque in every single town and village. This "renaissance" of Islam, sponsored by the Saudi king, is paying dividends as there is now a common proverb in the nation: "To be Kazakh is to be Muslim."[71] The government of nearby Kyrgyzstan came under fire in 2008 for "... passing a law designed to restrict non-Muslim religions from establishing themselves in the country."[72]

Myanmar (Burma)

Myanmar is a strongly Buddhist country ruled by a strict military dictatorship. There was a series of democratic rallies led by Buddhist monks in Myanmar in

2007 propelling the country into the news briefly, although the protests were crushed by the military. It was somewhat rare for this extremely closed nation to even make the news due to its closed-door policies. In 2008 the cyclone Nargis killed 150,000 Burmese, barely attracting attention in the West. When the United Nations sent food to the country, the government seized it. These events illustrated just how isolated Burma had become from the rest of the world. Christianity has been in Myanmar for over a millennium, beginning with the Nestorians in the 900s. Catholics arrived in the 1500s and Protestants in the early 1800s. The American Baptist missionary Adoniram Judson (1788-1850) famously worked for forty years in Burma in the first half of the nineteenth century. Judson had considerable success in his evangelism efforts, particularly amongst the persecuted Karen tribe. Christianity in Burma, as in Southeast Asia, tends to grow when tribes or regional ethnic groups convert en masse. This same pattern has occurred in Northeast India where tribes tend to convert as a community, rather than individually. Christianity is growing slightly in Burma, but there is little reason to think that any other religion will rival Buddhism in the foreseeable future.

Philippines

The Philippines is one of the more important strongholds of the Roman Catholic Church. This is a densely populated country—around 100 million people. It is also very Catholic. Christianity is the religion of nine out of ten Filipinos, and the vast majority of them are Catholic. Protestantism, particularly Pentecostalism, is growing in the Philippines, however. In fact, Pentecostalism was in the 1980s and 1990s growing at such a rapid pace that it seemed to be the wave of the future. However, in 1982, a Catholic by the name of Mario ("Brother Mike") Velarde started the El Shaddai movement, which today claims the allegiance of millions of Catholics. El Shaddai was begun by Brother Mike as a radio program. Velarde was a real estate businessman and had acquired a radio station as part of a deal. His Bible teaching on the radio soon acquired a following as people claimed he had healed them from various problems.[73] Brother Mike's movement continued to grow and today the huge gatherings have the atmosphere of,

> ... a 1960s rock festival. ... There is a firm belief in God's direct intervention in everyday life ... followers raise their passports to be blessed at services, to ensure that they will get the visas they need to work overseas. Many open umbrellas and turn them upside down as a symbolic way of catching the rich material blessings they expect to receive from on high.[74]

Philip Jenkins has noted that the El Shaddai movement is one shining example of how the Roman Catholic Church can possibly compete with the rising tide of Pentecostalism all over the world. Movements like Velarde's El Shaddai provide Catholics with a way of preserving the flock from mass defections that have occurred elsewhere, like in Latin America. The Philippines will continue to be a major player in world Christianity. Its large population is complemented by a high fertility rate (3.32 children born per woman) as well as very high active participation rates when it comes to Christianity. This nation is strongly Christian, evinced by the political involvement of some of the most prolific Christians in the country. For example, Catholic cardinal and archbishop of Manila Jaime Sin (1928-2005) famously led the overthrowing of Ferdinand Marcos from the presidency in 1986 due to nepotism and corruption. What was unique was Cardinal Sin's emphasis on using the teachings of Jesus to change the nation, rather than violence. Sin's "People Power Revolution" was known to emphasize nonviolence, prayer, and readings from the gospels.

Singapore

Formerly a British colony, Singapore is a highly developed nation—one of the few remaining city-states in the world. Singaporeans are some of the wealthiest people per capita in the world; over 90% of them own their own homes.[75] Singapore has the lowest fertility rate in Asia, an alarming 1.08 children born per woman. It is a unique country in terms of religious demographics. About 40% are from Chinese Universal religion—a syncretistic mixture of Buddhism, Confucianism, Taoism, and ancient Chinese folk religion. After that there is a fairly even distribution between Muslims, Christians, and Buddhists. About 5% of Singaporeans are Hindu. The largest Christian denominations in Singapore are the Catholics, Methodists, Assemblies of God, and Anglicans.

South Korea

Korea, historically known as the hermit kingdom, opened up in the 1880s. Japan conquered Korea in 1910 and colonized it until its defeat in 1945. During these years, the Christians took a leading role in the Korean resistance to the Japanese. Christianity was harshly suppressed during these years; however, it continued to grow and became increasingly linked to liberation movements. This led to a very favorable view towards Protestantism. Japan was forced out after their defeat in World War Two, and American troops secured Korean independence in the South. Russia took control of the North. South Korea's economy boomed after the Korean War (1950-1953); it is today one of the top economies in the world. North Korea is officially communist, but South Korean Christians have their eyes set to evangelize their northern counterparts when the timing is right.

The largest Christian congregation in the entire world is located in Seoul, South Korea. It is an Assembly of God Pentecostal Church and has become something of a tourist destination for those who go to this country. The Yoido Full Gospel Church, founded in a slum area of Seoul in 1958 by Pastor David Yonggi Cho, continues to amaze students of world Christianity—most notably with its nearly one million members! In a country of 50 million people, one out of every 50 is a member of this one church. Cho has become a celebrity of sorts in the world Christian scene. For a time he was the chairman of the World Pentecostal Assemblies of God. His younger brother, Yongmok Cho, is the pastor of the second largest congregation in Korea. Pentecostalism came to Korea in the 1930s, but Protestantism has been there since the 1880s. Today, South Korea is over 40% Christian, and the vast majority is Protestant, making Korea "... the most fruitful field in Asia for Protestant missions."[76] Presbyterianism is the preferred form of Christianity in South Korea; even the Pentecostal churches operate within a strongly Presbyterian context.

Three Questions for Analysis

1. How could someone consider Christianity to have been a "failure" in Asia?

2. What would a Christian form of communism look like?

3. As China's global influence continues to rise, how will the nation relate to Western culture, especially in terms of religion? Will Christianity make inroads into China, or will the West adopt historically Chinese attributes such as religious pluralism? Who will have the greater impact on whom?

Africa

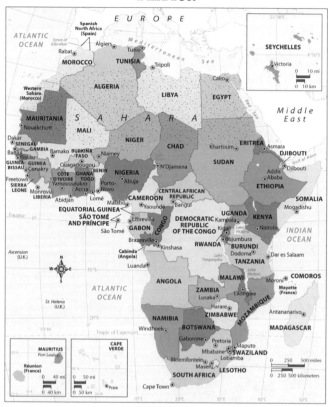

PEOPLE

Total Population:	973,699,893
Total Median Age:	19.4 years
Life Expectancy:	50.05 years
Fertility Rate:	4.72 children born/woman

RELIGION

Top Religion Percentages:	Christian (46.53%)
	Muslim (40.46%)
	Indigenous Religions (11.80%)
Number of Christians:	453,085,307
Major Christian Groupings:	Protestant/Independent (58%)
	Catholic (32%)
	Orthodox (10%)

AFRICAN CHRISTIANITY

Rarely do entire people-groups change religion. Under normal circumstances, people believe something similar to what their parents believed. If one's parents were Hindu, then there is a good chance—estimated by John Hick to be about 99 percent—that person will live life as a Hindu. In Africa, something remarkable happened in the twentieth century. It is one of those rare times in the history of humankind when entire families, tribes, and even nations began practicing a different religion. This happened in Africa in the twentieth century. It is still happening. The story of how this rapid acceptance of Christianity came about is quite complicated. The bare statistics, however, are breathtaking.

In 1900, Africa had 10 million Christians. By mid-century, the numbers of Christians were slowly rising—roughly on pace with fertility rates. In 1945, there were about 30 million Christians in Africa. In the second half of the twentieth century however, something amazing happened. Africans began to convert to Christianity en masse. Today, Africa has well over 450 million Christians, and due to fertility rates that number will pass 500 million soon.[1]

Put another way, in 1900, only 2% of the world's Christians lived in Africa. In 2005, nearly 20% of the world's Christians lived in Africa.[2]

Today, Africa ranks second to Latin America as having the most Christians for a cultural block. However, due to fertility rates—Africa's 4.72 children per woman dwarfs Latin America's 2.42 children per woman—Africa will soon become the continent with the most Christians.

What triggered this rapid conversion rate? Some experts predicted that once the European powers left Africa, Christianity would wither away. The reverse happened: "Africa's most dramatic Christian growth, in other words, occurred *after* decolonization."[3] This is especially the case with Protestant/Independent Christianity in Africa, where the growth rates have been exponential.

Christianity has very deep roots in North Africa, due to the connection between Judaism and Ethiopia. The Christian faith was embedded in the continent during apostolic times. Indeed, the Bible teaches that Christ himself was in Africa during his youth. The greatest theologians of early Christianity were Africans, and many Christian movements and ideas that Christians take for granted were in fact born first in the African church.

What Is Africa?

It is about 5,000 miles from Ras ben Sakka, Tunisia—Africa's northernmost point—to Cape Agulhas at the southern tip of this vast continent. It is a land of geographical superlatives. The largest hot desert is in Africa, the Sahara, which is roughly the size of the United States. The world's longest river is in Africa, the Nile. Africa is easier to define than most other cultural blocks due to its relatively clear geographical outline. It is often divided into two sections, North Africa and sub-Saharan Africa. North Africa tends to be Islamic and sub-Saharan Africa is dominated by Christianity, although there are many exceptions to this generalization. Historically, North African geography was divided into two: the Maghreb—the western side of North Africa which is dominated by Mauritania, Morocco, Algeria, Tunisia, and Libya; and the Nile River Valley which is on the east side of North Africa and is dominated by Egypt, Sudan, and Ethiopia. Sub-Saharan Africa simply means south of the Sahara desert. In several African countries such as Sudan, Chad, Niger, and Mali, the Sahara desert occupies the barren north while the southern part of the nation is lush. Sub-Saharan Africa is dominated by the Democratic Republic of the Congo in the center, and South Africa forms the southern base. There are many countries in this expanse including Kenya, Tanzania, Angola, Zambia, Mozambique, Namibia, Zimbabwe, and Botswana. Madagascar is a large island off the east coast directly opposite Mozambique.

Africa has been entirely surrounded by water since 1869, when the Suez Canal—connecting the Mediterranean and the Red Sea—was completed. The Mediterranean Sea separates North Africa from Europe. The Red Sea separates Africa from Saudi Arabia. To the east of Africa is the Arabian Sea as well as the Indian Ocean. To the west is the Atlantic.

If the geography is vast, the varieties of people-groups are vaster still. Africa is generally considered to be the birthplace of humans, according to recent scholarship. There are approximately one billion people in Africa today. The African continent is also a land of languages—around 2,000 of them according to UNESCO.[4]

Only one African nation today makes the top ten of the world's most populated countries—Nigeria, with nearly 150 million people. However, there are several countries in Africa with significant populations. The top ten populated countries in Africa are, in order: Nigeria, Ethiopia, Egypt, D.R. Congo, South Africa, Sudan, Tanzania, Kenya, Morocco, and Algeria. Both Ethiopia and Egypt are not far from the 100 million mark. Ethiopia, in particular, will hit the 100 million mark soon because its fertility rate is over six children born per woman. Egypt's fertility rate has slowed significantly in recent years and is today less than three children per woman. Africa's fourth most populated country, the D.R. Congo, is also growing fast due to its high fertility rate.

Fertility rates are extremely significant when it comes to projecting religious demographics, the sufficiency of natural resources for a population, and the projected growth of economies. Africa's fertility rate is much higher than anywhere else in the world. The world's average fertility rate is 2.61 children born per woman. However, in Africa, the average woman will have five children during her lifetime. Fertility rates can fall suddenly and drastically—as in the case of several Middle Eastern countries—but for now Africa's fertility is surprisingly high, stunning in some cases. The most fertile countries in the world are Mali, Niger, Somalia, and Uganda: in those countries the average woman will have seven children in her life. There are several African countries with fertility rates around six children born per woman: Angola, Benin, Burkina Faso, Burundi, D.R. Congo, Ethiopia, Liberia, Malawi, Mauritania, Republic of the Congo, and Sierra Leone. Many African countries have fertility rates in the four or five range. The continent's average is 4.72, making it easily the most fertile of the cultural blocks.

People tend to associate high fertility rates with Islam. It has become cliché to call Islam the fastest growing religion in the world. However, this assumption may not necessarily be true. The data are not extremely clear. In Africa, trends do not point to a faster-growing Islamic population. There are Islamic nations with high fertility rates in Africa and there are Christian nations with high fertility rates. Of the fifteen most fertile nations in Africa mentioned above, nine are more Christian and six are more Islamic. Of the four most populated countries in Africa—Nigeria, Ethiopia, Egypt, and D.R. Congo—Christianity has a higher constituency in three. In fact, when looking at the rapid increase of Christians in Africa in the twentieth century, there are ample reasons for predicting Christianity's market share to grow.

There are two more important conspicuous data to point out when looking at overall trends in Africa: median age and life expectancy. They are interrelated of course. Africa may have the highest fertility rate in the world, but it also has the lowest life expectancy. Africans, on average, barely reach the age of 50. This fact is glaring and unfortunate. Eastern Europe, the cultural block with the second lowest life expectancy in the world, has a life expectancy 20 years higher than in Africa. This fact alone points to the sad state of affairs in Africa. Similarly, the low life expectancy brings down the median age in Africa to less than 20 years—the lowest in the world. There are many reasons for this situation: HIV/AIDS, wars, and rampant diseases. Poor water quality, underdeveloped medical facilities, a shortage in medical and scientific personnel, malnutrition, and famine are some of the reasons Africans are, on average, the most impoverished, dangerously unhealthy cultural block in the world.

In many ways, the African continent is in disarray. Africa is marginal in global affairs, except as a land of resources to be exploited by well-off societies. Of the world's top 20 GDP countries, no African countries are represented, in spite of its being a land teeming with valuable goods and natural gifts.[5] Many African economies seem hopelessly dependent on Western aid, causing some to ask, "Is there life after debt?"[6] Ghanian theologian Mercy Oduyoye outlines a whole slew of problems, both historical and contemporary, that have contributed to the difficulties[7]:

- Low literacy rates, especially in West African nations. Africa's literacy rates are the lowest in the world.[8]
- A pervasive fear of witchcraft: "It is a sustained pressure of mental torture that reduces its victims to a state of permanent terror. And once they start on you they don't know where to stop, until you become stark, raving mad. Then they grin."[9]
- A colonial legacy that has many residual effects of dependency, corruption, and powerlessness: "We have been incorporated into a Euro-centered world culture."[10] For example, Africans must learn a European language in order to have any impact on global affairs.
- Systemic racism towards Africans has taken a dehumanizing toll on the consciousness of a continent, first by Arabs and later by Europeans. The trauma of centuries of slavery does not recover quickly.

Oduyoye cries out for justice to seemingly deaf ears, degrading an already low self-esteem:

> We are faced with how to reduce the West's stranglehold over Africa. ... At the moment we continue bound under the Western sphere of influence and seem unable to highlight our interdependence so as to build up the self-esteem of our children. ... The West continues involvement in how we run our economies and prosecute our politics because they need us for a market and for investment space. Our resources helped to develop their world so we can make them strengthen our regional structures. ... The world extracts minerals from Africa ... Should we not use this to make the transnational corporations more responsible? Could we in Africa keep our diamonds, gold and oil in the bowels of the earth, if we cannot make them speak for the good of Africa?[11]

Mercy Oduyoye represents a firm posture in Africa towards the West. However, the problems extend far beyond that. Africa's struggles are often within.

Whether the sad state of Africa's political ethos is a result of European colonialism, or whether it stems from corruption in the post-independence era, can be debated. One thing that is beyond debate however is the sad reality that year after year, nation after nation, African politics continue to disappoint the people, dashing hopes all along the way. The examples are numerous. Lamin Sanneh writes, "Corruption and despotic rule despoiled countries, divided society, and failed the national cause."[12]

The Atlantic slave trade lasted from the fifteenth to the nineteenth centuries, finally declining in the early nineteenth century due to pressure from Evangelicals and Quakers.[13] However, the idea of dominance over Africa took a new shape in the "Scramble for Africa"—a movement by imperial powers in Europe to occupy the continent and profit from its extremely fruitful land. While we may here make a brief list of areas of European influence, it is important to point out that colonial powers often fought with each other, resulting in many African regions changing hands among European governments.

- France consolidated control over much of West Africa including modern-day Morocco, Algeria, Mauritania, Senegal, Mali, Ivory Coast (Cote d'Ivoire), Burkina Faso, Benin, Niger, and others.
- British Africa was mainly in the East and South, although Nigeria and Ghana (formerly Gold Coast) are in the West. Britain exerted control over the modern-day nations of Kenya, Zimbabwe and Zambia (known in colonial times as Rhodesia), Uganda, Tanzania, South Africa, Sudan, Malawi, Lesotho, Botswana, and Swaziland.
- The Portuguese colonized modern-day Mozambique and Angola.
- The Spanish-occupied territory was limited to modern-day Western Sahara—a territory that is today in dispute.
- The Italians held Somalia, Libya, and Eritrea.
- Belgium controlled that massive swath of land in the center of Africa, the Congo.

Virtually all of Africa was colonized, with two exceptions: Ethiopia and Liberia. Ethiopia was never fully colonized, although the Italians invaded and were eventually defeated in the Battle of Adwa (1896). Ethiopia has for this reason become emblematic across Africa for independence, freedom, and resistance to European domination. Many independent churches in Africa to this day proudly include Ethiopia in their title since it represents something significant; it is a rejection of European origin. The other exception to colonial rule was Liberia, although it would be somewhat misleading to say the land was never colonized. It was in fact colonized by freed African slaves from the United States in the 1820s through the 1840s.

Why does all of this matter? The period of colonialism matters a great deal for a number of reasons. First, and perhaps most obvious, is that Africans were in fact ruled by Europeans for a very long time. Some interpreters of African history see this as the fundamental reason Africa remains in shambles. When

African independence movements began to happen in the 1950s, there was the sense that Africa's long period of subjugation would soon end. Beginning with Libya in Northern Africa, an avalanche of independence movements overwhelmed Africa in the 1950s and 1960s. Ghana took the lead in the southern half of the continent, declaring independence from Britain in 1957— the first sub-Saharan nation to throw off colonial rule. Seventeen African nations declared independence in the year 1960 alone. Postcolonial Africa was a victory for autonomous rule, but it was not necessarily a victory across the board. Some of the revolutionary leaders abused their respective countries, raping the land nearly as badly as the European powers had done. Some African leaders proved despotic and corrupt—a bane in African politics up to the present. For example, Robert Mugabe has held power in Zimbabwe since 1980, absolutely refusing to relinquish his tight hold on this collapsed country. Idi Amin famously declared himself "President for life" and became known for his excesses, although he was eventually overthrown. Omar Bongo ruled Gabon in west-central Africa for 41 years, accumulating vast riches due partially to his relationship with France. He died owning "... dozens of luxurious properties in and around Paris, a $500 million presidential palace, fancy cars," while his people remained in abject poverty.[14] In Zambia, ex-President Frederick Chiluba (in power from 1991 to 2001) became emblematic of a pan-African tendency for despotism and lavishness at the same time—his wardrobe included scores of Italian shoes made of exotic skins—while the national populations barely subsist on less than a dollar a day. Corruption continues in several African governments, and there are but few signs that relief is in sight. A *New York Times* article lamented the situation:

> The fight against corruption in Africa's most pivotal nations is faltering as public agencies investigating wrongdoing by powerful politicians have been undermined or disbanded and officials leading the charge have been dismissed, subjected to death threats and driven into exile. ... Experts, prosecutors and watchdog groups say they fear that major setbacks to anticorruption in South Africa, Nigeria and Kenya are weakening the resolve to root out graft [bribery], a stubborn scourge that saps money needed to combat poverty and disease in the world's poorest region.[15]

African poverty is a scourge on humanity and there is no end in sight. The United Nations' "List of Least Developed Countries" is always mainly comprised of African nations.[16]

Africa has also had its share of atrocities in the postcolonial era, again begging the question of whether the colonial legacy may have put in place some of the tensions that periodically become full-blown:

- Civil war in Liberia between the years of 1989 and 2003 became infamous for the use of child soldiers;

- The D.R. Congo has been crippled by wars and conflicts since the 1990s;
- Rwanda erupted into genocide in 1994, resulting in the brutal murders of perhaps a million people and the displacement of millions more;
- Civil wars in the Sudan have wracked the region virtually since independence, resulting in the deaths of perhaps two million people.[17]

Thus, the deplorable state of much of Africa today begs the question: To what extent is the Western world responsible? Scholars answer that question in different ways, ranging from the most vitriolic indictments of the West to the view that European colonialism actually may prove helpful to Africa in the long run. Generally, there is a combination of the two interpretive poles: while Africa may indeed have inherited much good from the West such as medicine, European educational institutions, European languages, and attempts at democratic government, the colonial scars are deep, complex, and painful.

Most African Christians would express gratefulness to the Western missionaries who attempted to bring good news, although even missionaries are frequently implicated in the postcolonial critique. The Mau Mau fighters of Kenyan independence in the 1950s may have been the first to utter that now-famous invective on imperial missions:

> When the white man came, he had the Bible and we had the land. He told us to close our eyes and pray, and when we opened our eyes he had the land and we had the Bible.[18]

This condemnation is not altogether justified, although it is not altogether false either. Missionaries came in all shades and sizes. Some enjoyed living the life of kings, employing scores of Africans in the name of Christianity and civilization—a phrase coined by David Livingstone during his explorations of Africa—while others lived meager existences, founding small churches and passing leadership to Africans within a short time. In a secular age, this second paradigm often goes ignored. Many Western missionaries gave their truncated lives to their adopted African homes, devoting their years to witnessing for Christ in an isolated corner of the world, and dying young usually because of malaria. Many highly trained Catholic priests devoted their energies towards establishing a safe community for freed slaves; many Protestant teams spent decades trying to provide communities with the Bible in their own language. It was an age of conviction and higher purpose. For those who believed Christ must be encountered for salvation, it made perfect sense to give one's life in that task. In a context of Western secularization, however, missionaries often become the subject of scorn—brainwashers from a bygone era.

The missionary legacy in Africa is significant. African religion today can be divided into three groups: Christians, Muslims, and those from indigenous religions. It is important to reemphasize that prior to European missions, Christianity was marginal, relegated to Ethiopia—which was largely Christian, and the Copts of Egypt, who were a significant minority. For better or for worse, Africa would not be half Christian today without that massive period of European missions. It would have been inconceivable in 1900 to predict that Africa would be the heartland of Christianity in a century or so. It would have sounded nonsensical to tell an African in 1900 that in a century Islam would actually be ranked second to Christianity in terms of followers on the African continent. The modern Christianization of Africa can be rather accurately dated: in 1491 the king of Kongo, Mbanza, was baptized a Christian.[19] That touched off a flurry of missionary efforts lasting nearly 500 years. While missionaries may have brought the faith to sub-Saharan Africa, the spreading of the faith was done by Africans. Missionaries relied on strategic converts— usually Africans who had influence in their communities—in order to Christianize people-groups.

Let us now take a step back in time and look at the origins of Christianity in Africa. We must go way back, as African Christians have existed since shortly after the death and resurrection of Christ.

Background: Christianity in Africa

Africa's Nile Valley has many connections to Jewish culture, historically. First of all, the Nile Valley and the Middle East were not two distinct regions in ancient times. Even today, the languages of Ethiopia—such as Ge'ez and Amharic—have Semitic roots. The Bible (1 Kings 10 and 2 Chronicles 9) tells a fascinating story about the Queen of Sheba visiting Solomon in the 900s BC. Apparently, the Queen—known to Ethiopians as Queen Makeda—noticed all of Solomon's riches and was overwhelmed. She was impressed by his wisdom and presented him with gold, spice, high-quality wood, and precious stones. Solomon returned the favor and gave to her "all she desired." In the Ethiopian tradition, Solomon and Makeda actually had an affair and Makeda returned to Ethiopia pregnant with Solomon's child. This boy, named Menelik I, became the first Jewish Emperor of Ethiopia. Ethiopian Christians believe Menelik eventually returned to Jerusalem to meet his father, who received him warmly and sent him back with the Ark of the Covenant—a very sacred symbol in Ethiopia today. The dynasty created by the Solomon-Makeda union lasted all the way until Emperor Haile Selassie's death in 1974.

Evidently, African Christianity has its roots in Ethiopian Judaism, or at least in significant Ethiopian-Jewish contacts before Jesus. Africa plays a role in several New Testament documents as well. Jesus went to Africa when he was a baby. Matthew 2:14 records that Joseph took Mary and Jesus to Egypt in order to escape Herod, who was going to try to have Jesus killed. Matthew is keen to point out that this was to fulfill the prophet Hosea. Herod required that all baby boys two years old and under in the small village of Bethlehem should be killed. Joseph realized the danger and did not return with his family until after Herod died. In other words, according to Christian scriptures, Jesus may have spent his first few years of life living as a refugee in Egypt.

Africa appears in Jesus' earliest days, and it also appears in the last days of Jesus on earth. In the synoptic gospels, Simon of Cyrene—modern-day Libya—was forced to carry Jesus' cross for him when he became too weak to do it himself. Thus, it was an African who first took up a cross and followed Jesus, up the hill to Golgotha. In Acts chapter two, on Pentecost Sunday, we read of Libyans and Egyptians at the birth of Christianity. Christianity has thus from day one been partly African. One of the earliest individual conversion stories in the New Testament involves an African. In Acts 8, an Ethiopian eunuch, "... an important official in charge of all the treasury of Candace, queen of the Ethiopians" had gone to Jerusalem to worship. This story is significant on a number of levels. It reveals the ancient Ethiopian-Jewish connection, it reveals a pilgrimage culture on behalf of Ethiopians, and it states that the Ethiopian man was acquainted with the Hebrew Bible—as he was reading the book of Isaiah. This text has become famous because it is one of the very first biblical accounts of a foreigner converting to Christianity. Philip the apostle explained to the Ethiopian that the Messiah had come, and after a discussion the eunuch requested baptism.

There are several other African highlights in the New Testament:

- Africans were among the first to preach the gospel to non-Jews. Acts 11:19 discusses evangelists from Cyrene preaching to Greeks in Antioch, and "the Lord's hand was with them."
- Paul was probably ordained for ministry by a group that included Africans (Acts 13:1–4).
- One of the great evangelists of the New Testament was Apollos, a native of Alexandria, Egypt (Acts 18:24).

Church tradition states that Mark—the New Testament writer—evangelized Egypt in the AD 40s and became the first Pope of the Coptic Orthodox Church. Whether that story is true or not, it is an established fact that Christianity entered Africa very early on in history.

Africa's pedigree is revered in early Christianity. One of the most important Christian movements took root in Egypt before the year AD 300. Saint Anthony the Great, revered today as the father of Christian monasticism, was an Egyptian who retreated to the desert for prayer, meditation, and spiritual warfare. While he was not the first monastic ever—Christian monasticism probably began before the year AD 100—he became the archetype. His fame was in large measure due to a biography of him written by the famous Egyptian theologian Athanasius. Athanasius' *Life of St. Anthony* was one of the most widely read Christian texts in the 300s; it spawned the monastic movement that has been so prominent throughout Christian history. Athanasius (lived 293–373), one of the most influential Christians in history, was largely responsible for fleshing out Christian belief prior to the Council of Nicea in 325. Athanasius's work proved critical in defining the Christian faith: doctrine, church polity, organization, and the Christian canon of texts. Several important early church fathers were African: Clement of Alexandria, Origen, Arius, Cyprian, and Tertullian. The city of Alexandria was well known as "the leading academic center of the ancient world." Indeed the early African universities of Alexandria and Carthage were pivotal in shaping the earliest medieval Western Universities at Padua, Paris, Salamanca, and Oxford. [20] Perhaps the most important theologian in Christian history, Saint Augustine (lived 354–430), was an African Berber from modern day Algeria.

One of the very first Christian states was a kingdom called Axum, in modern-day Ethiopia. Historically this region was known as Abyssina. It all began when a young Syrian Christian from Lebanon by the name of Frumentius was captured while sailing home from India. He was sold to the kingdom of Axum and ended up working closely to the king. Eventually Frumentius had a tremendous influence in the king's household, particularly in his assistance to the king's son, named Ezana. Frumentius was eventually released by the monarch and went immediately to bishop Athanasius of Alexandria. Athanasius consecrated Frumentius bishop. Bishop Frumentius—known to Ethiopians as Bishop Salama—returned to Axum and started a thriving mission work under the new king, his childhood friend Ezana. Within a short time the entire kingdom was hearing the gospel without impediment. The Bible was translated into Ge'ez and Christianity began to indigenize in Ethiopia. Ethiopian Christianity is ancient and well-documented due to royal inscriptions and coins minted during Ezana's reign.[21] Many of the traditions from the earliest days of the faith are still honored, giving Ethiopian Christianity a much more Jewish ethos than in Catholic and Eastern Orthodox Christianity. For example their church architecture and arrangements of the sanctuary are heavily dependent upon the Jewish synagogue. The amazing city of Lalibela, Ethiopia's New Jerusalem, was structured on the layout of Jerusalem, and meant to replace the old Jerusalem when it fell to Muslims in the 600s. Ethiopians also have strong dietary restrictions such as refusing pork or the mixing of meat and dairy, they mandate circumcision for boys, emphasize Old Testament laws, keep both the Jewish Sabbath and Christian Sunday, and allow polygamy.[22]

While North Africa was one of the epicenters of Christianity for several centuries, matters changed when the Islamic Arabs swept across the region in the 600s. When the dust settled, the region was firmly under the control of Islamic leaders and the process of Islamization began. In the centuries since, Christianity has receded in North Africa to the point it is nearly gone in most of the Arab-influenced countries. It lingered on yet declined for hundreds of years in various places in North Africa, particularly in the Nile Valley: Sudan, Egypt, Eritrea, and Ethiopia. As in the case of the Middle East, it was as if lamps were being put out all across the northern part of the continent. As Islam strengthened, Christian churches shut the doors, one by one. As far as North Africa goes, only in Ethiopia is Christianity still the leading religion of the nation—and Ethiopia is not really considered Northern Africa since it is just outside the Sahara desert. Somalia, which borders a huge portion of the Eastern Ethiopian border, is almost 100% Islamic. Ethiopia is almost completed surrounded by Islam, restricting its missionary capabilities over the centuries. This leads to a puzzling reality: how has this nation remained Christian in spite of being surrounded by Islam? How did this little country stand up not only to Islamization through the years, but also to European colonialism? Ethiopia is a proudly Christian country that remained almost completely isolated from Christendom for centuries. This had the effect of its being disconnected from many of the developments that took place in larger Christian areas, leading to some of the idiosyncrasies foreigners notice today. When contact with Ethiopia was restored in the 1400s, Portuguese Jesuit missionaries were appalled at their arrogance, "They are possessed with a strange notion that they are the only true Christians in the world; as for us, they shunned us as heretics."[23]

The Islamization of North Africa presents many difficult questions. How could this Christian heartland have converted to Islam, apparently without too much difficulty? The greatest theologians of Christianity were African. The great Christian schools of learning and libraries were in Africa. The battles for Orthodoxy were there. Christian monasticism—which came to dominate medieval Christianity—has African roots. There are several theories, all of which fall short of being fully convincing. First of all, it is possible that the doctrinal controversies between Athanasius' school of thought and the Arian school caused a deep fracture in Christianity that never really recovered. Arius had argued that there was once a time that Jesus was not begotten. In other words, Jesus was not eternally present with God the father in the past. Athanasius rebuffed this vehemently, and many Christians were caught in the middle. What may seem like impractical semantics became crucial. Some have argued that the confusion arising from these debates might have opened the door for the ardent "No" to Trinitarian thought by Muhammad's followers. Perhaps the Christological controversies in the 300s backfired when Islam came along offering a monotheism that was much clearer: "There is no God but God, and Muhammad is God's prophet."

It is also important to point out that in the year 451 a deep fracture occurred in Christendom: the Council of Chalcedon. This council essentially declared the Egyptian (Coptic) and Ethiopian Christians to be heretics—along with the Armenians, Indians, and some Syrians. These groups were anathematized at that council and have since been known as the "Oriental Orthodox" Christians. The Eastern Orthodox and Roman Catholic churches consider them to be fundamentally misguided in their understanding of the nature of Christ. This fissure remains to the present day, although there are many attempts to reunite the Oriental Orthodox with both Catholics as well as Eastern Orthodox Christians. Nevertheless, the point is that when African Christians received this chastisement from the larger church in 451, it may indeed have marginalized them to the point that Muhammad's fierce monotheism cut to the chase and resonated with the laity in the region—Christians who would have been confused by theological semantics. Islam rejected all of this by claiming God did not have a son; Jesus was only a prophet and God never sired any children.

The arrival of European powers in Africa was pivotal. It touched off a mad scramble for resources—including humans—that deeply impacted the African consciousness. The humiliating and violent business of slavery impacted Africa in profound ways. African-based slavery was lucrative for many, but came at an immeasurable cost to others. One of the many points of conflict during European contact with Africa was this: while many Europeans needed slave labor, many other Europeans tried to save African souls. Deep philosophical differences between missionaries, businessmen, and colonial administrators were common.

Roman Catholic missionaries did have some success in converting Africans, most notably in the Congo area, where Mbanza, an indigenous king, became Catholic in the year 1491. The Christianization of the Kingdom of Kongo, however, occurred during the reign of King Afonso (ruled 1509 to 1543). Afonso was probably under political pressure from the Portuguese in many ways, although it does indeed seem to be the case that he was devoutly Catholic. He began Christian schools, attempted to create a Catholic state-church, and proved effective at merging Christianity into the culture of his kingdom. The capital city of the kingdom was even christened Sao Salvador (known today as M'banza-Congo, in modern-day Angola). A cathedral was erected in 1549, one of the oldest in sub-Saharan Africa. What promised to be a central hub for Catholic Christianity all over the African continent proved to be a story of "missed opportunities." The Dutch defeated the Portuguese in the early 1600s, and the Dutch Protestants did not share the missionary zeal of the Jesuits. "By 1700 the Christian presence in Kongo ... was fading." [24] It did not completely die out, however. There were various indigenous movements that occurred until Baptist missionaries arrived in force in the 1870s.

One of the indigenous movements of the Kongo was led by a woman named Kimpa Vita, also known as Dona Beatriz.[25] She lived from 1684–1706 and became an important precedent for African Christianity. Baptized by Italian Capuchin missionaries, she forged an indigenous Christianity that became a fountainhead for the AICs: the African Independent Churches. Vita believed the European missionaries were not upholding African ways sufficiently, and she wanted to Africanize the faith. She believed herself to be a prophetess, receiving a vision from St. Anthony that urged her to strip the European colonial baggage away from Christianity. The Europeans dismissed her as a witch. She made startling claims such as her belief that Jesus was a black African from the Kongo. Her followers became known as Antonians. She became politically influential but eventually was arrested and condemned a heretic. She was burned at the stake and her movement suppressed. Many of the slaves who were sent to the New World, chiefly Brazil and South Carolina, were Antonian Christians. Her legacy lived on and her rejection of colonial Christianity was ahead of its time. Kimpa Vita can rightly be called one of the very first pioneers of that massively successful phenomenon in African Christianity known by its acronym: the AICs.[26] Philip Jenkins writes, "If the rising independent churches ever decide to identify a patron saint, they could do no better than to choose ... Kimpa Vita."[27]

In the 1700s, Africa was seen by Europeans as mainly a land that provided an abundance of slaves. When the British abolished the slave trade in 1807, they began intercepting the slave ships of other colonial powers. However, there was the problem of what to do with the intercepted slaves? The British had already in the 1780s begun a program in West Africa that was aimed at removing poor Africans from Britain and granting them freedom in modern-day Sierra Leone. Thus, when slave ships were intercepted by the British, they were taken to Freetown, the capital of Sierra Leone. Tens of thousands of slaves were settled there. Many African-Americans, some who had fought for the British during the American Revolution, were rewarded by getting their taste of Freetown. In 1792, a large group of 1200 freed American slaves on 15 ships sailed from Nova Scotia to Freetown. These were Christian people, usually from evangelical backgrounds. Some of them dreamed of preaching Christ to the tribes from which they originally came. This was the ambition of one of the most remarkable African Christians in history: Samuel Crowther (lived 1806 to 1891).

Samuel Ajayi Crowther was born in modern-day Nigeria around 1806.[28] As a teenager he was captured for the slave business by Muslim invaders in 1821. The Muslim slave traders sold him to the Portuguese who intended to ship him across the Atlantic. The ship was intercepted by the British navy, however, and Crowther was resettled at Sierra Leone, where he became a Christian. He was a brilliant young man and gained quite a reputation for it. He attended the newly established Fourah Bay College in Freetown and was also sent to England on two occasions for more education, including ordination into the Anglican priesthood. In 1843 he went out as a missionary to his own people, the Yoruba of Nigeria. He did tremendous work in translation of the Bible and the *Book of Common Prayer* throughout his career. In 1862 Crowther was about to retire when he was called to become bishop in the backlands of Nigeria. His elevation in 1864 was a watershed moment: Crowther became the first African bishop in the Anglican Church. For twenty years he worked among the people of Nigeria, only to be disgraced in the twilight of his ministry. In 1889 a group of European missionaries went out to Crowther's mission station and outright condemned him and his ministry. They believed the experiment in African clergy was a failure. Crowther's replacement was a European. Ward writes,

> The furor which these events created gave new impetus to the growth of "Ethiopian" Churches—that is, Churches led by Africans independent of missionary control ... determined to fulfill in authentically African terms the biblical prophecy that "Ethiopia [i.e. black Africa] shall stretch forth his hand to God." (Psalm 68:31)[29]

Crowther represents many significant events in African church history. Here was a bishop who rose from a slave ship to the Episcopal throne, only to be disgraced after a life of committed service to the church. Here was a man who "... had audience with Queen Victoria, and answered all Prince Albert's intelligent questions about commerce in Africa," only to become humbled and his efforts curtailed.[30] It was as if an African had become the perfect British clergyman, and it was still not enough. After Crowther, it became clear that what was needed in Africa was a clean break from European forms of faith. However, this was not to be for several decades, as this was the era that Europe began scrambling to put the colonial albatross around the neck of nearly the entire African continent.

Probably the best known European missionary to Africa was David Livingstone (lived 1813-1873). Livingstone was a Scotsman from a poor family and he spent his youth working in a cotton mill. As a young man he felt called to ministry, so he trained for ministry as well as medicine. In 1841 he arrived to Cape Town, South Africa and began a career traveling, exploring, creating maps, publishing books, and stirring an overall excitement for African missions. Livingstone was not a great evangelist on the ground, despite spending three decades in Africa as a missionary. While his books inspired millions in the West, he only managed to convert one person, and that person relapsed later. Livingstone knew his role was less about personal evangelism and more about opening up Africa for Christianity and commerce. Perhaps most of all,

Livingstone was appalled by the slave trade, which was still going on surreptitiously during his life. In fact, one of Livingstone's sons died fighting against slavery on the side of the Union in America's Civil War, largely because of his father's abolitionist views. David Livingstone believed that by helping Westerners understand this vast, difficult continent of Africa, more people would come and invest in it, helping to pull it out of its darkness, heathenism, and poverty. When Livingstone died in Zambia in 1873, his heart was buried by his two African companions, Susi and Chuma, in Zambia. These two faithful friends—former slaves that had been freed by Livingstone—over the course of a year carried his body to the coast of Africa so it could be shipped back to England where it is buried at Westminster Abbey today. His funeral was a huge, state affair. Livingstone is far more famous in southern Africa than in England today. Cities are named after him; even the capital of Malawi—Blantyre—is named after Livingstone's birthplace in Scotland. However, in his day, he was a superhero in the U.K., greatly admired for his manly treks across interior Africa—where no European had dared to venture before him. Livingstone's family paid a dear price for his devotion to exploration. His dogged commitment to Africa cost him a great deal. Two of his children and his wife died in Africa. It was uncommon for Westerners to travel into interior Africa in those days; the risks were too many. Livingstone was a survivor and was even criticized by his African helpers for wanting to travel at too fast a pace. His curiosity was well-known; more than anything he wanted to find the source of the great river Nile. Alas, he never fully understood the various sources of it.

Livingstone's missionary successes were few, but it depends upon how one looks at it. Zambia is today a Christian nation, and has been called "David Livingstone's greatest legacy."[31] Livingstone probably realized he would never live to see the fruits of his missionary labors. He said as much: "The end of the geographical feat is the beginning of the missionary enterprise."[32] He is probably best known in the West by the words of explorer Henry Morton Stanley, who found Livingstone in Tanzania after Livingstone had gone missing for two years and was presumed dead. When Stanley found Livingstone, he uttered four words that have become a catch phrase in the English language: "Dr. Livingstone, I presume?" Successes and failures aside,

> He was such an important figure that the history of southern Africa can be divided into B.L. (Before Livingstone) and A.L. (After Livingstone). When he arrived in 1841, Africa was as exotic as outer space, called the "Dark Continent" and the "White Man's Graveyard." ... African maps had bland unexplored areas—no roads, no countries, no landmarks. Livingstone helped redraw the maps, exploring what are now a dozen countries. He is the stuff of legend, indeed.[33]

Livingstone died in a mud hut in 1873, kneeling in prayer beside his cot. By the time of his death, Christianity was making major inroads into Africa. This

had a lot to do with the enthusiasm—as well as the maps—created by Livingstone. The Protestant missionary enterprise in Africa was enormous. Livingstone's dreams were in many ways being fulfilled: "One month after his death,
the British forced the Sultan of Zanzibar to close the largest slave market on
the east coast of Africa."[34]

Catholic missionaries were active in Africa as well, although their heyday
was in the sixteenth to eighteenth centuries. In the nineteenth century, one of
the great Roman Catholic missionary endeavors was spearheaded by a famous
missionary named Cardinal Charles Lavigerie (lived 1825-1892). Lavigerie
founded the Missionaries of Our Lady of Africa, known as the White Fathers
because of the white robes they wore. He was an outspoken abolitionist and
traveled extensively across Africa as well as all over Europe. He rose to the rank
of Archbishop when he accepted the bishopric of Algiers, North Africa. Pope
Pius IX—the Pope who codified papal infallibility in 1870—elevated Lavigerie
yet again by making him the primate of all Africa. Lavigerie's White Fathers
carried out their work mainly in Islamic North Africa, but they also established
a hub for their missions in Uganda—which is nearly half Catholic today. The
White Fathers had great success in the Congo region, testified today by strongly Catholic populations. The D.R. Congo is half Catholic and Republic of the
Congo is majority Catholic—one of the more Catholic regions in Africa. The
North African missions were not nearly as successful as the ones further south
due to strongly Islamic, fiercely traditional peoples in the Sahara. The Roman
Catholic Church is today the faith of about one-third of all African Christians,
a testament to the White Fathers, the earlier Portuguese colonies, and various
orders such as the Jesuits and Capuchins. Of the 29 Christian majority nations
and territories in Africa today, 13 of them have more Catholics than Protes-
tant/Independent Christians. Several countries in Africa are strongly Roman
Catholic: Angola, Burundi, Cape Verde, Equatorial Guinea, Gabon, Republic
of the Congo, Reunion, Sao Tome & Principe, Seychelles, and Spanish North
Africa.

It is an easy mistake to get the impression that European missionaries converted the Africans. By and large, this is untrue. Typically, European missionaries converted strategic individuals who would then do the ground work,
making connections, reaching the hearts of the people through their own dialects, and translating the Bible into indigenous languages. European missionaries often get credit for the conversions, translations, and great institutions
in Africa; however, it was indigenous agency that provided the lion's share of
the work. How could a European figure out an African language without an
African translator? How could a university or hospital be built without local
labor? Today, Africa's European denominations such as the Roman Catholic
Church, the Anglican Communion, the Lutheran and Baptist Churches are
thoroughly led by Africans. Colonial leadership is a part of history. The Afri-

can church—even in the guise of European-originated denominations—was only inspired by Europeans. It is today an African affair.

However, we would be remiss to downplay the great contributions the European Christians made to African society: technological advancements, improved farming techniques, methods and capabilities for introducing literacy, medical treatments, and sophisticated weaponry. One striking example of European contribution was quinine, known as Jesuit's Bark because of their work with Peruvians who used "quina" in the treatment of malaria. Jesuits introduced the medicinal bark to Europe where it proved effective in the treatment of the disease. African missions often spelt disaster for Europeans because of malaria; however, the introduction of quinine radically affected Christian missions in Africa. No longer was Africa destined to be the White Man's Graveyard. Quinine was introduced to Africans as well and proved to be one of the powerful attractions to Christianity. Why wouldn't Africans give Christianity a hearing? The tangential benefits could be huge: literacy, education, improved health care, and better crop production.

There is an important phenomenon that we must here reemphasize. The AICs—African Initiated Churches—are strong today, and have little connection to Europe. While a British citizen will be comfortable in an Anglican church in Africa, the AICs are thoroughly African to the core. Their leaders do not look back to Europe or America for their history. They were begun by Africans, for Africans, and often have a worldview dissimilar to Westerners. Many of these independent Christians include the name "Ethiopian" in their title to emphasize their disconnectedness from the West.

The concept of the AIC has fascinated scholars of Christianity, both for its rapid growth as well as its unique practices that are sometimes way outside the norm for Christians in the West. Philip Jenkins provides one of the best, most succinct introductions to the AIC:

> Across Africa, a common prophetic pattern has recurred frequently since the late nineteenth century. An individual is enthusiastically converted through one of the mission churches, from which he or, commonly, she, is gradually estranged. The division might arise over issues of church practice, usually the integration of native practices. The individual receives what is taken as a special revelation from God, commonly in a trance or vision. This event is a close imitation of one of the well-known New Testament scenes in which God speaks directly to his people, as at Pentecost or on the road to Damascus. The prophet then begins to preach independently, and the result might well be a new independent church. Particularly where the movement originates from a founder's revelation, such churches place a heavy premium on visions and charismatic gifts.[35]

These churches do not receive financial support from Americans or Britons, they do not attend European conferences, and they do not feel compelled to follow the Christianity that was imported from the West. They emphasize healing, the power of the Holy Spirit to defeat demons, and God's direct intervention in the lives of people today. The names of these churches are unrecognized in the West and little is known about them outside of academics whose researches take them to Africa.

In colonial times, these people aroused suspicion, as witnessed earlier in the condemnation and murder of Kimpa Vita, perhaps the archetypal AIC Christian leader. However, there were, and are, many others. The most famous, and arguably most successful, AIC leader was William Wade Harris (lived c. 1865 to 1929).[36] Harris was from Liberia and converted to Methodism as a student. He taught for ten years in an American Protestant School and became married. In 1910 he received a call from God while in prison for demonstrating against the colonial, Afro-American government. He wanted the British to be in charge. While in prison, he had a vision of the Archangel Gabriel urging him to become like an Old Testament prophet and abandon European ways. After release from prison he set out with a Bible, a cross, a gourd rattle, and a baptismal bowl, preaching first in Liberia and then in the Ivory Coast and Gold Coast (Ghana) regions. He established many churches as thousands of people came to repentance through his miracles and preaching. He baptized tens of thousands of people. He ventured into places where Europeans had never gone before him. His sermons were laden with condemnations of fetishism and the overpowering of evil spirits. He called for an immediate repentance, focusing on the Ten Commandments and the authority of the Bible. He wrote many songs. He offended the European missionaries because they thought he was undermining their authority. Additionally, he had no problem with polygamy—he had several wives. Colonial authorities had him arrested in 1915 and he was put under house arrest until his death in 1929. By that time, however, he had amassed a large following and he had appointed twelve apostles to carry on his work. His ministry paid handsome dividends for the European missionaries who came in his wake. Harris's significance is only now coming into full view. Philip Jenkins remarks, "He might in fact be one of the most glaring omissions from the various lists of the world's great Christian leaders."[37] Others have called him "... the most successful missionary in West Africa," claiming his ministry "... represents a movement from traditional religion to a form of New Testament Christianity."[38] Harris was a powerful witness for Christ in Sierra Leone, Ivory Coast, Ghana, and Liberia; his ministry led to an unprecedented openness to Christianity. Both Catholic and Protestants are deeply indebted to his seed-sowing work in the region, while they reaped most of the harvest.

Harris is only the most conspicuous of a whole host of African AIC leaders in the early twentieth century who form an African tradition that is strong and vibrant today:

- Garrick Braide became well-known as a healer in West Africa—people flocked to him as the second Elijah.
- John Chilembwe preached armed resistance to the British in Malawi (Nyasaland)—in the name of Christ!
- Simon Kimbangu often invoked the ancestors in his preaching, claiming that "God was changing the baton from whites to blacks."[39] His "Church of the Lord Jesus Christ on Earth of the Prophet Simon Kimbangu" numbers in the millions.
- Zulu prophet Isaiah Shembe's Nazarite movement hailed him as a messianic figure, capable of all manner of miracles, especially healing. He purportedly resurrected from the dead and appeared to his followers after death.[40]
- Engenas Barnabas Lekganyane established the Zion Christian Church in 1910—today it boasts the largest annual gathering of Christians on earth. Taking place at Moria in South Africa, the ZCC's Easter gathering is attended by over a million people and has featured Nelson Mandela as a speaker.[41]

Today the African Independent Church tradition continues. The list of prophets, healers, and larger than life preachers is lengthy. The important Kenyan theologian John Mbiti once described the AIC movements as being,

> ... [A]n African opportunity to mess up Christianity in our own way. For the past two thousand years, other continents, countries, nations and generations have had their chances to do with Christianity as they wished. And we know that they have not been idle! Now Africa has got its chance at last.[42]

Mbiti has argued that Christianity in its African guise is thoroughly Christian. He is part of a growing body of African scholars who claim Christianity as their own and resent colonial charges which imply African Christianity may be less authentic.

So convinced of this message, many Africans now missionize the West, former Christendom. In 2009 an intriguing, lengthy article in the *New York Times* proclaimed:

> Pastor Daniel Ajayi-Adeniran is coming for your soul. ... He is on a mission to save you from eternal damnation. He realizes you may be skeptical, put off by his exotic name—he's from Nigeria ... but he's not deterred. He believes the Holy Spirit is working through him.[43]

The article goes on to discuss how the Redeemed Christian Church of God, based in Lagos, already has millions of members and is growing exponentially. It is a far cry from the declining memberships in mainline Protestant denominations in North America or stale, empty churches in Europe. Africa is in the process of becoming Christian, and the revitalization of Christianity that occurred during the period of colonial missions has come back around. The empire has struck back, and it has brought Christianity back with it.

African Christianity Today

Today, Africa has 58 countries and territories. In 31 of those countries/territories, Christianity is the largest religion. In 21 of them, Islam ranks first. In five of them, indigenous religions form the largest group. Mauritius is unique in that Hinduism ranks first there.

In the countries where Christianity or Islam ranks first, this is often by an outright majority. For example, in 29 countries/territories, Christianity claims the allegiance of over half of the population. In some cases, a country is almost entirely Islamic or Christian. Algeria is 98% Muslim and Angola is 94% Christian. Overwhelmingly (over 90%) Muslim countries tend to be in the north: Algeria, Libya, Mauritania, Morocco, Niger, Somalia, Tunisia, and Western Sahara. The overwhelmingly (over 90%) Christian nations are in the south: Angola, Burundi, D.R. Congo, Gabon, Lesotho, Namibia, and the Republic of Congo.

Year after year, Christianity and Islam continue to gain converts from the practitioners of indigenous religions. The five countries that have indigenous religions as ranking first are: Benin, Guinea-Bissau, Ivory Coast, Liberia, and Mozambique. Christianity ranks second in all of these except Guinea-Bissau. According to the statistics, there are about 15 or 16 countries/territories that could go either way in the future—assuming conversion to Christianity or Islam is inevitable. These countries will doubtlessly receive intense focus by missionary strategists in both Christianity and Islam: Benin, Burkina Faso, Cameroon, Chad, Eritrea, Ethiopia, Ghana, Guinea-Bissau, Ivory Coast, Liberia, Mauritius, Mozambique, Nigeria, Sierra Leone, Tanzania, and Togo. Looking at a map, one will quickly realize most of these nations are on the belt of Africa, separating the primarily Islamic north from the mainly Christian south. West Africa, the region emanating around Nigeria, will be a particularly active hot spot for missionaries from both Islam and Christianity in the future. In many of these nations, it is difficult to predict which way the nation will tilt. For example, Benin is half indigenous, around 30% Christian, and around 20% Islamic. Ivory Coast is 35% Christian, 30% Islamic, and 35% indigenous. Surprisingly, in Liberia—a land colonized by African-American Christians—the leading category is indigenous religions. Nigeria is already a hot spot for religious activity; it is split almost evenly between Christians and Muslims. Each claims a 45% market share. Approximately 10% of Nigerians are members of indigenous religions; no doubt that small 10% will receive maximum attention by both Christian and Islamic missionaries in the future.

The majority of Africa's Christians are Protestant/Independent. The Catholic Church, however, is significant, claiming almost exactly a third of the continent's Christian population. The ancient Orthodox Christians of Africa—based mainly in the Nile Valley—account for one-tenth of the Christian population on the continent.

Africa is today a major player in world Christianity:

- Two of the six General Secretaries of the World Council of Churches (established in 1948) were African. Samuel Kobia, from Kenya, served from 2004 to 2009. Philip Potter, of African descent but from the West Indies, served from 1972 to 1984. Two of the nine General Assemblies of the World Council of Churches were held in Africa: in Kenya (1975) and Zimbabwe (1998).

- Africa has half a billion Christians and, within a generation or two, it will have more Christians than any other cultural block, surpassing Latin America and the Caribbean.

- The African diaspora is huge, and is changing world Christian demographics. African immigrants to secularizing nations are making impacts. For example, the second highest ranking cleric in the Church of England—the Archbishop of York—is John Sentamu, from Uganda. Sunday Adelaja, the pastor of Kiev's megachurch Embassy of God, is a Nigerian. The church holds 40 services weekly and claims to have planted congregations in 45 countries.[44]

- International denominations are being significantly impacted by the leverage of the African churches. A widely publicized debacle in the Anglican Communion highlighted this. Peter Akinola, the conservative, former primate of the Anglican Church in Nigeria, has led a charge to divide the global Anglican Communion along lines of liberal and conservative. He is staunchly opposed to homosexuality and has repeatedly condemned the Anglican churches in the West for liberalism and flagrant disregard of scriptural authority. His voice is highly influential in that denomination—the world's third largest after Catholicism and Eastern Orthodoxy. Some North American churches, the Convocation of Anglicans in North America (CANA), have actually joined themselves to Akinola's Nigerian diocese.

Probably the most important aspect of African Christianity is that it represents the turning over of a new leaf in world Christianity. While Christianity in the West declines, Christianity in Africa grows at a staggering speed. While Christianity in the West liberalizes, African Christianity tends to be conservative. While Western societies deepen the divide between Christianity and culture,

Africa seems to represent what may emerge as a new Christendom. While Western youth continue to become disillusioned with Christianity, breaking faith with their grandparents' form of worship, African youths seem to be highly religious (although it should be kept in mind that Africa is much younger: the median age in Western Europe is 41, Africa's median age is 19). The center of gravity for Christianity is moving south. This cliché is no more true anywhere else than in Africa.

The character of Christianity in Africa is also quite different than in the Western world. Africans are more charismatic in their worship than Western-ers, and they meet far more often than do their Western counterparts. Their instruments are different: drums are preferred to electric guitars. As an under-developed continent, they relate far more to the worldview of the Bible—where poverty, disease, and corrupt governments are ubiquitous. Christian theology and practice is very different in Africa than in the West. For example, Africa's historic deference for ancestors is upheld in the context of African Christiani-ty. Ancestors are called upon in prayer, they help us, they communion with us in the Eucharist, they interceded to God on behalf of humans, they should be placated for future blessings. This all sounds very medieval to a Westerner—when the veneration of saints was so common and everyone kept track of my-riad saint days.

Westerners who travel for any significant time in rural Africa often come back mesmerized by just how religious African people are. Church attendance can be a daily event! Rural life tends to revolve around the function of the church. Religious leaders are highly influential. Prayers are constant, whether for rain, fertility, safe travels, thanksgiving, or blessings upon guests. There is a belief in the spiritual realm that is far less common in Western consciousness. Houses are regularly blessed to send away bad spirits; angels and demons are assumed; exorcism is not at all uncommon; Satan is considered real. Simply put, secularization has not found a foothold in Africa. Africa is religious.

Algeria

One can scarcely read a history of Christianity without encountering the to-wering theologian Saint Augustine—perhaps the most influential theologian in the history of Christianity. Today, Christianity has virtually vanished from Au-gustine's homeland. Algeria is almost entirely Sunni Muslim. North Africa's Christian community was hit hard in the first several centuries by three differ-ent hammers. First was the Donatist schism. Named after the Berber Christian Donatus Magnus who died around 355, the controversy was essentially an ar-gument over the nature of the church: Is it a group of sinners saved by grace, or is it a group of saints who might only occasionally sin? Donatus preferred the later. He argued that clergy who had apostatized during the days of rampant persecution (before Constantine) were unfit for performing the Christian sacraments. Others disagreed, arguing that lapsed Christians did not affect the efficacy or worthiness of the rituals. In other words, the rituals were validated not by human purity but by God's ordinance. When the powerful theologian Augustine (lived 354–430) came along, the Roman Catholic Church gained the upper hand and condemned Donatus' view. The second hammer to hit was the decline of the Roman Empire. Algeria was an important part of the Roman Empire's grip on the Mediterranean Sea trade business. Vandals invaded in the 400s and 500s while the Byzantine Empire tried to come to the rescue and keep Roman North Africa within the fold. Byzantium never was able to secure firm control so when the Arabs came blazing across North Africa in the late 600s there was only meager resistance. The blow delivered by this third hammer reverberated through the centuries and Christianity in Algeria today is reduced to only a tiny fraction, in spite of its illustrious history in the region. What is ironic is that among the Christians that do exist in Algeria, the vast majority (over 90%) are Protestants. There is little hope for the growth of Christianity in Algeria due to severe Shari'a laws as well as outright persecution, most famously in the 1990s when many Christians, especially monks and nuns, were martyred. Many fled the violence and moved abroad. Famously, one Catholic bishop, Pierre Claverie, "... was assassinated by Islamic militants in a booby trap explosion at the entrance to his house" in 1996.[45]

Cameroon

Cameroon is a Christian-majority nation with significant Indigenous Religion and Muslim populations. The Christian population is well over 10 million and is nearly split between Catholic and Protestant/Independent. Cameroon honors several Christian holidays including Good Friday, Ascension Day, Assumption Day, and Christmas. There are two national holidays commemorating Islam: the Feast of the Lamb and Eid al-Fitr, the end of the Ramadan fast.[46] Cameroon has a history of tolerance between Christians and Muslims. Witchcraft—the attempt to harm someone through spiritual means—is illegal in Cameroon, punishable by two- to ten-year prison terms.

Chad

Chad has a Muslim majority but strong Indigenous religions and Christian minorities. It sits at the very center of the northern half of Africa. It is one of those countries on the belt of Africa that is strongly Muslim in the north with a significant Christian presence in the south. Like Cameroon, Chad has a fairly ecumenical history; religiously motivated tension is relatively rare considering the country's constituency and geographical location. However, political tensions are rife. Upon independence in 1960, Chad descended into a long civil war lasting three decades. The nation's stability continues to be threatened by rebels and lingering conflicts. Religion plays a major role in Chad, particularly in the overseeing of the allocation of oil revenues. A religious leader sits on the Revenue Management College, alternating every four years between a Christian and a Muslim.

Democratic Republic of the Congo

D. R. Congo is one of the more Christianized countries of Africa, at around 95%. It is also a highly populated country (around 70 million) with a high fertility rate (over six children per woman). Christians are split almost evenly between Catholics and Protestant/Independents. Kimbanguism is extremely popular in the D. R. Congo; it is the Christian sect founded by Simon Kimbangu (lived c. 1890–1951) in the 1920s. His healings (including resurrections of the dead) and preaching became legendary. Kimbangu was initially a Baptist, but his followers elevated him to prophet status. His teachings were puritanical: only one wife, no alcohol, no fetishism, and ardent monotheism. He is considered one of the greatest preachers and most powerful miracle-workers in African Christian history.[47] The Congo was a colony of Belgium between 1908 and 1960 and thus conducts its business in French. From 1971 to 1997 the country was known as Zaire. It is a vast country—the third largest in Africa. The D. R. Congo has been profoundly affected by the horrible violence of the 1990s that spilled over from Rwanda and Uganda and has only recently begun to see peace.[48]

Egypt

Egypt is today strongly (85%) Muslim. Christians are discriminated against in this former Christian heartland. There are still some significant Christian communities, particularly in Alexandria—one of the five pentarchies of early Christianity. However, the precarious nature of being Christian in Egypt is evident. The government does not normally recognize conversions, making the statistics problematic. It was not always this way. In 1968, after the famous apparitions of Mary in the Zeitoun region of Cairo, many Muslims converted to Coptic Christianity.[49] However, during the 1970s and 1980s Egypt became much more sensitive to conversion. In 1998, Mohammed Hegazy made headlines when he and his wife converted to Christianity and the government repeatedly refused to recognize it. Christians are routinely persecuted on account of their faith in Egypt. In 2009, amidst the universal hysteria of swine flu, the Egyptian government ordered the slaughter of hundreds of thousands of pigs. Many interpreted this as an Islamic government's attempt to eradicate the livelihood of many Christian pig farmers in the nation, since Muslims are forbidden from eating pork. The problem was that swine were not known to have swine flu. The World Health Organization condemned Egypt's move as having no scientific basis.[50]

Gabon

This small, Christian nation in southwest Africa is associated with Albert Schweitzer (lived 1875–1965). Schweitzer's was a renaissance intellect. He became known chiefly for his book *The Quest of the Historical Jesus* (1906) as well as his Nobel Peace Prize, awarded in 1953 for his "Reverence for Life" philosophy. Schweitzer, a gifted theologian, philosopher, physician, and musician, spent the majority of his life doing medical work in this small nation. He founded a hospital in Lambarene in 1913 and through the years served thousands of patients. In 1953 he started a leprosarium with his Nobel Prize money. He died in the hospital he founded and is buried in the ground of the nation he gave his life to.[51]

Ghana

Ghana, in West Africa, is known as the first Sub-Saharan African nation to declare independence. Its independence from the U.K. in 1957 touched off a new era in Africa as nation after nation declared independence. Ghana is majority Christian, but Indigenous Religions and Islam each claim about 20% of the country's inhabitants. The Pentecostal movement is strong and growing in Ghana. A form of prosperity gospel is common, according to Paul Gifford who has written several books on Ghanian Pentecostalism.[52] Gifford's work has been widely celebrated for its depth and breadth. However, some of his conclusions have been controversial. Gifford critiques the rising charismatic Christians of Ghana on three accounts: first, they focus too much on success coming miraculously to the believer; second, they de-emphasize hard work; and third, they avoid the rational in favor of focusing on the demonic.[53] Gifford also argues that Pentecostal preachers do little to help the situation, preferring to focus on their own gifts, constantly urging the people to give more to the church.

Ivory Coast

Religion in Ivory Coast is about evenly split between Indigenous Religions, Christianity, and Islam. The future of religion in this small, densely populated nation could go either way, presuming Christianity and Islam continue to gain market share. Most scholars believe the mass defection from Indigenous Religions to either Christianity or Islam in Africa will continue unabated for decades. Ivory Coast will prove to be one of those important case studies for trends in African religious growth. The nation's claim to Christian fame comes in the form of a church building. The Basilica of Our Lady of Peace of Yamoussoukro is believed by many to be the largest church building in the world.[54] It should be noted this is far from unanimous however. Others claim that the Winners' Chapel in Nigeria may in fact be larger; still others claim St. Peter's Basilica in Rome is still the largest.

Kenya

Kenya was part of the British Empire and is a largely English-speaking nation. It has served as a beacon of peace and political progress in Africa for many years. However, Kenya's reputation as a nation of stability took a beating in 2007 and 2008 when 1500 people died as a result of a disputed election. Kenya is a Christian-majority nation with a vibrant, growing Pentecostal community. The Protestant/Independent community in Kenya, particularly the Evangelicals, has become so strong that it wields the ability to steer national votes.[55]

Madagascar

Africa's largest island was under French control during colonial times but gained independence in 1960. About half of the 20 million citizens are Christian. Perhaps somewhat surprisingly the majority of the Christians are Protestant/Independent. Islam is very small in Madagascar although the island was strongly influenced by Arab Muslim traders and settlers for centuries prior to European contact. Madagascar's national holidays include several Christian celebrations.

Morocco

Morocco became largely Islamic during the Arab expansion in the 600s and 700s. Today it is one of the most Islamic nations in the world (99%). It was coveted by the Spanish and French during colonial times, although there are few vestiges of Europeans today outside of tourists. Morocco is Arabic, and tends to elevate its Arabic character above its Africanness: it has consistently refused to join the African Union—the only African country not to do so. Islam is the official state religion of Morocco and proselytizing of any kind is forbidden. There are penalties for "... anyone who employs incitements to shake the faith of a Muslim or to convert him to another religion."[56] There are Christian missionaries in Morocco, but their abilities to function are severely hamstrung. Additionally, it is estimated that it costs approximately $50,000 in

U.S. funds to achieve one baptism, making Morocco, along with other North African nations, a very expensive place to do missionary work.[57] As a comparison, it only takes around $7,000 to achieve a baptism in Nigeria. However, this all pales in comparison to Saudi Arabia, where $200,000 is needed to accomplish a baptism; or in secular Norway, where it takes $2 million to accomplish one Christian baptism!

Nigeria

Nigeria, by far Africa's most populous country, was under British rule from 1900 to 1960. It has been a democracy since 1999 when 33 years of military rule came to an end. Nigeria is almost evenly split between Muslims and Christians, and tensions peak daily. What is at the core of the conflict is a legal matter: Shari'a law was introduced in the Islamic north in 1999, causing deep concern in the Christian community. Violence has continued apace ever since. In 2002 clashes surrounding the planned Miss World contest led to over a thousand deaths and numerous churches and mosques were destroyed. In 2004 at least 78 Christians and 660 Muslims were killed. "Each of these attacks resulted in large movements of population."[58] Mass migrations—either Christians or Muslims moving to other areas on account of religious discrimination—have been common since 1999. Shari'a-based dress codes and travel restrictions have been introduced in many places, causing resentment amongst Christians. Women have been banned from riding motorcycles in several Islamic areas. The 1999 law was in many ways a regression for Nigeria, which had seen widespread and chaotic massacres in the 1960s and 1970s. The future of Nigeria is unclear due to the tinderbox it has become since 1999. The U.S. Department of State describes the Nigerian clash of religion in dire terms, listing a catalogue of human rights violations based on religious prejudice.[59]

Nigerian Christianity is strongly Protestant/Independent. The Pentecostal movement has been particularly influential in the spread of Christianity in that nation. One of the most important Pentecostal denominations in Nigeria, and in all of Africa for that matter, is the Redeemed Christian Church of God, established in 1952. The pastor, E. A. Adeboye, made Newsweek magazine's list of the most powerful people in the world in 2009.[60] Adeboye claims to have five million members in Nigeria alone, although his denomination is truly global. It has around 400 branches in both the USA and in Britain.

Rwanda

Perhaps no African nation has received more attention than Rwanda in recent times. In 1994 genocide ripped this tiny nation apart. It was based on tribal animosities between majority Hutu and minority Tutsis. The tensions had been elevating in the early 1990s and all of a sudden erupted in 1994 and lasted for over three months. The explosion of violence came when the country's President was assassinated—his plane was shot down just after taking off. The death toll is usually estimated to be around a million people. This was all very strange to Westerners who read that Rwanda was a Christian-majority nation. The atrocities from these events are legion: displaced persons, mass emigration out of the country, and continued armed conflicts spilling over the borders into Uganda, Burundi, Tanzania, and D. R. Congo. Huge refugee camps sprung up in the surrounding nations, but the squalid conditions often led to rampant and deadly diseases. All told, it was one of the most egregious disasters of the late twentieth century; anger is still directed at the United Nations who did little to stop the genocide while it was happening. There are currently many efforts going on that are directed at helping this nation recover such as justice tribunals, church work, and widespread humanitarian aid. The American mega-church pastor Rick Warren of Saddleback Church in California has forged good relations with the Rwandan government and has spearheaded an extensive program, "... aimed at promoting reconciliation, equipping servant leaders, assisting the poor, caring for the sick and educating the next generation."[61]

South Africa

South Africa is a strongly Protestant Christian nation. It is a land of vast natural resources, highly coveted by the Dutch and British during European colonization. South Africa has become nearly coterminous with the concept of racial division—apartheid— that separated people into three groups: whites, blacks, and colored (mixed race). While an informal policy for years, it became law in 1948, brutally suppressing blacks by revoking their citizenship and basic rights. This became one of the great humanitarian causes of the 1980s and early 1990s. In 1994 the racist system fell apart under the leadership of Frederik Willem de Klerk, Nelson Mandela and Desmond Tutu; it was a bloodless revolution. Philip Jenkins writes,

> The world's best-known Anglican cleric is probably former Cape Town Archbishop Desmond Tutu, who (alongside Nelson Mandela) became the symbol of the South African liberation movement. ... Tutu tried to reconcile the nation's old rivals through a Truth and Reconciliation Commission, an innovative attempt to apply Christian ideas of repentance and forgiveness to national secular politics.[62]

While South Africa's recovery from apartheid has been admirable, the country continues to deal with severe problems. Johannesburg, the largest city, is known for its frequency of violent crimes. The BBC once reported that "It is a fact that a woman born in South Africa has a greater chance of being raped, than learning how to read."[63]

Sudan

Africa's largest country is strongly Islamic—over 70%. The nation is in shambles, being one of the most unstable places on earth. Since independence from Britain in 1956 it has been mired in civil wars. War casualties, famine, and displacement have wreaked havoc to the point that many head for nearby countries, choosing to live in squalid refugee camps as opposed to living under the constant threat of getting caught in the crossfire of war. Human rights are a sham in Sudan. Religious tensions were evinced in 2007 when a British schoolteacher named the class teddy bear after Muhammad, leading to a national outcry. The Christian woman was pardoned by the president and promptly departed the country. Forced conversions, stealing of property, pillaging of villages, mass executions, child abduction, slavery, and torture for various reasons are all commonplace in Sudan. Shari'a law penalizes those who apostatize from Islam. This also curtails Christian missions in the country, particularly in the north. "Muslims in the north who express an interest in Christianity or convert to Christianity faced severe social pressure to recant," according to the U.S. Department of State.[64] One of the most severe human conflicts today is in Sudan, where the Darfur region has deteriorated to the point of near hopelessness. The situation was labeled genocide by the U.S. government in 2004.

Zimbabwe

Zimbabwe was a British colony known as Southern Rhodesia during colonial times until 1965. The country has become coterminous with President Robert Mugabe, the dictator who has ruled with an iron fist since 1980. Mugabe was at one time an African hero, leading the charge against white-minority rule in the region. The nation has collapsed on his watch, however, and Mugabe today is seen largely as leading this one-time prosperous country into disrepair. The Zimbabwean currency is essentially useless, elections are rigged, poverty and unemployment are widespread, and due to Mugabe's tyranny other nations are virtually powerless to help the situation. Like most of the southern African nations, Christianity is the predominant religion in Zimbabwe. Angola, Zambia, Namibia, South Africa, Lesotho, and Swaziland are all at least 80% Christian. There is an interesting trend however in a swath of territory that includes Botswana, Zimbabwe, Mozambique, and Madagascar. While all four of these nations have a strong Christian presence, there is also a strong Indigenous Religion presence in each of them. This was clearly demonstrated in

Zimbabwe in 2006 when the Witchcraft Suppression Act made several amendments such as criminalizing witch hunts and rejecting the killing of a witch as a defense for murder.[65] This is surely to be one of the busiest areas for Christian missions in the first half of the twenty-first century. If trends continue, these countries will continue to see large numbers of Christian converts. Islam is not strong in any of these four countries and thus Christian advance will be somewhat accelerated. Prior to independence, Zimbabwe was a prosperous nation. Even in 1998 the country was stable enough to host the World Council of Churches gathering in Harare. Today, that all seems a far cry away. Zimbabweans are amongst the poorest and unhealthiest people in the world. The HIV/AIDS crisis is most acute in sub-Saharan Africa, and Zimbabwe is a case in point—it is ranked number six in the world with about 15% of the population being infected. The ten most prevalent HIV/AIDS countries are in sub-Saharan Africa, conspicuously in the very south.[66]

Three Questions for Analysis

1. Does Africa seem set for a titanic clash of civilizations between an Islamic north and a Christian south? Why or why not?

2. Why do Indigenous Religions continue to decline in Africa? Is this trend inevitable? Why or why not?

3. Will African Christianity lead the way to a post-denominational era in Christianity? Why or why not?

Oceania

PEOPLE
Total Population: 34,373,095
Total Median Age: 33.1 years
Life Expectancy: 77.77 years
Fertility Rate: 2.26 children born/woman

RELIGION
Top Religion Percentages: Christian (79.74%)
Nonreligious (11.95%)
Buddhist (1.62%)
Hindu (1.58%)
Atheist (1.21%)
Muslim (1.20%)
Number of Christians: 27,410,997
Major Christian Groupings: Protestant/Independent (65%)
Catholic (32%)
Orthodox (3%)

CHAPTER NINE

OCEANIC CHRISTIANITY

Oceania is highly Christianized today. Christianization has been a fairly recent development, however. The Christian culture of this region of the world is complex and varied due to the many forms of the faith that took root on these islands and atolls throughout the eighteenth, nineteenth, and twentieth centuries. Oceania does not have a long history of being united in one form of faith or another, such as Orthodoxy in Eastern Europe or Roman Catholic Christianity in Western Europe. One form of Christianity has never been dominant in Oceania. The Oceanic experience of Christianity occurred rather late in history, and Christianity had already proliferated a great deal prior to European dominance in the region. Quite suddenly, the region changed from an animistic, totemic, and traditional context with stringent taboo systems, to a Christianized context. While the largest denominations were Anglican, Methodist, Presbyterian, and Catholic, there were smaller denominations such as the Churches of Christ, Seventh-Day Adventists and Mormons already well-established in Oceania by the end of the nineteenth century.[1]

Many scholars today believe Oceania represents "a latter-day Christendom" due to the strongly Christian character of the three sub-regions of Melanesia, Micronesia, and Polynesia.[2]

> Since the early part of the 20th century, the island populations of the Pacific have been overwhelmingly Christian in allegiance. Church buildings are to be found wherever there is human habitation and Christianity is an important feature of Pacific life almost everywhere. The religion of Christ … appears to have been more universally accepted and integrated here than in any other comparable region in modern times. Pacific people have incorporated Christian ideas, practices and structures into their cultures and communities.[3]

Australia and New Zealand are somewhat exceptional here; they were settled by Europeans and have thus developed similarly to Western Europe in many ways, particularly in terms of religiosity. Both of those countries, while nominally Christian, are in reality quite secular. This circumstance is statistically meaningful because the combined population of Australia and New Zealand is over 25 million, while the population of the entire region of Oceania is only about 35 million.

Oceania may not seem particularly significant globally because of its tiny population in comparison with the other cultural blocks represented in this book. The population of this vast region is almost exactly the same as the population of Canada. Only about one percent of the world's Christians live in Oceania.[4] However, this region is highly significant in the study of Christianity for several reasons.

First, the study of Christianity in Oceania is enmeshed with fascinating anthropological data unique to this region of the world because of its distinct people-groups. Every inhabited island contains a culture that has developed in its own unique way. Migration and cultural interactions remained relatively low due to the isolated nature of the islands. Thus, a study of Christianity in Oceania is intrinsically an overview of case studies.

Second, this region was marred with conflict between indigenous peoples and incoming colonizers for many years. However, perhaps surprisingly, the indigenous peoples accepted the faith of Christianity to the point that today the second and third largest religions in the region—Buddhism and Hinduism—together account for only 3% of the population. Oceania also represents an example of the drastic decline in indigenous populations in a small amount of time. For example, in 1800, the aboriginal population of Australia was 650,000. By 1900 it was a paltry 90,000 due primarily to European diseases such as smallpox and measles. While these catastrophes were devastating to indigenous populations, the colonial populations flourished. In 1800, Australia had only a few thousand Europeans, but by 1900 there were nearly four million! Similar trends prevailed in New Zealand during that century.[5]

A third reason Oceanic Christianity is highly significant is because it is severely understudied. There is much work to be done on understanding just precisely how this region so swiftly Christianized. There has been ample anthropological work on Oceanic peoples, but Christianity's role has been overlooked. One key reason for the dearth of study here is because anthropologists, historically, have neglected to look at the interaction of Christianity and indigenous cultures, instead preferring to study the indigenous religion and discredit Christianity as a colonial imposition on a victimized people. One scholar put it this way:

> The marginalization of Christianity in ethnographic writing on Melanesia is long-standing. That famous pioneer of salvage anthropology, Bronislaw Malinowski [lived 1884 to 1942], wrote many substantial volumes about the Trobriand Islanders of Papua New Guinea in which he scarcely mentioned Christianity, even though the Methodist Church was firmly established ... Malinowski's rare allusions to Christianity were mostly negative, suggesting that missionaries were engaged in the destruction or corruption of indigenous culture and social organization. What

Malinowski never seriously considered was that, like it or not, Trobrianders were making Christianity part of their culture.[6]

Today, the field of anthropology's long neglect of Christianity's impact on culture is receding. For one, it is becoming clearer that Christianity never was, and never will be, simply a Western faith; it has always interacted with culture in nuanced and culturally sophisticated ways as it migrated from the Middle East to Africa, Asia, Europe, and beyond. Secondly, anthropologists have become less reactive towards the work of missionaries as their discipline has settled into its own. Since the era of the circumnavigators, the greatest ethnographic work was done mainly by missionaries, who had a genuine—if vested—interest in understanding newly encountered peoples in order to make Christians of them. As the field of anthropology took off with the work of Edward Tylor (lived 1832–1917) and James Frazer (lived 1854–1941), it became important for these scholars to distance themselves from the missionaries. Thus, early anthropology contains within it a reactive mood towards Christianity, and could often—as in the case of Malinowski's work—appear anti-Christian in ways.

What Is Oceania?

Variously known as Oceania, Australasia, or the South Pacific, this waterlogged region of the world is defined as much by the Pacific Ocean as by the land. The term "Oceania" has only recently emerged as the preferred designation for the area. As in virtually all cultural or geographical blocks, there is considerable disagreement over the precise borders of this area of the world.

The Pacific Ocean is by far the largest body of water on the planet—twice the size of the Atlantic Ocean. It is somewhat difficult for people today to understand its grandeur and sheer incomprehensibility to people in the past: "The Pacific Ocean is so vast that it took European explorers almost three centuries to chart its features."[7] It is usually split into equatorial halves by cartographers, a North Pacific Ocean and a South Pacific Ocean. Oceania as a cultural block, however, includes around 10,000 islands from both sides of the equator.[8] The northernmost border of Oceania consists of the Northern Mariana Islands—a commonwealth of the United States—and the Marshall Islands, an independent republic whose territory nearly bumps up against the International Date Line. Theoretically, the Hawaiian Islands should also share the northernmost border of Oceania, but since Hawaii is one of the official 50 states of the U.S., this book locates it in North America. The eastern edge of Oceania consists of the Pitcairn Islands and French Polynesia—which includes the famous island of Tahiti. The southern edge of Oceania is New Zealand— "the last large, habitable region of the earth to receive members of the human species."[9] The Western side of Oceania is dominated by the continent of Australia in the south. Moving up from there is Papua New Guinea—which constitutes the eastern half of New Guinea, the world's second largest island after Greenland. The island of New Guinea is an extremely diverse land that is politically divided.[10] While the eastern half, Papua New Guinea, is an independent republic, the western half—known variously as Irian Jaya, Irian Barat, or Papua—belongs to Indonesia. Since the 1960s, West Papuans have struggled against Indonesia for independence. West Papua is home to rich resources, thus Indonesia keeps the region under heavy guard. It has been described as a human rights travesty involving:

> ... social and ethnic tension ... harsh treatment of Papuans by the Indonesian armed forces ... extra-judicial killing, intimidation, and a host of other horrendous actions to dissuade Papuans from pursuing political independence.[11]

On the northwest border of Oceania is the young nation of Palau—a close ally of the United States, as well as the U.S. territory of Guam.

Oceania consists of 25 countries and territories. In addition to the country/continent of Australia there are numerous island countries and territories that fit into one of three geographic divisions: Melanesia, Micronesia, or Polynesia. Indonesia is not usually considered part of this region of the world for various reasons; it is considered to be more of a link between Oceania and Asia, rather than an intrinsic part of an identifiable Oceanic culture. However, we must not push this way of thinking too far, as Indonesian culture shares much with Oceania.

Melanesia, Micronesia, and Polynesia are not indigenous divisions; they were superimposed by European voyagers. Nevertheless, these terms live on and are frequently cited in historical and geographical writings today. They all come from Greek words and they are meant to be "... a way of clustering the multitude of Pacific ethnic and cultural groups. They do so very loosely and often misleadingly, but they are still convenient."[12] Melanesia—meaning "Black Island" because of the skin color of the people—is the largest and most diverse of these three regions. It encompasses six nations/territories: Papua New Guinea (the Indonesia side is usually included here), the Solomon Islands, New Caledonia, Fiji, Norfolk Island, and Vanuatu. On the map, the Melanesian region, based in Papua New Guinea, extends southeastward to Fiji and Norfolk Island. Micronesia—meaning "small islands"—generally includes seven nations/territories: Guam, Kiribati, Marshall Islands, Micronesia (Federated States of Micronesia), Nauru, Northern Mariana Islands, and Palau. This region is distinguishable on a map as being the northern part of Oceania. Polynesia—meaning many islands—means just what it says. It is the largest of the three regions and includes over a thousand islands, organized into eleven countries and territories: American Samoa, Cook Islands, French Polynesia, Hawaii (although a U.S. state), New Zealand, Niue, Pitcairn Islands, Samoa, Tokelau Islands, Tonga, Tuvalu, Wallis and Futuna Islands, and Easter Island (part of Chile). On a map Polynesia can be discerned as anchored by New Zealand and including the islands located between Tuvalu and Pitcairn Islands.[13]

Oceania's land mass is dominated by Australia, Papua New Guinea, and New Zealand, which also happen to be the most populated nations in the region. Australia is by far the most populated with over 20 million people. The rest of Oceania is comprised of small islands with low populations. Fiji has a million people and Solomon Islands have over half a million. French Polynesia has around 300,000 people. There are twelve nations and territories in Oceania that have less than 100,000 people. The population of Oceania is basically keeping steady with a fertility rate of 2.26 children born per woman. Australia's European-like fertility rate (1.78) really brings down the fertility average for the region.

Overall, the people of Oceania enjoy good health and long lives. After Western Europe and North America they live longer than any other people-group. In fact they basically live as long as North Americans; their average life span differs from North Americans by less than a year. However, there is quite a disparity in many categories when comparing Australia and New Zealand to the rest of Oceania. As mentioned above, Australia and New Zealand are comparable in many ways to Western Europe: they are highly developed societies with good education and strong health care systems. Some of the islands do not always enjoy these same standards however. Kiribati, Nauru, and Vanuatu have life expectancies in the low 60s for example.

Human history in Australia and New Guinea goes back 60,000 years. A major migration from Southeast Asia to Oceania occurred about 5,000 years ago. These seafaring people created settlements all over the region. By the year A.D. 1000 virtually all of the inhabitable islands of Oceania had human settlements. The peoples of Australia remained hunters and gatherers until European contact. The people of New Guinea however followed a different trajectory; they turned to agriculture around 5,000 years ago, possibly due to the influence of the Southeast Asians who had immigrated there. Archaeologists have discovered one of the people-groups who settled the Pacific Islands—the Lapita peoples (named after an archeological site on New Caledonia)—were highly advanced. They had communication and trade networks, agriculture, jewelry, and stone tools. Vast amounts of their distinctive pottery have been unearthed. The Lapita peoples built societies in the Pacific islands that were hierarchical, with a chief at the top. Evidence shows that when a group of people became dissatisfied with a particular chief's leadership, they would build canoes and move to another island—sometimes at a great distance—in order to begin afresh. Over time, this pattern led to widespread human civilizations all over the region, and in many cases these groups developed along unique lines without much interference from other societies. The extensive Lapita trade networks fell into disuse around the year B.C. 500 thus creating rather autonomous societies that Europeans sometimes found perplexingly unique.[14]

Background: Christianity in Oceania

Christianity first came to Oceania by means of Western Europeans. Oceania was a whole new world to them when they arrived. There had been speculation of a southern continent known in Latin as *terra australis incognita* ("unknown southern land") since the second century A.D. The Portuguese and Dutch, highly involved in the spice trade, had approached Australia from the northwest. It was not until 1606, however, that the Dutch realized what they had run into. Indeed, most of the entire region of Oceania was fuzzy and considered rather worthless in the European consciousness until British Captain James Cook's (lived 1728–1779) arrival to Australia in 1770. Cook's accomplishments were great, but his ending was not; he was killed by Hawaiians after a misunderstanding went terribly wrong. He was stabbed and clubbed to death, as were several of his crewmen. These events happened just days after the islanders had hailed him as a hero. Cook had broken several taboos, however, especially when he tried to take a high-ranking chief hostage.[15] Captain Cook essentially added eastern Australia, New Zealand, New Caledonia, Vanuatu, and Hawaii to the European map. He was a student of Polynesian society and introduced a whole new world to the European mind. "By the time Cook's voyages had come to an end, European geographers had compiled a reasonably accurate understanding of the world's ocean basins, their lands, and their peoples."[16]

Explorers prior to Cook considered Australia a desolate wasteland that "... contains no metals, nor yields any precious woods... [It is] the most arid and barren region that could be found anywhere on earth."[17] When Australia finally was settled by Europeans in 1788, it was as a penal colony. Around one thousand Britons—eight hundred of them convicts—arrived to Sydney in that year, supporting themselves primarily through sheep herding. Only in the mid-nineteenth century did Australia begin to receive large numbers of settlers from less dubious circumstances.

Backing up a bit, it was Ferdinand Magellan (lived 1480–1521) in 1521 who became the first European to cross the vast Pacific Ocean. Magellan is considered one of the great circumnavigators in history, primarily because of his heroic accomplishment of finding a passage from the Atlantic to the Pacific—via a waterway in southern Chile that today bears his name, the Strait of Magellan. Magellan himself believed the lucrative spice islands of Indonesia were located not too far from America. His prediction proved terribly wrong, as he and his crew sailed for four months, many of them dying of scurvy along the way, until they happened upon Guam. "Immediately surrounded by the Chamorro people in their agile *proas* canoes, the Spaniards were the first Europeans to make contact with an Oceanic society."[18] Cultural misunderstandings were immediate. The Spaniards had superior firepower however and killed seven Chamorros. They burned several homes and desperately helped themselves to the local resources due to their near-starvation at sea. Three turbulent days after landing, Magellan and his ships again set sail for the Philippines, where trouble finally caught up with them—Magellan and 40 of his crewmen were slain after he got involved in a local political dispute.[19]

Magellan's legacy remains, however. He was one of the very first circumnavigators, and is without doubt one of the greatest discoverers of all time. His explorations had an indelible impact on succeeding geographers and maritime explorers. His voyages had demonstrated beyond a doubt that Ptolemy's (second century A.D.) understanding of the size of the world—which had dominated for nearly a millennium and a half—were vastly underestimated. It was Magellan who gave the Pacific Ocean its name because of his belief that it was a relatively calm body of water for sailing. After crossing the peaceful ocean however, and making contact with Micronesian people, the encounter between Oceanic and European would prove to be everything but peaceful. Magellan's journeys touched off centuries of conflict between the two cultures—a fairly predictable outcome when two cultures collide so suddenly.

It is one thing to say that Magellan's landing at Guam on March 6, 1521, was the introduction of *Christians* to Oceanic peoples. It is quite another to say that this debacle of an encounter represents the introduction of *Christianity* to Oceanic peoples. Whatever the inhabitants of Guam may have heard about Christ, little happened in that encounter that would have encouraged the islanders to follow the religion of these emaciated, ravenous, thieving sailors.

Christianity entered Oceania in two waves: the first wave was the Roman Catholic faith coming from imperial Spain—represented by Magellan. The second wave was by British Protestantism, as represented by Captain Cook. Many of the encounters between Oceanic peoples and Europeans ended up, sadly, with violence. This is what prompted the island of Tahiti to offer its women to British crew members in the late eighteenth century, touching off a frenzy in what would become a European stereotype of Tahitian women: sexually carefree, and peculiarly open to conjugal relations. Tahiti quickly became a hot destination place for European sailors.

The Europeans' sheer insatiable appetite for Tahitian women produced one burning concern for Tahitians: Could it be that European shores abounded with men and had few or no women? Armed with curiosity that equaled their European counterparts', several Tahitians made the long voyage to the mysterious continent. Unfortunately many died in transit, partially debilitated by the new diseases arriving into the Pacific Ocean. ... In short, these "noble savages" as Europeans called them, made a considerable impression on Europe.[20]

Even Britain's most honorable Royal Navy Captain James Cook could not rein in his men in the face of Polynesian women. In the earliest surviving record of a European visit to the Hawaiian Islands, Cook recorded the following in his journal in the year 1778:

We were agreeably surprised to find them of the same nation as the people of Otahiete [Tahiti] and the other [Polynesian] islands we had lately visited. ... As there were some venereal complaints on board both the Ships, in order to prevent its being communicated to these people, I gave orders that no Women, on any account whatever were to be admitted on board the Ships. I also forbid all manner of connection with them, and ordered that none who had the venereal upon them should go out of the ships. But whether these regulations had the desired effect or not time can only discover.[21]

The spread of sexually transmitted diseases became a horrific chapter in the history of Euro-Oceanic contact, especially after the whaling industry took root in the early 1800s. Hundreds of whalers brought with them diseases that Polynesians had no resistance to, leading to a catastrophic population decline in several island societies. Hawaii's population, it is estimated, was depleted by as much as 80% in the decades following Cook's arrival there.[22]

Tahiti's women captivated European men at sea, even driving them to bizarre extremes. On one occasion, in 1789, mutiny broke out aboard the HMS Bounty when crew members, led by Fletcher Christian, overtook Captain William Bligh. They set their captain adrift with some of his loyal supporters, and proceeded to kidnap several Tahitian women, taking them to the remote Pitcairne Islands in order to create their own isolated paradise. The experiment ended in disaster as all of the mutineers except one—John Adams—died of murder, alcoholism, or disease. Pitcairne Islands' capital is named after this man—Adamstown.[23] The famous mutiny was portrayed in movies and literature many times throughout the twentieth century, most notably in 1935 when the film Mutiny on the Bounty, starring Clark Gable, won the coveted Academy Award for Best Picture.[24]

The frenzied "Scramble for Africa" was actually preceded in the South Pacific during the 1800s. One by one, imperialist powers from Europe staked their claims in the region, beginning with France's grabbing of, perhaps predictably, Tahiti, in 1841. French Polynesia is a legacy of the French influence there. France also annexed New Caledonia. The British established a colony in Australia, known as New South Wales. In a show of force, the British

> ... [U]ndertook brutal military campaigns to evict aboriginal peoples from lands suitable for agriculture or herding ... displacing most indigenous Australians from their traditional lands and dispersing them throughout the continent.[25]

It was a similar story in New Zealand as the indigenous people, known as Maori, were in 1840 persuaded to allow British colonial rule. In exchange, however, they were given sovereignty of their land. The agreement, known as the Treaty of Waitangi, is still today a contentious matter in the country. New Zealand in the second half of the nineteenth century was a war zone as Maori attempted time and again to win their land back from British rule in what is known today as the New Zealand Land Wars.

Britain continued its dominance in the region, annexing Fiji in 1874. Germany took control of the Marshall Islands in the 1870s. The USA claimed Hawaii in 1875 and went on to take possession of Guam (and the Philippines) in 1898 after the Spanish American War.

> By 1900 only the kingdom of Tonga remained independent and even Tonga accepted British protection against the possibility of encroachments by other imperial powers.[26]

As the Western world continued to take political charge of the Oceanic nations, Christianity inevitably took root. Missionaries were ubiquitous in the South Pacific and with official European presence, albeit meager in places, they were able to present the gospel to the people more fluidly. Christianity's foundations were nevertheless secure by 1900. It was only a matter of time before the entire region would become perhaps the most Christianized region in the world as indigenous peoples adopted the faith and created missionaries of their own to take the good news to the most remote parts of Oceania. Indeed, one of the most important aspects of Oceanic Christianity is the indigenous role played in the transmission of faith.[27]

Devout Christians in Europe read wild reports of barbarism, cannibalism, flagrant sexuality, and a world without Christ, and thus flocked to Oceania during the nineteenth and twentieth centuries. Generally speaking, Christianity was introduced in the Pacific islands from east to west, beginning with Polynesia and moving west toward Micronesia, and finally down to Melanesia and New Guinea.

Roman Catholic priests were aboard some of the Spanish explorer ships in the 1500s, but they did little more than teach locals the sign of the cross and baptize a few young people. Their presence had little effect. The first formal missionaries to the South Pacific were Spanish Jesuits from the Philippines.

They conducted mission work in the Mariana Islands and in Micronesia, beginning in 1668. Again, however, the work petered out and nothing permanent was established.

The British colonies of eastern Australia—New South Wales, Victoria, and Queensland—were founded between 1788 and 1859. The Church of England was the primary form of Christianity. These were penal colonies and thus were largely populated by convicts who were rather irreligious back in England. About a third of the convicts were Catholics from Ireland. Thus, there was a double-barreled resentment toward the established church. Clergy correspondence shows that the outback in the first half of the nineteenth century was "godless" and "immoral." In the latter half of the century, however, free settlers began to migrate from Britain to Australia. Many of these were churchgoers. Church buildings began to be erected, and, along with a post office, bank, and railway stop, represented British civilization. Various missionary societies such as the evangelical CMS (Church Missionary Society), LMS (London Missionary Society) and the Wesleyan Methodists all spent huge resources to evangelize Australia and New Zealand. These early missions were transplanted European churches and functioned almost entirely according to British ways. Only much later, in the twentieth century, did a truly indigenous ethos begin to emerge in the churches.

In the Pacific Islands, Tahiti became the focus of missionary endeavor, beginning in 1797.[28] Within a few years there were missions in greater French Polynesia, Tonga, Cook Islands, and Samoa. Missionaries focused on two goals: first, converting tribal leaders, especially chiefs; and, second, literacy. It was crucial for these Protestants to get the Bible into the language of the people. Combined, these two factors often led to mass conversions to the faith. It was a pattern that was oft-repeated in the history of Christianity in the region as it worked its way westward.

One unique characteristic of the expansion of Christianity in the Pacific was that competition between denominations was intentionally kept to a minimum. Methodists were given this island, the evangelical Anglicans that one, and so on, in evangelistic agreements:

> From 1795 several Protestant missions began work in the region, agreeing among themselves to concentrate on different island groups, with the result that today the islands still reflect a patchwork of denominations: British Congregationalists in eastern Polynesia, the Cook Islands and Samoa, English Methodists in Tonga and Fiji, New England Congregationalists in Hawaii, Kiribati and Micronesia, Anglicans in the smaller Melanesian islands. After the Napoleanic Wars [1803 to 1815], there was competition from French Catholics.[29]

Missionaries in those days often stayed in one place for life. Christianity profited from this model as missionaries introduced technology, literacy, and religion, while islanders provided these Europeans with the means for survival such as food and shelter. It was a reciprocal relationship that more often than not resulted in the community adopting the form of Christianity brought to them by the individual or group willing to establish roots on a given island, with a particular community. The islanders would become the new family to the missionary. The missionary would, in a very real sense, become dependent upon them, albeit with a very high social status. To this day in Oceania, ministers and priests are considered very esteemed in the community, certainly much more so than in the West.[30] Clergy came to know their communities extremely intimately, often taking detailed notes of the manners and customs of the people. It was common for them to publish these writings later. These writings were some of the earliest forms of what would eventually become the field of social anthropology. Today, anthropologists study in the field for perhaps less than five years. In Oceania, during the heyday of Christianization in the nineteenth century, missionaries often lived the duration of their lives in the field.

Why did the islanders of the Pacific convert to Christianity? This question is extremely complex. A materialistic explanation would be that the region was deluged with changes going on all about them—mass death through European-borne diseases, a complete disruption of traditional village life, new economic realities due to European interests, philosophical clashes over which god was greater or truer. In some cases, it was fairly clear to islanders that the Europeans represented a more sophisticated civilization. One Samoan chief said the following:

> Only look at the English people. They have noble ships while we have only canoes. They have strong, beautiful clothes of various colours while we have only *ti* leaves; they have iron axes while we use stones; they have scissors, while we use the shark's teeth; what beautiful beads they have, looking glasses, and all that is valuable. I therefore think that the god who gave them all things must be good, and that his religion must be superior to ours. If we receive this god and worship him, he will in time give us these things as well.[31]

This longing to have what the Europeans possessed led to a phenomenon known as "cargo cults," something that still goes on in Oceania. To this day, in Papua New Guinea, certain tribes believe the vast cargo brought to their island comes from the gods or from their ancestors. In order to attract the planes to their village, they build makeshift landing strips, far too small to accommodate any manned aircraft. However, they wait, in the hopes that a plane will come to them. The name John Frum, or John From [America], is often, mysteriously, associated with the cargo cults, especially in Vanuatu. The John Frum Movement's believers reject Christianity and maintain their ancient customs by and large. The cult is believed to be traced to World War II, when American planes brought food, weapons, and medicine as replenishment for troops. Villagers believe a tall, white, American man called John Frum appeared to them in the 1930s and encouraged them to stick with their own traditions and stand firm against Western influence. John Frum has become a god to them. The movement's leader on the island of Tanna, Vanuatu—Chief Isaac Wan—said, "John Frum is our God, our Jesus."[32] Another cargo cult in remote Vanuatu believes Prince Philip—husband to the U.K.'s Queen Elizabeth II—is a divine being, the brother of John Frum. They believe he speaks to them, and while they know he lives in England, they believe his spirit remains with them. This cult formed in the 1950s and seems to stem from the British soldiers' respect for the royal couple. Somehow, this was blended into Christian messianic beliefs. Prince Philip visited Vanuatu in 1971, and has since sent autographed pictures, correspondence, and other tokens of respect, much to the delight of the tribe. The tribe believes Prince Philip is immortal, but if he dies, they might transfer allegiance to Prince Charles or perhaps his sons.[33]

The gist of the cargo cult is that through magic, the islanders can direct the cargo to themselves, as it was originally intended for them anyway. The white people have somehow managed to intercept the cargo from the divine ancestors. As a result, various rituals are performed by the natives in order to make the ancestors aware of where the cargo is actually supposed to go. In time, the ancestors will eventually figure out the mistake and will begin showering the tribe with the manufactured goods. Historian Stephen Neill called cargo cults "a resurgence of pagan ideas, often in partly Christian dress":

> Basically the Cargo cult represents an attempt to accept western civilization and to make use of it—on the Papuan's own terms. ... The question that lies at the root of the Cargo cult in New Guinea is this: How does it come about that the white man is so astonishingly rich, when he is not seen to work particularly hard? His ships go on and on bringing him goods without measure ... The white man is never seen to pay for these things: apparently he gets them all free. They are sent out from inexhaustible storehouses which belong to a higher power. There is a connexion between the wealth of the white man and his religion. The white man through the missionaries has passed on the Gospel to the Papuan; but he has not passed on to him the secret of access to all this wealth. The Papuans must, therefore, somehow or other discover this secret for themselves.[34]

While cargo cults—for all their exotic idiosyncrasies—continue in Oceania to present times, it would be a mistake to assume them as being common. Without doubt, the vast majority of Oceanic peoples are Christians, albeit in their own unique and indigenous ways.

Cargo cults represent something fundamental to the history and expansion of Christianity: syncretism—a blending of Christianity with preexisting beliefs. "Appropriated Christianity" is really the only way Christianity is ever "received" by a non-Christian culture.[35] There is no alternative. The receiving culture *must* accommodate Christian teachings within the context of the worldview they have inherited as it is impossible to immediately change one's inherited social culture with all of its nuanced meanings. In the transmission of faith from missionary to recipient, there are things jettisoned, but much remains, such as in the case of the fire dance of the Baining peoples—a ritual that has roots in tribal New Guinea, but has been modified by Christian teaching.

Unlike the early contact with Africa, Asia, and Latin America, in the context of Oceania, European missionaries always outnumbered government officials. This proved critical to the success of Christianity in the region. Government officials rarely exhibited the respect and cultural sensitivity of missionaries, who were after all not only interested in converting these peoples, but they were often dependent upon them for survival. Government officials, however, relied less on indigenous inhabitants and were less dependent upon them.

In the early 1800s, it was becoming clear that Christianity was becoming indigenized as Oceanic peoples began to make Christianity their own:

> Beginning in the 1820s hundreds of Pacific Island Christians, with their wives, volunteered to be missionaries themselves in distant places. Tahitians went to the Cook Islands, Hawaii, Fiji and Samoa; Cook Islanders and Samoans worked in New Caledonia and the New Hebrides [Vanuatu]; Tongans largely evangelized Fiji.[36]

Missionaries became the supervisors, mainly concerned with infrastructure: schools, seminaries, mission compounds, churches, and even hospitals. The task of bringing the people to Christ, however, was much more commonly associated with indigenous catechists and pastor-teachers. Christianity's presence began to be seen in the large, thatched palm leaf church buildings that became ubiquitous in the South Pacific.

Working shoulder to shoulder, the indigenous Christians and the European missionaries—the majority of whom were single women—became highly successful in the effort to bring the gospel to some of the most remote places on earth.[37] The European heroes were the subjects of fantastic tales back home, and inspired a wealth of literature:

- Englishman John Williams famously evangelized French Polynesia and became perhaps the most famous missionary in Oceania. In 1839 he was killed and eaten by cannibals on the island of Erromango in modern day Vanuatu while attempting to evangelize the indigenous population.
- George Selwyn was the first Anglican Bishop of New Zealand, serving from 1841 to 1868. He played a major role in the expansion of his

church all over the Pacific Islands but is probably best known for his role in the Christianization of the Maori population of New Zealand.

- Scottish missionary James Chalmers served in the Cook Islands and New Guinea from 1866 to 1901. Chalmers, like Williams, met a brutal death. On an exploratory trip with a young missionary companion, Chalmers and his friend Oliver Tomkins "... had hardly landed when they were set upon, clubbed to death, cooked, and eaten."[38]

- Henry Venn, head of England's Church Missionary Society, and Rufus Anderson, head of the American Board of Commissioners for Foreign Missions (ABCFM), were already claiming in the 1830s and 1840s that mission work must become indigenized if it is to be successful, a concept known at the time as "native agency." These two distinguished statesmen were not missionaries, but they are widely recognized as the masterminds of Protestant missions in the nineteenth century. They oversaw huge budgets and were the primary shapers of mission philosophy in the Protestant world. Their belief that mission work should have indigenization as its goal was ahead of its time. Their views were highly influential, but not always popular.

Native missionaries went relatively unheralded in the West, but are revered in their homelands:

- Maheanui was a Tahitian of high rank. Ordained by the London Missionary Society in 1851 he ministered in French Polynesia for many years, eventually becoming President of the Legislative Assembly. He died in 1886 after a long and fruitful ministry.[39] Beginning in 1821, Tahiti was the fountainhead from which indigenous missions would flow.

- Jose Palomo (lived 1836–1919), a Chamorro from Guam, was the first indigenous Catholic priest in the Pacific Islands. Ordained in 1859 he carried a long ministry in the Mariana Islands. He was shipped by priests to be educated in the Philippines. During his studies he even learned to speak Spanish, French, and English. When Spain relinquished Guam to the U.S. in 1899, he took a leading role in transitioning his people to a new colonial situation. He was described by an American official as "a saint on earth."[40]

- Gucheng was an evangelist in Papua New Guinea who became known for his courage as much as his piety. When he arrived to the island of Erub in the Torres Strait between Papua New Guinea and Australia, he said to the people, "Do you think I am afraid of you? I come from a country of warriors. I come here to teach you, but remember I can fight."[41] The Erub people had already killed four Christian teachers on their island, but they stood in awe of Gucheng and his wife. They were both revered in the entire Torres Strait group of islands. Gucheng trained evangelists for many years until his death in the 1880s.

- The islands of Fiji were evangelized by three indigenous Christians from French Polynesia: Taharaa, Fuatai, and Faaruea. Arriving to Fiji in 1830, these three men—commissioned by the London Missionary Society—planted the first church in Fiji. They were respected by the local Fijians, serving them until 1846. They worked primarily on the island of Oneata and two of them are buried side by side at the local church. They are still today remembered and honored as the first pastors in the area.[42]

- In Vanuatu, formerly known as the New Hebrides islands, an indigenous missionary by the name of George Sarawia emerged as an important figure in the late nineteenth-century Anglican Church. Baptized in 1863 and ordained deacon on Norfolk Island in 1868, Sarawia became, at the age of 26, "the first Melanesian clergyman."[43] He was ordained priest in 1873 at Auckland's St. Paul's Cathedral. With his good wife he had the full confidence of both European missionaries and indigenous Melanesians. With his home base in the Banks Islands of Vanuatu, Sarawia established a Christian village complete with a school and church. His ministry was rather quiet and small scale, as his health prevented him from extensive travel. He died in 1901 on his home island of Mota, having served a small flock of Christians for 35 years.

Working in a complementary relationship, leadership in the Protestant churches gradually became indigenous in the early decades of the twentieth century. The Roman Catholic Church, however, remained heavily dependent on Western leadership well into the second half of the twentieth century.

One characteristic of Protestant Christianity in Australia and New Zealand in the early twentieth century was that it began to look ecumenical. Motivated somewhat by revivalist preachers coming from the United States, Methodists and Presbyterians in particular began to think in terms of a less-fractured form of faith. Communities were scattered, and this rural setting proved helpful in bringing people of various Protestant creeds together out of necessity if they wanted to have church services at all. It was not a particularly religious culture, however. It must be remembered the cynicism toward religion in Australia ran back to its days as a penal colony. Missionaries worked to overcome this with little success. Most early missionaries to Australia and New Zealand did not minister to aboriginals; they were originally sent to the European-stock peoples. Churchgoing Australians and New Zealanders in the rural areas had no option but to become ecumenical. One could not be overly scrutinizing when it came to social gatherings such as marriage, since communities were rather sparse and spread out. Sunday Schools were built up in each town to teach Protestant children, thus further nurturing interdenominational cooperation. This dynamic did not apply to Catholics, however:

> The Roman Catholics took a different course. ... Catholic schools were to be staffed by religious sisters and teaching brothers, recruited initially from Ireland and France, and funded by the Catholic laity. ... The Roman Catholics had a church of their own.[44]

Throughout the first half of the twentieth century, Australia and New Zealand's rates of church attendance were about one-third of the population, thus perpetuating the ecumenical zeitgeist.[45] As in North America and Europe, the 1960s witnessed major social and cultural shifts in Australia and New Zealand. Partly as a consequence of the ecumenical spirit, and partly for ecclesial survival, in 1977 the Uniting Church in Australia was formed, consisting of Methodists, Congregationalists, and Presbyterians. Today, however, Australia and New Zealand are two of the most secular countries on the planet.

World War II blew the Pacific Islands onto the world's stage as Japan worked to expand its empire in the region. The results were catastrophic, lingering on in various ways. After the war, the colonial empires began to break up, beginning with Samoa's independence in 1962. France and the U.S. held on to a few territories, but Britain's influence receded.

The Protestant churches of Oceania are thoroughly indigenized today, and the territories of the region—outside of Australia and New Zealand—are highly religious. Samoa's motto, for example, illustrates a larger trend in the South Pacific: "Samoa is founded on God." The first prime minister of Vanuatu, Walter Lini, was an Anglican priest. The Roman Catholic Church has been slower to indigenize; still today the majority of priests are expatriates.[46] It has nevertheless continued to grow and is today the largest denomination in Australia. Protestant-Catholic relations have improved drastically since 1976, when the Roman Catholic Church was welcomed into full membership in the Pacific Council of Churches.[47] Pentecostalism, as elsewhere, has made major gains in Oceania:

> The 1970s and early 1980s were a period of intense revival activity throughout many parts of Melanesia. Numerous communities were swept by waves of healing, prophecy, visions, tongue speaking, and other ecstatic phenomena ... In retrospect, this era might well be seen as something of a Melanesian "great awakening."[48]

The most sizeable gains in Australia and New Zealand, however, have been made in the ranks of the nonreligious, the secular. It has been suggested that Australia may indeed be "the first genuinely post-Christian society."[49]

An indigenous, unique form of Christianity has emerged in Oceania. It is something quite different from anywhere else in the world. A fusion of Pacific culture and Christianity, Oceania is today contributing to the world church in many ways. Samoans, for example, are known for their flowing, festive liturgical dances.[50] Tonga has produced a theologian of considerable stature by the name of Sione 'Amanaki Havea. Havea has spearheaded what has become known as "coconut theology," emphasizing the indigenous character of Christianity in Oceania today:

> Before, the gospel was foreign and western. Now it is relevant and meaningful. Before, our Christ had blue eyes and spoke English or French. Now we see him brown-eyed; he speaks our language, and is one of us inclusively. Before, it was wheat and grapes, bread and wine. But they are foreign to us. Today it is the coconut. ... Bread and wine come from two different plants, but from the coconut both are from the one and same plant, just as Jesus Christ offered his body and shed his blood from himself.[51]

Oceanic Christians have also proven to be effective witnesses for the integrity of the earth, critiquing unrestrained mining, global warming, and weapons testing; long-range missiles are routinely launched in the Marshall Islands. The mining industry in Nauru "... has left 80 percent of the island unusable, leading to overcrowding."[52] Global warming threatens to completely wipe out Tuvalu, Kiribati, the Marshall Islands, and Fiji, due to rising sea levels. Tuvalu is in particularly imminent danger as most of its land is only two meters above sea level.[53] French and American nuclear testing in the past has caused radiation sickness in French Polynesia and the Marshall Islands. Perhaps the most important contribution of the Pacific churches has been its critique of war. World War II wreaked havoc on the lives of virtually all peoples in the Pacific, propelling them into modernity with all of its consequences. The World Council of Churches (WCC) points to some of the concerns of this region:

> The western world brought [to Oceania] dramatic transformations over the last 150 years. Changes in technology, energy, social services, education and health care have trapped most island cultures in dependence on developed nations. While people on the islands were once able to lead simple and independent lives, in the midst of the world economy they have become marginalized and poor. ... In addition to economic difficulties, violence and political instability mark several of these island nations.[54]

Oceanic Christianity Today

Oceania is about 80% Christian today. This number would be much higher if it were not for the strong secularization trends occurring in Australia and New Zealand. All 25 of the nations and territories that make up Oceania have a

Christian majority. In fact, 16 of them are over 90% Christian. Australia has a fairly substantial (15%) "nonreligious" segment of the population, as does New Zealand, which brings down the overall number of Christians in Oceania. Fiji is really the only country with a strong religious minority presence—Hinduism represents about a third of the Fijian population. Chinese immigration has brought members of indigenous Chinese religions to French Polynesia, Nauru, and Northern Mariana Islands, but even these numbers are small. Overall, this is a very Christianized part of the world, dominated by Protestant/Independent forms of Christianity, representing about two-thirds of the population. About one-third of Oceania is Roman Catholic. The Orthodox churches are very small at around three percent.

Australia

As mentioned throughout this chapter, Australia is one of the most secular countries in the world. This, however, does not necessarily indicate there is widespread acrimony against Christianity. As in Western Europe, there is an historic appreciation for the role of the churches; many people are simply not attending anymore. While some have labeled Australia a post-Christian society, the majority of Australians nominally affiliate with Christianity, even if only for baptisms and Christmas. In 2002, Australia's secular bent manifested itself with the "Jedi religion" phenomenon when over 70,000 people declared on their census forms that they were followers of the Star Wars allegiance to "the force." It was orchestrated by a major email campaign, but underneath the silly headlines lays a significant reality: Australians are, increasingly, becoming nonreligious. Australian Christianity continues to liberalize, although not without resistance. In 2008 the Australian Anglican Church appointed its first two female bishops, Kay Goldsworthy and Barbara Darling.[55] The Uniting Church in Australia has allowed gay clergy since 2003.[56] In recent years Australian Christians have taken an admirable stance on reconciliation with indigenous communities, offering formal apologies for wrongs committed in the past.

Fiji

Fiji's population of a million people has seen its share of political turmoil in recent times. There were military coups in the years 2000 and 2006. The military takeover of 2006 is ongoing. In April, 2009, after effectively usurping the reins of the government, Josaia Bainimarama, Commander of the military, wrote an open letter to Fijians which said:

> To facilitate the holding of true democratic and parliamentary elections I hereby abrogate the 1997 Constitution. ... I appoint myself as the Head of the State of Fiji under a new legal order. ... All judicial appointments are no longer in place. ... I

would like to take this opportunity to wish you all a happy Easter. May God Bless Fiji.[57]

As a result, in July of 2009 Fiji was expelled from the Pacific Islands Forum.

There is an ongoing conflict involving the Melanesian population and the ethnic Indian population in Fiji. Melanesians constitute 60% of the population, while ethnic Indians constitute 40%. A former British colony—receiving its independence in 1970—Fiji has the unique statistic of being the only nation in the region that contains a significant religious minority—Hinduism. The British brought Indians to work the sugar plantations in colonial times and they have become an important presence in this troubled nation of over 300 islands—about a hundred of which are inhabited.

Fijian Christianity is dominated by Protestant/Independent forms of Christianity, although the Roman Catholic Church claims around 17% of the Christian population. The Methodist Church is by far the largest denomination although the Assemblies of God have made great gains in the last two decades.

French Polynesia

French Polynesia is closely identified with the famous island of Tahiti, in the Society Islands part of the territory. The other island groups of this French territory are: the Austral, Bass, Gambier, Marquesas, and Tuamotu Islands. French Polynesia gained a reputation shortly after European contact (by the British and then the French, both in 1767) for its sexually open women, leading to widespread European-borne diseases that ravaged the region and decimated the indigenous population.[58]

Missionaries began arriving to Tahiti in the late eighteenth century and Christianity grew slowly for the first several decades. The people of Tahiti and the surrounding islands are known as Ma'ohi. They are famous in the history of Christianity in Oceania—they are the first indigenous peoples of the Pacific to establish their own indigenous ministries. A Ma'ohi chief, named Pomare, converted to Christianity around 1812 and "an almost overwhelming flood" of Ma'ohi people followed suit. The Tahitians became zealous missionaries to their own people and within only a few years began to send missionaries to surrounding islands.[59] A national church was established in 1820 and endures to this day.

The most important European missionary to French Polynesia was John Williams. His innovative technique of equipping indigenous people to evangelize their own became a hallmark method of the missionary societies in Oceania. Tahitians gained a reputation throughout the 1800s as successful missionaries to the Pacific Islands. Great enthusiasm, however, is often accompanied by movements toward autonomy, and Tahitian Christianity has seen several splits in the Protestant groups. The 60% Protestant and 40% Catholic statistics are a legacy of shifting colonial influence in French Polynesia. The British and Spanish alternated control of the territory throughout the late eighteenth and nineteenth centuries. France gained control in the 1840s.

Kiribati

Kiribati (formerly known as the Gilbert Islands) consists of the Gilbert, Phoenix, and Line Islands. Whalers, merchants, and slave traders visited the islands during the nineteenth century. In the 1890s the islands came under British protection and influence. Straddling the equator as well as the International Date Line, Kiribati is also unique for being split almost exactly in half between Catholic and Protestant/Independent Christians. Protestant Christianity was introduced to Kiribati in 1857 by two couples: Americans Hiram and Clarissa Bingham, and Hawaiians J. W. and Kaholo Kanoa. They were Congregationalists but had broad support from the highly influential American Board of Commissioners for Foreign Missions (ABCFM). Since Kiribati is just south of Hawaii, native Polynesians from Hawaii took a leading role in the evangelization of the region. Between 1857 and 1903 there were nineteen native Hawaiians sent as missionaries to Kiribati. While the churches indigenized rapidly, missionaries continued to come, especially native Samoans, who "made an enormous contribution" to the growth and development of Protestant Christianity in the late nineteenth and early twentieth centuries. Samoa provided scores of missionaries throughout that period.[60]

Roman Catholic Christianity was introduced to Kiribati by two natives of the islands—Betero Terawati and Rataro Tiroi. They had worked in Tahiti in the 1870s and 1880s, converted to Catholicism while away, and then brought the faith back home with them. They "... baptized hundreds of their countrymen and built places of worship."[61] These two unofficial missionaries lobbied France for proper missionaries, and in 1888 their wishes were granted when three Missionaries of the Sacred Heart (MSC) arrived. Protestant missionaries began arriving around the same time and Protestant/Catholic hostility lasted well into the twentieth century.

Micronesia

Micronesia (known historically as the Caroline Islands), Guam, and the Northern Mariana Islands are unique in the region as they became mainly Catholic due to early Spanish influence. Magellan landed on Guam in 1521, touching off what would become the earliest presence of Christianity on Oceanic soil. Official mission work did not begin for a century and a half however, when Jesuits established a mission on Guam in 1668. Spanish colonial rule was virtually immediate after the Jesuit missions began, leading to an influx of immigrants from Spanish territories. Many explorers and traders began intermarrying with the locals:

> Intermarriage with Spanish, Filipino and Mexican arrivals modified the Chamorro genetic inheritance, and the uniqueness of their colonial experience in this era cut the people of the Marianas off from their Micronesia neighbors.[62]

The strong Spanish influence declined rapidly when Spain sold the islands to Germany in 1899. Japan conquered the region during World War I. The United States began to assert control of the islands after defeating Japan in World War II. The Federated States of Micronesia continue a strong relationship with the U.S. to the present. The Catholic legacy of the Spanish, however, continues. Protestant Christianity arrived to Micronesia in 1852 through Congregationalist missionaries. These Congregationalists were from America and Hawaii. Only six years later, in 1858, there began to emerge an indigenous ministry in Micronesia.[63]

Nauru

The island nation of Nauru (formerly known as Pleasant Island) was for years "by far the wealthiest in the area," due to phosphate mining profits as well as offshore banking in more recent times.[64] Nauruans were unique for their wealth in the Pacific for many years, although this has changed recently. They are also unique for their distinct ethnicity. The CIA records, "The exact origins of the Nauruans are unclear since their language does not resemble any other in the Pacific."[65] Nauru is the world's smallest independent republic—only about eight square miles. In spite of Nauru's historic high per capita income, its life expectancy is not as high as one would expect, a fact blamed mainly on obesity according to the World Health Organization.[66] Nauru's population was for years among the richest and most obese in the world. Today, however, the mines—the origin of their national wealth—are nearly depleted and Nauru is scrambling for help, relying almost completely on Australian aid. The unemployment rate is presently 90% and the outlook is grim for this tiny country.[67]

Christianity arrived to Nauru by means of an indigenous Christian from Kiribati named Timoteo Tabwia. He arrived there in 1887 and worked for five years. One of Tabwia's colleagues committed adultery with the wife of a chief and this resulted in the expulsion of the missionaries. The ministry however indigenized and even today the movement started by Tabwia is the largest on the island; it goes by the name of the Nauru Congregational Church.[68]

New Caledonia

Also known as Kanaky, New Caledonia was home to the influential Lapita peoples beginning around B.C. 1500. Politically, this French territory is divided into three provinces: North, South, and the Loyalty Islands. The local government in New Caledonia has been in disarray since the 1980s, chiefly over the issue of whether it should declare complete independence from France or not.

Christianity in New Caledonia is dominated by the Roman Catholic Church, which represents over 70% of the population, obviously reflecting the French influence. Along with Guam, Federated States of Micronesia, Northern Mariana Islands, and Wallis and Futuna Islands, New Caledonia is one of the few Catholic majority nations/territories in the region. New Caledonia's people are Melanesian, but they were first evangelized by Polynesians. The first Protestant missionary was a native from Tonga who arrived in 1834.[69] The second wave, in 1840, was from Polynesian Christians from the Cook Islands and Samoa. French Catholic missionaries arrived in 1843. Evangelization took time because the people in New Caledonia were scattered into more than 20 language groups and many political units.[70]

New Zealand

New Zealanders, known as Kiwis, enjoy one of the highest standards of life in the world. Populated by the Polynesian Maori people around A.D. 800, New Zealand (also known as Aotearoa) came under British influence after the voyages of James Cook. Cook reached New Zealand in 1769 and mapped much of the country's coastline, stoking British interest. The controversial Treaty of Waitangi was signed between the British and Maori in 1840 and effectively ceded control to England, although Maori were supposedly able to keep their land and overall rights. Broken treaties led to a series of wars between the British and Maori. Those years, approximately 1840 to 1872, were fraught with difficulty for missionaries as well as the Maori who had converted to Christianity.

Christianity in New Zealand began in 1814 with an Anglican mission to the large numbers of Maori—approximately 100,000—as well as to the few white settlers.[71] It grew steadily and by 1838 included 35 full-time workers, 21 schools, and over 2,000 people in regular church attendance. Methodist missionaries arrived in 1822 in the north of the country. An Irish Catholic priest began work in New Zealand in 1828, representing the first Roman Catholic presence. Presbyterians began work there in 1839.[72] British missionaries worked with Maori to construct a written language in the 1830s, resulting eventually in a complete Maori-language Bible. Literacy proved to be an effective tool for evangelism as Maori were taught to read and write by using the

Christian scriptures. British sources show that the Maori were quick learners and by 1831 they were preaching, teaching, and conducting missionary efforts all over New Zealand.[73] The first ordination of a Maori however did not occur until 1853, when Rota Waitoa was ordained a deacon. The slow progress of Maori ordination was due to the reluctance of the powerful bishop George Selwyn who exerted tremendous authority in all ecclesial matters in New Zealand for three decades in the 1840s through the 1860s.[74] Towards the end of his career, Bishop Selwyn began ordaining Maori, but many thought he should have taken the step much earlier.

The largest denominations in New Zealand today are, in order: Anglican, Presbyterian, Catholic, and Methodist. The fastest rates of growth, however, are in the Pentecostal and Evangelical churches.[75]

Papua New Guinea

Papua New Guinea is the eastern half of the island of New Guinea and includes many surrounding islands as well. (The Western side was annexed by Indonesia in the 1960s and its status remains highly controversial.) With a population of around six million, Papua New Guinea is the second most populated country in Oceania. Many of the islanders, especially in the interior, have only been in significant contact with the outside world for a few decades. Some of the most remote people-groups in the world are in Papua New Guinea. In the early days of European contact this large island was treacherous:

> Missionary losses due to cannibalism were not uncommon in the early days; and during World War II, other missionaries together with their Christian followers were killed and their buildings destroyed. The stone-age peoples of the Highlands were not reached until after 1950, and little progress was made for another decade.[76]

Catholic missionaries arrived to Papua New Guinea in 1847, although the work did not last. A continuing Catholic presence took root in 1881 through the work of Sacred Heart missionaries. Protestant Christian missionaries associated with the London Missionary Society (LMS) arrived to Papua New Guinea in 1871. They were Lifou Christians, from the Loyalty Islands, in modern-day New Caledonia. These years seem rather late, but this lateness was largely because the Papuan peoples were Melanesian, black-skinned, and culturally different from the Southeast Asian peoples of the East Indies. The Dutch, who had a major, colonial presence in the region, came to regard the Melanesians as primitive, backward, and on the far reaches of their empire. The tribes were disunited, the region was dangerous, and communication was difficult because each tribe—often hostile and xenophobic—spoke a language known only to their members. As a result, the Europeans made little effort in Papua New Guinea until 1898, when Dutch government stations were finally set up. Prior to that, the mission work was scant and baptisms were scarce. By the year 1900, there were only 200 Christian converts in this entire, vast island.[77] Within a few years of a colonial establishment, however, large numbers of Papuans converted to Christianity, primarily under the influence of Malay-speaking teachers, known as "gurus." The Malay Christians were highly effective not only in planting churches, but also in indigenizing Christianity in the region by training leading men for ministry.

Papua New Guinea is today a highly Christianized country. There are scores of denominations doing ministry and mission work in the region, especially Bible translators intent on increasing literacy rates so that the locals can read the word of God in their own tongue. Cargo cults, although relatively uncommon, have fascinated Westerners due to their strange mixtures of primitive magic with Christianity. It is estimated there are around 35 cargo cults in Papua New Guinea. This number is deceptive, however, as defining a cargo cult is not always easy, and these indigenous movements often transition into more orthodox forms of Christianity through the years.

Papua New Guinea is today around 95% Christian, primarily Protestant. The leading denominations, in order, are: Catholics, Evangelical Lutheran, United Church, and Seventh-Day Adventists. When Pentecostals are all added together they amount to around 10% of the country's population.[78]

Samoa

Samoa, historically the Navigator Islands, is known for two important facts in the history of Christianity in Oceania. First, Samoans have an illustrious history of "native agency," or, conducting indigenous mission work without assistance from Europeans. The brainchild of the London Missionary Society, native agency proved remarkably successful in winning converts in the Pacific. Second, Samoa was the first Pacific nation to declare independence, in 1962, touching off a new era in the churches of Oceania.

Like several nations and territories in the South Pacific, Samoa fell under German rule for a time in the late nineteenth and early twentieth centuries, although that ended in World War I when New Zealand administered the region. Part of the Samoan Islands, known as American Samoa, remains a territory of the United States.

Christianity arrived in 1830 with the work of LMS missionary John Williams along with a group of Tahitian teachers commissioned for ministry in Samoa by Williams. The legacy left by this early group is still alive, as the Congregational Church is still the largest in the country. After that are the following, in order of membership: the Catholic Church, Methodists, Mormons, Assemblies of God, and Seventh-Day Adventists. Samoa is almost entirely Christian.[79]

Solomon Islands

Named by the Spanish navigator Alvaro de Mendana de Neira (lived 1542–1595), the Solomon Islands were initially thought to be the location of Ophir—a biblical port that, according to legend, had provided King Solomon with abundant riches. Quite a capable seaman, Mendana de Neira was an utter failure in his attempts to get along with islanders. His encounters with local peoples nearly always ended violently.[80]

Christianity took root in the Solomon Islands in the 1880s. As in most places in the Pacific Islands, the work was conducted primarily by fellow Oceanic peoples. One important example of indigenous missions comes from the Solomon Islands, the Melanesian Brotherhood, "... the largest male religious community in the Anglican Communion."[81] The Melanesian Brotherhood was founded in 1925 by Ini Kopuria, a policeman in the Solomon Islands. In 1925 Kopuria decided to renounce his possessions and conduct missionary work to the remotest villages that he could manage to find. Six men joined him the following year, establishing an important, indigenous venture that quickly made an impact in the region.[82]

> In a pattern which is also reminiscent of Jesus' disciples (Lk. 10), the lay brothers went out to the communities, accepting their hospitality and offering practical help with fishing, house-building and other tasks, as well as sharing Christian teaching. Many responded to the message when they saw that the brothers were unafraid of devils and ancestral spirits.[83]

The Melanesian Brotherhood continues to be a significant presence in the region, particularly through their peacemaking efforts.

The Melanesian Solomon Islands are almost entirely Christian today, dominated by Protestant forms of the faith which, as in most Oceanic countries, operate ecumenically. In close relations with the government of the U.K. since 1890, this nation of over 1000 islands has been unstable for the last several years due to "ethnic violence, government malfeasance, and endemic crime."[84] There was a coup in the Solomon Islands in the year 2000 that rendered the government ineffective. Still today the status of the government is in transition and a multinational peacekeeping force led by Australia works to quell the ethnic violence.

Tonga

Christianity in Tonga began disastrously when three missionaries were massacred in 1799. Several Wesleyan missions attempted work in the region during the early nineteenth century to little avail until 1834, when a chief by the name of Taufa'ahau became a Christian after hearing the gospel from Pita Vi, one of the first Tongan Christians. Chief Taufa'ahau later became King of all Tonga and took the name George Tupou I. He played a huge role in the evangelization of Tonga's 160 or so islands. Taufa'ahau effectively Christianized his people due to his keen interest in the new faith, as well as the fact that he ruled from 1845 to 1893. During these years, Christian missionaries, both Oceanic as well as Western, were welcomed to Tonga. Literacy was strongly advocated by the king and Tongans quickly gained a reputation for being among the most literate and capable amongst the Pacific peoples.[85]

Tongans are largely Christianized, although there is a fairly substantial (7%) presence of the Bahai Faith. By and large, Tongans are Protestants. The Wesleyan Church is the largest there. One interesting aspect of Christianity in Tonga is that the Church of Jesus Christ of Latter-Day Saints has a strong presence—about 14% of Tongans are Mormon. The LDS church has had a presence since 1891 and even has a temple there. The LDS church is very proud of this island nation due to its having "... the largest number of Mormons per capita of any nation in the world."[86]

Tonga, known popularly as "the Friendly Islands," is the only Constitutional Monarchy in Oceania today. The current king, George Tupou V, educated at Oxford and Cambridge, has taken steps to lead Tonga into a new era of democracy after the citizens rioted in 2006, demanding a more democratic government.[87]

Three Questions for Analysis

1. What are the core reasons Christianity proved so successful in Oceania?

2. What impacts does water make on Oceanic society? In what ways are island identities different from mainland identities?

3. What larger human truths are revealed by the cargo cult phenomenon?

AFTERWORD

What does Christianity mean? If Jared Diamond is correct, human origins go back seven million years, although the first five or six million years occurred in Africa.[1] Christianity has only been around for about two thousand years. Is Christianity simply a blip on the radar of human history, or is it the fulfillment of humanity? Obviously there is no way to gauge this sort of thing, but for Christians, the question cannot be denied. One in three humans roaming the world today bears the label Christian. According to predictions, the combined total of Christians and Muslims—already at over 50% of the world's population—will continue to grow. It remains to be seen which of these religions will grow faster. It is perplexing, however, to wonder why the human population is not more diverse. Why have Christianity and Islam emerged to become so influential on a global scale? Clearly, the life of Jesus has had a mammoth influence on human societies in a relatively short amount of time.

It is striking how many basic facts about world religions are not generally known. I suppose most scholars experience a similar reaction regarding fundamental knowledge in their own fields. Nevertheless, during the writing of this book, I was surprised to learn that many people do not realize just how globally prominent the Christian faith has become. This is shocking because the general statistics for world religions are in the public domain, and have been for decades. In *The Next Christendom*, Philip Jenkins wrote of the "dazzling levels of ignorance about the basic facts" of Christianity:

> Whatever the value of Christian claims to truth, it [Christianity] cannot be considered as just one religion out of many; it is, and will continue to be, by far the largest in existence. A generation ago, the neglect of Christianity in academic teaching made more sense than it does today, in that students could be expected to absorb information about the faith from churches, families, or from society at large. Today, though, that is often not a realistic expectation.[2]

The fact that, globally, one in three people calls him or herself a Christian warrants at least a basic understanding of this faith. It is increasingly vital that university students learn the basic tenets of the world religions, including global trends and general statistics such as those outlined in this book. Religion is not peripheral to human experience and current affairs. It is critical to know, for instance, why the Israel-Palestine problem has continued for so long. It is important to understand the root causes of the Marxist revolutions in the twentieth century. It should be assumed that university students will be exposed to the Quran and the Christian Bible, simply to understand the daily news, which is increasingly of a global nature.

My job, as a historian of religion, is to help people contextualize their reading of history by providing direction in the field of religion. In my case, Christianity is the religion I am most familiar with and have spent the most time studying. Therefore, it is incumbent upon me to cast light on the written record, and on current events, by illustrating just how, and in what ways, Christianity plays a part in the larger discourse. How did Christianity shape a particular debate? What does the history of Christianity have to say to this or that issue? How deep are the roots of a particular cultural phenomenon? For example, why are bombs going off in Pakistan as I write this? Why does Mahmoud Ahmadinejad continue to deny the Jewish holocaust? Why was it so controversial for Galileo to argue that the sun, not the earth, was at the center of the universe? How did the Protestant Reformation impact the rise of the nation-state, capitalism, and European secularization? Why is Latin America almost entirely Christian today? Why is Christianity so closely linked to the state in many sub-Saharan nations? Why isn't transatlantic slavery still legal? How did the university become so central in the development of human societies in the modern era? These are crucial matters, not peripheral. Understanding the Christian components involved in each of these big issues helps to better contextualize why things evolved the way they did, and not another way.

In 1968, anthropologist Clifford Geertz published an excellent little volume called *Islam Observed: Religious Development in Morocco and Indonesia.*[3] Geertz took an immensely complicated topic, Islam, and, by using two case studies, outlined the intricate developments of a transcontinental faith. The result was a carefully reasoned comparison of a faith that is both united yet highly variegated in different social contexts. Today, it is possible for scholars to do the same thing, yet on a larger scale, with Christianity. It is now possible to analyze how Christianity functions in Oceania, North America, Africa, Latin America, Western Europe, Asia, the Middle East, and Eastern Europe. Amidst the vast complexity, there is unity. All Christians hold to some fundamental texts, beliefs, and rituals. Today, "Christianity Observed" would be a study of humans in all inhabited parts of the world. No other religion presents quite the same opportunities for studying human life as does Christianity. Islam comes to mind, but Islam is statistically insignificant in Latin America and the Caribbean. In North America and Oceania it is tiny, only one or two percent. Thus, it would be difficult to offer a truly global understanding of Islam because Islam has yet to significantly impact several cultural blocks in the world.

The academic study of Christianity will become, I believe, more important in the study of human civilizations in the future. The social sciences and the humanities can scarcely avoid dealing with Christianity. Christianity presents a very helpful lens for observing human culture. Endless comparative analyses can be made by looking at Christianity as a global institution. Marriage, government, language: these are all excellent perspectives for understanding humans. However, there is something very interesting about this comparatively recent phenomenon—Christianity—and observing how it interacts with people from all eight of the world's cultural blocks. There is an ever-growing body of research that is attempting to do this, and it is fascinating. Christianity has affected the ethos of human cultures profoundly, yet very differently. The end result is a religion that spans the globe, united in some things, yet marvelously variegated in others.

We are still left with the question: What does Christianity mean? No doubt, to some readers, Christianity will be seen as having played a critical role in many great human achievements: scientific advance, the university, endless human relief efforts across the globe, increased literacy, and expanded opportunities for women. Others will see Christianity as a concomitant to what is perceived as being the atrocious nature of European expansion. These readers might understand Christianity to have promoted slavery, oppressed women, suppressed human freedom and expression, and stifled scientific advance from Roman times until the chains of religion began to be unlocked during the so-called enlightenment. Such is the nature of any historical movement or institution; there are two ways of seeing it. Like Mark Twain's "Two Ways of Seeing a River," some will see disease underneath the rose-tinted surface while others will be mesmerized by the providential stamina, grace, and beauty of the Christian faith. I suppose the twin temptations of unequivocal praise and wholesale rejection have always been the polar responses to a potentially volatile topic like religion. A historically sophisticated approach, however, demonstrates the messiness of an epoch or institution, yet in the clearest way possible.

One thing seems certain, at least in the short term. Christianity will continue to grow in the global South, while it recedes in the Euro-American world. The jury is still out on what trends may actually be going on in the USA, but a strong sense of secularization has already settled into the social fibers of Western Europe. Probably the most conspicuous trend that all scholars of Christianity should be coming to terms with is how different Chinese Christianity, African Christianity, and other non-Western Christianities have become. While there are certainly Anglicans in India that practice the faith in the distinctly British way they were taught, there are far more examples of new experiences that defy Western conceptions of Christianity. Many books and films are documenting a very interesting development: global South Christians seem to have little connection to the West. In fact, global Southerners often see the West as a grand mission field, a spiritual wasteland in need of the gospel. What goes around has come around indeed! The interplay of globalization and world Christianity will continue to yield fruit for academic research. From a larger perspective, there are two ways to interpret this: globalization is radically changing the nature of Christianity; however, Christianity has deeply impacted globalization, resulting in what we may call Christobalization. Those mission-minded idealists in the late nineteenth and early twentieth century who envisioned world evangelization may not have been so unrealistic after all.

Recently, one of my colleagues, with whom I frequently play basketball, finished a major project. I asked him how he felt about it. His response was vivid: "I left it all on the court." I suppose that is how I feel about this project. I left it all there. The problem, however, is that I cannot leave it there. By studying the history of Christianity through the lenses of population trends, conversion rates, immigration, fertility, geographical diversity, politics, persecution, oppression, colonialism, and war, I have only created more questions for myself. In addition, the data changes often, and those changes can significantly impact interpretations of World Christianity.

Dyron B. Daughrity
Malibu, California
Reformation Day/All Hallows' Eve, 2009

NOTES

World Rankings

1. The sources for statistical data are: the CIA World Factbook, the World Christian Database, and the U.S. Department of State's 2008 Report on International Religious Freedom. Statistics were accessed throughout the year 2009.

Chapter One: Christianity the Largest Faith

1. Most scholars believe Jesus was probably born in the year 4 BC and died around 30 AD.

2. See David B. Barrett, *World Christian Encyclopedia, 2nd edition* (Oxford: Oxford University Press, 2001), p. 7.

3. The percentages of world religious adherents are widely available and there is slight variation in reputable sources as there is no one authoritative database. Currently, three of the most comprehensive sources for worldwide religious statistics are the Central Intelligence Agency (CIA) of the government of the United States of America, the *World Christian Encyclopedia*—a resource originally intended for Christian academics in the 1980s but has evolved into a major source for world religion due to its statistical rigor, and the website Adherents.com. The *CIA World Factbook* lists Christianity as 33.32%, Islam as 21.01%, Hinduism as 13.26%, Buddhism as 5.84%. Every other religion is less than half a percent. For example, Sikhism is listed fifth with .35%. See https://www.cia.gov/library/publications/the-world-factbook/. The *World Christian Encyclopedia* (WCE) was last printed in the year 2001 but continues to update its statistics through an academic website associated with Brill Publishing called "The World Christian Database." See: http://www.worldchristiandatabase.org/wcd/. The 2001 edition of the WCE lists Christianity as 33.0%, Islam as 19.6%, Hinduism as 13.4%, and Buddhism as 5.9%. The WCE also groups the various Chinese religions under one heading "Chinese folk-religionists" and has that category listed as 6.4%. A scholarly review of the WCE was completed recently by Becky Hsu, Amy Reynolds, Conrad Hackett, and James Gibbon, of Princeton University. See: http://www.princeton.edu/~bhsu/Hsu2008.pdf. Adherents.com has two advantages: it draws from 43,000 different surveys into its overall numbers, and it rounds off the numbers in order to avoid tenths of percentages. Adherents.com lists Christianity as 33%, Islam as 21%, Hinduism as 14%, and Buddhism as 6%. It is important to note that the

well-known and respected Pew Forum has begun a major research project to map the religious world, country by country. Pew injected new life into the religious statistics early on in their study when they figured Islam constitutes 23% of the world's population. This statistic for Islam is rather high and is attracting major scholarly attention. Pew Forum plans to generate statistics for world Christianity in the year 2010. See www.pewforum.org.

4. Harm De Blij, *The Power of Place: Geography, Destiny, and Globalization's Rough Landscape* (Oxford: Oxford University Press, 2008), p. 57.

5. Donald Johnson and Jean Elliot Johnson, *Universal Religions in World History: The Spread of Buddhism, Christianity, and Islam to 1500* (New York: McGraw Hill, 2007).

6. It should also be noted that Armenia, known to Armenians as Hayastan, is a strongly Christian country.

7. It should be noted that this fact is debatable. Some scholars argue that the Indonesian government has for political reasons actually superimposed the identity "Muslim" on people who have little to do with Islam, particularly those from tribal and rural areas of Indonesia. Pakistan may well have the most Muslims in the world.

8. The Iberian Peninsula consists primarily of Spain and Portugal.

9. Wilbert R. Shenk, ed., *Enlarging the Story: Perspectives on Writing World Christian History* (Maryknoll: Orbis, 2002), xii. We must point out that Christianity was actually more of an "Eastern" faith until well into the second millennium AD. In other words, Christianity was more affiliated with the Eastern side of the Roman Empire and Central Asia until 1100 or so. We will unpack this "Eastern" part of the story in chapters two and three.

10. Shenk, Enlarging the Story, xi–xiii.

11. Mary Farrell Bednarowski, ed., *Twentieth-Century Global Christianity* (Minneapolis: Fortress Press, 2008), 32–33.

12. Paul Freston, "The Changing Face of Christian Proselytizing: New Actors from the Global South Transforming Old Debates," ch. 5 in *Proselytization Revisited: Rights Talk, Free Markets and Culture Wars* (London: Equinox, 2008) ed. by Rosalind Hackett.

13. See Dyron B. Daughrity, *Bishop Stephen Neill: From Edinburgh to South India* (New York: Peter Lang, 2008).

14. Tim Stafford, "Historian Ahead of His Time," *Christian History and Biography* 51:2 (February 2007), 87.

15. Today it is known as the Centre for the Study of World Christianity.

16. Philip Jenkins, *The Next Christendom: The Coming of Global Christianity* (Oxford University Press, 2007).

17. Lamin Sanneh and Joel Carpenter, eds., *The Changing Face of Christianity: Africa, the West, and the World* (Oxford: Oxford University Press, 2005).

18. CIA World Factbook.

19. *CIA World Factbook*. France hovers just under the two-children-per-woman mark, but the others are far from that benchmark.

20. Stephen Neill, *A History of Christian Mission*, p. 559.

21. See Franklin Foer, "Baptism by Celluloid," *New York Times*, February 8, 2004, http://www.nytimes.com/2004/02/08/movies/baptism-by-celluloid.html?pagewanted=all (accessed August 27, 2009). See also Giles Wilson, "The Most Watched Film in History," *BBC News Online Magazine*, July 21, 2003, located at: http://news.bbc.co.uk/1/hi/magazine/3076809.stm (accessed August 27, 2009).

22. See: http://www.jesusfilm.org/.http://www.jesusfilm.org/.

Chapter Two: Middle Eastern Christianity

1. The Palestinian Authority governs the Gaza Strip and the West Bank and is not normally recognized as an official country; it is generally viewed as a partially self-governing region.

2. For world fertility rates, see the Web site for the Population Reference Bureau (PRB): www.prb.org. See also Christine Eickelman, "Oil, Fertility, and Women's Status in Oman," in *Everyday Life in the Muslim Middle East* (2nd edition), ed. by Donna Lee Bowen and Evelyn A. Early (Indianapolis: Indiana University Press, 2002).

3. Donna Lee Bowen and Evelyn A. Early, eds., *Everyday Life in the Muslim Middle East* (2nd edition), p. 1.

4. See http://travel.state.gov/travel/cis_pa_tw/cis/cis_1012.html (accessed September 26, 2009).

5. CIA World Factbook. The BBC reports that in the United Arab Emirates less than one percent of the population votes. Furthermore, those voters are selected by the government. See http://news.bbc.co.uk/2/hi/middle_east/6185199.stm (accessed September 26, 2009).

6. Esposito and Mogahed, *Who Speaks for Islam?: What a Billion Muslims Really Think* (New York: Gallup Press, 2007), pp. 47–48.

7. Esposito and Mogahed, *Who Speaks for Islam*, p. 49.

8. For an advanced analysis of the similarities and differences of Christianity and Islam in the Middle East, see Sidney H. Griffith, *The Church in the Shadow of the Mosque: Christians and Muslims in the World of Islam* (Princeton, New Jersey: Princeton University Press, 2008).

9. Sidney H. Griffith, *The Church in the Shadow of the Mosque*, p. 11.

10. Philip Jenkins, *The Lost History of Christianity*, pp. 155–156.

11. Noel Davies and Martin Conway, *World Christianity in the 20th Century*, p. 95.

12. For a study of Christianity among the Arabs prior to the advent of Islam, see J. Spencer Trimingham, *Christianity Among the Arabs in Pre-Islamic Times* (Immeuble Esseily, Place Riad Solh, Beirut: Librairie Du Liban, 1979).

13. Sidney H. Griffith, *The Church in the Shadow of the Mosque*, p. 48.

14. Sidney H. Griffith, *The Church in the Shadow of the Mosque*, p. 50.

15. Sidney H. Griffith, *The Church in the Shadow of the Mosque*, p. 60.

16. Sidney H. Griffith, *The Church in the Shadow of the Mosque*, p. 63.

17. Sidney H. Griffith, *The Church in the Shadow of the Mosque*, p. 2.

18. Sidney H. Griffith, *The Church in the Shadow of the Mosque*, p. 4.

19. See Robin E. Waterfield, *Christians in Persia: Assyrians, Armenians, Roman Catholics, and Protestants* (New York: Harper & Row Publishers, 1973).

20. Philip Jenkins, *The Lost History of Christianity*, p. 61.

21. Robin E. Waterfield, *Christians in Persia: Assyrians, Armenians, Roman Catholics, and Protestants*, p. 17.

22. The School of Edessa's history is closely related to the history of a nearby city known as Nisibis. Both of these cities are today in Turkey along the Turkey-Syria border. The School of Nisibis gave birth to many other centers of learning. The best study of the School of Nisibis is Adam H. Becker, *The School of Nisibis and Christian Scholastic Culture in Late Antique Mesopotamia* (Philadelphia: University of Pennsylvania Press, 2006).

23. Robin E. Waterfield, *Christians in Persia: Assyrians, Armenians, Roman Catholics, and Protestants*, p. 17. Eventually the Syriac churches favored the *Peshitta*, or, the Syriac Bible.

24. Robin E. Waterfield, Christians in Persia: Assyrians, Armenians, Roman Catholics, and Protestants, p. 17.

25. For the most part I have followed the typology outlined by Betty Jane Bailey and J. Martin Bailey in *Who Are the Christians in the Middle East?* (Grand Rapids, Michigan: Wm. B. Eerdmans, 2003).

26. The Assyrian Church of the East has been placed into the Orthodox family of Churches in this book in order to avoid confusion. Nevertheless, we may point out here that the Assyrian Church of the East, also known as the Nestorian Church, is unique. Part of the Church joined the Roman Catholic family in the sixteenth century, but many did not. The Assyrian Church has been one of the more persecuted Christian bodies in history, which accounts for why the Patriarch residence was moved from Iraq to the USA around the year 1940, where it remains indefinitely.

27. Noel Davies and Martin Conway, *World Christianity in the 20th Century*, p. 92.

28. Betty Jane Bailey and J. Martin Bailey, *Who Are the Christians in the Middle East?* p. 52.

29. Philip Jenkins, *The Lost History of Christianity*, p. 156.

30. Philip Jenkins, *The Lost History of Christianity*, pp. 158–161.

31. Philip Jenkins, *The Lost History of Christianity*, p. 163.

32. Philip Jenkins, *The Lost History of Christianity*, p. 149.

33. Betty Jane Bailey and J. Martin Bailey, *Who Are the Christians in the Middle East?* p. 160.

34. Betty Jane Bailey and J. Martin Bailey, *Who Are the Christians in the Middle East?* p. 161.

35. See: http://2001-2009.state.gov/g/drl/rls/irf/2008/108482.htm.

36. See http://news.bbc.co.uk/2/hi/middle_east/7294078.stm (accessed September 26, 2009).

37. Added together, Christians and Muslims constitute over half of the world's population.

38. Betty Jane Bailey and J. Martin Bailey, *Who Are the Christians in the Middle East?* pp. 155–156.

39. Betty Jane Bailey and J. Martin Bailey, *Who Are the Christians in the Middle East?* p. 182.

40. Betty Jane Bailey and J. Martin Bailey, *Who Are the Christians in the Middle East?*, p. 192.

41. See: http://2001-2009.state.gov/g/drl/rls/irf/2008/108493.htm.

42. Betty Jane Bailey and J. Martin Bailey, *Who Are the Christians in the Middle East?*, p. 196.

Chapter Three: Eastern European Christianity

1. Carl Haub, "Tracking Trends in Low Fertility Countries: An Uptick in Europe?" "Over the long term, TFRs (total fertility rates) below 2.1 children per woman can eventually lead to population decline because couples are not replacing themselves in the population. Many European countries have been far below the 2.1 replacement level for years and some are experiencing population decline as a result." See: http://www.prb.org/Articles/2008/tfrtrendsept08.aspx.

2. James Rodgers, "Putin Shines Spotlight on Population Fears," May 10, 2006. See the BBC News website: http://news.bbc.co.uk/1/hi/world/europe/4758695.stm.

3. The Population Reference Bureau reports that it is too early to predict whether or not the historically low fertility rate trends have "hit bottom." Carl Haub, "Tracking Trends in Low Fertility Countries: An Uptick in Europe?" See: http://www.prb.org/Articles/2008/tfrtrendsept08.aspx.

4. Clifford J. Levy, "Its Population Falling, Russia Beckons Its Children Home," *New York Times*, March 21, 2009, located at: http://www.nytimes.com/2009/03/22/world/europe/22believers.html?hp.

5. Clifford J. Levy, "Its Population Falling, Russia Beckons Its Children Home," *New York Times*, March 21, 2009, located at: http://www.nytimes.com/2009/03/22/world/europe/22believers.html?hp (accessed September 29, 2009).

6. See the "Transnational Issues" for the CIA World Factbook site for Kosovo: https://www.cia.gov/library/publications/the-world-factbook/geos/kv.html.

7. Jerry Bentley, Herbert Ziegler, Heather Streets, *Traditions and Encounters: A Brief Global History* (New York: McGraw Hill), p. 590.

8. Serge Schmemann, "Russian Orthodox Church: Soul of Russia," *National Geographic* (April, 2009). This quotation comes from page seven of the online version: http://ngm.nationalgeographic.com/2009/04/orthodox/schmemann-text.

9. Erik Kulavig, *Dissent in the Years of Khrushchev* (New York: Palgrave Macmillan, 2003), p. 39.

10. While Communist, the Yugoslavian countries led by long-time dictator Josip Tito (ruled 1953–1980), at least in theory tried to steer a "non-aligned" middle path between the Western allies and the Soviet Union. Tito's regime was officially socialist and for a brief time connected itself to the USSR. The former country of Yugoslavia is broken today into several countries including Bosnia and Herzegovina, Croatia, Macedonia, Montenegro, Serbia, Slovenia, and Kosovo.

11. David Melling, "Autocephalous," in *The Blackwell Dictionary of Eastern Christianity* (Oxford: Blackwell, 1999), p. 73.

12. Paul Mojzes, "Orthodoxy under Communism," p. 152.

13. Timothy Ware, *The Orthodox Church*, p. 85.

14. Serge Schmemann, "Russian Orthodox Church: Soul of Russia," *National Geographic* (April, 2009). This quotation comes from page seven of the online version: http://ngm.nationalgeographic.com/2009/04/orthodox/schmemann-text.

15. Timothy Ware, *The Orthodox Church*, p. 115.

16. Paul Mojzes, "Orthodoxy under Communism," in Mary Farrell Bednarowski, ed., *Twentieth-Century Global Christianity* (Minneapolis: Fortress Press, 2008), pp. 138, 142.

17. Paul Mojzes, "Orthodoxy under Communism," in Mary Farrell Bednarowski, ed., *Twentieth-Century Global Christianity* (Minneapolis: Fortress Press, 2008), p. 155. I am indebted to this chapter by Mojzes—a long-time scholar of Eastern Orthodoxy in Eastern Europe—for this section of the chapter. There are many introductory books and articles intended to help the Western mind understand Eastern Orthodoxy. Mojzes's article is one of the best due to its focus on the common worshiper and larger trends among the Orthodox people during the twentieth century. This is a departure from the traditional historiography which tends to highlight patriarchs and major leaders.

18. Mojzes, "Orthodoxy under Communism," p. 141. Italics are mine and are intended to contrast Orthodox priests martyred with Roman Catholic priests currently serving in America.

19. *Missionary Research* 33.1 (January 2009). Presently, there are approximately 44,700 Catholic priests serving in the United States of America.

20. Paul Mojzes, "Orthodoxy under Communism," p. 145.

21. Timothy Ware, *The Orthodox Church*, p. 167.

22. "Atheization" is a neologism used by some scholars to refer to the Marxist policies of the Soviet Union against religion. See Paul Mojzes, "Orthodoxy under Communism," p. 146.

23. Timothy Ware, *The Orthodox Church*, pp. 311–12.

24. See the CIA World Factbook entry for Greece:
https://www.cia.gov/library/publications/the-world-factbook/geos/gr.html.

25. See the U.S. Department of State's International Religious Freedom Report 2008 (IRFR 2008) and its entry for Greece. See:
http://2001-2009.state.gov/g/drl/rls/irf/2008/108449.htm.

26. Kenneth Scott Latourette, *A History of Christianity: Reformation to the Present* (Peabody, MA: Prince Press, 1975), p. 740.

27. Margaret Macmillan, *Paris 1919: Six Months that Changed the World* (New York: Random House, 2003), pp. 247, 263.

28. See BBC News, "Timeline: Hungary" at
http://news.bbc.co.uk/1/hi/world/europe/country_profiles/1054642.stm.

29. See *Ecumenical News International*, December 17, 2007:
http://www.eni.ch/highlights/news.shtml?2007/12.

30. For drop in vocations, see *Ecumenical News International*, February 11, 2008: http://www.eni.ch/featured/article.php?id=1621. For Polish priests' attitudes on celibacy, see Adam Easton, "Polish Church under growing pressure," February 15, 2009, BBC News, located at: http://news.bbc.co.uk/2/hi/europe/7884472.stm (accessed September 26, 2009).

31. Timothy Ware, *The Orthodox Church*, p. 168.

32. Mircea Pacurariu, "Romanian Christianity," chapter 9 in *The Blackwell Companion to Eastern Christianity*, ed. Ken Perry (Oxford: Blackwell, 2007). For the quotations, see pp. 202–203.

33. Timothy Ware, *The Orthodox Church*, p. 168.

34. Mircea Pacurariu, "Romanian Christianity," in *The Blackwell Companion to Eastern Christianity*, ed. Ken Perry (Oxford: Blackwell, 2007). On the ancient sources for Romanian Christianity, see pp. 186–89.

35. G.E.H. Palmer, Philip Sherrard and Bishop Kallistos (Timothy) Ware, *Philokallia: The Eastern Christian Spirituality Texts* (Woodstock, Vermont: Skylight Paths, 2006).

36. G.E.H. Palmer, Philip Sherrard and Bishop Kallistos (Timothy) Ware, *Philokallia: The Eastern Christian Spirituality Texts*, p. vii.

37. One of the best, recent articles on the current state of the church in Russia is Serge Schmemann, "Russian Orthodox Church: Soul of Russia," in *National Geographic* (April, 2009). Much of this section comes from that splendid article. It is located online at: http://ngm.nationalgeographic.com/2009/04/orthodox/schmemann-text.

38. Serge Schmemann, "Russian Orthodox Church: Soul of Russia," in *National Geographic* (April, 2009). This quotation comes from p. 4 of the online version: http://ngm.nationalgeographic.com/2009/04/orthodox/schmemann-text/4.

39. Serge Schmemann, "Russian Orthodox Church: Soul of Russia," *National Geographic* (April, 2009). This quotation comes from p. 7 of the online version: http://ngm.nationalgeographic.com/2009/04/orthodox/schmemann-text/7. Alexy II

was the previous Patriarch of all Russia. He died in 2008. The new Patriarch is Kirill I, elected in 2009.

40. John Binns, *An Introduction to the Christian Orthodox Churches* (Cambridge: University Press, 2002), p. 198.

41. Timothy Ware, *The Orthodox Church*, p. 169.

42. Paul Mojzes, "Orthodoxy under Communism," p. 152.

43. Timothy Ware, *The Orthodox Church*, p. 95; see also pp. 164–66.

44. Timothy Ware, *The Orthodox Church*, p. 165.

45. Peter Galadza, "Easter Catholic Christianity," in *The Blackwell Companion to Eastern Christianity*, ed. by Ken Parry (Oxford: Blackwell, 2007). The numbers come from the table on p. 292. The Syro-Malabar Catholic Church of South India, the Maronite Catholic Church of Lebanon, and the Melkite Greek Catholic Church of the Middle East are the Eastern-Rite (Greek) Catholic Churches that have over a million members. In all, there are over 20 Greek Catholic denominations.

46. Philip Jenkins, *The Next Christendom* (Oxford: University Press, 2007), p. 247.

47. See Alan Cullison, "WSJ: Man With a Mission," *Wall Street Journal*, July 21, 2006, pg. A.1.

Chapter Four: Western European Christianity

1. Philip Jenkins, The Next Christendom: The Coming of Global Christianity (Oxford: Oxford University Press, 2002), p. 1.

2. Mary Farrell Bednarowski, "Multiplicity and Ambiguity," in *Twentieth-Century Global Christianity* (Minneapolis: Fortress Press, 2008), p. 32.

3. Mary Farrell Bednarowski, "Multiplicity and Ambiguity," in *Twentieth-Century Global Christianity*, p. 33.

4. Mary Farrell Bednarowski, "Multiplicity and Ambiguity," in *Twentieth-Century Global Christianity*, p. 33.

5. Ian Fisher, "Pope Warns Against Secularization in Germany," *New York Times*, September 10, 2006, located online at:
http://www.nytimes.com/2006/09/10/world/europe/11pope.web.html?pagewanted=1&_r=1.

6. Philip Jenkins, *The Next Christendom, Revised and Expanded Edition* (Oxford: Oxford University Press, 2007), p. 3.

7. Philip Jenkins, *God's Continent: Christianity, Islam, and Europe's Religious Crisis* (Oxford: Oxford University Press, 2007), p. 6.

8. A good American example of this tendency was covered in a *New York Times* series called "Remade in America" that ran in 2009. This quotation comes from Denise Grady, "Foreign Ways and War Scars Test U.S. Clinic," *New York Times*, March 28, 2009.

9. Rowan Williams's lecture can be found on the Web site for the Archbishop of Canterbury: http://www.archbishopofcanterbury.org/1575.

10. See "Sharia Law in UK is 'Unavoidable'" on the BBC website, dated February 7, 2008: http://news.bbc.co.uk/2/hi/uk_news/7232661.stm.

11. See Dipesh Gadher, Abul Taher and Christopher Morgan, "Rowan Williams faces backlash over sharia," *The Times Online*, February 10, 2008, located at: http://www.timesonline.co.uk/tol/comment/faith/article3342059.ece.

12. Another interesting example, albeit rather statistically insignificant, is Svalbard. Svalbard is a protectorate of Norway way up in the north. It has a tiny population of just over 2,000 people. Interestingly, the Christians are split about half and half between Protestants and Orthodox. However, a large part of them, roughly 40%, are nonreligious.

13. One of many examples here is Andrew Thompson, *The Empire Strikes Back? The Impact of Imperialism on Britain from the Mid-Nineteenth Century* (Harlow, U.K.: Pearson Longman, 2005).

14. The prediction was published in an interview with Lewis by the German paper *Die Welt*. The interview was initially published July 28, 2004, and is posted on the online version in the article "Europa wird islamisch." See: http://www.welt.de/print-welt/article211310/Europa_wird_islamisch.html.

15. Philip Jenkins, "Demographics, Religion, and the Future of Europe," *Orbis: Foreign Policy Research Institute* 50, no. 3 (2006): p. 523.

16. The conference was held at The Center for Vision and Values at Grove City College, Pennsylvania, in April 2007.

17. Dale Irvin and Scott Sunquist, *History of the World Christian Movement Vol. I* (Maryknoll, NY: Orbis, 2004), p. 373.

18. Dale Irvin and Scott Sunquist, *History of the World Christian Movement Vol. I* (Maryknoll, NY: Orbis, 2004), pp. 374, 378.

19. Dale Irvin and Scott Sunquist, *History of the World Christian Movement Vol. I* (Maryknoll, NY: Orbis, 2004), p. 375.

20. James Burge, *Heloise and Abelard: A New Biography* (New York: HarperSanFransisco, 2003), p. 21.

21. James Burge, *Heloise and Abelard: A New Biography* (New York: HarperSanFransisco, 2003), p. 20.

22. Peter Berger, Brigitte Berger, and Hansfried Kellner, *The Homeless Mind: Modernization and Consciousness* (New York: Random House, 1973), pp. 163-67. Accessed in Noel Davies and Martin Conway, *World Christianity in the 20th Century: SCM Reader* (London: SCM Press, 2008), p. 203.

23. Peter Berger, Brigitte Berger, and Hansfried Kellner, *The Homeless Mind: Modernization and Consciousness*, pp. 163-67. Accessed in Noel Davies and Martin Conway, *World Christianity in the 20th Century: SCM Reader* (London: SCM Press, 2008), p. 204.

24. Sigmund Freud, *The Future of an Illusion*, trans. by James Strachey (New York: W. W. Norton, 1961), pp. 38, 56.

25. Sigmund Freud, *The Future of an Illusion*, p. 55.

26. Sigmund Freud, *The Future of an Illusion*, p. 47.

27. Sigmund Freud, *The Future of an Illusion*, p. 63.

28. On the decline of church attendance throughout the 19th and 20th centuries, see Grace Davie, *Believing Without Belonging* (Oxford: Wiley Blackwell, 1994), and Hugh McLeod, *Secularization in Western Europe, 1848-1914* (New York: St. Martin's Press, 2000).

29. Grace Davie, "Europe: The Exception That Proves the Rule?," in Peter Berger, ed., *The Desecularization of the World: Resurgent Religion and World Politics* (Grand Rapids: Eerdmans, 1999), p. 69.

30. Grace Davie, "Europe: The Exception That Proves the Rule?," p. 83.

31. Graeme Smith, *A Short History of Secularism* (London: I.B. Tauris, 2008), pp. 2–3.

32. See Jonathan Benthall, *Returning to Religion: Why a Secular Age is Haunted by Faith* (London: I.B. Tauris, 2008).

33. Grace Davie, *Believing Without Belonging* (Oxford: Wiley Blackwell, 1994).

34. See Dietrich Bonhoeffer, *Letters and Papers from Prison, New Greatly Enlarged Ed.* (New York: Macmillan, 1972), pp. 280-281, 285-286, 380-381.

35. David Martin, *Pentecostalism: The World Their Parish* (Oxford: Blackwell, 2002), p. 57.

36. Alister McGrath, *The Twilight of Atheism* (New York: Doubleday, 2004), p. 1.

37. David Martin, *Pentecostalism: The World Their Parish*, p. 57.

38. Philip Jenkins, *The Next Christendom* (Oxford: Oxford University Press, 2007), 211.

39. Grace Davie, "Europe: The Exception That Proves the Rule?," p. 69.

40. In February 2009, Philip Jenkins spoke at Pepperdine University—the institution of the author—and argued that perhaps Western Europeans may not be as thoroughly de-Christianized as much evidence suggests. He claimed that while church attendance is down, pilgrimage statistics are way up. This evidence suggests Grace Davie's thesis of "believing without belonging" may provide a highly plausible corrective to a radically secular understanding of Western Europe.

41. Ian Fisher, "Pope Warns Against Secularization in Germany," *New York Times*, September 10, 2006, located online at:
http://www.nytimes.com/2006/09/10/world/europe/11pope.web.html?pagewanted=1&_r=1.

42. The IRFR reports are on the U.S. Department of State website. See the discussion of Germany at: http://2001-2009.state.gov/g/drl/rls/irf/2008/108448.htm.

43. See Ecumenical News International (ENI), "Protestants in northern Germany to form united church by 2012," April 1, 2009, news article 09-0262, located at: http://www.eni.ch/news/item.php?id=2870.

44. This was the title of an article on the World Council of Churches (WCC) affiliated news site Ecumenical News International (ENI) on 15 April 2008. See article number 08-0307, located at: http://www.eni.ch/news/item.php?id=1820.

45. For the predictions of decline, see ENI article 07-0846, "Numbers of priests continue to decline in Catholic Ireland," (November 1, 2007) and the IRFR 2008 entry for Ireland located at: http://2001-2009.state.gov/g/drl/rls/irf/2008/108452.htm.

46. IRFR 2008, "Italy," located at:
http://2001-2009.state.gov/g/drl/rls/irf/2008/108453.htm.

47. Philip Jenkins, *The Next Christendom* (2007), p. 110.

48. David Martin, *Pentecostalism: The World Their Parish*, p. 58.

49. The Spanish Inquisition, while horrific, is often associated with egregious crimes of genocidal proportions. In reality the numbers of deaths has been estimated around 3000 people—a surprisingly low number compared with other ethno-religious persecutions of modern times.

50. See IRFR 2008, "Spain," located at:
http://2001-2009.state.gov/g/drl/rls/irf/2008/108473.htm.

51. See for example Bill Weir and Sylvia Johnson, "Denmark: The Happiest Place on Earth," *ABC News*, January 8, 2007, located at:
http://abcnews.go.com/2020/story?id=4086092&page=1.

52. Phil Zuckerman, *Society Without God* (New York: New York University Press, 2008), pp. 3-4.

53. Christine Demsteader, "Say a little prayer for Sweden," *The Local: Sweden's News in English*, August 11, 2006, located at: http://www.thelocal.se/article.php?ID=4579.

54. See IRFR 2008, "Sweden," located at: http://2001-2009.state.gov/g/drl/rls/irf/2008/108474.htm.

55. IRFR 2008, "United Kingdom," located at: http://2001-2009.state.gov/g/drl/rls/irf/2008/108478.htm.

56. Noel Davies and Martin Conway, *World Christianity in the 20th Century* (London: SCM Press, 2008), p. 206.

Chapter Five: Latin American and Caribbean Christianity

1. There is a good possibility that Leif Ericson (c. 970-1020) was already a Christian when he arrived to Newfoundland, but the evidence is inconclusive at this point in time. For the Oct. 12 date, see Klaus Koschorke, Frieder Ludwig, Mariano Delgado, eds., A History of Christianity in Asia, Africa, and Latin America 1450-1990 (Grand Rapids: Eerdmans, 2007), p. 277.

2. Jared Diamond, *Guns, Germs, and Steel* (New York: W.W. Norton, 1999), p. 46.

3. Johannes Meier, "The Beginnings of the Catholic Church in the Caribbean," in *Christianity in the Caribbean*, ed. by Armando Lampe (Barbados: University of the West Indies Press, 2001), p. 2.

4. Justo and Ondina Gonzalez, *Christianity in Latin America* (Cambridge: Cambridge University Press, 2008), p. 27.

5. The events that began in 1492 are probably the clearest and most extreme example of genocide the world has ever known. See Adrian Hastings, "Latin America," in A World History of Christianity, ed. by Adrian Hastings (Grand Rapids: Eerdmans, 1999), p. 331.

6. Christopher Columbus, *The Diario of Christopher Columbus's First Voyage to America*, trans. Oliver Dunn and James E. Kelly Jr. (Norman: University of Oklahoma Press, 1989), pp. 65–69, 143–145. Quoted in Jerry Bentley and Herbert Ziegler, *Traditions and Encounters*, 4th ed. (New York: McGraw Hill, 2008), p. 669.

7. Justo and Ondina Gonzalez, *Christianity in Latin America*, p. 302.

8. Dale Bisnauth in Oscar L. Bolioli, ed., *The Caribbean: Culture of Resistance, Spirit of Hope* (New York: Friendship Press, 1993), p. 16.

9. David Carrasco, *Religions of Mesoamerica* (New York: HarperSanfrancisco, 1990), p. 15.

10. David Carrasco, *Religions of Mesoamerica*, p. xvi.

11. David Carrasco, *Religions of Mesoamerica*, p. xvi.

12. Adrian Hastings, "Latin America," in Hastings, ed., A World History of Christianity (Grand Rapids: Eerdmans, 1999), p. 331.

13. Jared Diamond, *Guns, Germs, and Steel*, p. 210.

14. Jared Diamond, *Guns, Germs, and Steel*, pp. 74–75.

15. Adrian Hastings, "Latin America," in Hastings, ed., A World History of Christianity, p. 331.

16. Adrian Hastings, "Latin America," in Hastings, ed., A World History of Christianity, p. 333.

17. Dale Bisnauth in Oscar L. Bolioli, ed., The Caribbean: Culture of Resistance, Spirit of Hope, p. 20.

18. Dale Bisnauth in Oscar L. Bolioli, ed., *The Caribbean: Culture of Resistance, Spirit of Hope*, pp. 21–22.

19. See "Slave labourers freed in Brazil," *BBC News*, 3 July 2007, located at: http://news.bbc.co.uk/2/hi/americas/6266712.stm.

20. Justo and Ondina Gonzalez, *Christianity in Latin America*, p. 4.

21. Justo and Ondina Gonzalez, *Christianity in Latin America*, p. 4.

22. Meier records that Columbus was reprimanded by Queen Isabella more than once for taking slaves. See Johannes Meier, "The Beginnings of the Catholic Church in the Caribbean," in *Christianity in the Caribbean*, p. 5.

23. Harvey Cox in "Volume 5: Jesus in Latin America," *The Jesus Experience And Christianity Around the World* (Chicago: Questar, 2002), produced by Paulist Productions, 6 hours total for series, DVD.

24. Jared Diamond, *Collapse: How Societies Choose to Fail or Succeed* (New York: Viking, 2005), p. 159.

25. Adrian Hastings, "Latin America," in Hastings, ed., *A World History of Christianity*, p. 334.

26. David Carrasco, *Religions of Mesoamerica*, p. 6.

27. For an excellent discussion of the Great Debate at Valladolid, see David Carrasco, *Religions of Mesoamerica*, pp. 6–10. This quotation comes from p. 8.

28. Adrian Hastings, "Latin America," in Hastings, ed., *A World History of Christianity*, p. 338.

29. Bartolome De Las Casas, *A Short Account of the Destruction of the Indies*, trans. by Nigel Griffin (London: Penguin, 1992), p. xxxi.

30. Bartolome De Las Casas, *A Short Account of the Destruction of the Indies*, trans. by Nigel Griffin, p. xvii.

31. Bartolome De Las Casas, *A Short Account of the Destruction of the Indies*, trans. by Nigel Griffin, p. 127.

32. Adrian Hastings, "Latin America," in Hastings, ed., *A World History of Christianity*, p. 338.

33. Charles Lippy, "Slave Christianity," in Amanda Porterfield, ed., *Modern Christianity to 1900 (People's History of Christianity)* (Minneapolis: Fortress Press, 2007), p. 291.

34. Philip Jenkins, *Next Christendom (Revised and Expanded)*, p. 37.

35. See for example "Haiti makes voodoo official," April 30, 2003, located at: http://news.bbc.co.uk/2/hi/americas/2985627.stm.

36. William Wroth, "Santuario de Chimayo," located at: http://www.newmexicohistory.org/filedetails.php?fileID=505.

37. Philip Jenkins, *Next Christendom (Revised and Expanded)*, p. 146.

38. Amanda Porterfield, *Healing in the History of Christianity* (Oxford: Oxford University Press, 2005), p. 123.

39. For an excellent overview of Pentecostalism in Latin America, see Harvey Cox, *Fire From Heaven: The Rise of Pentecostal Spirituality and the Reshaping of Religion in the Twenty-First Century* (Cambridge, MA: Da Capo Press, 1995), chapter nine, "We Shall Do Greater Things: Pentecostalism in Latin America."

40. Timothy Steigenga and Edward Cleary, *Conversion of a Continent: Contemporary Religious Change in Latin America* (New Jersey: Rutgers University Press, 2007), p. 107.

41. Quoted in Philip Jenkins, *Next Christendom*, rev. ed., p. 103.

42. Philip Jenkins, *Next Christendom (Revised)*, pp. 165-166.

43. See especially David Lehmann, *Struggle for the Spirit: Religious Transformation and Popular Culture in Brazil and Latin America*, accessed in Noel Davies and Martin Conway, *World Christianity in the 20th Century: SCM Reader* (London: SCM Press, 2008), p. 169.

44. Paul Sigmund, Religious Freedom and Evangelization in Latin America: The Challenge of Religious Pluralism (Maryknoll, NY: Orbis, 1999), p. 3.

45. Paul Sigmund, Religious Freedom and Evangelization in Latin America, p. 2.

46. Donald E. Miller and Tetsunao Yamamori, Global Pentecostalism: The New Face of Christian Social Engagement (Los Angeles: University of California Press, 2007), p. 125.

47. Paul Sigmund, ed., Religious Freedom and Evangelization in Latin America, p. 172.

48. Some scholars put Protestant numbers much higher, such as David Martin, who argues that in 1990 Argentina may have been as much as 10% Protestant. There are several questions that arise here, for example, how many conversions to Pentecostalism eventually return to the Catholic Church? See David Martin, Pentecostalism: The World Their Parish (Oxford: Blackwell, 2002), p. 84.

49. "Argentina," IRFR 2008, located at:
http://2001-2009.state.gov/g/drl/rls/irf/2008/108511.htm.

50. "Argentina," IRFR 2008, located at:
http://2001-2009.state.gov/g/drl/rls/irf/2008/108511.htm.

51. "Brazil," IRFR 2008, located at:
http://2001-2009.state.gov/g/drl/rls/irf/2008/108516.htm.

52. See the Assemblies of God official website:
http://worldmissions.ag.org/regions/latinamcab/overview.cfm.

53. See the Assemblies of God official website:
http://worldmissions.ag.org/regions/latinamcab/overview.cfm. See the official AOG statistics for the USA at:
http://ag.org/top/About/statistics/Statistical_Report_Summary.pdf.

54. For Senator Crivella's Web site, see
http://www.senado.gov.br/web/senador/marcelocrivella/index.htm.

55. See BBC News, November 18, 2004, "Chile introduces right to divorce," at:
http://news.bbc.co.uk/2/hi/americas/4021427.stm.

56. An excellent discussion of the Chilean Pentecostal Revival is in Gonzalez, Christianity in Latin America, pp. 271–280.

57. See Jeffrey Gros, "Struggle and Reconcilation: Some Reflections on Ecumenism in Chile," International Review of Mission 97.384/385 (January/April 2008): p. 59.

58. Ibid., p. 64.

59. Gonzalez, Christianity in Latin America, p. 280.

60. Gonzalez, Christianity in Latin America, p. 262.

61. Gonzalez, Christianity in Latin America, p. 262.

62. Timothy Wadkins, "Getting Saved in El Salvador: The Preferential Option for the Poor," in International Review of Mission 97.384/385 (January/April, 2008): p. 31.

63. Timothy Wadkins, "Getting Saved in El Salvador: The Preferential Option for the Poor," p. 32.

64. Philip Jenkins, Next Christendom (Revised), p. 180.

65. Philip Jenkins, Next Christendom (Revised), pp. 183–184.

66. "Jamaica," IRFR 2008, located at:
http://2001-2009.state.gov/g/drl/rls/irf/2008/108531.htm.

67. See the encyclical Sollicitudo Rei Socialis by John Paul II, located at:
http://www.vatican.va/holy_father/john_paul_ii/encyclicals/documents/hf_jp-ii_enc_30121987_sollicitudo-rei-socialis_en.html.

68. See Kenneth MacHarg, "Mexico: Healing the Violence: Presbyterians, Catholics try to reconcile as expulsions persist in Chiapas," in *Christianity Today*, July 25, 2000, located at: http://www.christianitytoday.com/ct/2000/august7/17.30.html. See also James Smith, "Chiapas Gunmen Kill at Least 45 Churchgoers," *LA Times*, December 24, 1997, located at: http://www.christianitytoday.com/ct/2000/august7/17.30.html.

69. Gonzalez, *Christianity in Latin America*, p. 293.

Chapter Six: North American Christianity

1. See Harvey Cox, The Secular City (New York: Macmillan, 1965), and Peter Berger, ed., The Desecularization of the World: Resurgent Religion and World Politics (Grand Rapids: Eerdmans, 1999). Berger famously recanted his earlier thesis that the world would secularize although he continues to believe Western Europe has remained consistent with his earlier work in secularization theory. Cox, too, has modified his views and in 2001 explored the phenomenal growth of global Pentecostalism in his book Fire From Heaven (Cambridge, MA: Da Capo Press, 2001).

2. Vinson Synan, The Century of the Holy Spirit: 100 Years of Pentecostal and Charismatic Renewal, 1901–2001 (Nashville: Thomas Nelson, 2001).

3. Saint-Pierre and Miquelon are territories of France and are included at the end of this chapter only because of their geographical proximity to the North American mainland.

4. Desmond Morton, A Short History of Canada (Toronto: McClelland & Steward, 2001), p. 62.

5. Stephen Neill, A History of Christian Missions (Harmondsworth, England: Penguin Books, 1964), p. 107.

6. Cartier had already been to North America prior to 1534. He had accompanied the Italian explorer Giovanni da Verrazzano in the 1520 as they explored the east side of North America.

7. In North America the war was known as the French and Indian War, although this was merely an extension of the hostilities based primarily in Europe.

8. Mark Noll, The Old Religion in a New World (Grand Rapids: Eerdmans, 2002), p. 37.

9. Jared Diamond, Guns, Germs, and Steel (New York: W. W. Norton and Company, 1997), p. 44.

10. In fact the archaeological find is closer to Portales, New Mexico—home to the Blackwater Draw Museum.

11. Jared Diamond, Guns, Germs, and Steel, p. 45.

12. Catherine Albanese, America Religions and Religion (New York: Thomson Wadsworth, 2007), p. 20.

13. See Christopher Columbus, Diario of 1492, "Esta tierra vido primero un mariner que se dezia Rodrigo de Triana." Diary located at the King's College London Early Modern Spain Electronic Texts site:
http://www.ems.kcl.ac.uk/content/etext/e019.html#d0e393.

14. CIA World Factbook, "United States," located at:
https://www.cia.gov/library/publications/the-world-factbook/geos/us.html#People.

15. See CIA World Factbook, located at:
https://www.cia.gov/library/publications/the-world-factbook/geos/us.html#People.

16. For an introductory article to Canadian immigration, see: http://www.statcan.gc.ca/daily-quotidien/080402/dq080402a-eng.htm.

17. "U.S. Population Projections: 2005–2050," located at: http://pewhispanic.org/files/reports/85.pdf.

18. See, for example, Alan Wolfe's excellent study *One Nation, After All* (New York: Penguin, 1999).

19. Martin Marty, *The Christian World: A Global History* (New York: The Modern Library, 2007), pp. 162–163.

20. Martin Marty, *The Christian World: A Global History*, pp. 161–162.

21. Martin Marty, *The Christian World: A Global History*, p. 164.

22. Mark Noll, *The Old Religion in a New World*, p. 36. Italics are his.

23. There are two excellent articles on the Rehoboth mission written by James Calvin Schaap in the journal *Books and Culture: A Christian Review*. See "Rehoboth" dated Jan. 9, 2009, and "Every Knee Shall Bow," dated April 20, 2009. The articles can be accessed at: http://www.christianitytoday.com/bc/2009/janfeb/5.31.html?start=1 and http://www.christianitytoday.com/bc/2009/marapr/21.16.html. The descriptions of the cemetery come from the article "Rehoboth."

24. See "Rehoboth," p. 5.

25. See Mark Noll, *The Old Religion in a New World*, p. 36.

26. Theodora Kroeber, *Ishi: In Two Worlds* (Berkeley: University of California Press, 1976).

27. For a timeline of Ishi's life and ordeal, see http://history.library.ucsf.edu/ishi.html.

28. See Robert Worth, "A Black Imam Breaks Ground in Mecca," *New York Times*, April 11, 2009, located at: http://www.nytimes.com/2009/04/11/world/middleeast/11saudi.html. The article deals with the first Black man to lead prayers in Mecca, which occurred in 2009. See also the CIA World Factbook, "Saudi Arabia," located at: https://www.cia.gov/library/publications/the-world-factbook/geos/sa.html. "Saudi Arabia is a destination country for workers from South and Southeast Asia who are subjected to conditions that constitute involuntary servitude including being subjected to physical and sexual abuse, non-payment of wages, confinement, and withholding of passports as a restriction on their movement; domestic workers are particularly vulnerable because some are confined to the house in which they work unable to seek help." See also the BBC article "The child slaves of Saudi Arabia" at: http://news.bbc.co.uk/2/hi/programmes/this_world/6431957.stm.

29. A good overview of the recent discoveries pertaining to British North America slavery is Lisa Rein, "Mystery of Va.'s First Slaves Is Unlocked 400 Years Later," in *The Washington Post*, section A01, September 3, 2006. The article is located online at: http://www.washingtonpost.com/wpdyn/content/article/2006/09/02/AR2006090201097_pf.html.

30. See the U.S. census results for 1860 at: http://www.civil-war.net/pages/1860_census.html.

31. Martin Marty, *The Christian World: A Global History*, p. 165.

32. "Sinners in the Hands of an Angry God" is widely available online, for example: http://www.jesus-is-lord.com/sinners.htm.

33. Mark Noll, *The Rise of Evangelicalism: The Age of Edwards, Whitefield and the Wesleys* (Downers Grove, IL: Intervarsity Press, 2003), p. 13.

34. George Whitefield, quoted in Mark Noll, *The Rise of Evangelicalism: The Age of Edwards, Whitefield and the Wesleys*, p. 15.

35. See Robert Bruce Mullin, "North America" in Adrian Hastings, ed., *A World History of Christianity* (Grand Rapids: Eerdmans, 1999), p. 429.

36. Robert Bruce Mullin, "North America," p. 429.

37. See "Protestant churchgoers are no more loyal to their church denomination than they are to brands of toothpaste or bathroom tissue," Ellison Research, January 12, 2009, located at: http://ellisonresearch.com/releases/20090112.htm.

38. Robert Bruce Mullin, "North America," p. 429.

39. See Wency Leung, "Polygamist leader wed girls under 16, he tells Larry King," *Vancouver Sun*, December 9, 2006, located at:
http://www2.canada.com/vancouversun/features/polygamy/story.html?id=87ab93bb-b16c-4ab7-b488-0187b55b70ef&k=71593.

40. See "One Million Missionaries, Thirteen Million Members," located at:
http://newsroom.lds.org/ldsnewsroom/eng/news-releases-stories/one-million-missionaries-thirteen-million-members.

41. Robert Owens, "The Azusa Street Revival: The Pentecostal Movement Begins in America," in Vinson Synan, ed., *The Century of the Holy Spirit* (Nashville: Thomas Nelson, 2001), p. 41.

42. Solange Lefebvre, "History of Religion in Quebec," *Religious Studies News* 24, no. 1 (January 2009), p. 20.

43. Reginald Bibby, *Restless Gods: The Renaissance of Religion in Canada* (Toronto: Stoddart, 2002), p. 32.

44. Reginald Bibby, *Restless Gods*, p. 28.

45. Canadian religious demographics come from Reginald Bibby, *Restless Gods* and Statistics Canada, located at:
http://www12.statcan.ca/english/census01/Products/Analytic/companion/rel/contents.cfm.

46. See Bruce Hindmarsh, "Let the Little Children Come to Me: Young people have been the lifeblood of evangelical Christianity since its earliest revivals in central Europe," May 27, 2009, located at:
http://www.christianitytoday.com/ch/byperiod/earlymodern/letthelittlechildrencome.html.

47. See Rob Bell, Sex God: Exploring the Endless Connections between Sexuality and Spirituality (Grand Rapids: Zondervan, 2007).

48. The quotation comes from Thabit Anyabwile at the website: http://www.christlesschristianity.org/. Horton's book is *Christless Christianity: The Alternative Gospel of the American Church* (Ada, MI: Baker Books, 2008).

49. See Michael Horton, "Christless Christianity: Getting in Christ's Way," located at his Web site: http://www.christlesschristianity.org/ (accessed September 28, 2009).

50. See: http://www.adherents.com/rel_USA.html#families.

51. See for example the respected "Pew Forum on Religion and Public Life" which estimates Pentecostals and Charismatic Christians to be about 23% of the U.S. population: http://pewforum.org/surveys/pentecostal/.

52. See for example Alan Wolfe's book *One Nation, After All*.

53. For the transcript for the interview where MLK said this, see: http://www.wmich.edu/library/archives/mlk/q-a.html.

54. See "Clergywomen Find Hard Path to Bigger Pulpit," *New York Times*, August 26, 2006, located at:
http://www.nytimes.com/2006/08/26/us/26clergy.html?th&emc=th.

55. Alan Wolfe, *One Nation, After All*, p. 153.

56. View the results of the survey at: http://pewresearch.org/pubs/1159/homosexuality-protestant-view.

57. See: http://www.hellyeahchurchofloveandmiracles.org/ for the Hell Yeah Church. For "the cussing pastor," see Molly Worthen, "Who Would Jesus Smack Down," *New York Times*, January 6, 2009, located at:
http://www.nytimes.com/2009/01/11/magazine/11punk-t.html.

Chapter Seven: Asian Christianity

1. Robert Strayer, The Communist Experiment: Revolution, Socialism, and Global Conflict in the Twentieth Century (New York: McGraw Hill, 2007), p. 177.

2. See the CIA's publication "Global Trends 2015," December 2000, located at: http://www.dni.gov/nic/PDF_GIF_global/globaltrend2015.pdf. See p. 37 for CIA predictions. See p. 16 for the quotation.

3. John Hick, "Believable Christianity," a lecture delivered on October 5, 2006. It is located on Hick's Web site: http://www.johnhick.org.uk/article16.html.

4. See the World Gazetteer for 2009 population statistics for Indian metropolitan areas: http://www.world-gazetteer.com/wg.php?x=&men=gcis&lng=en&dat=80&geo=-104&srt=pnan&col=aohdq&msz=1500&va=&pt=a.

5. See http://www.citypopulation.de/world/Agglomerations.html.

6. See Guan Xiaofeng, "Most people free to have more Child," at chinadaily.com, 2007-07-11, located at: http://chinadaily.com.cn/china/2007-07/11/content_5432238.htm.

7. Peter Phan, "World Christianity and Christian Mission: Are They Compatible? Insights from the Asian Churches," in Asian Christian Review 1.1 (Spring, 2007): p. 28.

8. See the Web version of the Ethnologue: http://www.ethnologue.com/ethno_docs/distribution.asp?by=country.

9. Ambani and Mittal were in 2009 ranked numbers 7 and 8 on Forbes' wealthiest list. See: http://www.forbes.com/2009/03/11/worlds-richest-people-billionaires-2009-billionaires_land.html.

10. See the panel discussion: "Dalits in India 2000: The Scheduled Castes more than a half century after Independence," New York: September 27, 2000. Located at: http://www.asiasource.org/asip/dalits.cfm.

11. "Dalits in India 2000: The Scheduled Castes more than a half century after Independence," New York: September 27, 2000. Cited above.

12. "Dalits in India 2000: The Scheduled Castes more than a half century after Independence," New York: September 27, 2000. Cited above. For the preference for males, see Elisabeth Bumiller, May You Be the Mother of a Hundred Sons (New York: Ballantine, 1991).

13. Mark Landler, "Colonialism Ending in Asia As China Reclaims Macao," New York Times, December 19, 1999, located at: http://www.nytimes.com/1999/12/19/world/colonialism-ending-in-asia-as-china-reclaims-macao.html.

14. David Lumsdaine, ed., Evangelical Christianity and Democracy in Asia (Oxford: Oxford University Press, 2009), p. x.

15. Mary Farrell Bednarowski, ed., Twentieth Century Global Christianity (Minneapolis: Fortress Press, 2008), p. 32.

16. Peter Phan, "World Christianity and Christian Mission: Are They Compatible? Insights from the Asian Churches," p. 26.

17. David Lumsdaine, ed., Evangelical Christianity and Democracy in Asia, p. xiii.

18. See Philip Jenkins, The Next Christendom (Oxford: Oxford University Press, 2002), pp. 175-185.

19. Philip Jenkins, The Next Christendom (2002), p. 176.

20. See Babu Thomas, "Chargesheets drawn up against suspected Orissa attackers," June 10, 2009, located at:
http://www.christiantoday.com/article/chargesheets.drawn.up.against.suspected.orissa.att ackers/23567.htm.

21. See V. Venkatesan, "The Staines case verdict," Frontline, 20.21 (October 11-24, 2003), located at: http://www.hinduonnet.com/fline/fl2021/stories/20031024003902400.htm.

22. Stephane Courtois, et al., The Black Book of Communism: Crimes, Terror, Repression (Harvard: Harvard University Press, 1999), p. 4. Statistics for deaths in this section come from this book.

23. See Stanley Wolpert, Shameful Flight: The Last Years of the British Empire in India (Oxford: Oxford University Press, 2006).

24. Samuel Moffett argues, on coin evidence, that the possibility of Christianity arriving to India in the first century is entirely possible. The central issue revolves around the existence of a King Gundaphar who is mentioned in the Acts of Thomas. However, King Gundaphar was thought to be mythical until a treasure of coins was discovered in 1834 that proved beyond dispute that a king by this name did indeed exist in the first century AD. See Moffett, volume 1, pp. 27-30, cited below.

25. The authoritative work on the general history of Christianity in Asia is Samuel Hugh Moffett's two-volume (so far) A History of Christianity in Asia (Maryknoll, NY: Orbis, 1998, 2005) that covers the beginnings to 1900. A shorter overview history up to 1500 is John England, The Hidden History of Christianity in Asia (Delhi: ISPCK, 2002). See also Philip Jenkins, The Lost History of Christianity.

26. John England, The Hidden History of Christianity in Asia, p. 15.

27. Moffett, vol. 1, p. 58.

28. Philip Jenkins, Lost History of Christianity, p. 6.

29. See Moffett, volume 1, pp. 291ff.

30. David Aikman, Jesus in Beijing (Washington, D.C.: Regnery, 2003), pp. 20-25.

31. John England, The Hidden History of Christianity in Asia, pp. 103-104. Moffett writes that archaeological evidence—graves with Nestorian crosses—prove Nestorian Christianity was in the region of Korea, but it depends on what is meant by Korea, since the border has shifted through the years. He writes, "All we can say with certainty, therefore, is that as early as 1000 there were Nestorian Christians in what had not long before been Korean territory." See Moffett, vol. 1, p. 462.

32. Moffett, vol. 1, p. 314.

33. Moffett, vol. 1, p. 471.

34. Christoph Baumer, The Church of the East (New York: I.B. Tauris, 2006), p. 272.

35. Jenkins, Next Christendom (2002), p. 31.

36. Shusaku Endo, Silence (New York: Taplinger, 1980) trans. by William Johnston. The Kirishitan were also the subject of an intriguing documentary by Christal Whelan entitled Otaiya: Japan's Hidden Christians (1997).

37. Noel Davies and Martin Conway, Christianity in the 20th Century (London: SCM Press, 2008), p. 158.

38. Moffett, vol. 2, pp. 132–133.

39. Moffett, vol. 2, pp. 133, 130. For a description of the controversy, see pp. 120–133.

40. Moffett, volume 2, p. 128.

41. R. G. Tiedemann, "China and its Neighbours," in Adian Hastings, ed., A World History of Christianity (Grand Rapids: Eerdmans, 1999), p. 374.

42. R. G. Tiedemann, "China and Its Neighbours," p. 374.

43. R. G. Tiedemann, "China and Its Neighbours," p. 374.

44. David Aikman in Jesus in Beijing, p. 39, goes with the lower estimate of 20 million, but some estimates are as high as 30 million. The Taiping Rebellion has been called the bloodiest civil war in history.

45. Moffett, vol. 2, p. 483.

46. Moffett, vol. 2, p. 487.

47. Mark Galli, "Fury Unleashed: The Boxer Rebellion revealed the courage of missionaries—and the resentment they sparked," Christian History on ChristianHistory.net, October 1, 1996, located at: http://www.christianitytoday.com/ch/1996/issue52/52h031.html.

48. Moffett, vol. 2, p. 487.

49. The Jesus Experience, "Asia," DVD, Paulist Productions, 2002.

50. R. G. Tiedemann, "China and its Neighbours," pp. 395–396. See also Daniel Bays, ed., Christianity in China: From the Eighteenth Century to the Present (Stanford: Stanford University Press, 1996), pp. 310ff.

51. For an excellent discussion of the Back to Jerusalem movement, see David Aikman, Jesus in Beijing, pp. 194–205.

52. The documentary is available from Chinasoul: http://www.chinasoul.org/e/cs-e.htm.

53. The Local Churches are associated with the publishing house Living Stream Ministry located in Anaheim.

54. See R. G. Tiedemann, "China and its Neighbours," p. 406.

55. See R. G. Tiedemann, "China and Its Neighbours," pp. 407–408.

56. Leroy Seat, "The Future of Christianity in Asia," Review and Expositor 103 (2006): p. 548.

57. See, for example, "Death Tolls for the Major Wars and Atrocities of the Twentieth Century, located at: http://users.erols.com/mwhite28/warstat2.htm.

58. See the Department of State's Report on International Religious Freedom, 2008, located at: http://www.state.gov/g/drl/rls/irf/2008/108497.htm.

59. See: http://www.state.gov/g/drl/rls/irf/2008/108497.htm.

60. See, for example, Rob Moll, "Want More Growth in China? Have Faith," The Wall Street Journal Online, August 8, 2008, p. W9, located at: http://online.wsj.com/article/SB121815556386722667.html. See also David Aikman, Jesus in Beijing, pp. 13–18.

61. Geoffrey York, "Jesus Challenging Marx for soul of China," Globe and Mail, February 21, 2004, A3.

62. Kim-Kwong Chan, "The Christian Community in China: The Leaven Effect," in David Lumsdaine, ed., Evangelical Christianity and Democracy in Asia, p. 49.

63. David Martin, "Issues Affecting the Study of Pentecostalism in Asia," in Allan Anderson and Edmond Tang, eds., Asian and Pentecostal: The Charismatic Face of Christianity in Asia (Oxford: Regnum Books, 2005), p. 29.

64. Gail Coulson, The Enduring Church: Christians in China and Hong Kong (New York: Friendship Press, 1996), p. 33.

65. David Barrett, Todd Johnson, George Kurian, World Christian Encyclopedia Second Edition (Oxford: Oxford University Press, 2001), p. 373.

66. Philip Jenkins, The Next Christendom, Revised Edition (Oxford: Oxford University Press, 2007), pp. 190–191.

67. See "Shariah Spreads," March 11, 2009, at: http://www.christianitytoday.com/ct/2009/april/4.13.html.

68. See IRFR 2008, "Indonesia," located at: http://www.state.gov/g/drl/rls/irf/2008/108407.htm.

69. See Philip Jenkins' discussion of the Jemaah Islamiyah in The Next Christendom, Revised Edition, pp. 206–207.

70. Leroy Seat, "The Future of Christianity in Asia," pp. 561–562.

71. For the renaissance of Islam in Kazakhstan, see David Barrett, et al., World Christian Encyclopedia (2001), "Kazakhstan."

72. Ecumenical News International, article ENI-08-0941. Located at: http://www.eni.ch/highlights/news.shtml?2008/11.

73. Allan Anderson, An Introduction to Pentecostalism (Cambridge: University Press, 2004), pp. 131-132.

74. Philip Jenkins, The Next Christendom, Revised Edition, pp. 77-78.

75. David Barrett, et al., World Christian Encyclopedia (2001), "Singapore."

76. David Barrett, et al, World Christian Encyclopedia (2001), "South Korea."

Chapter Eight: African Christianity

1. These statistics come from Terence Ranger, ed., Evangelical Christianity and Democracy in Africa (Oxford: Oxford University Press, 2008), p. x, but they are rooted in David Barrett and Todd Johnson's World Christian Database.

2. Mary Farrell Bednarowski, ed., Twentieth Century Global Christianity (Minneapolis: Fortress Press, 2008), pp. 32–33.

3. Terence Ranger, ed., Evangelical Christianity and Democracy in Africa, p. x.

4. "Africa is known to be by far the most linguistically diverse continent. The number of African languages is usually put at around 2000." See "Africa" on the UNESCO "Communication and Information/Culture" portal, located at: http://portal.unesco.org/ci/en/ev.php.URL_ID=8048&URL_DO=DO_TOPIC&URL_SECTION=201.html.

5. See the CIA World Factbook Publications: "Country Comparison: GDP (Purchasing Power Parity)," located at: https://www.cia.gov/library/publications/theworldfactbook/rankorder/2001rank.html?countryName=South%20Africa&countryCode=SF&regionCode=af#SF.

6. Mercy Oduyoye in Nicholas Otieno with Hugh McCullum, *Journey of Hope: Towards a New Ecumenical Africa* (Geneva: WCC, 2005), p. XIX.

7. In Nicholas Otieno with Hugh McCullum, pp. XIX-XXII. Oduyoye's "A Letter to My Ancestors" (pp. XV-XXII) is essentially a conversation with the ancestors in which she vows to help change Africa's trajectory through renewed spiritual commitment.

8. See, for example, the Oxfam publication "From Closed Books to Open Doors—West Africa's Literacy Challenge," April 2009, located at: http://oxfam.qc.ca/en/policy/2009-04-21_closed-books.

9. Oduyoye's "A Letter to My Ancestors" p. XIX.

10. Oduyoye's "A Letter to My Ancestors" p. XX.

11. Oduyoye's "A Letter to My Ancestors" p. XXI.

12. Lamin Sanneh, quoted in Terence Ranger, ed., *Evangelical Christianity and Democracy in Africa*, pp. 11–12.

13. Denmark was the first European nation to abolish slavery, but the British Empire was so expansive that abolition in British parts was particularly significant.

14. See Adam Nossiter, "Omar Bongo, Gabon Leader, Dies at 73," *New York Times*, June 8, 2009, located at: http://www.nytimes.com/2009/06/09/world/africa/09bongo.html.

15. Celia Dugger, "Battle to Halt Graft Scourge in Africa Ebbs," *New York Times*, June 9, 2009, located at: http://www.nytimes.com/2009/06/10/world/africa/10zambia.html?_r=1&scp=1&sq=battle%20halt%20graft%20scourge&st=cse.

16. Access the list at: http://www.un.org/special-rep/ohrlls/ldc/list.htm.

17. See "Millions dead in Sudan Civil War," December 11, 1998, BBC News, located at: http://news.bbc.co.uk/2/hi/africa/232803.stm.

18. This statement has been attributed to many African sources. See Nicholas Otieno with Hugh McCullum, *Journey of Hope*, p. 7.

19. Timothy Yates, *The Expansion of Christianity* (Downers Grove, IL: Intervarsity Press, 2004), p. 73.

20. Thomas C. Oden, *How Africa Shaped the Christian Mind* (Downers Grove, IL: Intervarsity Press, 2007), pp. 43–44.

21. See Dale Irvin and Scott Sunquist, *History of the World Christian Movement*, vol. 1 (Maryknoll, NY: Orbis, 2001), pp. 217–218.

22. Dale Irvin and Scott Sunquist, *History of the World Christian Movement*, vol. 1, p. 474.

23. Philip Jenkins, *The Lost History of Christianity* (New York: Harperone, 2008), pp. 146–147.

24. Timothy Yates, The Expansion of Christianity, p. 73.

25. Most of the information on Kimpa Vita in this section comes from Philip Jenkins, *The Next Christendom* (2002), pp. 47–48.

26. AIC originally meant "African Independent Churches," although the "I" in the acronym has taken on many variations: Indigenous, Initiated, Instituted, etc.

27. Philip Jenkins, *The Next Christendom* (2002), p. 47.

28. Much of the biographical data comes from Jehu Hancile, "In the Shadow of the Elephant: Bishop Crowther and the African Missionary Movement," the inaugural lecture at the opening of the Crowther Centre for Mission Education in Oxford, published by the Church Missionary Society, Oxford, March 2008. See also Kevin Ward, "Africa," in Adrian Hastings, ed., *A World History of Christianity* (Grand Rapids: Eerdmans, 1999), pp. 207–209.

29. Kevin Ward, "Africa," in Adrian Hastings, ed., *A World History of Christianity*, p. 208. Brackets are his.

30. Andrew Walls, *The Missionary Movement in Christian History* (Maryknoll, NY: Orbis, 1996), p. 104.

31. Ted Olson, "One African Nation Under God," *Christianity Today*, Feb. 4, 2002, located at: http://www.christianitytoday.com/ct/2002/february4/3.36.html.

32. Quoted in Timothy Yates, *The Expansion of Christianity*, p. 82.

33. Alvyn Austin, "Discovering Livingstone," *Christian History*, Oct. 1, 1997, located at: http://www.christianitytoday.com/ch/1997/issue56/56h010.html.

34. Alvyn Austin, "Discovering Livingstone," *Christian History*, Oct. 1, 1997, located at: http://www.christianitytoday.com/ch/1997/issue56/56h010.html.

35. Philip Jenkins, *The Next Christendom* (2002), p. 48.

36. See Graham Duncan and Ogbu Kalu, "Bakuzufu: Revival Movements and Indigenous Appropriation in African Christianity," in Ogbu Kalu, ed., *African Christianity: An African Story* (Trenton, NJ: Africa World Press, 2007), pp. 250–253.

37. Philip Jenkins, *The Next Christendom* (2002), p. 48.

38. Graham Duncan and Ogbu Kalu, p. 252.

39. Ogbu Kalu, ed., African Christianity: An African Story, p. 36.

40. See Isabel Mukonyora, "The Dramatization of Life and Death by Johane Masowe," *Zambezia* XXV, no. ii (1998): p. 205. See also G.C. Oosthuizen, "Isaiah Shembe and the Zulu World View," *History of Religions* 8.1 (August 1968), pp. 1–30.

41. For a transcript of Mandela's 1992 lecture, see: http://www.sahistory.org.za/pages/people/special%20projects/mandela/speeches/1990s/1992/1992_zcc_conference.htm.

42. John Mbiti, quoted in Noel Davies and Martin Conway, *World Christianity in the 20th Century* (London: SCM Press, 2008), p. 118.

43. Andrew Rice, "Mission From Africa," *New York Times*, April 8, 2009, located at: http://www.nytimes.com/2009/04/12/magazine/12churches-t.html.

44. See the church's website: http://www.godembassy.org/en/embassy.php.

45. Aylward Shorter, "Claverie, Pierre," in *Dictionary of African Christian Biography*, located at: http://www.dacb.org/stories/algeria/claverie_pierre.html.

46. See "Cameroon" in the U.S. Department of State's International Religious Freedom Report, 2008 (hereafter IRFR 2008), located at: http://2001-2009.state.gov/g/drl/rls/irf/2008/108357.htm.

47. See "Kimbangu, Simon," in *Dictionary of African Christian Biography*, located at: http://www.dacb.org/stories/demrepcongo/kimbangu4_simon.html.

48. See Eale Bosela Ekakhol, "Justice and Poverty in the Democratic Republic of the Congo: A Challenge to the Church," Doctor of Theology Dissertation, University of South Africa, June 2009.

49. See Thomas Brady, "Visions of Virgin Reported in Cairo," *New York Times*, May 5, 1968, p. 71.

50. See Nadim Audi, "Culling Pigs in Flu Fight, Egypt Angers Herders and Dismays U.N.," *New York Times*, April 30, 2009. Located at: http://www.nytimes.com/2009/05/01/health/01egypt.html.

51. See "Albert Schweitzer," at Nobelprize.org.

52. See Paul Gifford, *Ghana's New Christianity: Pentecostalism in a Globalising African Economy* (Bloomington: Indiana University Press, 2004).

53. Ogbu Kalu, *African Pentecostalism* (Oxford: Oxford University Press, 2008), pp. 193–194.

54. Jason Beaubien, "Ivory Coast Cathedral is World's Largest Christian Church," *National Public Radio*, March 24, 2005.

55. See John Karanja, "Evangelical Attitudes toward Democracy in Kenya," in Terence Ranger, ed., *Evangelical Christianity and Democracy in Africa*.

56. Morocco," IRFR 2008.

57. See "Morocco" in David Barrett, ed., *World Christian Encyclopedia*, 2nd ed. (Oxford: Oxford University Press, 2001).

58. See Ludwig Frieder, "Christian-Muslim Relations in Northern Nigeria since the Introduction of Shari'ah in 1999," *Journal of the American Academy of Religion* 76.3 (September 2008): 602–637. Quotation from p. 618.

59. "Nigeria," IRFR 2008. See also Philip Jenkins, *Next Christendom*, rev. ed. (2007), pp. 201–204.

60. See the RCCG website at: http://www.rccg.org/. See the article by Lisa Miller at: http://www.newsweek.com/id/176333.

61. Cynthia McFadden and Ted Gerstein, "Rick Warren's 'Long-Term Relationship' with Rwanda," *ABC News*, July 31, 2008, located at:
 http://abcnews.go.com/Nightline/story?id=5479972&page=1.
 See also David Van Biema, "Warren of Rwanda," *Time*, August 15, 2005, located at: http://www.time.com/time/magazine/article/0,9171,1093746,00.html.

62. Philip Jenkins, *Next Christendom*, rev. ed. (2007), pp. 68, 170.

63. Carolyn Dempster, "Rape – Silent War on SA Women," *BBC News*, April 9, 2002, located at: http://news.bbc.co.uk/2/hi/africa/1909220.stm.

64. "Sudan," IRFR 2008.

65. "Zimbabwe," IRFR 2008.

66. CIA World Factbook: "Country Comparison: HIV/AIDS - Adult Prevalence Rate."

Chapter Nine: Oceanic Christianity

1. Sebastian Kim and Kirsteen Kim, Christianity as a World Religion (London: Continuum, 2008), p. 198.

2. Noel Davies and Martin Conway, *World Christianity in the 20th Century* (London: SCM Press, 2008), p. 145.

3. Raeburn Lange, *Island Ministers: Indigenous Leadership in Nineteenth Century Pacific Islands Christianity* (University of Canterbury, New Zealand: Macmillan Brown Centre for Pacific Studies, 2005), p. 8.

4. Mary Farrell Bednarowski, *Twentieth-Century Global Christianity* (Minneapolis: Fortress Press, 2008), p. 32.

5. Jerry Bentley and Herbert Ziegler, *Traditions and Encounters: A Global Perspective on the Past*, 4th ed. (Boston: McGraw Hill, 2008), p. 925.

6. Harvey Whitehouse, "Appropriated and Monolithic Christianity in Melanesia," in *The Anthropology of Christianity*, ed. Fenella Cannell, (London: Duke University Press, 2006), pp. 296–297.

7. Jerry Bentley and Herbert Ziegler, *Traditions and Encounters*, p. 608.

8. Rainer Buschmann, *Oceans in World History* (Boston: McGraw Hill, 2007), p. 70.

9. Jerry Bentley and Herbert Ziegler, *Traditions and Encounters*, p. 557.

10. The island has around eight million people and over 1000 distinct, mutually unintelligible languages which are spoken, causing this to be a hot spot for Bible translators. See Sebastian Kim and Kirsteen Kim, *Christianity as a World Religion*, p. 201.

11. Charles Farhadian, "Worship as Mission: The Personal and Social Ends of Papuan Worship in the Glory Hut," in *Christian Worship Worldwide: Expanding Horizons, Deepening Practices*, ed. Farhadian (Grand Rapids: Eerdmans, 2007), p. 176.

12. Lange, *Island Ministers: Indigenous Leadership in Nineteenth Century Pacific Islands Christianity*, p. 8.

13. For the fourfold organization of Oceania, see Rainer Buschmann, *Oceans in World History*, p. 76.

14. Jerry Bentley and Herbert Ziegler, *Traditions and Encounters*, pp. 149–152.

15. Rainer Buschmann, *Oceans in World History*, p. 93.

16. Jerry Bentley and Herbert Ziegler, *Traditions and Encounters*, p. 609.

17. Dutch explorer Jan Carstenzs, quoted in Jerry Bentley and Herbert Ziegler, *Traditions and Encounters*, p. 687.

18. Rainer Buschmann, *Oceans in World History*, p. 78.

19. Rainer Buschmann, *Oceans in World History*, p. 78.

20. Rainer Buschmann, *Oceans in World History*, p. 92.

21. Captain James Cook, quoted in Jerry Bentley and Herbert Ziegler, *Traditions and Encounters*, p. 690.

22. Rainer Buschmann, *Oceans in World History*, p. 93.

23. See "History of Pitcairn Island," a long article taken from the Pitcairn government's *Guide to Pitcairn*, located at: http://library.puc.edu/pitcairn/pitcairn/history.shtml.

24. See http://www.oscars.org/awards/academyawards/oscarlegacy/bestpictures/.

25. Jerry Bentley and Herbert Ziegler, *Traditions and Encounters*, p. 926.

26. Jerry Bentley and Herbert Ziegler, *Traditions and Encounters*, p. 927.

27. One of the most important books on this topic is Raeburn Lange's *Island Ministers: Indigenous Leadership in Nineteenth Century Pacific Islands Christianity* (University of Canterbury, New Zealand: Macmillan Brown Centre for Pacific Studies, 2005).

28. David Hilliard, "Australasia and the Pacific," Ch. 13 in Adrian Hastings, ed., *A World History of Christianity* (Grand Rapids: Eerdmans, 1999), p. 511.

29. Sebastian Kim and Kirsteen Kim, *Christianity as a World Religion*, p. 199.

30. Lange writes, "Almost everywhere the minister, pastor or priest occupies a place of high social status and considerable social importance—certainly a more prominent place in social and cultural life than in today's West." See Raeburn Lange, *Island Ministers: Indigenous Leadership in Nineteenth Century Pacific Islands Christianity*, p. 9.

31. David Hilliard, "Australasia and the Pacific," p. 511.

32. Phil Mercer, "Vanuatu cargo cult marks 50 years," *BBC News*, February 15, 2007, located at: http://news.bbc.co.uk/2/hi/asia-pacific/6363843.stm.

33. Nick Squires, "South Sea tribe prepares birthday feast for their favourite god, Prince Philip," *Telegraph*, February 19, 2007, located at:
http://www.telegraph.co.uk/news/worldnews/1543156/South-Sea-tribe-prepares-birthday-feast-for-their-favourite-god-Prince-Philip.html. See also Richard Shears, "Is Prince Philip a god?," *MailOnline*, June 3, 2006, located at:

http://www.mailonsunday.co.uk/news/article-388901/Is-Prince-Philip-god.html;jsessionid=A757E74C86713B7A90C8DAB62404E996.

34. Stephen Neill, *A History of Christian Missions* (Harmondsworth: Penguin, 1964), p. 476. The long quotation, cited by Neill, is from G.F. Vicedom, *Church and People in New Guinea* (World Christian Books no. 38, 1961), pp. 59ff.

35. See Harvey Whitehouse, "Appropriated and Monolithic Christianity in Melanesia," Ch. 10 in *The Anthropology of Christianity*.

36. David Hilliard, "Australasia and the Pacific," p. 515.

37. David Hilliard, "Australasia and the Pacific," p. 526.

38. Stephen Neill, *A History of Christian Missions*, p. 354.

39. Lange, *Island Ministers: Indigenous Leadership in Nineteenth Century Pacific Islands Christianity*, pp. 49, 57.

40. Lange, *Island Ministers: Indigenous Leadership in Nineteenth Century Pacific Islands Christianity*, p. 223.

41. Lange, *Island Ministers: Indigenous Leadership in Nineteenth Century Pacific Islands Christianity*, pp. 293–294.

42. Lange, *Island Ministers: Indigenous Leadership in Nineteenth Century Pacific Islands Christianity*, p. 128.

43. Lange, *Island Ministers: Indigenous Leadership in Nineteenth Century Pacific Islands Christianity*, p. 275.

44. David Hilliard, "Australasia and the Pacific," pp. 524–525.

45. David Hilliard, "Australasia and the Pacific," p. 528.

46. David Hilliard, "Australasia and the Pacific," p. 530.

47. Davies and Conway, *World Christianity in the 20ᵗʰ Century*, p. 148.

48. Joel Robbins, *Becoming Sinners: Christianity and Moral Torment in a Papua New Guinea Society* (Los Angeles: University of California Press, 2004), p. 122.

49. David Hilliard, "Australasia and the Pacific," p. 532.

50. Thomas A. Kane, "Celebrating Pentecost in Leauva'a: Worship, Symbols, and Dance in Samoa," in Farhadian, ed., *Christian Worship Worldwide: Expanding Horizons, Deepening Practices* (Grand Rapids: Eerdmans, 2007).

51. Sione 'Amanaki Havea, quoted in *The Ecumenical Movement: An Anthology of Key Texts and Voices*, ed. by Michael Kinnamon and Brian Cope (Grand Rapids: Eerdmans, 1997), p. 262.

52. See "Annual focus 2008: Pacific Region Profile," located at:
http://www.overcomingviolence.org/en/about-dov/annual-focus/2008-pacific/pacific-region-profile.html.

53. See Eoin O'Carroll, "Climate change could redraw national borders," *Christian Science Monitor*, July 14, 2009, located at:
http://features.csmonitor.com/environment/2009/07/14/climate-change-could-redraw-national-borders/.

54. See "Annual focus 2008: Pacific Region Profile," located at:
http://www.overcomingviolence.org/en/about-dov/annual-focus/2008-pacific/pacific-region-profile.html.

55. See: "Australia appoints woman bishop," located at: http://news.bbc.co.uk/2/hi/asia-pacific/7414979.stm. See also "From rookie to Melbourne bishop, meet Barbara Darling," located at: http://www.theage.com.au/news/national/from-rookie-to-melbourne-bishop-meet-barbara-darling/2008/04/25/1208743253124.html.

56. See Barney Zwartz, "Uniting Church votes for gay clergy," *The Age*, 18 July 2003, located at: http://www.st-francis-lutheran.org/theage_030718.html.

57. See the Fiji government's website: http://www.fiji.gov.fj/publish/page_14712.shtml.

58. See Howard M. Smith, "The Introduction of Venereal Disease into Tahiti: a Re-examination," in *The Journal of Pacific History* 10:1 (1975), pp. 38-45.

59. Lange, *Island Ministers: Indigenous Leadership in Nineteenth Century Pacific Islands Christianity*, pp. 37–39.

60. Lange, *Island Ministers: Indigenous Leadership in Nineteenth Century Pacific Islands Christianity*, p. 211.

61. Lange, *Island Ministers: Indigenous Leadership in Nineteenth Century Pacific Islands Christianity*, p. 215.

62. Lange, *Island Ministers: Indigenous Leadership in Nineteenth Century Pacific Islands Christianity*, p. 222.

63. Lange, *Island Ministers: Indigenous Leadership in Nineteenth Century Pacific Islands Christianity*, p. 224.

64. See "Annual focus 2008: Pacific Region Profile," located at: http://www.overcomingviolence.org/en/about-dov/annual-focus/2008-pacific/pacific-region-profile.html.

65. CIA World Factbook, "Nauru."

66. See *Obesity in the Pacific: Too Big to Ignore* (Manila: Secretariat of the Pacific Community, 2002).

67. CIA World Factbook, "Nauru."

68. Lange, *Island Ministers: Indigenous Leadership in Nineteenth Century Pacific Islands Christianity*, p. 216.

69. "New Caledonia" in the *World Christian Encyclopedia*, ed. by David Barrett and Todd Johnson (Oxford: Oxford University Press, 2001).

70. Lange, *Island Ministers: Indigenous Leadership in Nineteenth Century Pacific Islands Christianity*, p. 232.

71. Lange, *Island Ministers: Indigenous Leadership in Nineteenth Century Pacific Islands Christianity*, p. 149.

72. Barrett and Johnson, *World Christian Encyclopedia*, 2nd Ed., "New Zealand," pp. 540–541.

73. Lange, *Island Ministers: Indigenous Leadership in Nineteenth Century Pacific Islands Christianity*, p. 150.

74. Lange, *Island Ministers: Indigenous Leadership in Nineteenth Century Pacific Islands Christianity*, pp. 164, 167.

75. Barrett and Johnson, *World Christian Encyclopedia*, 2nd Ed., "New Zealand," pp. 540–541.

76. Barrett and Johnson, *World Christian Encyclopedia*, 2nd Ed., "Papua New Guinea," p. 583.

77. Lange, *Island Ministers: Indigenous Leadership in Nineteenth Century Pacific Islands Christianity*, p. 291.

78. See U.S. Department of State "Papua New Guinea," in the International Religious Freedom Report 2008, located at: http://www.state.gov/g/drl/rls/irf/2008/108420.htm.

79. U.S. Department of State "Samoa," in the International Religious Freedom Report 2008, located at: http://www.state.gov/g/drl/rls/irf/2008/108422.htm.

80. Rainer Buschmann, *Oceans in World History*, p. 87.

81. Kim and Kim, *Christianity as a World Religion*, p. 200.

82. See the official site of the Melanesian Brotherhood at: http://orders.anglican.org/mbh/.

83. Kim and Kim, Christianity as a World Religion, p. 200.

84. CIA World Factbook, "Solomon Islands."

85. Lange, Island Ministers: Indigenous Leadership in Nineteenth Century Pacific Islands Christianity, p. 103.

86. See the official LDS Web site: http://www.newsroom.lds.org/ldsnewsroom/eng/contact-us/tonga.

87. See "Tongan king to give up absolute rule," July 31, 2008, located at: http://www.cnn.com/2008/WORLD/asiapcf/07/29/tonga.king/.

Afterword

1. Jared Diamond, Guns, Germs, and Steel (New York: W. W. Norton and Company, 1999), p. 36.

2. Philip Jenkins, The Next Christendom, Rev. Ed. (Oxford: Oxford University Press, 2007), p. 255.

3. Clifford Geertz, Islam Observed: Religious Developments in Morocco and Indonesia (Chicago: University of Chicago Press, 1968).

INDEX